Sociology in
Post-Normal Times

Sociology in Post-Normal Times

Charles Thorpe

LEXINGTON BOOKS
Lanham • Boulder • New York • London

Published by Lexington Books
An imprint of The Rowman & Littlefield Publishing Group, Inc.
4501 Forbes Boulevard, Suite 200, Lanham, Maryland 20706
www.rowman.com

86-90 Paul Street, London EC2A 4NE

British Library Cataloguing in Publication Information Available

Library of Congress Cataloging-in-Publication Data Available

ISBN 9781793625977 (cloth) | ISBN 9781793625991 (paperback) | ISBN 9781793625984 (ebook)

For my father
David Charles Thorpe

It is hard for thee to kick against the pricks.
Acts 9:5

Contents

Acknowledgments

I would like to especially thank Lauren Langman for his comradeship, inspiration, infectious curiosity and excitement, and political hope. I have learned a great deal from the participants that Lauren brings together in the Self & Society workshops every year, and I feel very lucky to be part of this intellectual community. UCSD in the nineties: Falk Müller, Eileen Crist, Ryan Moore, Ralph Wheaton, Patrick Carroll, Bart Simon, Takashi Hatanaka, Rampaul Chamba. Hugh Mehan, Chandra Mukerji, Harvey Goldman, Andrew Scull, Alan Houston: ethnomethodology, technology, Weber, social control, American thought. Jerry Doppelt: the stakes, and the very soul of the Science Studies Program. Bennett Berger read and took time to discuss with me over coffee a very early iteration of some of the ideas presented here. Bennetta Jules-Rosette, Richard Biernacki and Christena Turner have been culturally inspirational. I appreciate Ricardo Dominguez's advice to trust my process. I am grateful to Gershon Shafir for his friendship and gentle, constructive skepticism. Bob Westman has been a true friend, model scholar, and embodiment of the best of Science Studies. Harry Collins, Robert Evans, Ian Welsh, William Housley, Finn Bowring, Gabrielle Ivinson, and Barbara Adam—what they gave me during three years at Cardiff University is incalculable. What I know about science policy owes to Brian Balmer and Jane Gregory at UCL. Kean Birch and David Tyfield of CPERI (Cultural Political Economy of Research and Innovation) brought back what was missing for much too long in Science & Technology Studies. Early iterations of these ideas were presented at conferences of the Science & Democracy Network, and I am indebted for comments and conversations with Sheila Jasanoff, Kaushik Sunder Rajan, Les Levidow, and Brian Wynne. Radical Theory Reading Group, an extraordinary phenomenon, Debra Shaw, Christian Garland, Helen Jackson. Sanjoy Mahajan kickstarted some of the thoughts presented here, not least by recommending Jeff Schmidt's *Disciplined Minds*. Mimi Yang and Robert Carley opened up what is valuable and exciting in American cultural studies. My understanding of Marxism has been deepened and clarified by Emanuele Saccarelli and I have been fortunate to witness what a remarkable teacher he is. I have learned more from my PhD students Christine Aicardi, Brian Lindseth, and Brynna Jacobson than they did from me. Zachary Frailey read and commented helpfully on this work in draft. Robert Merton's term "role model" has been too trivialized to express what I would like to about Steven Shapin.

Introduction

This book looks sociologically at today's post-normal times and looks at sociology from the vantage point of these times. Sociology is the institutional space carved out within the university for the scientific study of society *as society*. Among the social sciences, sociology is unique in studying the social itself, that is, the nature and constitution of society itself. The institutional weakness of sociology within the bourgeois university, and the intellectual limitations, contradictions, and conflicts within sociology as a discipline, reflect the deep ambivalence toward the social within bourgeois ideology.[1] This book explores these contradictions.

Sociology matters. The marginality and confusion of the sociological voice today constitutes the blindness of contemporary society, the inability of society to understand itself, its inability to see itself as a society, the inability of people to see themselves as society. This reflects and further reproduces human beings' actual inability to create themselves as society, since the requisite forms of solidarity are blocked by the prevailing social interests and relations of power. These relations of power also occlude society's, and sociology's, self-understanding.

Sociology is the scientific understanding of society, that is to say, science's understanding of society; therefore, sociology is science's understanding of itself. Sociology is the reflexivity of science and the reflexivity of modern society.[2] This capacity for reflexivity is blocked by bourgeois ideology, which is the reflection and expression in ideas of bourgeois social relations. Bourgeois atomism (both real and imagined) blocks the development of sociology. Under capitalism, sociology can only ever be bourgeois sociology. As such, it can only ever be a partial and distorted knowledge of an incomplete and malformed reality.

The primary focus of analysis will be on the United States, but the American context is explored in dialogue with, and historical relation to, classical and contemporary European sociology and social thought. Rather than being a history of sociology *per se*, the book examines historical transformations of sociology in order to theorize and understand the nature of modern societies and, in contrast, the present post-modern and post-normal condition. It examines changes in the content and status of sociology in order to elicit how changes in sociological worldview, and in the place of sociology within the hegemonic culture, reflect fundamental social transformations in capitalist society. It argues that sociology and its transformations replicate the change in the relationship between capital and social solidarity. The contradictions, crises, and transformations of sociology signify the ever more explosive contradiction between capitalism and human sociality itself. The organization of normalcy in modernity has given way to the disorganization of post-modern post-normalcy.[3]

Alvin W. Gouldner's 1970 book *The Coming Crisis of Western Sociology* is the central reference point for understanding these contradictions and transformations.[4] The publication of Gouldner's book was the pivotal historical moment signifying the end of sociology's peak of coherence and influence (which will be called *the sociological moment*) and the onset of the fracturing of sociology.[5] However, the cause of the crisis was not, as Gouldner thought, the continued growth in power of the welfare state and its dominance over sociology but, rather, the beginning of the demise of the welfare state. This should be understood more broadly as the end of the precarious normalcy of the period of Fordism-Keynesianism, which lasted only a quarter of a century from the end of World War II and was also the period of peak modernity.[6] The origins of post-normal times, which have marked the experience of the Covid-19 pandemic, must be sought in the 1970s. It was then that the political-economic roots of post-normalcy began to develop.

The fact that sociology entered into crisis in this period was indicative of the unity, identified by Gouldner, between the domain assumptions of sociology and the solution to the problem of capitalist order represented by Fordism-Keynesianism in the postwar period. The fragmentation and theoretical incoherence that marks contemporary academic sociology, manifested in the current forms of hyper-normal and (what Stephen P. Turner has termed) "post-normal" sociology, reflect the breakdown of the real social conditions for bourgeois sociology.[7] The social conditions no longer exist for a sociological discipline that provides a coherent account of the social world and that can simultaneously accommodate the interests of the capitalist ruling class and, therefore, find a niche in the bourgeois university.

The university is bourgeois and reproduces bourgeois ideology because, as Ernest Mandel put it, "In the long run the university as an institution remains bound with golden chains to the power of the ruling class." In terms of the ultimate constraints of structural and institutional power, the higher learning in America is, just as in the subtitle that Thorstein Veblen ultimately chose for his 1918 book, "the conduct of universities by businessmen."[8] Today, that control is filtered through a growing and increasingly powerful managerial layer of university administration.[9]

Gouldner regarded sociology as "New Class" ideology, that is, reflecting the interests of the intellectuals as a rising class. It is clear, however, that the intellectuals who produce sociology are not the same as the intellectuals who gave rise to Marxism, and that Gouldner's critical hope for the intellectuals as a progressive, or even revolutionary, class has less salience than his view of sociologists as bureaucratized intellectuals inextricably bound up within the structures of the welfare state. Academic faculty, in employment relations, lifestyle, family relationships, and outlook, and above all in their position within the capital-labor contradiction, are socially situated within the broader social stratum that Jeff Schmidt calls salaried professionals, or what Barbara Ehrenreich and John Ehrenreich have called the Professional-Managerial Class (PMC).[10] Gouldner's analysis of sociology as New Class ideology is best understood, therefore, in terms of its being the ideological emanation of the PMC. Hence, Gouldner says, "Talcott Parsons' vast *oeuvre* can best be understood as a complex ideology of the New Class, expressed by and through his flattering conception of *professionalism*."[11] Parsonian functionalism reflected the social outlook, interests, and aspirations of the PMC. In particular, in its conception of professionalism (with which Robert K. Merton's notion of the normative structure of science was closely aligned), it stressed the dimension of autonomy in relation to the power of capital. However, as the managerial dimension of the PMC would suggest, this autonomy has only ever been relative and, as Mandel observes about the university, the PMC is tied to capital by its position as employee and by its managerial relationship in employment hierarchies. As Catherine Liu has stressed, today the more professionally oriented members of the PMC are at a distinct disadvantage in relation to the more managerially oriented and this reflects what Mandel called "golden chains." Liu writes:

> PMC centrism is a powerful ideology. Its priorities in research and innovation have been shaped more and more by corporate interests and the profit motive, while in the humanities and social sciences, scholars are rewarded by private foundations for their general disregard for historical knowledge, not to mention historical materialism. The rewards for following ruling class directives are just too great.[12]

So, just as it makes sense to speak of the bourgeois university, it makes sense to speak of bourgeois sociology, even though this sociology is directly produced by members of the PMC and most directly reflects the condition and dilemmas of the PMC within bourgeois society.[13]

Sociology, as it is institutionalized today, is bourgeois, because it reifies and normalizes what exists.[14] In this way, sociology reflects the prevailing capitalist social relations, into which sociology is itself integrated by the university. This is necessarily true of positivism, since it recognizes no other reality than what empirically appears.[15] Positivist sociology must necessarily mirror bourgeois actuality.

This means that there is critical potential within bourgeois sociology because it has the power to expose the actuality of bourgeois society, warts and all. To the extent that sociology participates in the broader intellectual "culture of careful and critical discourse" which, Gouldner argued, characterized and wove together the New Class, it has the power to do more than merely reflect a class worldview.[16] Gouldner's notion of the culture of critical discourse intersects with, and draws out the more radical potential of, the organized skepticism that his mentor, Merton, identified as part of the normative structure of science.[17]

At the same time, sociology's very means of detaching its knowledge from particularistic and everyday perspectives, through positivist methodology, also prevent sociology from doing other than reflecting the prevailing appearances of things. Its anti-septic scientism is also its anodyne middle-class professional complacency and unseeingness. It is the kind of "know-ingness" or "well-informed superiority" that keeps reality at bay, of which Max Horkheimer wrote, "It is the well-informed, farsighted judgments, the prognoses based on statistics and experience, the observations which begin 'I happen to be an expert in this field,' it is the well-founded conclusive statements which are untrue."[18] Sociology is bound to a bourgeois perspective on bourgeois actuality, even while it contains the possibility of exposing the falsity of this perspective.

Bourgeois sociology only briefly cohered around a conception of the social totality. This was in the paradigmatic form of Parsonian functionalism in the first two decades after World War II. Functionalist sociology corresponded to the precarious hegemony of Keynesian social democracy under the conditions of the post-war boom. Gouldner summed up the relationship: "Academic Sociology flourishes in a period when Keynesian economics permit effective intervention with respect to the more traditional economic factors."[19] American imperial hegemony and the class compromise enabled by the postwar boom allowed the intellectual formulation of forms of universalistic nationalism.[20] The sociological idea of society was a key form of universalistic nationalism, to the extent that it reified abstract society as nation-state. Sociology rendered the nation as social universe and rendered abstract "society," the social universe, as nation-state.

The period of sociological coherence was also the height of the broader cultural influence of sociology. This was the era in which the bourgeois nation-state was engaged in a project of social reform. This created opportunities but also imposed political limitations.[21] Sociology may be understood as the bourgeois science of social reform. Its fate as a discipline and intellectual project is inextricably tied to the fate of social reform under capitalism.

Gouldner stated the close relationship between sociology as a discipline, middle-class social reformism, and the welfare state. Sociology, he clearly indicates, emerged as the bourgeoisie became a hegemonic class, freeing itself from the domination of the pre-capitalist landed aristocracy or, in the case of the post-Civil War US, facing the problem of organizing and integrating a nation of immigrants in a continent-wide, capitalist society. Gouldner writes:

> Modern sociology emerged most fully when the middle class was free of the threat from the past or where it never regarded it as a threat. It is apparent that sociology becomes most fully *institutionalized* under the sponsorship of a powerful middle class that has freed itself of the hegemony of older elites.

Sociology emerged under conditions of bourgeois hegemony, but crucially also, a hegemony immediately challenged by the emergence of the working class as a political force. The hegemonic bourgeoisie was haunted by the specter of communism. Gouldner observes, "Still, if an industrial society were totally secure, if it had no social problems that needed to be understood and managed, it would merely appreciate but would not liberally endow a sociology." The welfare state, as the, at least partial, recognition and integration of the needs of the working class and a stabilizing influence on the class tensions of capitalism, was also the crucial institutional basis for state support for, and the public voice of, sociology. Goulder writes, "It was the burgeoning of the Welfare State after World War II, with its massive financing and its emphasis on a broader *social* utilitarianism, that provided the most favorable context for the institutionalization of sociology."[22]

The brief *sociological moment* after World War II corresponded to the height of the project of using the bourgeois nation-state as a vehicle for social reform. Significant redistributive social reform, capable of a generalized stabilization of social order, is no longer possible under capitalism. Sociology, therefore, has reached its limit as an intellectual project. Universalistic nationalism is no longer possible under globalization. It is no longer possible to imagine the nation as social universe. But bourgeois class power, expressed in imperialism, allows for no higher, more global, social universe to appear as such. Yet, that higher social universe is materializing within capitalism.

The current period is one in that can be described in Antonio Gramsci's words, "[T]he old is dying and the new cannot be born; in this interregnum, a great variety of morbid symptoms appear."[23] The Covid-19 pandemic is a morbid symptom of the contradiction between the material globalization of social relations, such that humanity is a single organism on a global scale, and the organization of society and protection of collective well-being by the institution of the nation-state.[24] Social relations today are global in scope, and the human species is materially interconnected as a planet-wide social entity.[25] However, the conscious political organization of social life takes place in the institution of the nation-state. The nation-state is increasingly incapable of organizing society. Imperialism, the capitalist solution to the contradiction between nation-state and global economy, threatens a catastrophic world war. Trotsky's words on the brink of World War II have renewed urgency: "The objective prerequisites for the proletarian revolution have not only 'ripened'; they have begun to get somewhat rotten. Without a socialist revolution, in the next historical period at that, a catastrophe threatens the whole culture of mankind."[26]

Post-normal times are the volatile interregnum that exists as the emergence of global humanity is blocked by the contradiction between the forces and relations of production within capitalism. Private appropriation prevents socialized production from being utilized for the well-being of this human, social, global force of production. Competition between nation-states produces war and continual armaments buildup, while preventing cooperation in meeting the problems that face humankind. The class contradiction had, to a certain extent, been rendered "latent," as Jürgen Habermas put it, in the first two decades after World War II.[27] However, with globalization the contradiction between private appropriation and socialized production has returned with a vengeance, sending continual shocks throughout social life.

Sociology is inextricably bound up with the inherently self-contradictory project of constructing a bourgeois society. The very notion of bourgeois society is self-contradictory because the class power of the bourgeoisie is rooted in the *anti-social* individualist logic of the market. Liberalism, the bourgeoisie's classical and essential legitimizing ideology, emerged from the atomized relations of buyers and sellers on the market.[28] The contradictory anti-social competitive sociality of the market, whereby what brings people together is what holds them apart, is reflected in the contradictions of liberalism and of liberal sociology.[29] Liberalism, writes Alan Wolfe, "is the philosophy par excellence of the capitalist mode of production."[30] As Christopher Caudwell argued, the essential core of bourgeois ideology is the idea of the pre-social, unattached, negatively free individual, as expressed in social contract theory. Therefore, bourgeois thought has at its core a metaphysical conception of individual freedom that is fundamentally anti-social and anti-sociological. Caudwell writes:

Yet in bourgeois economy the market is the only way in which human desires can appear as active forces realizing themselves, and dictating the machine process. Hence human desire appears to the bourgeois as "spontaneous," that is, anarchic and undetermined and certainly not as determined by the machine, whose laws (as he thinks) he precisely knows. Hence the subject and object have become completely separated.[31]

Bourgeois thought is essentially anti-sociological in positing the negatively free, unattached individual with their spontaneous desires as uncaused cause. This metaphysical assumption at the core of bourgeois culture and ideology comes into conflict with, and creates contradictions within, all attempts to construct a human science or social science and to situate the human being in relation to the rest of the material universe studied by science. The assumption lurks behind the "two cultures" problem of the relationship between the humanities and the natural sciences in the bourgeois university. It lies behind the essential, albeit tension-ridden, position of the social sciences in the mediation between dichotomies of nature and spirit, object and subject, and free will and determinism.[32]

The dichotomies that rive the university entail splits between and within the social sciences and the humanities. These dichotomies are at the root of the conflict-ridden position of sociology. Among the social sciences, sociology is the discipline that is concerned with the social in and of itself. Therefore, it is the discipline most troubled by the contradictions of the very idea of the social with the presuppositions of bourgeois thought. There is no way to reconcile the metaphysically free individual human subject with the causality of material processes. All bourgeois thought, and its institutionalization within the university, is caught on the horns of this dilemma.

This dilemma is not purely intellectual but is a contradiction in the project of constructing a bourgeois society, the real purpose that underlies and motivates bourgeois sociology as an academic field, its latent function within capitalist society. Sociology emerged in the nineteenth century, and was institutionalized from the beginning of the twentieth century. Sociology grew out of the social, political, and intellectual demands of legitimation that followed from the sedimentation of the bourgeoisie as a hegemonic ruling class. Sociology offered solutions to the problem that bourgeois liberal ideology faced of shifting from expressing the aspirations of a revolutionary class to the maintenance of order as a ruling class. Wolfe writes, "Though it originated in protest, liberalism rapidly became a theory of power."[33] This means being tasked by its power with ordering not only particular other people to its benefit but ordering order as such: in other words, asserting and establishing hegemony. The relations of power become more subtle and more diffuse the more this is power over social order itself rather than over particular individuals or groups.

The development of sociology followed the path of development of the capitalist state. The bourgeoisie secured, through (and within the framework and boundaries of) the nation-state, power over the entire society (equivalent to the area capable of being fused together militarily and through the solidarizing force of nationalism). Wolfe explains clearly the process by which the bourgeoisie, through the state, turned from eliminating social obstacles to laissez-faire to the constructive task of making social order in which laissez-faire could be sustained. The latter was a task that necessarily involved constraining as well enabling the market. Wolfe draws attention to the contradiction between the need of the bourgeois class for the state "to provide the necessary materials for the expansion of capital" and the desire for the state to "leave the capitalists alone to continue from there." The bourgeoisie used the state "to destroy the feudal structure, which was based on proximity and common interest." The capitalist state produced the conditions for "laissez-faire" by alienating the population from land and community, producing a proletariat. And the bourgeoisie again had to turn to the state in order to transform this alienated population into a cohesive society capable of being managed and regulated in the interests of capital:

> [C]apitalism itself changed the whole nature of the arrangement, because, with large scale production, it brought workers together and increasingly provided them with a common interest . . . Therefore only an expansion of the alienated power of the state can preserve the society.

With large-scale production came the development of the working class into a political force, in the labor and socialist movements. Wolfe writes,

> Those who wished to . . . preserve capitalism had two choices: they could repress workers and radicals once they organized or they could attempt to provide concessions so that they wouldn't organize. Either alternative required an expansion of the capitalist state.[34]

Wolfe describes the shift from using state power to create the conditions for the market, in the ad hoc way of the nineteenth century, to using state power to systematically construct capitalist order.[35] This use of the state to order *order itself* corresponded to the development of scientific solutions in the form of sociology.

The role of the state in securing order supported what Zygmunt Bauman terms the role of the "legislator intellectual" in defining culture. The nation-state took on the role of what Bauman, following Ernest Gellner, calls a "gardener," responsible for cultivating, or culturing, the nation. The state also, through exclusion and social control, trims the weeds. Bauman writes:

"Wild cultures" . . . reproduce themselves . . . without conscious design, super-vision, surveillance or special nutrition. "Cultivated" or "garden" cultures, on the contrary, can only be sustained by literary and specialized personnel . . . The emergence of modernity was . . . a process of transformation of wild cultures into garden cultures.[36]

Therefore, the idea of culture was the basis for the power of intellectuals and for state support for their role. It is related to this that Gouldner calls the New Class a "new *cultural* bourgeoisie whose capital is not its money but its control over valuable cultures."[37] Culture was the arena and resource of intel-lectual power and also the value that the intellectuals offered the ruling class. Culture was a program for remaking order in the form of the modern nation. Hence, Bauman writes, "The intellectual ideology of culture was launched as a militant, uncompromising and self-confident manifesto of universally bind-ing principles of social organisation and individual conduct."[38]

The gardening role of the nation-state was the construction of hegemony. Hegemony is power universalized. Hegemony is power *as* order. This is in the sense of Stephen Lukes's third dimension of power, whereby power shapes not only the action, and not only sets the agenda in terms of limiting the available choices, but also makes even the thought of certain choices impossible.[39] In other words, hegemony is a condition in which the ruling class is able to affect and, to a greater or lesser extent, determine not only what gets done, and not only what gets talked about doing, but also what gets *thought* about doing. Hegemony is power over what it is possible to think. "The foundation of a ruling class," writes Gramsci, "is equivalent to the creation of a *Weltanschauung* [worldview]."[40] Hegemony is power over consciousness. It is also, it must be remembered, power over what is done. These things go together. Quintin Hoare and Geoffrey Nowell-Smith write,

The fact that, more than any other great revolutionary Marxist thinker, [Gramsci] concerned himself with the sphere of "civil society" and of "hegemony" . . . can-not be taken to indicate a neglect of the moment of political society, of force, of domination.[41]

In order to exist as a ruling class, it must be possible to exert power not only by force but also by voice, by command. And that command is most efficient when it is done by other people, who give commands to others. And commands are most powerful when they are internalized, when they become the individual commanding this to themselves. Commands are most power-ful when they become command. In other words, commands can become detached from the original commander, when they become passed along so far that the original commander is forgotten and the command is no longer associated with that person. And it is possible for commands to be made *on behalf of* a person, without the awareness of, or reference to, that original person. There can be commands on behalf of the commander that are not at any point issued by the commander. Commands may be highly mediated by chains of individuals such that the command does not appear to be on behalf of anyone and does not even appear to be a command and the commander does not know that they are issuing a command or that it is being issued on their behalf. Hegemony has been achieved when such secondary, or de-personalized, commands are accepted as readily or even more readily than commands from the original commander (the charismatic individual or group charismatic ruling clique, status group, class).

It is through the institutional and ideological mediation of command that power becomes hegemony. Mediation is particularly important for bourgeois rule because of the separation and protection from direct violence of a distinct economic sphere under capitalism, and therefore the institutionalized separation of economy from polity. In his study of Gouldner's work, James J. Chriss writes, "As the economic class loses direct control of the coercive power of the polity, which is now in the hands of a new stratum, the political class, they must attempt to exert their influence through more indirect means." Hence, as Chriss writes, "This special kind of ruling class, unique to late capitalism, is what Gramsci termed a *hegemonic* class."[42] As power extends in space and time, it becomes the abstract framework of what is right. This is expressed in laws of the state. It is also expressed in a variety of formal institutionalized rules.

The formal mediation of commands is done in modern societies by bureaucracies.[43] And there is also informal mediation of commands, through ideology and culture, and internalized attitudes and habitual practices. Hegemony is expressed in what is taken for granted as the very difference between right and wrong, and therefore not questioned. This is the background and fabric of social life itself. So class hegemony consists of the commands of that class becoming taken for granted as the way of social life. Hegemony is the making of social order. The project of stabilizing bourgeois rule by embedding it in life as the social order is also the process of the societalization of capital, in the sense of making a capitalist everyday life or what Antonio Negri calls "the social factory."[44]

Hegemony is legitimacy in the sense used by criminologist Gary LaFree: "*legitimacy* refers to the ease or difficulty with which institutions are able to get societal members to follow . . . rules, laws, and norms." Institutions channel behavior into "preestablished 'grooves'," as Peter Berger put it.[45] Therefore, bourgeois hegemony may be regarded as the condition in which the grooves of everyday life are carved in such a way as to reproduce the interests of the dominant class.

Sociology, as the bourgeois science of society, is the science of bourgeois hegemony. It is the science of the reconstruction of society under capitalist conditions and, therefore, within the parameters of bourgeois rule. However, sociology is not merely bourgeois, but scientific, and participates in what Gouldner calls "the culture of critical discourse."[46] It is a completely disenchanted look at the world as profane. Sociology is a perception that banishes the sacred from shared life and leaves only disenchanted everyday life. It, further, exposes the precariousness of that everyday life, as ethnomethodological accomplishment.[47] Ethnomethodology is profoundly realist in that it is an exposure of the unreality, in the sense of artificiality, of the socially constructed *Umwelt*.[48]

Sociology conspires with the natural attitude in constructing and maintaining a reified *Umwelt*.[49] However, sociology also fundamentally undermines that reified world image simply by calling attention to it as such. Sociology is an expression of the culture of critical discourse as a disenchantment of the social. Gouldner argues that the essential task of sociology

> is to exhibit the ordinary group's everyday life [EDL]. In other words, sociology's distinct function is to liberate EDL from the neglect that is the fate of the commonplace. Which is to say, its task is to focalize the seen-but-unnoticed. Sociology's task, then, is to transform the common perspective on the common and, as a special case, to heighten the stable accessibility of the common: to make it visible. Sociology's task is thus to liberate subjugated reality, to emancipate underprivileged reality.[50]

Thus, Gouldner argues that sociology's task is not so much to *dis*cover reality as to *re*cover everyday reality, in other words to go about "*the display of the already known.*" This means to display what is known, but hitherto "known" only in the sense of "seen-but-unnoticed."[51] As such, sociology is in constant tension between its scientific desire to see beyond or differently from an everyday "folk" perspective and its own reifying practices that create its own specialized professional folk perspective.[52] This, in turn, cannot help but replicate the contours of the everyday natural attitude.

Gouldner argues that sociology's role in buttressing the ontological stability of twentieth-century capitalist normality consisted precisely in excluding what the stability of this normality required be excluded and repressed:

> This has one small merit as characterization of normal, academic sociology: it helps explain how it is possible to have a "science of man" that lived through continual catastrophes and people-devouring wars without speaking of war, of imperialism, of conflicts, tensions, poverty, of racism, of sexism, of hunger, of

false promises, viciousness, and envy. These, after all, are scarcely the furnishings of a homey world.[53]

The worlds made in the *American Journal of Sociology* and *American Sociological Review* are sanitized of that which would trouble the reality of society as sociology conceives it and seeks to make it.

Ted R. Vaughan argues that Gouldner overlooked a crucial development in sociology, already taking place when *The Coming Crisis* was written, which was the emphasis on technique as being the key to science. The commitment "to uncovering natural and universal invariant relationships through an emphasis on quantitative techniques and procedures" became the prevailing "methodological hegemony," replacing Parsonian structural-functionalism as the defining center of the "mainstream" of the discipline in the United States.[54] No substantive theoretical consensus replaced functionalism, only a stringent policing of a methodological definition of the discipline in which quantitative methods would be maintained as the core through what Turner calls "cartel" control of the journals and the job market.[55] Vaughan develops Gouldner's argument into a critique of this methodological hegemony precisely for the way in which it blocks reflexivity. He writes that "the current methodological procedures are self-serving. They protect sociologists from having to confront the issues associated with the social conditions of their own activities."[56] The procedures allow sociologists to accommodate themselves to what exists, especially the agendas of the existent funding agencies, through which the boundaries of legitimacy imposed by capital and the state are channeled. Sociology is an intellectual extension of the nation-state, engaged in legitimizing the nation-state and urging and guiding the state in its role as "gardener" of modern society. Sociology must affirm the legitimacy of what exists and thereby participate in de-problematizing, regularizing, and stabilizing what exists.

The stable order, of which sociology is the science, is normalcy. Notions of the normal human being and of normality as a condition of social life historically map onto the development of modern medicine, psychiatry, statistics, the human and social sciences, and the increasing regulation of the market and administration of social life by the state.[57] Lennard Davis notes the relationship between the idea of the normal and modernity:

> [T]he constellation of words describing this concept "normal," "normalcy," "normality," "norm," "average," "abnormal"—all entered the European languages rather late in human history. The word "normal" as "constituting, conforming to, not deviating or differing from, the common type or standard, regular, usual" only enters the English language around 1840 . . . Likewise, the word "norm," in the modern sense, has only been in use since around 1855, and "normality" and "normalcy" appeared in 1849 and 1857 respectively.[58]

It is bound up with the processes of regulation, administration, control, and sequestration that give rise to a specifically modern everyday life. Davis says that "the very term that permeates our contemporary life—the normal—is a configuration that arises in a particular historical moment. It is part of a notion of progress, of industrialization, and of ideological consolidation of the bourgeoisie."[59]

The notion of normal, especially as constructed through the statistical principle of the normal curve of distribution, situates and measures the individual by reference to a population. The ideal became redefined in relation to the "general population" as peoples were being carved out according to the principle of nationalism.[60] Davis discusses how the eugenics movement's definitions of deviance versus normality emphasized national fitness. "[T]he eugenic notion," he writes, was "that individual variation would accumulate into a composite national identity."[61] George Mosse has shown the relationship between nationalism and the control of sexuality as the idea of middle-class respectability took hold with the rise of capitalism and the hegemony of the bourgeoisie. He writes:

> Respectability and nationalism established themselves in the late eighteenth and early nineteenth centuries at the identical time when bourgeois society was taking hold . . . Respectability was thought essential for the maintenance of an ordered society. The bourgeoisie had created the age of commerce and industry and it feared what it had created . . . Industrialization was accompanied not only by the pastoral, . . . but also by a nostalgia for an intimate society that could sustain a manageable world. . . . Respectability met this need for order and security in an ever more disordered world. It provided the middle classes with a solid base from which to make the leap, not into moral purification—this they now possessed—but into the not-so-clean world of debit and credit.
>
> Nationalism claimed to be unchanging and eternal, and through this claim gave to the middle-class way of life an appearance of immutability.[62]

Julian B. Carter argues that in the United States, between 1890 and 1940, the conception of normality that developed was in the racial image of "white," and "whiteness" was closely linked, in this cultural imagery, with heterosexuality and the nuclear family.[63]

Nationalism (with its corollary forms of racism and xenophobia), defines the boundaries of values and the context for their application. It defines "we" who hold these values and to whom these values apply. The construction of insiders is the construction of outsiders, who are not regarded as sharing our values and who do not deserve to benefit from our values—for example, the "enemy combatants" the Bush administration defined as outside the scope of the Geneva Convention. Chris Hedges quotes the Yugoslav writer

Danile Kis's argument that "The nationalist is by definition an ignoramus," since nationalism is (in modern societies) the most simple, uncritical way of defining "us" versus "them" and constructing ontological security within the boundaries of "us":

> Nationalism is the line of least resistance, the easy way. The nationalist is untroubled, he knows or thinks he knows what his values are, his, that's to say national, that's to say the values of the nations he belongs to, ethical and politi-cal; he is not interested in others, *they are of no concern of his*, hell—it's other people (other nations, another tribe).[64]

The nation-state is a set of institutions which is itself embedded within a broader arrangement of cultural meanings that the institutions of the nation-state themselves go about shaping. So nationalism as ideology is actively involved in making the nation-state.

The nation-state is the container of what is normal. Normality emerged between the 1840s and 1860s, the period in which the bourgeoisie was estab-lishing itself as the hegemonic class and the relations of society as bourgeois relations. This was the period of the 1848 Revolutions and the American Civil War. Normalcy arose with, and is equivalent to, bourgeois society. During the first two decades after World War II, affluence and consumer culture (especially American, as other advanced countries were still recovering from the war) contributed to period of maximal concern with normalcy. This was also the peak of the cultural significance of sociology, in the sense in which sociology meshed with the ruling ideological assumptions embedded in the political economy of Fordism and Keynesianism.[65] The forces of industrial Fordism supported the homogenizing, within its geographic boundaries, of citizens in the nation-state.[66]

With the transformation from citizenship to consumerism as the primary form in relation to which self-identity is shaped, the emphasis on homog-enization gave way to an emphasis on differentiation of self from the mass, through conspicuous consumption. Globalized consumption creates new cos-mopolitan identities not anchored in the nation-state. At the same time, global media culture, carrying consumerist cultural cosmopolitanism, relativizes national identities and values, exacerbating the de-traditionalizing force of modernity.[67] The disruption of ontological security by relativizing of values goes along with the way in which the global market creates new insecurity, temporariness, and mobility.

In the period of neoliberal globalization, what Henri Lefebvre called "the bureaucratic society of controlled consumption" gives way to more chaotic, uncontrolled and vicious competition in the face of the ever-present threat of being removed from the ranks of consumer into the faceless human "waste" that, as Bauman argues, globalized capitalism continually creates and casts aside.[68] Saskia Sassen contrasts the logic of mass consumerism with that of financialization. Finance, she writes

> is a radically different organizing logic from that of, for instance, the typical mass consumer oriented corporation. The latter needs and thrives on households doing well, and on the sons and daughters doing better than their parents, on governments supporting households via health subsidies so they can use private hospitals and buy prescribed medications, and so on. Finance, like mining, wants to extract value it can immediately put to work (that is, financialize) for specific aims, and once it has executed that operation, it leaves behind destruction and moves on to the next target.[69]

There is a dialectical quality to globalization between the local and the cosmopolitan because, in the face of the undermining of sources of ontological security, people turn with increased desperation and intensity to reassuring symbols and structures.[70] Nationalism takes on renewed virulence in the phase of the decline of the nation-state in relation to the power of the global economy. As Sassen writes, global capital "markets can now exercise the accountability functions formally associated with citizenship in liberal democracies: they can vote governments' economic policies out or in; they can force governments to take certain measures and not others."[71] Hence, today's nationalism is, Étienne Balibar observes, "an 'anachronistic' nationalism that it is tempting to call 'postnational nationalism' because it comes after all possibility of creating or re-creating autonomous nation-states has disappeared."[72] Lauren Langman and George Lundskow argue that, as the resulting legitimation crisis of the nation-state "worsens, and aggression increases, a culture and social character of destructive nihilism also increases correspondingly—a desperate effort to preserve the 'pure' communities, values, and authoritarian social characters of yesterday."[73]

As national sovereignty wanes, and virulent nationalism surges in response, the nation-state system is increasingly an obstacle to securing the future of humanity. The Covid-19 pandemic, which suspended everyday life, is one symptom of what authors such as Sivlio Funtowicz, Jerry Ravetz, and Ziauddin Sardar, coalescing around the journal *Futures*, are calling "postnormal times," characterized by growing uncertainty, unpredictability, and complexity arising at a fundamental level from globalization and the global transformations of the relationships between human society and the rest of nature.[74] It will be argued in the following chapters that the disruptions and insecurities of post-normal times arise from the contradiction between nation-state and global economy. This contradiction prevents a rational solution to any major societal problems.

The post-normal condition is bound up with the crisis of the gardening role of the nation-state and its mediating institutions. This has profound implications for universities and for sociology as an academic discipline. Sociology as a discipline has been oriented to the project of constructing normalcy in the form of a stable bourgeois society, within the boundaries and through the institutions of the nation-state. This reformist project of mediation is no longer viable. The demise of the gardening role of the nation-state has radically undermined the intellectual role of the sociologist.

NOTES

1. Cf. Göran Therborn, *Science, Class and Society: On the Formation of Sociology and Historical Materialism* (London: NLB, 1976); Robin Blackburn ed., *Ideology in Social Science: Readings in Critical Social Theory* (New York: Vintage Books, 1973); Stephen P. Turner and Jonathan H. Turner, *The Impossible Science: An Institutional Analysis of American Sociology* (Newbury Park, CA: Sage Publications, 1990); Terence C. Halliday, "Introduction: Sociology's Fragile Professionalism," in Terence C. Halliday and Morris Janowitz eds, *Sociology and its Publics* (Chicago: University of Chicago Press, 1992), 3–42; Alan Wolfe, "Weak Sociology/Strong Sociologists: Consequences and Contradictions of a Field in Turmoil," *Social Research* 59, no. 4 (1992): 759–779; Mark Solovey, *Social Science for What?: Battles over Public Funding for the "Other Sciences" at the National Science Foundation* (Cambridge: The MIT Press, 2020); James S. House, "The Culminating Crisis of American Sociology and Its Role in Social Science and Public Policy: An Autobiographical, Multimethod, Reflexive Perspective," *Annual Review of Sociology* 45 (2019): 1–26; Philip N. Cohen, "The American Sociological Association is Collapsing and its Organization is a Perpetual Stagnation Machine," Family Inequality (blog), March 21, 2021, https://familyinequality.wordpress.com/2021/03/28/the-american-sociological-association-is-collapsing-and-its-organization-is-a-perpetual-stagnation-machine/. For UK context, see John Holmwood, "Sociology's Misfortune: Disciplines, Interdisciplinarity and the Impact of Audit Culture," *British Journal of Sociology* 61, no. 4 (December 2010): 639–658.

2. Anthony Giddens, *In Defence of Sociology: Essays, Interpretations and Rejoinders* (Cambridge: Polity Press, 1996).

3. Cf. Zygmunt Bauman, *Intimations of Post-Modernity: On Modernity, Post-Modernity and Intellectuals* (London: Routledge, 1992); Ziauddin Sardar ed., *The Postnormal Times Reader* (Herndon, VA: International Institute for Islamic Thought and the Centre for Postnormal Policy & Futures Studies, 2017).

4. Alvin W. Gouldner, *The Coming Crisis of Western Sociology* (New York: Equinox, 1971).

5. Cf. Stephen Turner, "The Strange Life and Hard Times of the Concept of General Theory in Sociology: A Short History of Hope," in Steven Seidman and David G. Wagner eds, *Postmodernism and Social Theory: The Debate Over General Theory* (Cambridge, MA: Blackwell, 1992), 101–133.

6. Ian Welsh, *Mobilising Modernity: The Nuclear Moment* (London: Routledge, 2000).

7. Stephen P. Turner, *American Sociology: From Pre-Disciplinary to Post-Normal* (London: Palgrave Macmillan, 2014).

8. Ernest Mandel, "The Changing Role of the Bourgeois University" (June 1970), Speech delivered at Rijks Universiteit Leiden on the occasion of its 79th anniversary, June 1970. Published as a pamphlet by the Spartacus League, London 1971, https://www.marxists.org/archive/mandel/1970/06/university.htm; Thorstein Veblen, *The Higher Learning in America : A Memorandum on the Conduct of Universities by Business Men* (New York: A.M. Kelley, 1965). See also Louis Althusser, "Ideology and Ideological State Apparatuses," in *Lenin and Philosophy and Other Essays* (New York: Monthly Review Press, 1971), 127–186; Clyde W. Barrow, *Universities and the Capitalist State: Corporate Liberalism and the Reconstruction of American Higher Education, 1894-1928* (Madison: The University of Wisconsin Press, 1990); David Harvie and Massimo de Angelis, "Cognitive Capitalism and the Rat Race: How Capital Measures Immaterial Labour in British Universities," *Historical Materialism* 17, no. 3 (2009): 3–30; Alex Callinicos, *Universities in a Neoliberal World* (London: Bookmarks, 2006); Philip Mirowski, *Science-Mart: Privatizing American Science* (Cambridge, MA: Harvard University Press, 2011).

9. Benjamin Ginsberg, *The Fall of the Faculty: The Rise of the All-Administrative University and Why It Matters* (Oxford: Oxford University Press, 2011).

10. Jeff Schmidt, *Disciplined Minds: A Critical Look at Salaried Professionals and the Soul-Battering System that Shapes their Lives* (Lanham, MD: Rowman and Littlefield, 2000); Barbara Ehrenreich and John Ehrenreich, "The Professional-Managerial Class," in Pat Walker ed., *Between Labor and Capital* (Montréal, Canada: Black Rose Books, 1978), 5–45; Barbara Ehrenreich, *Fear of Falling: The Inner Life of the Middle Class* (New York: HarperPerennial, 1990). See also C. Wright Mills, *White Collar: The American Middle Classes* (New York: Oxford University Press, 1951); Donald Clark Hodges, *Class Politics in the Information Age* (Urbana: University of Illinois Press, 2000).

11. Alvin Gouldner, *The Future of Intellectuals and the Rise of the New Class* (New York: Continuum, 1979), 37 (emphasis in original).

12. Catherine Liu, *Virtue Hoarders: The Case Against the Professional Managerial Class* (Minneapolis: University of Minnesota Press, 2021), 13. See also interview of Catherine Liu by Ariella Thornhill and Jen Pan, Jacobin Show, Youtube, January 27, 2021, https://www.youtube.com/watch?v=D4WV7oswt3M.

13. Therborn, *Science, Class and Society,* 144.

14. Jürgen Habermas, *Legitimation Crisis*, trans. Thomas McCarthy (Boston, MA: Beacon Press, 1975), 36.

15. Herbert Marcuse, *Reason and Revolution: Hegel and the Rise of Social Theory* (Boston, MA: Beacon Press, 1960).

16. Gouldner, *Future of Intellectuals*, 27.

17. Robert K. Merton, *The Sociology of Science: Theoretical and Empirical Investigations* (Chicago: University of Chicago Press, 1973).

18. Max Horkheimer, "Against Knowingness," in Max Horkheimer and Theodor W. Adorno eds, *Dialectic of Enlightenment: Philosophical Fragments* (Stanford: Stanford University Press, 2002), 173. On authorship, see ibid, 224.

19. Gouldner, *Coming Crisis*, 161.

20. Cf. Gershon Shafir and Alison Brysk, "The Globalization of Rights: From Citizenship to Human Rights." *Citizenship Studies* 10, no. 3 (2006): 275–287.

21. David Paul Haney, *The Americanization of Social Science: Intellectuals and Public Responsibility in the Postwar United States* (Philadelphia, PA: Temple University Press, 2008). Cf. C. Wright Mills, *The Sociological Imagination* (New York: Oxford University Press, 1959).

22. Gouldner, *Coming Crisis*, 160–161 (emphases in original).

23. Antonio Gramsci, *Selections from the Prison Notebooks of Antonio Gramsci*, ed. and trans. Quintin Hoare and Geoffrey Nowell-Smith (London: Lawrence & Wishart, 1971), 276; Lauren Langman and George Lundskow, "Social Character, Social Change, and the Social Future," in Kieran Durkin and Joan Braune eds, *Erich Fromm's Critical Theory: Hope, Humanism, and the Future* (London: Bloomsbury Academic, 2020), 194–215, on 196.

24. Mike Davis, *The Monster Enters: COVID-19, Avian Flu and the Plagues of Capitalism* (New York: OR Books, 2020). Malcolm James and Sivamohan Valluvan, "Coronavirus Conjuncture: Nationalism and Pandemic States," *Sociology* 54, no. 6 (2020): 1238–1250. Cf. Leo Panitch and Colin Leys, *Morbid Symptoms: Health Under Capitalism* (New York: Monthly Review Press, 2010).

25. Nick Dyer-Witheford, "Digital Labour, Species-Becoming, and the Global Worker," *Ephemera*: *Theory & Politics in Organization* 10, no. 3/4 (2010): 484–503; Charles Thorpe, "Toward Species Being," *Logos: A Journal of Modern Society & Culture* (Summer 2021), http://logosjournal.com/2021/toward-species-being/.

26. Leon Trotsky, *The Death Agony of Capitalism and the Tasks of the Fourth International: The Transitional Program* (New York: Labor Publications, 1981), 2.

27. Jürgen Habermas, "Technology and Science as 'Ideology'," in Jürgen Habermas ed., *Toward a Rational Society: Student Protest, Science, and Politics* (Boston, MA: Beacon Press, 1971), 81–122, quoting 109.

28. C. B. Macpherson, *The Political Philosophy of Possessive Individualism* (Oxford: Clarendon Press, 1962).

29. Cf. Patrick J Deneen, *Why Liberalism Failed* (New Haven: Yale University Press, 2018), 43–77. Cf. Karl Polanyi, *The Great Transformation: The Political and Economic Origins of Our Time* (Boston, MA: Beacon Press, 1957), 111–162.

30. Alan Wolfe, *The Limits of Legitimacy: Political Contradictions of Contemporary Capitalism* (New York: The Free Press, 1977), 4. See also Rebecca Fisher, "The Paradox of Democratic Capitalism: An Historical View," in Rebecca Fisher ed., *Managing Democracy, Managing Dissent: Capitalism, Democracy and the Organisation of Consent* (London: Corporate Watch, 2013), 15–45.

31. Christopher Caudwell, *The Concept of Freedom* (London: Lawrence and Wishart, 1965), 211.

32. Christopher Caudwell, *The Crisis in Physics* (London: John Lane The Bodley Head, 1939); Cf. C. P. Snow, *The Two Cultures* (Cambridge: Cambridge University

Press, 1993); Frank Furedi, Roger Kimball, Raymond Tallis, and Robert Whelan, *From Two Cultures to No Culture: C. P. Snow's 'Two Cultures' Fifty Years On* (London: Civitas, 2009).

33. Wolfe, *Limits of Legitimacy*, 7.

34. Alan Wolfe, "New Directions in the Marxist Theory of Politics," *Politics & Society* (Winter 1974): 131–159, quoting 153–154. See also Habermas, *Legitimation Crisis*, 50–68.

35. See also Antonio Negri's discussion of the "planner state" and its crisis: Antonio Negri, "Crisis of the Planner-State: Communism and Revolutionary Organisation," Antonio Negri ed., *Revolution Retrieved: Writings on Marx, Keynes, Capitalist Crisis and New Social Subjects* (London: Red Notes, 1988), 97–148, esp. 119–123.

36. Zygmunt Bauman, *Legislators and Interpreters: On Modernity, Post-Modernity and Intellectuals* (Cambridge: Polity Press, 1987), 51. Cf. Chandra Mukerji, *Territorial Ambitions and the Gardens of Versailles* (Cambridge: Cambridge University Press, 1997); Patrick Carroll, *Science, Culture, and Modern State-Formation* (Berkeley: University of California Press, 2006).

37. Gouldner, *Future of Intellectuals*, 21 (emphasis in original).

38. Bauman, *Intimations of Post-Modernity*, 11.

39. Steven Lukes, *Power: A Radical View* (London: Macmillan, 1974).

40. Gramsci, quoted in Thomas R. Bates, "Gramsci and the Theory of Hegemony," *Journal of the History of Ideas* 36, no. 2 (April–June 1975): 351–366, on 351. See also Gramsci, *Selections*, 12, 53, 57, 160, 170, 182, 210; Robert F. Carley, *Culture & Tactics: Gramsci, Race, and the Politics of Practice* (Albany: State University of New York Press, 2019).

41. Quintin Hoare and Geoffrey Nowell-Smith, "Chapter 2: State and Civil Society: Introduction," in Gramsci, *Selections*, 206–209, on 207.

42. James J. Chriss, *Alvin W. Gouldner: Sociologist and Outlaw Marxist* (Aldershot, Hampshire, UK: Ashgate, 1999), 151 (emphasis in original).

43. Albert Dragstedt and Cliff Slaughter, *State, Power & Bureaucracy: A Marxist Critique of Sociological Theories* (London: New Park Publications, 1981); Ernest Mandel, *Power and Money: A Marxist Theory of Bureaucracy* (London: Verso, 1992): 153–188.

44. Finn Bowring, "From Mass Worker to Multitude: A Theoretical Contextualization of Hardt and Negri's Empire," *Capital & Class* 28, no. 2 (July 2004): 101–132. Cf. Stephen Campbell, "Anthropology and the Social Factory," *Dialectical Anthropology* 42 (2018): 227–239; Mario Tronti, *Workers and Capital*, trans. David Broder (London: Verso, 2019); Rosalind Gill and Andy Pratt, "In the Social Factory? Immaterial Labour, Precariousness and Cultural Work," *Theory, Culture & Society* 25 (7–8) (December 2008): 1–30. See also Heinz Sünker, "Childhood between Individualization and Institutionalization," in Georg Neubauer and Klaus Hurrelmann eds, *Individualization in Childhood and Adolescence* (Berlin: Walter de Gruyter, 2012), 37–52, on 39.

45. Gary LaFree, *Losing Legitimacy: Street Crime and the Decline of Social Institutions in America* (Boulder, CO: Westview Press, 1998), 6 (including Peter Berger quotation) (emphasis in original).

46. Gouldner, *Future of the Intellectuals*; Alvin W. Gouldner, *The Dialectic of Ideology and Technology: The Origins, Grammar, and Future of Ideology* (New York: The Seabury Press, 1976).

47. Cf. Richard A. Hilbert, *The Classical Roots of Ethnomethodology: Durkheim, Weber, and Garfinkel* (Chapel Hill: University of North Carolina Press, 1992).

48. Cf. Hugh Mehan and Houston Wood, *The Reality of Ethnomethodology* (New York: John Wiley and Sons, 1975).

49. Peter Winch, *The Idea of a Social Science and Its Relation to Philosophy* (London: Routledge & Kegan Paul, 1958); Aaron Cicourel, *Method and Measurement in Sociology* (New York: Free Press of Glencoe, 1967); Jack Douglas, *The Social Meanings of Suicide* (Princeton, NJ: Princeton University Press, 1967); Jack Douglas ed., *Understanding Everyday Life: Toward the Reconstruction of Sociological Knowledge* (Chicago: Aldine, 1970); Richard Biernacki, *Reinventing Evidence in Social Inquiry: Decoding Facts and Variables* (New York: Palgrave Macmillan, 2012).

50. Alvin Gouldner, "Sociology and the Everyday Life," in Lewis A. Coser ed, *The Idea of Social Structure: Papers in Honor of Robert K. Merton* (New York: Harcourt Brace Jovanovich, 1975), 417–432, on 425.

51. Gouldner, "Sociology and the Everyday Life," 425 (emphasis in original).

52. *Pace* Göran Therborn's Althusserian criticism of Gouldner's "refusal to acknowledge the specificity of the theoretical level": Therborn, *Science, Class and Society*, 24. Cf. Mehan and Wood, *Reality of Ethnomethodology*, 215–223.

53. Gouldner, "Sociology and the Everyday Life," 432.

54. Ted R. Vaughan, "Crisis in Contemporary American Sociology: A Critique of the Discipline's Dominant Paradigm," in Ted R. Vaughan, Gideon Sjoberg, and Larry T. Reynolds eds, *A Critique of Contemporary American Sociology* (Dix Hills, NY: General Hall, Inc., 1993), 10–53, quoting 21.

55. Turner, *American Sociology*, 60–63, 81–97. On the lack of theoretical coherence of post-Parsonian sociology, see Nicos Mouzelis, *Sociological Theory: What Went Wrong? Diagnosis and Remedies* (London: Routledge, 1995).

56. Vaughan, "Crisis in Contemporary American Sociology," 32–33. See also Gideon Sjoberg and Ted R. Vaughan, "The Bureaucratization of Sociology: Its impact on Theory and Research," in Vaughan et al. eds, *Critique of Contemporary Sociology*, 54–113.

57. Abram de Swaan, *The Management of Normality: Critical Essays in Health and Welfare* (London: Routledge, 1990); Peter Cryle and Elizabeth Stephens, *Normality: A Critical Genealogy* (Chicago: University of Chicago Press, 2017).

58. Lennard J. Davis, *Enforcing Normalcy: Disability, Deafness, and the Body* (London: Verso, 1995), 24.

59. Davis, *Enforcing Normalcy*, 49.

60. Davis, *Enforcing Normalcy*, 34,

61. Davis, *Enforcing Normalcy*, 36.

62. George L. Mosse, *Nationalism and Sexuality: Middle-Class Morality and Sexual Norms in Modern Europe* (Madison: University of Wisconsin Press, 2020), 184–185.

63. Julian B. Carter, *The Heart of Whiteness: Normal Sexuality and Race in America, 1880-1940* (Durham, NC: Duke University Press, 2007), 33.

64. Chris Hedges, *War is a Force that Gives us Meaning* (New York: Public Affairs, 2014), 45 (emphasis in original).

65. George Steinmetz, "Scientific Authority and the Transition to Post-Fordism: The Plausibility of Positivism in U.S. Sociology since 1945," In George Steinmetz ed, *The Politics of Method in the Human Sciences: Positivism and its Epistemological Others* (Durham, NC: Duke University Press, 2005), 275–323. See also George Steinmetz and Ou-Byung Chae, "Sociology in an Era of Fragmentation: From the Sociology of Knowledge to the Philosophy of Science, and Back Again," *The Sociological Quarterly* 43, no. 1 (January 2002): 111–137.

66. Boris Kagarlitsky, *Between Class and Discourse: Left Intellectuals in Defence of Capitalism* (London: Routledge, 2020), 42–43.

67. Lauren Langman, "From Subject to Citizen to Consumer: Embodiment and the Mediation of Hegemony," in Richard Harvey Brown ed, *The Politics of Selfhood; Bodies and Identities in Global Capitalism* (University of Minnesota Press, 2003), 167–188; Steve Hall, Simon Winlow, and Craig Ancrum, *Criminal Identities and Consumer Culture: Crime, Exclusion and the New Culture of Narcissism* (Devon, UK: Willan, 2013); Anthony Giddens, "Living in a Post-Traditional Society," in Ulrich Beck, Anthony Giddens, and Scott Lash eds, *Reflexive Modernization: Politics, Tradition and Aesthetics in the Modern Social Order* (Stanford, CA: Stanford University Press, 1994), 56–109.

68. Henri Lefebvre, *Everyday Life in the Modern World*, trans. Sacha Rabinovitch (London: Allen Lane The Penguin Press, 1971); Zygmunt Bauman, *Wasted Lives: Modernity and its Outcasts* (Cambridge: Polity Press, 2004).

69. Saskia Sassen, "Predatory Logics: Going Well Beyond Inequality," in Lauren Langman and David A. Smith eds, *Twenty-First Century Inequality and Capitalism: Piketty, Marx and Beyond* (Chicago, IL: Haymarket Books, 2017), 64–85, on 69.

70. Zygmunt Bauman, *Globalization: The Human Consequences* (New York: Columbia University Press, 1998). Cf. Peter Kloos, "The Dialectics of Globalization and Localization," in Don Kalb, Marco van der Land, Richard Staring, Bart van Steenbergen, and Nico Wilterdink eds, *The Ends of Globalization: Bringing Society Back In* (Lanham, MD: Rowman and Littlefield, 2000), 281–297; Lauren Langman, "The Dialectic of Populism and Cosmopolitanism," in Vincenzo Cicchelli and Syvlie Mesure eds, *Cosmopolitanism in Hard Times* (Leiden: Brill, 2020), 339–354. Cf. Alvin W. Gouldner, "Cosmopolitans and Locals: Toward an Analysis of Latent Social Roles-I." *Administrative Science Quarterly* 2, no. 3 (1957): 281–306; Alvin W. Gouldner, "Cosmopolitans and Locals: Toward an Analysis of Latent Social Roles. II." *Administrative Science Quarterly* 2, no. 4 (1958): 444–480. See also Daniel Rosenblatt, "Stuff the Professional Managerial Class Likes: 'Distinction' for an Egalitarian Elite." *Anthropological Quarterly* 86, no. 2 (2013): 589–623; Hans-Georg Betz, "Postmodernism and the New Middle Class," *Theory, Culture & Society* 9, no. 2 (1992): 93–114.

71. Sassen, "Predatory Logics," 72.

72. Étienne Balibar, *Violence and Civility: On the Limits of Political Philosophy*, trans. G. M. Goshgarian (New York: Columbia University Press, 2016), 15.

73. Langman and Lundskow, "Social Character, Social Change, and the Social Future," 196–197.

74. Sardar, *The Postnormal Times Reader*.

Chapter 1

Hypernormalization in Post-Normal Times

THE DECLINE OF AMERICAN IMPERIALISM AND THE END OF NORMAL

The year 2020 was characterized by the longing for a return to "normal." The promise of a return to normal has been, arguably, the one aspiration shared nationally, and even globally, amid the suspension of the regular routines of everyday life by the global Covid-19 pandemic. For many Americans, especially the politically liberal, the fear and mourning induced by the pandemic was experienced as overlaid on a prior suspension of the normal. This was the electoral victory of Donald J. Trump in 2016, which confounded opinion polls and induced shock and disorientation among those expecting a smooth transition, within the framework of the Democratic Party's culturally liberal neoliberalism, from President Barack Obama to his secretary of state, the former First Lady Hillary Clinton. Yet, Trump's appeal for his supporters also derived from an idea of the return to normal, the greatness of America being how things were and how things naturally ought to be. Trump would be a disrupter who would "drain the swamp" of corrupt Washington politics, but his supporters understood that he would do so in order to overcome the pathology of "this American carnage" and restore American prosperity and power. In that sense, Trump would restore the lost normalcy of how things were before liberals undermined the certainties of racial hierarchy and masculine authority, the jobs were sent to China, crime overran the cities and reached the suburbs, and a "foreign-born" black president occupied the White House.

In 2016, Clinton ran on continuity with the neoliberal economic policies of the Obama administration, the identity politics appeal of the first female president, and the projection of military power. America, she asserted, "is already great." Trump, in contrast, was the charismatic agent of change, declaring war on the regulatory bureaucracy of what his adviser and ideologue Steve Bannon called "the administrative state." In 2020, Trump as incumbent shifted to a rhetoric of continuity, claiming success in reviving the economy and fulfilling campaign promises such as a hard line against immigration. While continuing to use the slogan "Make America Great Again," Trump also asserted "Promises Made, Promises Kept." The Democratic Party establishment undermined, as it had in 2016, the social democratic candidacy of Bernie Sanders.[1] So, with Joseph Biden as their candidate, the Democrats also put forward a message of continuity, with the supposed normalcy of the pre-Trump era. Biden notoriously reassured a group of Wall Street executives that "nothing would fundamentally change" under his administration.[2] Portraying Trump as an aberration and highlighting the administration's chaotic response to the pandemic, Biden promised to "Build Back Better." Biden offered a steady, experienced hand and the protection of the legacy of the Obama administration. As the *New York Times* put it, "Joseph R. Biden Jr. never wavered from his central message: that President Trump was a danger to American democracy, while he was a stable, experienced leader."[3]

For Democrats, then, both senses of the return to normal—the chaos of the pandemic and the anti-democratic charismatic capriciousness of the Trump presidency—were interconnected. The very lack of charisma of the man Trump dubbed "Sleepy Joe" was itself his selling point. Even while aligning himself with the so-called racial reckoning called for by the Black Lives Matter protests of the summer of 2020, Biden did so in terms of healing and reconciliation. This aligned with Biden's political rhetoric of unity, consensus, and bipartisanship. Biden appealed to a unified stance by the ruling class in tamping down social tensions inflamed by Trump. Biden was the candidate for "cooling the mark out."[4]

When Biden announced his candidacy in May 2019, the journalist Ezra Klein observed that "What Biden is promising is a return to normalcy." Klein noted the parallel between Biden's rhetoric and that a hundred years earlier of Warren G. Harding in the 1920 presidential election. Harding coined the political language of "normalcy." Normalcy for Harding meant putting "America First" in the sense of replacing Wilsonian internationalist idealism with pragmatic domestic concerns. This resonated against the economic problems of postwar inflation and social turmoil including the race riots of 1919, a wave of strikes, and the Red Scare of that year. Harding cut a figure, as described in *The Nation*, as "A colorless and platitudinous, uninspired and uninspiring nobody."[5] In the speech for the Nation's Forum, for which he is most remembered, Harding promised a politics of "tranquility" and resumption of "the normal forward stride" of America after what he called "the madness of war and the wildness of its aftermath." He pronounced, "America's present need is not heroics, but healing; not nostrums, but normalcy; not revolution, but restoration; not agitation, but adjustment; not surgery, but serenity; not the dramatic, but the dispassionate; not experiment, but equipoise."[6] The word "normalcy" was not in wide currency before Harding's usage and it was mockingly said that he had created the variation on the more common "normality." The latter term itself is somewhat modern, its current meaning dating only from the mid-nineteenth century, prior to which "normal" was a geometrical term, connoting a right angle. The emergence of the terms "normality" and "normalcy" in their modern usage reflected the particular form of social order established and regulated within the capitalist nation-state, a form that is now in crisis and decline.

The crucial difference between Harding's return to normalcy and that of Biden is that the context of the former was the emergence of the United States of America as the leading imperialist power at the end of World War I.[7] This was itself based on the superiority of the productivity of labor achieved by American capitalism, in particular the new methods of Taylorist work discipline and managerial control and Fordist use of the assembly line and interchangeable parts, techniques pioneered in the United States. These new techniques and the increase in output, the mass production, that they made possible, required for their successful implementation new solutions to the problems of manufacturing consent both in the workplace and in the broader society.[8] They created new tensions and called for new solutions to the problem of securing a capitalist social order that could absorb this scale of production, solutions that were not possible in the 1920s.

The problem of social order as a problem within the nation-state was inherently bound up with the international situation. The United States's fate was to emerge as the leading imperialist power in the period after 1917, when the Russian Revolution had fundamentally called the future of capitalism into question and the working class emerged decisively as its own political force in world history.[9] The bourgeois normalcy proclaimed by Harding was, from that very point on, a precariously maintained normalcy. The descent of the bourgeois nation-states into a hellish maelstrom in World War I itself could not be forgotten as a reminder of the inherent precariousness of the social order achieved by the bourgeoisie within the framework of nation-states.

Harding's victory ushered in the conservatism, corruption, and economic boom of the 1920s. Jane Addams lamented the end of the progressive upsurge of the beginning of the century, saying that the 1920s were "a period of political and social sag."[10] It was a precarious normalcy, marked at the beginning by war and revolution and at the end by the Wall Street crash and the greatest economic collapse in the history of capitalism. It was a normalcy followed by another even more gigantic and terrible descent into imperialist mass violence as the advances in science and the productive forces were transformed into even more destructive weapons. Yet, this descent into chaos created the conditions for the solution that was lacking in the 1920s, but took the form of the Bretton Woods agreement and the decisive assertion of US hegemony over its decimated imperialist rivals as the world emerged from World War II.

It was the two decades after the end of World War II that established the model of the affluent consumer society as "normal." As James K. Galbraith argues, this was bound up with the idea that economic growth was "not only desirable but also normal, perpetual, and expected."[11] In the period between 1945 and 1970, capitalism appeared to have overcome its contradictions and established a stable capitalist everyday life capable of absorbing mass production.[12] This was the height of structural-functionalism in sociology. Gouldner argues that Parsons's sociological outlook was shaped by, and expressed, the twin normalcies of the 1920s and 1950s:

> Some of the most fundamental aspects of Parsons' personal reality had been shaped by the economic prosperity of the 1920s, during which time his own personal prospects and position coincided with the general success of the American economy . . . For Parsons, then, the Great Depression was an interlude between the prosperity of the 1920s and the later American triumph in World War II and postwar affluence. Linked to the experiences of a powerful and successful middle class, Parsons' optimism was the optimism of those for whom success, of and in the system, was the fundamental personal reality and for whom its failure was an aberration not quite personally real.[13]

The coming apart of this "powerful and successful middle class," and indeed the disintegration of the category in which this seemingly classless unity could be constructed, was a key dimension of the unraveling of this postwar Keynesian-Fordist hegemony.

It is the decline of the world position of US imperialism that was expressed in the events of January 6, 2021, when the Capitol was stormed by petit-bourgeois fascist Trump supporters. This was a desperate bid to stage a coup by stopping the certification of Biden's election victory and so, they hoped, allowing Trump to remain in power. The events of January 6 represent the domestic crisis of the American nation-state which is also in crisis in its foreign relations, and these are interconnected.[14] The military rampage that the United States has been on in the Middle East for the last thirty years, and what Max Blumenthal calls the "tidal wave of nationalist propaganda" that followed 9/11, has done a great deal to create an atmosphere of fascism in the national culture and to produce cadres of authoritarians, trained in arms: the American Freikorps.[15] The culture of militaristic nationalism of the American right wing reflects the strategy of American imperialism, to use military power to overcome the consequences of its relative economic decline, an impossible feat.[16] This is reflected in the magical use of nationalism by a lumpen American petit-bourgeoisie to compensate for, and restore, their lost ontological security.

The increasing role of violence in American politics was evidenced by the January 6 attack on the Capitol and by the rise of right-wing militias that have developed since the end of the Vietnam War.[17] These have now moved from the fringe to integration with the, now openly fascist, Republican Party. The role of violence is exemplified by militarized, highly repressive policing of protest and the routine murderousness of the police. The increasing prominence of violence for political power was also displayed by Trump the previous year, when Secret Service and federal Park Police brutally cleared Black Lives Matter demonstrators from Lafayette Square, opposite the White House, in order to give Trump a Bible-toting photo opportunity in front of nearby St. John's Church. As tear gas and flash-bang grenades were deployed against protesters, Trump emerged into the White House's Rose Garden, declaring "I am your president of law and order." Seeming to be preparing martial law, he added, "If a city or state refuses to take the actions that are necessary to defend the life and property of their residents, then I will deploy the United States military and quickly solve the problem for them . . . As we speak, I am dispatching thousands and thousands of heavily armed soldiers, military personnel and law enforcement officers to stop the rioting."[18]

What is indicated by this integration of American politics and violence is the advanced stage of the process that Wolfe identified in his 1977 book *Limits of Legitimacy*, as being that "the dominant forces within late capitalism are losing their ability to rule. Thus 'rule by force' is a contradiction in terms. Authoritarian solutions are an expression of the inability to rule." The turn by the ruling class to authoritarianism evidences its

> bankruptcy and impotence, not hardheaded realism; political extremism, not moderation and civility. Those who seek to replace liberal democracy by some sort of authoritarian structure are engaged, not so much in a strategy for the ruling class, as in voicing the decline of the ruling class.[19]

Biden's "Nothing will fundamentally change" administration does not offer any way out of the crisis of American imperialism and the long-term hollowing out of American democracy (in which the January 6 events represent a qualitative turning point in the loss of stability and legitimacy from the US governing institutions). Like Harding a hundred years earlier, Biden ran on a return to normalcy. While Biden's administration has even less chance than Harding's short-lived presidency of achieving "normalcy," there may prove to be parallels in corrupt corporatism. The age of social reform within capitalism ended with the failure of Lyndon Johnson's Great Society, and European social democracy ran out of steam in the 1970s. Gary Teeple writes,

Social democracy as we have known it has no future, because the conditions that
gave rise to it are being transformed and because its policies and programs—the
reforms of the nation-state era—were nothing more than what these conditions
allowed or even demanded.[20]

There has not been a single significant economically redistributive social
reform since then (Obamacare included) and there cannot be under conditions of declining US imperialism and a global capitalist system in structural
decline facing mounting insoluble contradictions.[21] The 2008 financial crisis
and "great recession" did not usher in new period of reform. Bastiaan van
Apeldoorn, Naná de Graaff and Henk Overbeek write,

> The enormous sums of public money being poured into the global economy to
> sustain demand . . . in 2008-2009 did not, we now know, announce a full-scale
> return to Keynesian demand management. Rather, they turned out to be an
> emergency measure soon to be replaced by a renewed and indeed even deeper
> neoliberal offensive of austerity and retrenchment.[22]

Biden's promise of normalcy is an example of what Adam Curtis calls
"hypernormalization," under technocratic neoliberalism. He adopts the term
from Alexei Yurchak's study of the last two decades of the Soviet Union:
Everything Was Forever Until It Was No More. Curtis's documentaries,
including his 2016 *HyperNormalisation*, expose the fantasy that global capitalism can be managed and sustained, by contrasting neoliberal nostrums with
images of mounting global chaos.[23] Hypernormalization may be understood
in terms of Erving Goffman's observation that one response to the disruption of everyday routines and expectations, and the sense of danger that such
disruption carries with it, is to deny that the rules, routines, and modes of
behavior of normalcy have ceased to apply. Hence, in elucidating Goffman's
account, Barbara Misztal writes,

> When Umwelt (the region of potential or real sources of alarm) suddenly
> ceases to maintain normal appearances we search for signs of danger, while
> concealing our suspicions by acting "normally," and subsequently we try to
> revert a disturbing event to the normal . . . As people employ various cre-
> ative accounts to render abnormalities unalarming, normal appearances can
> be faked. In such a case, normal appearances become a normalcy show, [as
> Goffman wrote] "a show in which all participants have the task of acting
> unfurtively."[24]

Hypernormalization as "a normalcy show" can be understood as an actively
(though not necessarily consciously) defensive normalization.

As Anthony Giddens has argued, in de-traditionalized modern societies, everyday life is rendered banal as the administrative and technological mechanisms of modernity, and the rise of positivistic thought, suppress existential dilemmas at the heart of the human condition. The banal routines of everyday life themselves become the major support of individuals' ontological security, or protection against dread and chaos. Ontological security (a term Giddens derives from R. D. Laing) is the ability to take for granted the continuity of self and world, and therefore to have stable expectations of the natural world, the technological infrastructure that we routinely use, and other people and their actions and meanings.[25] Giddens writes that

> ontological security . . . refers to the confidence that most human beings have in the continuity of their self-identity and in the constancy of the surrounding social and material environments of action. A sense of the reliability of persons and things, so central to the notion of trust, is basic to feelings of ontological security.[26]

It is, fundamentally, security in the knowledge that tomorrow will be another day, much like today. Harry Collins writes, "Mostly we have to rely on the normal being normal—we have to rely on the reliability and continuity of social life. Of course, all bets are off in times of war and revolution."[27]

As Lefebvre emphasized, modern everyday life is shaped by mass consumerism in "the bureaucratic society of controlled consumption." This sheds light on the context of Harding's phrase: this was the period in which the mass production technologies of the assembly line and the automobile were creating a new way of life, which Gramsci called "Fordism." This came to fruition, however, only after World War II in the "affluent society" of the postwar boom.[28] During this period, the working class was integrated into American capitalism within a Keynesian strategy of economic growth, with bureaucratic collective bargaining and wage increases tied to productivity growth, within the special conditions of US economic hegemony in the wake of World War II, with competitor capitalist nations recovering from the devastation of war.

Fordism-Keynesianism, as the combination of mechanization with mass consumption and the broader institutional apparatus of the welfare state replaced working-class culture based on surviving vestiges of preindustrial forms of community with a social democratic solidarity project reconstituting solidarity at the level of the nation-state as welfare state.[29] In this way, working-class solidarities and collective aspirations were co-opted by the nation-state through the construction of the welfare state. Social democracy thereby strengthened nation-state institutions and supported nationalism. In the United States, social democratic concessions to the working class in the form of welfare were limited in comparison with European nation-states, but for the integrated section of the working class this was compensated for by rising wages. Wolfe writes,

> The principle of using the power of the government to preserve the capitalist order solidified during the Wilson years and became a way of life under the New Deal. The same process occurs in Europe; in fact, by 1960 European welfare states are much more advanced in the breadth of their functions than the American. Capitalism . . . changed again and with it its state.[30]

Social democracy (and the US post-New Deal variant) was an essentially national project, but locked into a contradictory dependence on, and, therefore, integration with, global imperialism under US power. The Bretton Woods Conference of 1944 created an apparatus of fixed exchange rates tied to the dollar and stabilized by the transferability of the dollar into gold, and created organizational legacies of the General Agreement on Tariffs and Trade (GATT), the International Monetary Fund (IMF), and the World Bank. The peak of social democracy was under the umbrella of the institutional infrastructure of globalization. The contradiction between this overall framework of the organization of a global "free-trade" economy and the nevertheless primarily national character of economies in the postwar period prior to the 1970s was manageable only under the highly artificial and necessarily temporary conditions of postwar reconstruction in the wake of World War II. The fact that World War II left a single capitalist power, the United States, with such unrivalled superiority allowed for a temporary suppression of the contradiction between global economy and the nation-state through the imperialist logic of the domination of the world economy by a single national power.

However, the global economic dominance of the United States was undermined by the very logic of Bretton Woods and of the postwar reconstruction achieved through the Marshall Plan. The growth of international competition, as Germany and Japan reemerged as major manufacturing forces contributing to the global economy, was by the end of the 1960s eroding the US's economic hegemony and squeezing profit rates. The growth of imports was undermining the US balance of payments creating downward pressure on the value of the dollar.[31]

The Bretton Woods project of creating a capitalist global market, resting on a foundation of US dominance, was undermined by its own success, the global economy undermining the conditions for US hegemony. The turning point was the act by President Nixon, on August 15, 1971, of reneging on the dollar's exchangeability for gold and floating the dollar on international exchange rates, an event known as the "Nixon shock."[32] This marked the essential end of Bretton Woods and the opening of the era of globalization of production. It marked the beginning of the end of US economic hegemony.[33]

US imperialism was in the inherently contradictory position that it took its place as the world power in the period in which the contradictions of capitalism as a system encompassing the globe were producing increasingly devastating wars between states. The character of the United States as a "garrison state," and the growing power of the military-industrial complex, are expressions of the coincidence of US hegemony with the mounting contradictions of global capitalism that were manifesting themselves in war.[34]

Dan Glazebrook describes US strategy in the Middle East today as "divide and ruin":

> This is the natural result of Empire's declining economic influence. It cannot compete with the very generous terms of trade offered by China, and is thus at risk of losing all its contracts in the third world. For Western imperialism, today more than ever, strong independent third-world states are seen as a dangerous threat, because all are viewed as potential economic partners of China.
>
> Of course, during the Cold War, this was also true—every independent third world state was a potential Soviet ally. But at least anti-communist strongmen could be relied on to pick the U.S. as a partner rather than the USSR. The U.S. could ultimately "outbid" its Soviet rivals for the allegiance of third world states. This is what has changed. Backing the U.S. and the West is increasingly a game of diminishing returns.
>
> The West realizes this, and understanding that any genuinely strong state is unlikely to do its bidding anymore, prefers to see such states destroyed. It is only in this context that we can understand the apparently ludicrous policies pursued by the West across the Middle East . . . These policies are not designed to produce stable, compliant states, as in the past, because the West has realised that in its crisis phase such things are no longer possible. They are designed to produce weak, divided "failed states," unable to become regional powers in their own right, and unable to become powerful allies of China or anyone else. Thus, the much-criticised "failure to plan" in Iraq, was a plan in itself.[35]

Glazebrook points out that the big business of private security directly benefits from this violent chaos, as do arms manufacturers and infrastructure firms brought in to rebuild what is destroyed (though the rebuilding is less important than being funneled government money and minimal restoration takes place). War is, as Julian Assange put it in interview with John Pilger, a means of laundering money offshore, similar to tax havens of the kind exposed by the Panama Papers.[36] The proceeds of the legalized looting of the American state's coffers by private corporations are laundered via these contracts. Glazebrook contrasts this policy of destruction and chaos with the

Cold War policy of "installing 'complaint dictatorships' " such as those of the Shah in Iran, Mobutu in the Congo, Suharto in Indonesia, and Pinochet in Chile.

However, there is more continuity with the Cold War than Glazebrook implies and the point of intersection was President Carter and Zbigniew Brzezinski's Afghanistan policy. To the extent that American Cold War policies toward its client dictatorships were informed by, or ideologically presented in terms of, modernization theory (associated especially with Walt Rostow), Afghanistan represents a total contrast in that it had no goal other than destabilization.[37] This destabilization was justified by the Reaganite language of freedom, especially the emancipation of religion as the US underwrote Islamic fundamentalism, even though Washington would later claim to be freeing Afghan women from this fundamentalist backwardness.[38]

It is striking to what extent American divide and ruin policy in Afghanistan was the obliteration of modernity. The descent of the country into the chaos of civil war in the 1990s triggered a debate in the United States over the merits of what was called "nation-building." Announcing the withdrawal of US troops from Afghanistan in July 2021, Biden said, "We did not go to Afghanistan to nation-build."[39] What was left after the ousting of the modernizing Afghan Stalinists was the inevitable disintegration of the country into tribalism, warlordism, religious fundamentalism, and an economy fueled by the heroin trade. After the US 2001 invasion, it set up a government in Kabul, entirely dependent on US military funding and firepower. The United States accomplished little to nothing in terms of economic development. Its puppet regime collapsed immediately when the United States pulled out its forces in 2021, leaving the country again in the hands of the Taliban, the Pashtun tribal and Wahabi Islamist organization that formed the government prior to the US invasion.

The chaos of divide and ruin creates the conditions for what Norbert Elias terms a "decivilizing spurt."[40] This is a situation of weak to no centralized monopoly of violence, producing greater likelihood of violence breaking out in everyday life. This ramifies throughout social interactions and psychology, leading to a reduction in self-control and greater likelihood of resort to violence. De-civilizing was evident in, for example, a moment of cannibalism during the Syrian civil war, caught on video, where one of Washington's so-called moderate rebels pulled out an organ, perhaps the heart, from a dead body and took a bite out of it.[41] De-civilizing is also evident in US forces engaging in murder of prisoners and civilians for sport, the collection of body parts, and so on. De-civilizing is of course inherent to war, which makes a positive good out of overcoming civilized restraints on killing. This is the cultural-psychological complex promulgated by President Trump when he boasts of the "toughness" of his followers and associates his enemies with weakness, and when he threatens to "annihilate" the entire country of Afghanistan. War and fascism go together, in syn-necrosis. The US campaign of divide and ruin set into motion a global de-civilizing process, one that proliferates at all levels of society and psychology. US imperialism's de-civilizing divide and ruin policies entail ruling over chaos and ruling through the creation of chaos.

It is hard to say which horrors stand out; so many could be mentioned. On October 3, 2015, under Obama, a US Air Force AC-130U gunship airplane attacked a Medecins Sans Frontieres trauma hospital in Afghanistan, firing 211 shells on the hospital building "where patients were sleeping in their beds or being operated on in the operating theatre" killing 42 people and injuring 37.[42] In September 2019, a US drone killed thirty pine nut farmers and injured forty of the workers who were gathered together resting after a day's work.[43] Later that month, Afghan security forces killed forty civilians at a wedding party, while targeting Taliban next door.[44] At the end of 2019, President Trump pardoned Navy Seals war criminal Edward Gallagher, who used a hunting knife to stab a teenaged Iraqi fighter to death as he was being treated by a medic as well as committing multiple other atrocities. Trump praised Gallagher and had the murderer appear beside him at a rally for the far-right organization Turning Point USA.[45] US-supported Saudi bombing of Yemen has resulted in a cholera epidemic, ongoing since 2017, which has seen more than 1.2 million cases and is the largest in epidemiologically recorded history.[46] On January 13, 2018, with Trump ramping up threats and tensions with North Korea, a false alert of imminent nuclear attack caused a million people in Hawaii to say goodbye to their loved ones or try desperately and futilely to shelter their children.[47] There is also ecological horror. In November 2018, eighty-six people were killed and the town of Paradise, California, razed in what was the deadliest wildfire in California recorded history.[48] The end of 2019 saw climate change-fueled fires ravage Australia, causing thousands of people to seek shelter on the beach, awaiting a siren giving the alert to wade into the ocean.[49] In July 2021, with the Covid-19 pandemic not yet under control, Germany and Belgium have faced catastrophic flooding, for which climate change is the underlying cause.[50]

De-civilizing arises from divide and ruin pursued both in military destructiveness abroad and in economic and social destructiveness domestically within the United States. The government casts off the provisions for the well-being of the population that derive from the period of class compromise in the twentieth century. Instead, public power becomes a means of extraction from the mass of the population. Sociocide and ecocide are pursued actively through war and extraction and passively through abandonment of populations to brute nature. The capitalist state becomes the predator state. James K. Galbraith writes that "In the corporate republic that presides over the Predator

State, nothing is done for the common good. Indeed, the men in charge do not realize that public purposes exist." According to Galbraith,

> Hurricane Katrina illustrated this perfectly, as Bush gave contracts to Halliburton and at the same time tied up efforts to restore the city. The actual population of New Orleans was at best an afterthought; once dispersed, it was quickly forgotten.[51]

The contradiction between egalitarian and democratic ideals that are still powerful within the American population and the immense unequal concentration of power in what G. William Domhoff calls "the corporate rich (the owners and managers of large incorporated properties)" and at the intersection of the state and big business, has created tremendous pressures that have drastically undermined bourgeois democracy in the United States.[52] The universalistic Enlightenment ideals in the US Bill of Rights created a contradictory democratic nationalism, a universalistic particularism. The only resolution of this contradiction that capitalism allows is imperialism as the globality of the power of the particular, the US state as global bully.[53]

Under the pressure of war and inequality, American nationalism has shed its liberal democratic universalism. While nationalism had a progressive orientation in the period of the bourgeoisie's rise, by the twentieth century it had become an inherently regressive ideology, corresponding to the rise of imperialism and the transformation of the bourgeoisie from rising class to ruling class and the emergence of a fully global capitalist economy as imperialism integrated the world into a global market. Today the role of the capitalist class in the turn to fascism is personified in the figure of President Trump and in billionaires and multimillionaires such as the Mercer family and their agent of sorts, the hedge-fund manager Bannon.[54]

In fascism, the military power that the nation-state projects outward is projected also inward domestically, undoing the existence of a civil society, in other words, a sphere of relations from which violence and power differentials rooted in violence were removed. The inability of the bourgeoisie to create society above the level of the nation-state and, therefore, the limits of the civilizing process under capitalism, represent the inability of capitalism to overcome the contradiction between the nation-state and global economy.

THE SPECTACLE OF NORMALCY

Normalcy is always linked to return. Normalcy is a nostalgic idea, but what it is nostalgic for is modernity. What is normal is always what we have known (or imagine we have known) in the past. Normalcy consists of, as Harold

Garfinkel puts it, "points of departure and return for every modification of the world of everyday life." Everyday life, the template of normalcy, is as Gouldner says, the realm of those "commonly recurrent" experiences and "background assumptions" from which the extraordinary or "historical" represents a break and departure.[55] At the same time that normalcy is inherently nostalgic, it is quintessentially modern, precisely because, as Giddens has stressed, it is modernity that produces an everyday life that is entirely banal and purged of sacred significances. Normalcy, however, stands in essential tension with the other promises of modernity, the release of the freedom of the individual and the potential for dynamic creative destruction.[56] Hence the 1920s was a period of political repression, which had begun in the violent suppression of American leftists such as the IWW immediately after the end of World War I, and was also a period in which there was a cultural desire to throw off what Howard Brick calls "conformist restraint."[57] Consumerism provided a solution to this tension, by absorbing the nonconformist energies and channeling them into the conformist activity of buying commodities. Hence Edward Bernays's advertising of cigarettes as symbols of freedom to newly politically enfranchised and culturally assertive women. The emergence of consumerist capitalist normalcy was blighted by the disasters of the Great Depression and World War II, although significantly the latter left the United States of America relatively unscathed. While the project of normalcy was assembled and put into motion from around the turn of the century, it was only in the first two decades after World War II that it can be said to have come to fruition. And it is to this period that current nostalgia for normalcy attaches itself. Normalcy also has a place—the United States. This is for two reasons: first, that the early postwar period in America modeled the affluent society, the promise of which remains a key dimension of normalcy; second, that the US financially, militarily, politically, and culturally underwrote the stabilization of capitalism in the immediate aftermath of World War II and in this way provided not only the ideal but the infrastructure of normalcy.

Normalcy is everyday life. It is the quotidian, the ordinary. Ordinarily, one turns the faucet and potable water comes out. That is an accomplishment of science, engineering, bureaucratic organization, and industrial labor, that designed, planned, organized and implemented the infrastructure of modern urban life. One flicks the light switch and the lights come on. There is, of course, a massive energy infrastructure that makes that possible. But the energy infrastructure of modernity belies normalcy. The burning of coal and oil has thrown the climate out of balance. Nuclear power carries with it the dangers of the atomic bomb and the reactor meltdown.[58]

Normalcy was always uncanny. The chaos that it depended on excluding was never fully excluded. When facilely using the term "postwar," it is

possible to miss the meaning and significance of that term. The exclusion
of violence is essential to the concept of normalcy. And yet, the history
of modernity is a history of violence. If normalcy was "postwar," it had to
exclude from itself the maelstrom of World War II: the holocaust, the atomic
bombings of Hiroshima and Nagasaki, the horrific battlefield slaughter, the
destruction of cities, and the displacement of populations. Normalcy, made
possible by science and technology, entails the exclusion of the other side of
science and technology: destruction and violent death.[59]

Normalcy was an escape from, and denial of, the dark side of modernity.
It was a retreat into the quotidian, forcing horror backstage.[60] If the first two
postwar decades were the period of "normalcy," this relied on the possibility
of marking a break with war. The return to normalcy after the war was, in
Western Europe especially, a return to liberal democracy. The contradiction
in liberalism between the sovereignty of the individual and the sovereignty
of the state was solved by Locke with the notion of "tacit consent."[61] In
going about their business in society, the individual is relying on the order
that the state guarantees and using the infrastructures and facilities that the
state provides. Therefore, in the normal course of life, the individual necessarily grants consent to this ordering power of the state. This suggests the
rooting of the legitimacy of the state in the normal flow of everyday life.
Order is, in a sense, self-legitimizing. Life goes on, smoothly, quietly; the
system works, so the system is good. But this also suggests that the legitimacy of the state depends on the backgrounding of everything disruptive of
normalcy.

Bauman has called the modern nation-state a gardener because of the way
nation-states sought to produce and regulate a national population, in particular through the construction of a national culture and through the regulation of
individuals and groups.[62] The idea of normalcy, then, is very closely related to
civil society, in the sense that this counterposes civility to violence and entails
the absence of violent conflict. Balibar identifies civility with "the whole set
of political strategies (and conditions of possibility of politics) that respond
to the fact that violence, in various forms, always exceeds normality."[63] Civil
society, as the arena of everyday life, assumes and depends for its existence
upon the maintenance of civil peace. The state's ability to maintain peace,
as Hobbes argued, is the very purpose of the state and the basis for consent
to its authority. Writing of the demoralizing effect of counterrevolutionary
defeat, Trotsky said that "Force not only conquers but, in its own way, it
'convinces.' "[64] Drowning a revolution in blood convinces people that it was
a pipe dream all along. Correspondingly, the ability of the state to suppress
opposition and conflict, to impose its one-sided "peace," to shift violence
from manifest to latent, to thereby normalize rule, itself tends to convince the
ruled of the rightness of that rule, that it is simply the way of things.

The normalcy of the postwar period was dependent on "peace" under the threat of the atomic bomb, but this "peace" was also a state of permanent mobilization for war, the routinization of military preparation within a "permanent arms economy."[65] Not only did "cold war" become a hot war in Korea but the Vietnam War ultimately contributed to the end of the postwar boom and its social compact. Normalcy was, therefore, an uncanny presence/absence of war.

Yurchak coined the term "hypernormalization" to describe the standardized, authoritative forms of language and ceremonial forms of participation in the last two decades of the Soviet Union, alongside subcultural forms of irony and parody, often achieved by subtle hoax in the form what Yurchak calls ironic "over-identification." Legitimacy became attached not to the content of speech but to the form of words. Official modes of expression were valued as performances of adherence and allegiance, and adoption of them and participation in them were definitive of "normal." But due to the substantive emptiness of these standardized and routinized forms of official discourse and expression, the performance of these discourses often was repetitive and self-referential. Since all that mattered was following formal protocol, a self-reinforcing mimesis produced ever more hypernormalized performances of "normal" Soviet ideology and citizenship. At the same time, due to their emptiness, meticulous performance of these ritualistic modes of expression could cover for distancing the self from the performance and even deviating from the officially required behavior. Yurchak and Dominic Boyer draw parallels between late Soviet irony and parodic forms of political comedy in contemporary American television. Yurchak and Boyer suggest that such ironic distancing has political significance, but much of their argument would also support a view of such cynicism as a strategy of adaptation and accommodation.[66] What is probably most important in their analysis of parallels between the ebbing years of the Soviet Union and the current American condition is what they delineate as the structural causes of contemporary Western capitalist hypernormalization. They write in their 2010 article:

First, a high degree of monopolization of media production and circulation via corporate consolidation and real-time synchronization . . . Second, the active orchestration of public political discourse by parties and governmental institutions (the RNC's "talking points," paid spokespersons performing objective assessments, Pentagon "information operations," etc.) . . . . Third, the cementing of ideological (in this case, liberal-entrepreneurial) consensus in political news analysis . . . and the rapid thinning out of investigative reporting . . .; Four, the thematic and generic normalization of modes and styles of political performance and representation. In keeping with the general professionalization of political life and the definitive role of 24/7 news television in political communication, political performances in the United States are increasingly calculated and formalized, concerned more with the attainment of efficient and precise genres of political messaging then with exploration of the thematic substance of social issues. Put more provocatively, contemporary American political performance has come to resemble the formalist theatrics of late-socialist political culture.[67]

Boyer and Yurchak are describing what Guy Debord, in *Comments on The Society of the Spectacle*, called "the integrated spectacle." This, according to Debord, was the integration of the "concentrated spectacle" of single-party states like the Third Reich and the Soviet Union with the "diffuse spectacle" of the mass-mediatized consumer capitalist societies.[68] So there is a private corporate media that is integrated with the apparatus of the nation-state actively carrying out what Noam Chomsky and Edward Herman call "the manufacture of consent."[69]

Curtis's 2016 film *HyperNormalisation* suggests that the prevailing ideology of neoliberalism and modes of neoliberal governance have created a generalized complicity in unreality. Yurchak's concept resonated for Curtis with this unreality of life in capitalist societies today.[70] Curtis portrays the chasm between the fictions of normalcy promoted by elites who seek a managed neoliberalism and the realities of war and ecological collapse that neoliberal capitalism produces.[71] Curtis uses techniques of video collage similar to Debord's *Society of the Spectacle* film in order to expose the way in which a layer of unreality is imposed over the real world.[72] But whereas Debord's theory of the spectacle, like Herbert Marcuse's *One-Dimensional Man*, suggested the ability of advanced capitalism to stabilize and maintain itself in an almost totalitarian manner, Curtis's film contrasts the narrowness of vision of the status quo with a chaotic world of terrorism and war.[73]

Psychologist Matthew Adams suggests that Curtis's conception of hypernormalization

> can be used to make sense of the maintenance of a simplified, reassuring and fake version of the world in the face of unprecedented global challenges that incumbent governments and power alliances do not have the competence or inclination to address.

Adams argues that the concept applies particularly to contemporary society's state of inertia as it plunges into climate change.[74] Jean Baudrillard's "hyperreality" referred to the endlessly fascinating ultra-vivid spectacles that subsumed life in post-modern late capitalism, providing a sparkling world in relation to which the real was a desert, empty and inhospitable. Hypernormalization may be understood as being too normal to be true, a normalcy being purposively acted, as if to prevent recognition of its own precariousness.[75] Hypernormalization is an ethnomethodological normalcy. In that way, hypernormalization is the truth of normalcy, in that in its very weakness it exposes the always inherent fragility of normalcy. Hypernormalization is when normalcy is no longer lived experience but has become spectacle.

Normalcy becomes beset with what Frederic Jameson calls "nostalgia for the present." Normalcy is presentist while also longing for the past. It is presentist in its implication of a steady state and, therefore, the holding still of time. But it is also nostalgic because of its inherent connotation of "a return to." "I'm glad things are back to normal" cannot but carry with it nostalgia for the present in its very recognition of the specificity of the present in time and therefore of its potential nonexistence, its potential giving way again to the non-normal. Normalcy is confronted by the impossibility of a steady state: in other words, its own impossibility.

The returns to normalcy after both world wars were predicated on the suppression of the specter of 1917. It was an actively repressive normalcy. Curtis is obsessed with the origins of neoliberalism in Cold War technocratic attempts to create a society of individuals ordered by rational systems of the bureaucratically administered market. The point of these Cold War projects, he argues, was to create normalcy by eliminating the possibility of revolution and radical change. So this normalcy was based on the deliberate exclusion of all ideological and emotional forces that would disrupt the smooth operation of the market and of a consumer culture in the narrow freedom of which individuals would be trapped. Curtis may be understood as tracing a path from Daniel Bell's announcement of "the end of ideology" in 1960 to Francis Fukuyama's assertion of "the end of history" when the Berlin Wall fell in 1989.[76] Curtis is particularly interested in the development of a managerial style of politics that came to fruition in the 1990s and the first decade of the twenty-first century in Britain's New Labour government. This was a depoliticized, managerial politics precisely because it had expunged socialism, and therefore any vestige of ideological opposition to capitalism, and transformed the main left-wing party into one that fully accepted Margaret Thatcher's dictum that "there is no alternative" to capitalist society and neoliberal "free market" policies. In this way, New Labour served to normalize neoliberalism, accommodating the population to it.[77]

Curtis's fundamental point is that this hypernormalized, managed market individualist society is impossible because what it excludes returns in new form. Hence, he contrasts the image of hyper-normalcy with the intrusion of destabilizing and destructive realities and forces of war and terrorism. His point is that political forms that seek the transcendence of this banal normalcy cannot be suppressed. Nor, he suggests, can the violence of nature, disordered by the very technological basis of hyper-normalcy, be managed by the neoliberal experts. Hypernormalization creates a fake world, but one that must ultimately fail to exclude reality. The maintenance of this political-ideo-logical-imaginative stasis in which, as Jameson said, "the historical imagina-tion is paralysed and cocooned," will itself bring about the end of the world.[78]

The breakdown of hypernormalization is brought into focus in the writings of Roy Scranton. His novel *War Porn* moves between the settings of a Utah barbeque among laid-back post-college American left-liberal hipsters and the war zones of Iraq, where a mathematics student's life is ripped apart by the Americans' bombing and invasion.[79] The mathematician descends into the hellish de-civilized world of American occupation with its callous dehuman-izing contempt for the Iraqis. The uneasy ordinariness and sense of affluent boredom of the barbeque is troubled by the presence of a US military veteran, a torturer, who carries with him the sadism of American empire. Scranton portrays a sense of the banal unreality of quotidian American life, and the longing for reality. But the novel also shows the horror of Iraq's desert of the real, the violence of American empire, which is precisely what is excluded from consciousness to produce the eternal sunshine of the spotless American mind and the ordinary illusion of everyday life.[80] The conversational and behavioral patterns through which people keep civil interaction going, repairing and covering over uncivil breaches, prove incapable of handling the predatory violence of empire to which this everyday life is uncannily but inevitably attached. The narrative is interrupted by snatches of seemingly disordered words. A poem titled "Babylon" that is strewn through the novel is written in the language of military commands, protocols, news propaganda, and patriotic ideology. Empire's banality of evil, empty words, communicat-ing thoughtlessness, shout down and break up meaning into meaningless fragments.

Scranton again conveys the unreality of contemporary life in his nonfiction work *Learning to Die in the Anthropocene*, in which he states flatly that "this civilization is already dead." The world we have come to take for granted, "carbon-fueled capitalism," lives on only in "zombie" form. It has totally undermined its basis in the planets' natural systems and is dying and taking with it to the netherworld not only humanity but a vast number of the planet's other species. Scranton captures the strange stasis of the pattern of talk and action through which we go on even while knowing that we cannot go on, and through which we deny and deflect this truth of dying:

And while smart, dedicated, and thoughtful people fumble with political machinery that doesn't work, such as carbon-pricing markets, protests, and the United Nations, all of us in the Global North go about our business, driving, fly-ing, leaving lights on, running heaters and air conditioners, eating meat, charg-ing our devices, living unsustainable lives predicated on easy consumption.[81]

The situation that Scranton describes is what Ingolfür Bluhdorn and Ian Welsh call "sustaining the unsustainable" in which a "simulative politics" ensures that, even while the reality of climate change is recognized, and even when agreements are made and policies introduced, these are only minor adjustments to a system that is, in its very nature, voraciously unsustainable.[82] As Scranton says, these are ways of denying death in the combined sense of the threat to all our individual lives from fire, flood, storm, famine, and violence that climate change carries, and the death of this global capitalist civilization. We are collectively hurtling into the abyss.

Thomas Singer insightfully observes how the culture of reality-denial arises from the very recognition, too terrifying to acknowledge, of the morbidity of the prevailing way of life:

> Collective madness plays itself out in the denial of the pandemic of the virus, mass shootings at schools and climate change . . . At its core, I would suggest that these collective madnesses are based on the basic denial of the threat to existence itself.[83]

The sense of impending doom expresses a suppressed recognition of what cannot be recognized, that human civilization is on a path leading inexorably toward global collapse. The idea of a "return to normalcy" is a key form of contemporary reality-denial.[84] The expectation and hope that life will return to normal has become a mantra during the Covid-19 pandemic.[85] But the pandemic is only a symptom of the social forces that are closing the very possibility of normalcy and pushing us into a post-normal world. The institutionalized patterns that are regarded as normal are unsustainable and self-undermining.

In a *New York Times* op-ed published in the early new year of 2021, during the ongoing pandemic, Scranton points out that 2020 was not only the year in which normal life was suspended by the Covid-19 virus, but it was also the worst fire season on record for the West Coast of the United States and the most active Atlantic hurricane season; it saw massive fires devastating the Amazon rainforest, near-record lows of Arctic sea ice, record global temperatures, and large methane releases from melting Arctic permafrost signaling the onset of feedback loops that are likely to make climate change self-perpetuating. It is precisely what has been taken for granted as normal that is producing the end of normalcy. Scranton writes: "Going back to normal now means returning to a course that will destabilize the conditions for all human life, everywhere on earth."[86] Normal is, therefore, a nostalgic illusion. Not only can it never be restored, but it never truly was. Normal was always an illusion in the sense that it was an impossible condition, always undoing itself. "The first thing we need to do," says Scranton, "is let go of the idea that life will ever be normal again."[87] The return to normalcy can only be a return to hypernormalization.

GLOBALIZATION, NEOLIBERALISM, AND DISPOSABILITY

The end of normal has been particularly striking and painful in the United States of America. As the United States has reserved for itself the right to be a "global policeman," through the global war on terror and through its bogus humanitarian justifications for the destruction of entire societies, as in the Obama administration bombing of Libya, domestic policing of the internally excluded populations increasingly takes on the character of war. Militarized police were mobilized against protesters in the 1999 WTO protests, the so-called Battle of Seattle. An LRAD sound weapon was deployed against protesters at the G20 meeting in Pittsburgh in 2009. The transfer of military hardware such as Humvees and military rifles to the police was shockingly on display in the mobilization against anti-police protesters in Ferguson, Missouri, in 2014. Occupy Wall Street in 2011 and Black Lives Matter protests in 2020 faced brutal police repression. Veterans of the US neocolonial wars bring the wars home in their repression of working-class communities across the United States. The experience of these soldier-cops in the neocolonial occupation zones of Afghanistan and Iraq, combined with Israeli training that many police forces have engaged in since 2001, imports the methods and mentality of the colonial occupier to the bereft and excluded inner city, small town, and rural working-class populations across the United States.[88] The establishment by the Bush administration in 2002 of the US military's Northern Command, with responsibility for military operations in the US, Canada, and Mexico, effectively integrated the US domestic territory into the global battlefield. The internment and torture of US citizen Jose Padilla at Guantanamo Bay under the Bush administration was followed by President Obama's assassination of US citizen Anwar al-Awlaki and his US citizen son in Yemen in 2011, and the Obama administration asserted the right of the US president to assassinate US citizens anywhere in the world (refusing to rule out that this includes on US territory). These acts have cemented the integration of the US population into the target zone of the US state's military violence.[89]

Francis Fukuyama's "end of history" prognosis articulated the dominant ideological response, by the ruling class and its intellectual agents, to the liquidation of the Soviet Union. The triumphalist jingoist assertion of the superiority of "the West" and of the economic system of capitalism was the only response of which they were capable, despite having entirely failed to predict the collapse of the Stalinist regimes. Liberal democracy and capitalism had triumphed. The rest would be a mopping-up operation, drawing the rest of the world, inevitably, into the orbit of hegemonic American power. To the extent that this triumphalism was questioned among the pundits of the ruling class, it was in the arch-reactionary terms of Samuel Huntington's "clash of civilizations." Huntington's claim represented, in highly distorted ideological form, a recognition that the end of the Cold War only opened the way for the emergence of new conflicts and that, rather than a unipolar moment and inevitable convergence toward the model established and represented by the United States, the rise of new powers threatened this hegemony. If Fukuyama's universalistic liberalism resonated with expectations of a post–Cold War "peace dividend," Huntington's prediction of new conflicts was more in keeping with the martial character of American power.[90] Huntington's thesis provided a useful discourse for new ideological divisions of "us" versus them in order to justify what would be an eruption of militaristic violence projected across the planet.

The dominant ideology of post–Cold War American imperialism has been a combination of Fukuyama and Huntington, the appeal to the notion of a "rules-based international order" supposedly epitomized and defended by the United States, and at the same time the assertion of the inevitability of conflict with demonized "rogues" who "hate our freedoms" and who can only be dealt with by force. If Fukuyama was the high priest of America as Cold War "victor," Huntington constructed a philosophy for the 1990–1991 Persian Gulf War, which he called "the first post-Cold War resource war between civilizations." The war, he said, had succeeded in making the Persian Gulf "an American lake."[91]

Fukuyama and Huntington were combined within America's dominant ideology, providing the rhetorical weapons with which to justify the explosion of American militarism in the new millennium. Indeed, the combination of Fukuyama's universalism and Huntington's cultural nationalist particularism reflects the character of imperialism as the contradictory attempt to organize the world in the particular interests of the capitalist class of the dominant capitalist nation. As Trotsky wrote during the early stages of America's emergence as world power,

> US capitalism is up against the same problems that pushed Germany in 1914 on the path of war. The world is divided? It must be redivided. For Germany it was a question of "organizing Europe." The United States must "organize" the world. History is bringing humanity face to face with the volcanic eruption of American imperialism.[92]

The violent re-eruption of American imperialism began immediately, the moment it was no longer counterbalanced by Soviet power, in the move to control the oil-producing region of the Middle East, domination of which was also key to control of the geo-strategically essential Eurasian landmass, and, thereby, the world. Alfred W. McCoy makes clear that the US drive to control the "world island" of Eurasia was a key dimension of its hostility toward the Soviet Union during the Cold War, and that there was continuity from the US machinations in the Middle East against the Soviet Union to today's wars. It was Brzezinski who developed the strategy of funding Muslim fundamentalist fighters "to attack the Soviet Union's soft Central Asian underbelly," successfully drawing the USSR into a disastrous intervention in Afghanistan against the US-armed Mujahadeen.[93] In a 1997 article in the Council on Foreign Relations' journal *Foreign Affairs*, Brzezinski called Eurasia "the decisive geopolitical chessboard" and asserted that "America's emergence as the sole global superpower now makes an integrated and comprehensive strategy for Eurasia imperative."[94]

David North notes the significance of the coincidence of the Persian Gulf War, beginning with Saddam Hussein's annexation of Kuwait in August 1990, and the dissolution of the Soviet Union, which was declared in December 1991. The limits of that war were defined by the continued existence of the Soviet Union as the US carried out its air war in early 1991. North writes:

> The USSR was the principal military ally of Iraq, and there were months of diplomatic maneuvering between Secretary of State James Baker and Soviet Foreign Minister Eduard Shevardnadze while troops and weaponry poured into the battle zone. Ultimately, the Soviet bureaucracy did not oppose the US-led military action, as long as the Bush administration limited its strategic goals to the reconquest of Kuwait. Despite considerable pressure from the more hawkish sections of the Republican Party and the Pentagon, the White House did not order a "march on Baghdad" to overthrow the Iraqi regime, in large measure to avoid a direct confrontation with the Soviet Union.[95]

This demonstrates the significance of the subsequent absence of Soviet power, which enabled the United States to complete its destruction of Iraq in the war and occupation that began in 2003. Above all, it was the collapse of the Eastern European satellite states and the impending dissolution of the Soviet Union that provided the opportunity and the geopolitical necessity for US imperialism to plunge itself into a new attempt to organize the world in its capitalist interests. It was this project that George H. W. Bush notoriously signaled with the "big idea" that he proposed in his January 29, 1991, State of the Union address, of "a new world order."[96] Political scientist Jeffrey Haynes writes, "The thirty years since Bush's aspirations for a New World Order were expressed have led to its opposite: New World *Dis*order."[97]

The Persian Gulf War, under President George H. W. Bush, was the shape of things to come, followed by the Balkans War under President Clinton, the occupation of Afghanistan and the bombing and occupation of Iraq under President George W. Bush, the destruction of Libya, the destabilization of Syria and the US-supported coup in Ukraine under President Barack Obama, as well as numerous other interventions. The White House's war report of 2018 stated that the United States was fighting wars in seven countries: Afghanistan, Iraq, Syria, Yemen, Somalia, Libya, and Niger.[98] There was essential continuity from the Persian Gulf War initiated by George H. W. Bush to the Trump administration's actions such as dropping the largest non-nuclear explosive in existence on Afghanistan, the destruction of the city of Mosul in the fighting against ISIS in Iraq, threatening North Korea with nuclear annihilation, providing military support for Saudi Arabia's war in Yemen, intervening directly against the Syrian regime and carrying out bombing raids in Syria and stationing US troops on the ground in that country (which began under the Obama administration in the fall of 2015 and continued under Trump, under the pretext of fighting ISIS), as well as sending lethal military aid to Ukraine, and assassinating Iranian General Qasem Soleimani in Iraq.

There is bipartisan consensus within Washington, DC, on the core principle of using military power to assert American interests. What is called "American national interest" translates into the interests of US banks and corporations, for example, oil companies, weapons manufacturers and military-industrial infrastructure, and logistic firms such as Halliburton and technology-oriented companies such as Google and Amazon. These tech companies are increasingly tightly integrated into the military branches of the state. The military, police and intelligence apparatuses increasingly constitute the predominance of the US state. American national interest also includes the global interests of the American ruling class, the corporate rich in whose interests the state functions. There are, nevertheless, bitter disagreements about how, in terms of strategy, to achieve this, in particular between those who regard China as the primary focus and those pushing for a more immediate confrontation with Russia.[99]

There is bipartisan consensus in favor of sociocidal wars. The bipartisan-supported destruction of Iraq by the Bush administration was repeated under Obama in the destruction of Libya. In both cases, the US government and military carried out *sociocide*, the destruction of the fabric of the society, the destruction of physical infrastructure that makes civilized social life possible and the shattering of the social order into sectarian fragments.[100] The emergence of slave markets in Libya, enslaving refugees from the war in Syria and the horrors of sexual slavery perpetrated by ISIS on Yazidi women in Syria follow from US sociocide in Libya and Iraq and in Syria by the United

States, together with its regional allies Saudi Arabia, Qatar, and Israel, which have provided support (direct or indirect) to al-Qaeda-linked groups and the Islamic State (ISIS or ISIL).[101]

As opposed to Fukuyama's view that the global triumph of capitalism was also the triumph of liberal democracy, the period since the collapse of the Soviet Union has seen the global convergence of states toward authoritarian capitalism. Far from globalized production and the development of a consumer capitalist society creating an unstoppable impetus toward liberal democracy in China, the Chinese model of neoliberal capitalism combined with repressive state control is now less and less aberrant from the so-called liberal democracies. The 9/11 attacks on the World Trade Center and Pentagon, followed by the anthrax letters attacks against individuals, media outlets and Congress, and the inauguration by the Bush administration of the global "war on terror" provided the justification for the rapid passage of the Patriot Act which allowed mass surveillance and arbitrary detention.[102] The Authorization for the Use of Military Force passed by Congress in the immediate aftermath of 9/11 has been continually renewed up to the present and allowed the massive expansion of America's global military operations behind the backs of the American people.[103] Obama's enamorment with drones fit with this extension of America's war zones, in line with the way in which drones make the whole planet a battlefield in which war never needs to be declared. War becomes the all-pervading reality.[104] Today in America war has become completely normalized. It is accepted by the political establishment, and with varying emotions from Spartan, flag-waving enthusiasm to fatalism by the population, that America will always be at war.

The US government is primarily a machinery of war and repression. The reduction of the state to its core capabilities of violence goes together with the eschewing by the ruling class and aligned power elites of the state's responsibility for the well-being of the population. The twentieth century's connection between warfare and welfare has been undone.[105] In the wake of mass opposition to the Vietnam War and the erosion of military discipline that occurred in the final stages of the war, the United States shifted to an "all-volunteer force," relying on the declining economic position of the working class to drive a section of the population into military service.[106] This was accompanied by a concerted propaganda effort to counter so-called Vietnam Syndrome.[107] The US rapid victory in the 1990–1991 Persian Gulf War was important in reestablishing a belief in American invulnerability and in the rightness of waging war. Since then, the prestige of the military in American society has grown, such that the military is today treated as a sacred institution.[108] This sense of military invulnerability was combined with a deep sense of vulnerability among the American population, shocked by corporate downsizing, outsourcing, and offshoring that accompanied the mergers and acquisitions frenzy of the 1990s. The economic precariousness of the population contrasted uneasily with the jingoistic assertions of American power. That there was something very wrong beneath America's glittering fantasy image that it beamed around the world and to its own population was made evident in the phenomenon of workplace mass shootings that began in the 1980s and in the school shootings that have become a regular occurrence since the Columbine High School massacre in 1999. A society with this much seething anger against itself has a great need to project and displace these internal tensions onto others.[109]

The contrast between "socialism" within the military and the impoverishment of the mass of the working class signifies a shift from the warfare-welfare deal to a different relationship between the population and the state, which now takes the form of the predator state.[110] Galbraith describes the public-private nexus at the core of the predator state as

> a coalition of relentless opponents of the regulatory framework on which public purpose depends, with enterprises whose major lines of business compete with or encroach on the principal public functions of the enduring New Deal. It is a coalition, in other words, that seeks to control the state partly in order to prevent the assertion of public purpose and partly to poach on the lines of activity that past public purpose has established. They are firms that have no intrinsic loyalty to any country. They operate as a rule on a transnational basis, and naturally come to view the goals and objectives of each society in which they work as just another set of business conditions, more or less inimical to the free pursuit of profit. They assuredly do not adopt any of society's goals as their own, and that includes the goals that may be decided on, from time to time, by their country of origin, the United States. As an ideological matter, it is fair to say that the very concept of public purpose is alien to, and denied by, the leaders and the operatives of this coalition.[111]

Thus, what James Cypher calls "neoliberal militarism" is an integral part of the predator state, as it involves the abandonment of the needs of the population by the state and the integration into the state of an economic sector, the military-industrial complex, that profits entirely from its relationship to the state. Cypher notes that even the neoliberal aim of reducing the activities carried out by the state, when applied to the military, in fact enrich and enlarge precisely this sector, "a vast constellation of contractors employing a shadow military," which then lobbies for more military spending.[112]

The predator state entices people into its apparatuses of violence by the modicum of security that military life provides in contrast to the mass condition of economic precariousness. The military becomes associated with security and consistency; it becomes a haven in a heartless world, a setting where values of duty and self-sacrifice contrast with the cutthroat individualism of American economic life, and seemingly an ascetically moral contrast with the hedonism of consumer culture. In contrast with the historically American republican ideal of the citizen-soldier, the "volunteer" military forms a distinct subculture within American society. It is one that nurtures authoritarian values. Rape and domestic violence are particularly high in the military.[113] White supremacist and neo-Nazi ideology has become prevalent in the military. Following the involvement of a significant number of military personnel and former military personnel in the January 6 storming of Congress, the Department of Defense announced a stand-down of troops in order to address the spread of far-right ideology and support among armed forces personnel.[114] The militias that have grown in size and number since they began to develop in the 1990s are today the American Freikorps, composed of a large number of military veterans, plotting assassinations of anti-fascists and liberal politicians, and coming within a hair's breadth of taking congressional representatives and the vice president hostage and executing them until their demands to nullify the election result and leave Donald J. Trump in power were met.[115] They did succeed in breaking up and delaying the vote whereby Congress ratifies the election result, normally a mere formality.

Normalcy is a condition in which there can be "mere formalities," in the sense that actions are humdrum, repetitive, ritualistic and "merely" ceremonial. Formalities take place against the background of tacitly shared assumptions and mutual expectations. There is an integral relationship between formality, normality, and civility. De-civilizing renders social life and institutions less predictable.[116] It is a force toward deinstitutionalization, which is also why it is often linked with charismatic leadership. The de-civilizing spurt in America today, like that in Germany on which the Nazis rode to power, is a process that has been spearheaded by elites, especially through war and the cultivation of a culture of militarism, and as in Germany it draws its mass base from a lower middle class unsettled by economic crisis and decline.[117] The culture of militarism and xenophobic nationalism cultivated by the American ruling class and power elites, which saturated television after the 9/11 attacks, has been attractive to petit-bourgeois elements finding security and identity in the myths and symbols of military strength and a reactionary ethno-nationalism and nativism that are existential refuges from globalization.[118] These petit-bourgeois elements provide the foot soldiers for the particularly fascist elements of the ruling class that are aligned with Trump.[119] The service of the far-right militias to the needs of capital is evident in the fact that a key issue around which the militias have congealed is that of opposing public health lockdowns during the Covid-19 pandemic. This is a fascism that denies any duty of the state to provide care for the population. The militias sought to achieve with violence what the Republican Party has been advocating through rhetoric and what has been the real unofficial policy of the Trump administration (and in fact continues in the Biden administration's refusal to impose public health lockdowns)—the de facto policy of herd immunity. Lockdowns cannot be allowed to interfere with the extraction of surplus value from labor on which capital lives.

Karl Marx wrote of the capitalists' attitude to the physical health of the working class and their propensity to work their employees to death:

> Capital therefore takes no account of the health and the length of life of the worker, unless society forces it to do so. Its answer to the outcry about the physical and mental degradation, the premature death, the torture of over-work, is this: Should that pain trouble us, since it increases our pleasure (profit)?[120]

The raw expression of the capitalists' thirst to extract labor is evident today as it was in the nineteenth century before the development of the welfare state. Today, it takes the form of "return to normal," which means the rush under Biden to reopen schools during the still uncontrolled pandemic, to get workers back to work. A key difference is the level of development of the productive forces so that the contradiction between imposed scarcity and the wealth and technological capability of society is gaping. What is different is that this is capitalism in its malignant stage, or what John McMurty calls "cancer capitalism."[121] Its exploitation no longer serves any progressive historical dynamic but rather is a hindrance to all human development.[122]

The historically reactionary role of the bourgeoisie was an important implication of Lenin's theory of imperialism, as a characteristic of the highest stage of capitalism.[123] Lenin formulated his theory in the midst of World War I, in order to explain the war and its implications for socialist revolution. Imperialism is intrinsically connected with world war and, therefore, it marks the period in which the continued existence of capitalism calls into question the existence of the human species. This was made evident by the development of the atomic bomb and is so today in the impetus of American imperialism, long after the end of the Soviet Union and the Cold War, toward war with Russia and China. The epoch of imperialism is intrinsically linked to cancer capitalism and the development of what Erich Fromm identified as necrophilic cultural and social-psychological trends.[124]

In the United States, a form of "libertarian" fascism has developed, as the living death of American individualism under the regime of imperialism. It is a necrophilous ideology, hostile to the even most basic provision for the population.[125] This outlook was exemplified by the Colorado City, Texas mayor who posted on Facebook, during the 2021 winter storm that cut power to millions and led to approximately eighty deaths, the message that people should not ask the government for assistance:

No one owes you are [*sic*] your family anything; nor is it the local government's responsibility to support you during trying times like this! Sink or swim it's your choice! . . . Bottom line quit crying and looking for a handout! Get off your ass and look after your own family.[126]

While the mayor was forced to resign as a result of the online tirade, the statement is significant as an encapsulation of a key dimension of right-wing ideology in America.[127]

The Texas mayor's rhetoric of the responsibility of the head of the family resonates with Thatcher's assertion that "There is no such thing as society. There are just individuals and families." It represents an extreme atomic individualism, where the only collective is the private realm of the family. The individualism, therefore, combines with a patriarchal traditionalist and religious ideology of the family.[128] The mayor's tweet explicitly states the antisocial implications of neoliberal individualism and privatism: a repudiation of any governmental role as a vehicle for mutual aid and for the reproduction of society. The growth of this ideology and its particularly virulent expression in the US Republican Party is an indication of structural transformations in the relation of the capitalist state to society.

The predator state corresponds with the social policy, and broader social and cultural, paradigm that Henry Giroux calls "disposability." He points to the transformation of schools and the dominant political attitude toward childhood in which schools in working class and minority neighborhoods have become prison-like institutions, criminalizing youth through zero-tolerance policies and creating a school-to-prison pipeline feeding into mass incarceration.[129] Giroux locates the shift toward disposability as arising from the end of the social reform projects of the 1960s:

When the "War on Poverty" ran out of steam with the social and economic crisis that emerged in the 1970s, there was a growing shift at all levels of government from an emphasis on social investments to an emphasis on public control, social containment, and the criminalization of social problems. The criminalization of social issues—starting with President Johnson's Omnibus Crime and Safe Streets Act of 1968 (a bill that was debated in Congress after the assassination of Dr. Martin Luther King), entering a second phase with President Ronald Reagan's war on drugs and the privatization of the prison industry in the 1980s, and moving into a third phase with the passage of a number of anticrime bills by President Clinton's administration, including the Anti-Terrorism and Effective Death Penalty Act, coupled with the escalating war on immigrants in the early 1990s and the rise of the prison-industrial complex by the close of the decade— has now become a part of everyday culture and provides a common referent that extends from governing prisons and regulating urban culture to running schools. This is most evident in the emergence of zero-tolerance laws that have swept the nation since the 1980s, and gained full legislative strength with the passage of the Violent Crime Control and Law Enforcement Act of 1994.[130]

The paradigm of governance that emerged from the social and economic crises of the 1970s involved a shift from the inclusionary emphasis of the welfare state and, in Europe, of social democracy, to the exclusionary dynamic of neoliberalism.[131] Mass incarceration and zero-tolerance policies in the US treated the poor not as a reserve army of labor but as a surplus population to be shut out of legitimate economic activity and political participation and segregated through incarceration and crime control.[132] Giroux identifies in the hidden curriculum of schooling a fundamental shift away from the promotion of political citizenship and toward the treatment of education as a commodity, reflective of "a growing commercial culture that reduces social values to market relations, limits the obligations of citizenship to the act of consuming, and dismisses racial and economic justice as the product of a bygone era."[133]

As a socialization institution, the school is directly reproducing the culture of the society; it provides children with their first image of the world outside the home as forming a unified whole. It is society's formal self-representation to each new generation. In the United States, the ritual of pledging allegiance to the flag makes explicit that this whole is the nation and national flags in the classroom make clear that the school represents the nation and the government. In American political culture, there has been a particularly close relationship between democracy and the idea of a democratic education.[134] In American schools today, the democratic significance of education has been hollowed out. As schools are increasingly oriented toward corporations and law enforcement, traditions of democratic education are a direct threat to corporate power and to the growing authoritarianism of the state. The public school is in many ways the core civic institution in a community and brings coherence to a community through providing a focal point and being something truly shared and representing a social whole as opposed to the private worlds of shopping malls and the sectarian divisions of religion. In poor working-class neighborhoods, the school has largely been emptied of democratic and cultural content and become a holding pen for youth in which they are drilled on a narrow curriculum of basic literacy and mathematics, skills emptied of content, and accommodated to punitive policing.[135] As reality becomes increasingly contrary to the image the ruling class relies on sustaining, as little of that reality as possible is formally presented to youth.

Giroux traces disposability through the micro-spaces of the classroom to the macro-scale of Hurricane Katrina in 2005 and the abandonment of New Orleans, and in particular of its poor African American majority, by the Bush

administration and by local elites.[136] Katrina represented a horrific manifestation of the logic of disposability which had been developing at more subter-
ranean levels in American society for decades. The same disposability, or
"malign neglect" as *World Socialist Web Site* puts it, has subsequently been
evident in the lead poisoning of Flint, Michigan, where a city was deliberately
poisoned as a direct element of neoliberal policies imposed by a political
apparatus working for the financial oligarchy.[137] Disposability is evident in
the Trump administration's abandonment of Puerto Rico to its fate in the
aftermath of Hurricane Maria, in the stranding of millions without heat and
water in the Texas winter storm of February 2021, and, above all, in what by
the beginning of March 2021 had reached half a million deaths from Covid-
19 within the United States.

These events are indicative of processes of deindustrialization linked
to globalization (Flint and nearby Detroit), climate change (New Orleans,
Puerto Rico, and Texas), and globalization in the form of air travel and the
consequent rapidity of the spread of disease in what is an increasingly globally interconnected collective human organism (Covid-19). They indicate
that the nation-state has lost its ability and willingness to organize the social
in the context of globalization processes that cut across and exceed national
boundaries, disorganizing social life that remains represented and regulated
within the institutional framework of nation-states.[138] At all levels, from the
growing insecurity of everyday life to the destruction wrought by the war on
terror and the impetus toward major power conflict between the United States
and both Russia and China, to the slide toward human extinction caused by
climate change, the mismatch of scales between the nation-state and the globalization of economic and social life that capitalism has wrought, creates
growing disorganization.

The Trump administration's acrimonious withdrawal from the World
Health Organization at the height of the Covid-19 pandemic, and the broader
phenomenon of "vaccine nationalism" whereby states have sought national
advantage through control over vaccine manufacture and distribution, have
been particularly stark expressions of the conflict between nation-state organization and the globality of the human species woven together through
myriad communication, technological, economic, and cultural networks.[139]

The Trump presidency cannot be understood apart from the intertwined
crises of global capitalism and of the global hegemony of the United States.
In particular, this presidency is a manifestation of the failure of the project of
establishing the United States as the sole world-dominating power after the
collapse of the Soviet Union, a project the hubris of which was encapsulated
by Fukuyama's "end of history" thesis. This project necessitated the use of
military force to offset America's relative economic decline in the face of
increased global competition. The very forces of globalization that rendered

the autarkic economies of the eastern bloc no longer viable, precipitating the collapse of Stalinism, and that undermined the national reformist policies of social democracy, also showed up the weaknesses in the economic basis of American power. The response of the American ruling class to the contradiction between their hubristic imperialist ambitions and the real structural weakness of their power has been increasingly irrational and destructive. Trump, in his bullying chauvinism and malignant narcissism, is merely an expression of the irrationality of US imperialism in terminal decline.[140]

Rather than representing an abnormal in relation to some standard of normality (either some imagined rules-based order or consistent imperialist strategy), the twists and turns of the Trump administration and opposition to it from the Democratic Party and from within the deep state reflect divisions over imperialist strategy within the American political establishment and ruling elite. These have become more bitter and destabilizing as the hubristic project of securing "a new American century" founders on the rocks of the global contradictions of imperialism in the era of capitalist decline.

The Trump administration represented a qualitative deepening of the ongoing degradation of American bourgeois democracy. The most powerful country in the world, which presents itself as the bastion of democracy, has now had a fascist president who has cultivated a fascist movement in his heavily armed base of enraged lumpen petit-bourgeois and working-class supporters and in sections of the military, police, and within the already fascistic Homeland Security apparatus.[141] This, together with his frequent mooting of the possibility of outstaying the constitutionally mandated term limits, culminating in his January 6 coup plot, brought America to the brink of dictatorship. The danger of this far-right movement, embedded in the Republican Party, remains high. However, the creation of the conditions for fascism in the United States long precedes the Trump presidency, which is an outcome of the intensifying contradictions of US imperialism within the context of globalization.[142] The erosion of democratic rights accelerated significantly in the wake of the legalized theft of the 2000 election that brought the Bush administration to power, and amid the events of Fall 2001 (the September 11 airplane attacks and the subsequent anthrax letters attacks) that led to the passage of the Patriot Act, the secret initiation of mass electronic surveillance, and the illegal invasions of Afghanistan and Iraq.[143] A pervasive climate of xenophobia has inexorably accompanied the US wars in the Middle East, spawning the fascistic racism that motivates Trump's die-hard followers.

In all essentials, these policies of war and authoritarianism have been supported and carried out continuously by the Democratic Party. Attacks on the living standards of the American working class have been carried out by both parties: from Clinton's welfare anti-reforms (The Personal Responsibility and Work Opportunity Reconciliation Act of 1996) and NAFTA to Obama's

restructuring of the auto industry and the Republican Congress's refusal
to extend unemployment insurance in the wake of 2008 financial crisis, to
Trump's cuts to food stamps and the expiry of the pandemic eviction moratorium so that millions of working-class Americans are in the summer to fall
of 2021 facing imminent eviction during an ongoing pandemic with the dan-
gerous "delta variant" of Covid spreading.[144] The drop in life expectancy of
the US population in recent years, beginning prior to the Covid-19 pandemic
and exacerbated by it, is a clear indication of the worsening living conditions
of the majority of Americans.[145] Anthropologists Alya Ansari and Mitch
Hernandez observe that

> to speak of the pandemic solely in these terms—of sensationalized exception,
> of a radically novel state of existence—obscures the profound normalcy of
> the present moment, particularly with regard to the inequitable distribution of
> resources in our highly stratified capitalist society and the deplorable conditions
> of labor at the root of this inequity.[146]

These policies of immiseration and the growth of social inequality contributed to Trump's rise. Precarious non-higher-educated, "independent" petit-
bourgeois and equally precarious working-class Americans, deeply alienated
from the Washington political establishment, were attracted to the manufactured image of Trump as an "outsider" who would shake up the system and
"drain the swamp." And social inequality is behind the ability of a billionaire
to self-fund an election campaign, while real representation of working-class
interests is structurally blocked. Denied political expression, the pent-up anger
of the working class is easily exploited by fascism.[147] Trump combines support
from the disillusioned working class with the petit-bourgeoisie's panicked
Chicken Little rush into the den of a charismatic authoritarian Foxy Loxy.

Normalcy was inextricably related to the growth of the middle class, to the
politically mediating and stabilizing role of the middle class, and to both the
reality and ideal of the middle-class way of life as integrating and supporting
an image of American "classlessness."[148] The decline of the American middle
class is, therefore, a crucial dimension of the end of normalcy. Sheri Berman
writes in *Foreign Policy*: "The collapse of the middle class—long viewed as
the bedrock of American democracy—has also been dramatic . . . Making
matters worse, inequality has become increasingly hereditary; as it has risen,
social mobility has declined."[149] The decline of normalcy is inextricably
related to the decline of the middle class under post-Fordist and neoliberal
conditions. This has produced the chronic and deepening legitimation crisis
of the state and its mediating institutions.

The Democratic Party did everything it could to prevent the emergence
of mass struggle against the Trump regime by the American working class,

putting on a "normalcy show" by making out that Trump was abnormal, and therefore that the rest of the system, which was normal, would sort things out. The official so-called resistance represented by the Democratic Party used the methods of palace intrigue in order to avoid mobilizing the mass of the population and unleashing the anger and power of the working class which has the potential to turn from Trump to the financial aristocracy which funds, and is represented by, the Democratic Party. Hence the narrowness of the articles of impeachment drawn up by the Democratic-controlled House of Representatives, focusing entirely on the withholding of military aid to the Ukraine, the transcript of a conversation leaked by a CIA agent, and the allegation that Trump sought foreign interference in US elections by soliciting derogatory information on the corruption of Hunter Biden, son of former vice president, and Democratic primary candidate Joe Biden. The fact that Hunter Biden's $50,000 per month sinecure on the board of a Ukrainian gas company represents blatant corruption, precisely of the kind that disgusts the mass of the American population with the political elite, has been strenuously but ineffectively suppressed by the Democratic Party and its allied media. In mid-September 2021, Hillary Clinton's lawyer was charged with lying to the FBI in relation to "Russiagate."[150] Official reality seems to consist of sandcastles, or smoke and mirrors. In place of mass struggle, there is elite-managed spectacle.

Paradoxically, the impeachment was a normalcy show. It was a spectacle of legal proceduralism that promulgated the fiction that Trump was, as Supreme Court Justice Ruth Bader Ginsburg put it, "an aberration" after which there could be a return to legal-rational constitutionalism.[151] The entire political establishment is deeply implicated in the criminality of a declining American empire. The CIA, which initiated the action leading to the impeachment, illegally spied on the Senate Intelligence Committee investigating its illegal torture program and threatened Senate staffers involved in the investigation with prosecution for espionage. Gina Haspel, CIA director during the Trump administration, was herself involved in torture and the destruction of evidence of torture.[152] Yet, the Democrats, in their impeachment drive, represented the intelligence agencies as defenders of constitutionality. Indeed, the Democratic majority leader and Speaker of the House of Representatives, Nancy Pelosi, was briefed by the Bush administration on its torture program and, therefore, complicit in that.[153] Far from Trump's contempt for the law being an aberration, it is the normality of the American elite in the era of imperial decline. As the bipartisan passage of record military spending at the same time as the articles of impeachment were being passed by the House showed, Trump's impeachers are as much agents of imperial aggression as the president. Trump is the personification of the normal abnormal, the normal pathology, of American empire in decline.[154]

THE POST-NORMAL CONDITION

The term "post-normal" was introduced in the early 1990s by Silvio Funtowicz and Jerome Ravetz, in book chapters published in 1991 and 1992, and became widely known based on the 1993 article "Science for the Post-Normal Age," in the journal *Futures*. Funtowicz and Ravetz used the term to designate the new kind of science that they argued was emerging, and was needed, in response to challenges of environmental risks produced by modern technology.[155] They draw on Thomas Kuhn's term "normal science," which he described as "puzzle-solving" within a paradigmatic framework of assumptions and contrasted with scientific revolutions in which paradigms are overturned.[156] Functowicz and Ravetz's suggestion is that normal science is itself a paradigm, rooted in unquestioned assumptions of the possibility of knowing and controlling the world through instrumentally rational techniques and formal systems.[157] These techniques and systems, however, through their very effectiveness in transforming the material world and, therefore, the deep and far-reaching character of these transformations, produce feedbacks and unintended consequences that make for inherently uncertain outcomes. The world that the natural sciences study is increasingly a world that is already mixed with human action and its consequences in a chaotic spiral. This is the meaning of the Anthropocene, in which the dominant cause affecting the planet's processes is the human species. What produces these far-reaching effects on nature is human activity as manifested in technology. Technology is the medium through which humanity interrelates with nature, therefore, it follows that it is through technology that human social activities (in all their dimensions, including economic and political) have their impact on the material world of nature.

The concept of "post-normal science" has affinity with Ulrich Beck's notion of the "risk society" and Beck and Giddens's conception of "reflexive modernization."[158] Awareness of the environmental hazards created by modern technological society had been growing since Rachel Carson's landmark book *Silent Spring*, published in 1962, drew attention to the toll of toxic synthetic pesticides in poisoning flora and fauna including, ultimately, human beings.[159] Environmental consciousness was also raised by activist scientists who sought to educate the public about the dangers of nuclear war and radiation that governments sought to cover up.[160] Growing recognition of the danger of nuclear fallout from the hundreds of nuclear bombs exploded above ground as tests during the early Cold War culminated in the Partial Test Ban Treaty of 1963. Outcry against the US poisoning of Vietnam with the deadly dioxin-containing defoliant chemical Agent Orange, resulting in ecological destruction and horrific human birth defects also fed into concern about the more general environmental effects of chemicals. The Santa Barbara oil spill of 1969, at that time the largest in US waters, was another event that consolidated environmental activism. Twenty years later, the Exxon Valdez ran aground and released catastrophe in Prince William Sound, Alaska. The Three Mile Island nuclear reactor accident in 1979 was followed by the Chernobyl meltdown in 1986. In 1984, the Union Carbide India Limited plant in Bhopal, majority owned by the US firm Union Carbide and Carbon, released poisonous methyl isocyanate killing thousands.

In Britain, the *Royal Society*'s report on *The Public Understanding of Science* (known as the Bodmer Report), published in 1985, expressed the concern of the scientific establishment that public trust in science was declining and that this was due to deficient public knowledge of science. This was followed by the government's mishandling of the BSE outbreak in the late 1980s and into the 1990s, along with protests against genetically modified crops in the 1990s. The sociologically oriented field of Science & Technology Studies, which had developed since the 1970s, became highly involved in the UK in debates concerning relations between science and the public and academics in this field were widely critical of the hierarchical technocratic ways in which the British scientific community had traditionally approached communication with the public about technological risks and hazards.[161] Technocratic discourse, sociologists of science and technology argued, presented an aura of certainty which elided the uncertainties that always accompanied such problems of untested interaction of toxic materials with complex and chaotic interacting systems of nature and human society. Technocratic discourse suppressed the ethical and political issues that inter-sected in complex ways with technical concerns in any such problems of decision-making concerning environmental risk.[162] Funtowicz and Ravetz argued that such problems of environmental risk required a new philosophical framework for understanding science as an activity, encapsulating the new modes of scientific thinking and practice that were emerging as scientists sought to understand increasingly complex systems and as they became less institutionally sheltered from public involvement and criticism. They intro-duced their seminal article "Science for the Post-Normal Age," as follows:

> After centuries of triumph and optimism, science is now called on to remedy the pathologies of the global industrial system of which it forms the basis . . . In response, new styles of scientific activity are being developed. The reductionist, analytical worldview . . . is being replaced by a systemic, synthetic and human-istic approach. The old dichotomies of facts and values, and of knowledge and ignorance, are being transcended. Natural systems are recognized as dynamic and complex; those involving interactions with humanity are "emergent" . . . The science appropriate to this new condition will be based on the assumptions of unpredictability, incomplete control, and a plurality of legitimate perspectives.[163]

Post-normal science confronts problems for which no single paradigm is prepared and questions that are inherently value-laden such as what level of risk
is acceptable. It speaks in controversies that are not contained within core sets
but spill out into much broader publics in which these intersect with moral
and political conflicts.

The material consequences of science and technology are so global, far-
reaching, deeply integrated into the practices of everyday life, and inescap-
able for individuals, that they cannot be taken for granted as unproblematic
goods. The modern rationalist ideas of science and technology as value-
neutral failed to capture the ways in which science and technology are guided
by human purposes, in other words collective or social purposes. The idea of
"pure science," with its idealist roots in religion, came into contradiction with
the interdependency of science and instrumentation and the dependency of
instrumentation on the level of development of the productive forces, and the
role of science in transforming those very productive forces.[164] The very questions that natural sciences address and open up arise within a much broader
web of productive human interrelations with nature that are expressed in the
Marxian notion of a mode of production.

John Ziman terms "post-academic science" the contemporary situation in
which the ideal of value-free pure science is eroded and science is increasingly assessed on the basis of its utility.[165] This shift from the value-free ideal
to an instrumental-utilitarian framework corresponds to the imposition of
scarcity under neoliberalism and the increasing privatization of science.[166] In
this context, what Ziman calls "the norm of utility" that replaces the value-
free ideal is occluded by the mediation of money. Precisely the process of
marketization by which science is directed toward certain tasks rather than
others and placed into the service of certain institutions and organizations,
and therefore goals and values, rather than others, occludes the fact that these
directions do involve definite goals and values and therefore that they involve
judgments of utility. Money reifies values such that they do not appear as values subject to human deliberation but as determining commands, yet with the
human commander obscured. The command appears impersonal, as that of
rationality, but merely in a different guise, as economic rationality. Therefore,
the connection between post-academic science and the norm of utility and
politicization of science is not as direct as Ziman supposes. The market still
operates as a depoliticizing relation, unless the politics become not only
about "values" conceived in the moral sense, but value and the relations of
exploitation that produce it, in other words unless the impersonal rationality
of the market is called into question as well the impersonal rationality of
technocratic science.[167]

This suggests an understanding of "normal science" more critical
than Kuhn's in the sense that it examines the institutional and broader

political-economic context and preconditions for normal science. Steve Fuller has argued that Kuhn's conception of normal science must be understood as an expression of Cold War liberalism. Fuller argues that Kuhn paradoxically presents an image of scientific community insulated (except during periods of scientific revolution) from political power at the very historical moment when science was involved with government, industry, and the military to an unprecedented degree.[168] Normal science, with its faith in its own certainty and its Promethean technological attitude, was the product of a particular historical period, when science was highly enmeshed with the state, while this state support also insulated it from external criticism. As Brian Balogh has shown, the nuclear energy project itself produced a proliferation of nuclear experts such that the Atomic Energy Commission lost its monopoly on expertise and, therefore, its authority to define nuclear issues such as radiation safety. Brian Lindseth has shown specifically how the field of ecosystem ecology developed within in US Atomic Energy Commission ecological radiation studies, while such studies went on to become part of what ecologist Paul Sears called "the subversive science."[169] Normal science was inherently self-undermining, since the very conditions for its existence arose from the antithesis of normalcy—the atomic bomb. Normal science was inherently involved in producing the technical risks that brought its conditions to an end, and that necessitated the development of post-normal science.

There is a close relationship between the destabilizing effects of globalization and the concept of "post-normal times." The notion of "post-normal times" is closely related to the concepts of postmodernism and postmodernity, and it is evident today that the intellectual framework of postmodernism was itself a reaction to the transformations of globalization. Funtowicz and Ravetz note that their analysis of the "post-normal age" is "complementary" to their analysis of postmodernity, which was published in *Futures* in December 1992, "The Good, the True, and the Post-Modern."[170] In the latter article, they provide an interpretation of Baudrillard which draws out the implicit reference to technology in Baudrillard's postmodernism such that the technological development of the means of simulation create a hyperreality which degrades truth and reality. Funtowicz and Ravetz suggest, therefore, that postmodernism in science implies both the undermining of certainty and the rise of notions of uncertainty, complexity, chaos, and risk, while the modern quantitative increase in the number and power of technologies undermines the qualitative goods of social life.[171] Modernity, as quantitative increase in knowledge and technical capacity, culminates in the undermining of the quality of this knowledge, which becomes increasingly uncertain, and the social outcomes produced by technology, which increasingly degrade the natural and human environment.[172]

Funtowicz and Ravetz's notion of a post-normal age has been developed by Ziauddin Sardar, who argues that "the spirit of our age is characterized by uncertainty, rapid change, realignment of power, upheaval and chaotic behavior."[173] According to Sardar, uncertainty arises from "the three c's: complexity, chaos and contradictions—the forces that shape and propel postnormal times."[174] Having to make sense of a complex, chaotic, and contradictory world and make decisions about how to act in such a world, first evident in the science of technological risk, has now become a generalized condition.

The weakness of the literature on post-normal times lies in the fact that notions of uncertainty and complexity are used as if these themselves are the concrete social forces and actors. This obscures the social dynamics that produce contradictions and chaos and the real social forces at play. However, the notion of post-normal times is important in showing that what is at stake today and what increasingly is the object of study of the "natural sciences" is a complex mixture of the natural and the social.

Naomi Oreskes argues that the earth sciences are increasingly, of necessity, involved in producing social science. She writes that

> earth scientists have increasingly acknowledged—albeit mostly implicitly—that the problems that society supports them to address—water supply, climate change, seismic and volcanic risk—are hybrid problems, borne of the interaction between human activity and natural systems. Earthquakes have always existed, but they became a problem for human societies when we began to build rigid infrastructures. Water supply has famously challenged human cultures since ancient times, and the failure of some of ancient civilizations to manage their water supplies was a significant cause of difficulty for, if not actual collapse of, those civilizations. Climate change, as a natural phenomenon, has always existed, but climate change understood as "dangerous anthropogenic interference in the [natural] climate system" is a problem borne of our capacity to recover and exploit the energy stored in fossil fuels, coupled with our seeming incapacity to reform an economic system that fails to account for environmental damage as an accumulating cost.[175]

Oreskes is critical of the institutional barriers within academia that have prevented dialogue and intellectual collaboration between earth scientists and social scientists. She writes:

> At least some earth scientists are doing social science without quite acknowledging that this is what they are doing, without adequate training and understanding of social phenomena, and, in the worst cases, without respect for colleagues who have greater experience and insights into the workings of social systems.[176]

In making this argument, Oreskes draws on the work of historian of science Paul Forman, who has traced two shifts in science that, he argues, characterize postmodernity. Forman identifies the changed relationship between, and ascription of value within the university to, science and technology. The earlier model of the research university had as its core ideal the notion of pure science or basic research and viewed technology as an application of knowledge initially derived through curiosity-driven research (however erroneous that was as an explanation of the actual development of technology). The university at the end of the twentieth century and into the twenty-first century, values, above all, technology, and science is supported as a means toward technological goals. Related to this, Forman points to the growth of "antidisciplinarity," the increasing porousness of boundaries between academic disciplines and the sense that disciplinary boundaries are increasingly a fetter on the further development of knowledge. Oreskes embraces this implication in arguing that the complex relations between natural and social systems which science is increasingly tasked with understanding and responding to, require that knowledge exceeds the boundaries of disciplines. But Oreskes's argument has further implications for the overall structure of universities and knowledge. In addition to divisions between disciplines, there is the rigid divide, albeit largely informal, between what C.P. Snow famously called the "two cultures" of the natural sciences and the humanities.[177] The problem for sociology has always been to negotiate its position in between these two cultures and, therefore, within itself, between subjective *verstehen* and objective explanation.

NORMAL AND POST-NORMAL SOCIOLOGY

When sociology has presented itself as a science as opposed to the humanistic disciplines such as history, it is notable that it has done so on the basis of methodology. Hence, the adoption of quantitative methods has tended to be sociology's claim to scientificity, as opposed to humanistic qualitative research. This, as Collins has argued, conflates scientificity with certain methods that are applicable to certain questions and not others.[178] This methodological way of claiming scientificity is also one that in no way troubles the division of the university between *Naturwissenschaften* and *Geisteswissenschaften* that positions the study of the social on the side of the sciences of the *spirit*.[179]

Durkheim's demarcation of sociology as a discipline, distinguishing the level of the social from the individual focus of psychology, also placed sociology, while methodologically following the objectivist quantitative methods of the natural sciences, on the side of the sciences of spirit, in that what social facts revealed was a moral condition and that society was taken to be, most fundamentally, a system of shared values. The fact of suicide rates (even if representing material dead bodies) was an effect of a moral cause, and in effect therefore a moral sign.[180] An idealist conception of society in a one-sided way as a mental phenomenon has been a continuous theme in sociology, uneasily alongside the attraction of positivism to behaviorism, which seeks to eliminate mental life from scientific explanation.[181]

Society is consciousness, but it is also material practice and, as such, has a material foundation, as a collective body interacting with nature. As Frederick Engels said in his speech at Marx's gravesite:

> Just as Darwin discovered the law of development of organic nature, so Marx discovered the law of development of human history: the simple fact, hitherto concealed by an overgrowth of ideology, that mankind must first of all eat, drink, have shelter and clothing, before it can pursue politics, science, art, religion, etc.; that therefore the production of the immediate material means, and consequently the degree of economic development attained by a given people or during a given epoch, form the foundation upon which the state institutions, the legal conceptions, art, and even the ideas on religion, of the people concerned have been evolved, and in the light of which they must, therefore, be explained, instead of vice versa, as had hitherto been the case.[182]

The human being is a dialectical unity of opposites. As the cultural development of the species has alienated it from nature, mind as an accomplishment and expression of the human being as a social being has become capable of being experienced as separate from body. This has to do with the distance from necessity, and hence the immediate physical reality of the present, that the individual, and the species, is able to achieve.

The ability to conceive of society as its own realm existing apart from nature—indeed the common sense taken-for-grantedness of that way of thinking about society—is a function of the real exclusion of disruptive forces of nature from the domain of social life, in other words, everyday life. The sociologists' social is the material accomplishment of social life through the exclusion of the shocks of nature from rhythms and patterns maintained in defiance of nature. The ability to live through a winter storm by virtue of the fact that there is heating is a precondition for this meaning of "society."

"Society," as a protective cocoon between the biological human individual and brute natural scarcities and forces, rests on material foundations, and also political foundations in the sense of a balance of power between human beings, a balance of class forces. What Gouldner calls the extrusion of the economic from the social by the discipline of sociology was also the exclusion from the realm of study of the social of the material foundations of society, and therefore of the material, class forces that would undermine this formation.[183] Neoliberalism, proclaiming that "There is no such thing as society," has significantly undone the insulating wrappings of society that were the welfare state, and along with that the regulatory state, or what Bannon refers to as "the administrative state" which it is his goal to dismantle.[184] Post-normal times, just as they intrude the social into what were in the past understood as natural systems, also intrude nature, often violently, into the social, undoing in the process the metaphysical foundations of the discipline of sociology at the same time as throwing into question all the disciplinary divisions upon which normal science had been organized.

Gouldner was fundamentally correct, therefore, to argue that the problem posed by the collapse of the disciplinary consensus around Parsonian functionalism was not to come up with some other paradigm, but rather that the crisis of functionalism was something much more profound. It was the crisis not only of an intellectual paradigm but an ideological outlook which constituted the domain assumptions on which the discipline of sociology had rested as an intellectual-political project.[185] Therefore, the crisis required the development of a reflexive sociology that could comprehend the conditions for its own existence, including the social causes of its own domain assumptions.

What Gouldner identified as the crisis of Parsonianism was also the crisis of a model of the relationship between social science and the state. The relationship between sociology and the welfare state was, as Gouldner argued, closely bound up with positivist epistemology. Turner shows how what followed from this were assumptions about the relationship between social science and policy that reflected the "linear model" entailed by the modern university's pure science ideal. The collapse of reform with the end of the Johnson administration was bound up with the crisis of normal science in Ravetz's sense, with the intellectual crisis of positivism and the intellectual-social crisis of technocracy.

The response by the discipline of sociology entirely failed to acknowledge and address the depth of its crisis. The primary response by the discipline was to double down on the normal science model, in the production of what could be called hypernormalization of sociology, or the construction of hyper-normal science. As Turner devastatingly puts it, "'Mainstream sociology' lives on, no longer as a coherent idea, but more as the embodiment of the professional preferences of a status group."[186] This "mainstream" is defined by its use of quantitative methods, and the premium it places on statistical technique, so that in the absence of a shared conception of a social whole, there is now "methodological hegemony." This is maintained through the operation by the "top twenty" sociology departments of a "labor cartel," which operates in tandem with cartel control by these departments over the "top" two journals, *American Journal of Sociology* and *American Sociological Review*, publishing in which is necessary to get a job in a top twenty department, alongside having a PhD from a top twenty department. Hence, a hyper-normal science reigns, in which the collapse of the intellectual and social foundations from sociology as normal science has been responded to by further entrenching a disciplinary normal science model. This model is guarded rigorously despite the complete emptiness of content in terms of a coherent conception of society.[187] The institutional culture of "mainstream" American sociology is encapsulated by a graduate student interviewed by Schmidt, who describes being discouraged from questioning canonical assumptions: " 'So our whole goal is just to write articles for journals?' Basically the response was, There are only five good journals in sociology. You want to publish in those. And you're right, that's all your work in sociology is."[188] In the face of philosophical challenges from hermeneutics, phenomenology, ethnomethodology, reflexive sociology, feminism, and the sociology of scientific knowledge, positivism has dug itself in by simply refusing to engage with these ideas and by delegitimizing the entire discourse of theory. An anti-intellectual hostility to theory is the primary way in which mainstream sociology has maintained its boundaries in response to its theoretical weaknesses. In the process, it has become increasingly self-referential, insular, divorced from the broader intellectual culture, actively hostile to the humanities, and unquestioning of the technocratic liberalism which tacitly provides its taken-for-granted worldview, despite the growing crisis of this political outlook.[189] "Mainstream" sociology exhibits the hyper-formalized qualities of "performative acts of reproducing authoritative forms" which Yurchak suggests are aspects of hypernormalization.[190] Richard Biernacki suggests a ritualistic quality to the ways in which sociologists seek to mimic the techniques of the natural sciences and so reduce to measurable units the complexity of the meaningful cultural worlds made by human beings.[191]

Alongside hyper-normal sociology, there has been the development of what Turner calls "post-normal sociology." This is post-normal in that it is post-positivist. It results from the intellectual crisis of positivism, and the related crisis of Keynesian-welfarist technocracy. The Kuhnian critique of positivist philosophy inspired an anti-positivist sociology of scientific knowledge and undercut the intellectual justification for positivism both in its expression in functionalism and in the hyper-valuation of quantitative methods.[192] However, as Turner observes, "All of this was ignored by mainstream sociology." The way in which the critique of positivism did find expression in sociology was in the growth of gender studies and feminist sociology. Turner argues that feminist sociology was able to derive legitimacy within the field by presenting itself as an alternative paradigm alongside mainstream sociology, buoyed by ideas, outside the mainstream, of a "multi-paradigm" sociology. The feminist paradigm was justified by a standpoint theory of knowledge on the basis of which it was argued that women's experience had been hitherto excluded from the male-dominated profession, which clearly was true as the Schwendingers showed in their critique of early American sociology. On egalitarian and intellectual grounds (merged in standpoint theory), the claim was that only female sociologists, pursuing feminist methods, could give voice to women's experience. Multi-paradigm sociology was, therefore, justified on the ground of the incommensurability of standpoints in society. Kuhnian relativism fit with, and arguably entailed a conception of social life as made up of multiple incommensurable paradigms or forms of life. The implication is that it requires being a member of a particular identity category to understand and sociologically represent that category. In 1972, Merton criticized this view, as it had emerged especially in black studies, as a "new credentialism."[193] The new credentialism emerged with the collapse of structural-functionalism because both represent the breakdown of the conception of society as a coherent whole along the lines of Durkheim's conscience collective, or as an integrated system of meanings and values. The very topic field of sociology, society, splinters into a kaleidoscope of points of view which cannot be represented by sociology in any sense as a whole. Post-normal sociology has splintered off from sociology as a discipline into various forms of cultural studies (ethnic studies, black studies, chicano studies, women's studies, gender studies, disability studies, queer theory, critical race theory) which can be even more self-referential. They exhibit what Yurchak calls "hegemony of form" and "rhetorical circularity" over substance in their performative, ritualistic use of specialized jargon, which has made them an easy target for "over-identifying" hoaxes.[194]

In the process that Giddens calls the "double hermeneutic," the contorted language of these self-referential academic communities has become part of the institutional life of the post-normal nation-state and the mediating institutions.[195] Acceptance of a hypernormalized contortion of language becomes necessary for employment in PMC positions and the training of employees and supervision in their use of this language becomes a new angle of managerial surveillance and control of the workforce by the PMC.[196] The undermining of basic sex categories as "man" and "woman," which has gained traction from activism and legitimacy from academic queer studies, is profoundly destabilizing of ontological security, as well as the physical safety of women.[197] The pressure to accept the official anti-realism is a means of ensuring more generalized compliance. Hence post-normal sociology proves useful as mental shock doctrine, accommodating people to a new epistemology that, in its paradoxical "anti-essentialist" essentialism, absolutism, and intolerance for dissent, opposes and undermines the culture of critical discourse. The recent turn by the American power elite to the advocacy of internet censorship, euphemistically called "content moderation," is indicative of the potential that Gouldner identified for the "New Class" to turn away from its earlier opposition to censorship: "as a cultural bourgeoisie with its own vested interests, it may wish to limit discussion to members of its own elite"[198] As the twists and turns of official thought become increasingly jarring, compliance becomes increasingly performative. A general fog of mistrust, that is, legitimation crisis, spreads across people's relationship with the mediating institutions. Whereas Yaron Ezrahi points to Hans Christian Anderson's fable of "The Emperor's New Clothes" as the quintessential parable for modernity, the transformation traced in *The Descent of Icarus*, has now completed itself as the PMC gender ideology calls on people to distrust the evidence of their senses in favor of another's inappellable rendition of their authentic inner voice. The modern norm of transparency is inverted.[199] Correct usage of the official language is important for the PMC, since these are most fundamentally as Schmidt argues "ideological workers": "These jobs require strict adherence to an assigned point of view, and so a prerequisite for employment is the willingness and ability to exercise . . . ideological discipline."[200] Attacking vernacular realism and requiring phantastic jargon amplifies the power of this stratum, while tightening its ideological self-discipline.[201]

Turner argues that it is precisely the hypernormalization of sociology (or what Steven Shapin has equivalently referred to as its hyper-professionalism) that has prevented the discipline from having any answer to the fragmentation of its field of study into multitudinous identity-based concerns. Sociology's substantive domain of study fragments and dissipates. As a discipline, sociology becomes less of a voice on topics that are institutionalized in separate departments and interdisciplinary programs. Sociology commands its retreating boundaries via methodological hegemony. Turner suggests that sociology as a discipline turns a deaf ear to critiques that it has lost the theoretical ammunition to answer:

> The limited consequence of this critique for conventional sociology is explained by the fact that American sociology as it has developed has so little theoretical content . . . Despite the lack of impact [on the "mainstream"] of these feminist ideas, after Merton's abortive response to the claims of Black Studies, the idea of a standpoint distinctive to groups was never made a subject of contestation by elite sociologists.[202]

So hyper-normal sociology does not recognize that since Gouldner published *The Coming Crisis*, it has been running "a worker bee culture of productivity alone," producing statistically sophisticated articles without building any substantive theory.[203] Mainstream sociology is like a cartoon character running furiously in mid-air, staying aloft just so long as it doesn't look down.

Identity politics (including especially the fracturing intersectional post-modern forms of post-identity identity politics), expressed in post-normal sociology, reflect the crisis and transformation of the mediating role of the social sciences as a result of globalization: the decline of the social ordering functions of the nation-state and of the broad array of mediating institutions supported by the nation-state, including the universities. This crisis was reflected in the collapse of the sociological language of society as a whole and it is associated with the loss of the sense and reality of a public in the Deweyan and Habermasian senses as discussed by Giroux. The demise of the sociological language of the whole is bound up with the economic and political processes that have produced crisis in the public university.

THE UNIVERSITY CAUGHT IN THE CONTRADICTION BETWEEN NATION-STATE AND GLOBAL ECONOMY

The collapse of sociology's society, that is, society as a nation-state, under the pressure of neoliberalism and globalization, produces a crisis in the legitimacy of the mediating institutions that exist under the umbrella of the nation-state. The university is in particular tension in this regard. The research university developed in close relationship with the nation-state, both serving and deriving legitimacy from the nation-state.[204] Universities were, as George Caffentzis argues, a key institution in the "human capital strategy" of Keynesianism, as evident in the California Master Plan and Clark Kerr's conception of the "multiversity."[205] The reconfiguration of universities from providing public goods within a Keynesian context to privatizing education and commodifying knowledge is directly connected into the broader crisis of Keynesianism and reconfiguration of capital at the global level. Universities have globalized their operations as a response to declining state support (e.g., American and British universities with campuses in China and Dubai), as well as drawing increasing funding from international students.[206] The globalization of the university, a feature of the neoliberal model, corresponds with the globalization of the productive forces, an expression of the advanced socialization of the productive forces. The globalization of science has followed from the globalization of the productive forces.[207] As Marx said, "society's science," or "general intellect," or the "general productive forces of the social brain" integrates production into the social process extending beyond the factory, so that production far exceeds the wage relationship and the law of value.[208] This is a form of the contradiction between socialized production and private appropriation. This contradiction is ramified and reflected in the contradiction between global economy and the nation-state and, hence, in imperialism as the capitalist solution to this contradiction. The globalized university is caught up in this contradiction.

As universities became part of capital's solution to the problem of growing international competition and crises of productivity growth and the declining rate of profit, they were integrated into the processes of economic globalization, part of a global market in education, research, and scientific labor. The importance of science for military technology is a bond between the university and the military needs of the nation-state, which provides funding for those reasons. At the same time, the relationship between universities and high-tech corporations puts the university in a network that extends to the global weapons market.[209] The contradiction between the globalized economy of the university and its continuing integration with the nation-state puts the university in a tension-ridden position. This is expressed in, for example, current security scares about Chinese researchers in the United States. It may also be seen in extreme form in the conflict between the Trump administration and the World Health Organization and in the relation between vaccine skepticism and right wing extremely nationalistic politics. It may be seen in the ways in which, as Susan L. Robinson and Matias Nestore argue, the neoliberal knowledge economy manifested and promoted in universities shuts out a whole section of society who are not credentialed and whose humiliation is entailed by the self-sanctifying neoliberalism of the professional-managerial stratum.[210]

The neoliberal transformation of universities in service of economic competitiveness within the global economy refutes the claim of new class theory that intellectuals, scientific and technical experts, bureaucrats, and managers, who possess knowledge rather than capital, inexorably rise within capitalism to displace the owners of capital from the pinnacle of power. New class theory entails that knowledge, rather than capital, becomes the primary medium of power in modern society. While it has taken many forms, from Mikhail Bakunin's anarchist critique of Marx to Max Weber's theory of bureaucracy to theories of the Soviet Union as bureaucratic collectivist or state capitalist to New Left criticisms of technocracy to neo-conservative criticism of the welfare state and governmental bureaucracy, new class theory coheres around the notion of knowledge replacing capital as the primary source of social power. New class theory may be understood as a critical corollary of the sociological conceptualizations of modernity that treat modern societies as being primarily characterized by scientific rationality rather than capitalism. Put another way, it is the negative corollary of the positive technocratic utopian visions of post-industrial society and post-capitalism.[211] New class theory went along with convergence theories which conceptualized the capitalist societies of the West converging with the Soviet Union on a bureaucratic statist model.[212] This was a theoretical framework that emerged from the social-theoretical reflection of the social forms of welfarist capitalism or social democracy and Stalinism that characterized the mid-twentieth century. The conditions for plausibility of new class theory have been drastically undercut by the institutional transformations that have accompanied globalization, especially the transformation of the university which is the core institution of the scientific elites, credentialed experts, and professionals.

Gouldner developed his reflexive sociology along the lines of a theory of intellectuals as a new class that is set apart from other classes by its culture of critical discourse.[213] Gouldner saw a utopian dimension to the rise of the new class and argued that the new class was potentially a "universal class," in the sense of representing and carrying with it the universal interest of humanity. However, it was a "flawed universal class." Gouldner offered critical support to the new class project of the intellectuals:

> The New Class is elitist and self-seeking and uses its special knowledge to advance its own interests and power, and control its own work situation. Yet the New Class may also be the best card that history has presently given us to play.[214]

Whereas Weber's project was to give class consciousness to the German bourgeoisie, Gouldner's was to provide class consciousness to the emerging new class of intellectuals. To overcome its flaw, it needed to become conscious of itself, through reflexive sociology.

Gouldner explicitly rejected a view of intellectuals as allies of the "old" capitalist class or as "servants of power," views he associated with Noam Chomsky and Maurice Zeitlin. The New Class, Gouldner wrote, "is substantially more powerful and independent than Chomsky suggests."[215] Chomsky has withstood the test of time on this, while Gouldner has not. Lawrence King and Iván Szelényi assert, contra Gouldner, that "professionalism . . . is the ideology of the intellectual stratum that guarantees that this stratum does not represent any meaningful, significant challenge to the dominant capitalist class."[216] Gouldner's belief in the independence of interest of the New Class from the bourgeoisie was shaped in the context of postwar Keynesianism and the welfare state. As with the limitations of his understanding of the crisis of sociology, Gouldner failed to comprehend the transformation that was underway he was writing toward the reassertion of the primacy of the market. This reassertion involved undermining the mediating institutions that managed the compromise with the working class and supported the somewhat independent institutional base of power for knowledge elites or intellectuals. The underpinning, by the Keynesian welfare state, of the autonomous power of intellectuals (even while, as Gouldner argued, it tethered intellectuals to its structures) was connected with the welfare state's technocratic character.

Technocracy was attacked by both the New Left and the New Right.[217] An aspect of the rise of neoliberalism was the attack from the right, informed by neo-conservative iterations of new class theory combined with public choice theory, on the perceived power of the new class.[218] Another aspect of neoliberalism was the transformation of the universities to reorient them from the provision of public goods to the privatization and commodification of knowledge. In the process, a section of the technical intelligentsia has been integrated into the capitalist class, as "entrepreneurial scientists." At the same time, the university has a large precarious proletariat, or what Herb Childress calls the "adjunct underclass."[219] Hence, neoliberalism has pulled apart the professional-managerial class, particularly to the detriment of its more pro-fessionally oriented members, increasing this stratum's sense of insecurity.[220]

As opposed to the technocratic ethos of postwar Keynesianism, neolib-eralism as ideology holds that the superior processor of information is the market itself.[221] This ideology reflects and legitimizes the growing demand of the owners of capital to take control over the production of knowledge and to suppress the scope for independent action by producers of knowledge, that is, intellectuals. In so doing, the capitalist class sought to directly trans-fer their monetary capital into epistemic capital.[222] The commodification of science and the privatization of education is a direct assertion of capitalist class power.[223] The university and the PMC or so-called New Class is tied by chains of capital to the bourgeoisie. But this generates tension in the uni-versity's relationship to the nation-state. The university is caught between globalized capital and the nation-state. Independence of the "new class" from capital was made possible by the embedding of intellectuals within the institutional framework of the nation-state and the mediating institutions sup-ported by the nation-state. The decline of the independence of intellectuals from capital (and the emerging class division among intellectuals between the capitalized and the proletarianized) follows from the declining power of nation-state institutions in relation to global capital. Under globalization, the price system took back the ground it had lost to the social engineers.[224]

There is no solution within the framework of bourgeois relations to the contradiction between science as universal and national or between global economy and nation-state. This is because the nation-state is the bourgeoisie's only solution to the problem of order and nationalism is its only solution to the problem of meaning. However, the productive forces have outgrown the nation-state and science has along with them outgrown the national scale, with international collaboration and facilities. The Covid-19 pandemic not only demonstrates the contradiction between the real material global integration of the human species and the national political organization of the species. It also shows the contradiction between global science and national govern-ment. The mobilization of science by the nation-state always ties science to the dynamics of imperialism, whether in the form of vaccine nationalism or in the form of military research. The nation-state and nationalism are today clearly fetters on the development of the productive forces most clearly in the case of science. However, bourgeois society has no solution to the problem of order other than these. As a result, the advanced development of the productive forces and of science disorganizes rather than orders the world.

NOTES

1. Jared H. Beck, *What Happened to Bernie Sanders?* (New York: Hot Books, 2018).

2. Igor Derysh, "Joe Biden to Rich Donors: 'Nothing Would Fundamentally Change' If He's elected," *Salon,* June 19, 2019, https://www.salon.com/2019/06/19/joe-biden-to-rich-donors-nothing-would-fundamentally-change-if-hes-elected/.

3. Jonathan Martin, "Biden Always Had a Simple Message. He Rode It to the Nomination," *New York Times*, August 21, 2020, https://www.nytimes.com/2020/08/21/us/politics/Joe-Biden-Democratic-nominee.html.

4. Erving Goffman, "On Cooling the Mark Out: Some Aspects of Adaptation to Failure," *Psychiatry* 15, no. 4 (1952): 451–463. Cf. Jason Glynos, Robin Klimecki and Hugh Willmott "Cooling Out the Marks: The Ideology and Politics of the Financial Crisis," *Journal of Cultural Economy* 5, no. 3 (2012): 297–320.

5. *The Nation* quoted in Karl Schriftgiesser, *This was Normalcy: An Account of Party Politics During Twelve Republican Years: 1920-1932* (New York: Little Brown, 1948), 35.

6. Harding, quoted in Ezra Klein, "Joe Biden's Promise: A Return to Normalcy," *Vox,* March 20, 2019, https://www.vox.com/policy-and-politics/2019/5/20/18631452/joe-biden-2020-presidential-announcement-speech; Warren G. Harding, "Readjustment," June 29, 1920, Library of Congress, http://www.loc.gov/item/2016655168/. See also "Presidential Election of 1920," Library of Congress, https://www.loc.gov/collections/world-war-i-and-1920-election-recordings/articles-and-essays/from-war-to-normalcy/presidential-election-of-1920/#:~:text=Harding%20recorded%20several%20speeches%20for,.not%20surgery%20but%20serenity. See also Robert K. Murray, *The Politics of Normalcy: Governmental Theory and Practice in the Harding-Coolidge Era* (New York: Norton, 1973); Burl Noggle, *Into the Twenties: The United States from Armistice to Normalcy* (Urbana: University of Illinois Press, 1974).

7. David Emory Shi and George Brown Tindall, *America: A Narrative History* (New York: W.W. Norton and Co., 2016), 849.

8. Cf. Michael Burawoy, *Manufacturing Consent: Changes in the Labor Process Under Monopoly Capitalism* (Chicago: University of Chicago Press, 1979); Edward S. Herman and Noam Chomsky, *Manufacturing Consent: The Political Economy of the Mass Media* (New York: Pantheon Books, 2002); Olivier Zunz, *Why the American Century?* (Chicago: University of Chicago Press, 1998).

9. Emanuele Saccarelli and Latha Varadarajan, *Imperialism: Past and Present* (New York: Oxford University Press, 2015), 124–154. See also David North, *The*

Russian Revolution and the Unfinished Twentieth Century (New York: Mehring Books, 2014).

10. Jane Addams, quoted in Shi and Tindall, *America*, 854.

11. James K. Galbraith, *The End of Normal: The Great Crisis and the Future of Growth* (New York: Simon and Schuster, 2014), 21.

12. Habermas, "Technology and Science as 'Ideology'," 108; Habermas, *Legitimation Crisis*, 37–38.

13. Gouldner, *Coming Crisis*, 147–148.

14. Cf. Bob Woodward and Robert Costa, *Peril* (New York: Simon and Schuster, 2021).

15. Spencer Ackerman, *Reign of Terror: How the 9/11 Era Destabilized America and Produced Trump* (New York: Viking, 2021); Max Blumenthal, *The Management of Savagery: How America's National Security State Fueled the Rise of Al Qaeda, ISIS, and Donald Trump* (London: Verso, 2019), 44. See also Gershon Shafir, Everard Meade, and William J Aceves, *Lessons and Legacies of the War on Terror: From Moral Panic to Permanent War* (Abingdon, Oxon: Routledge, 2013).

16. David North, *A Quarter Century of War: The U.S. Drive for Global Hegemony 1990-2016* (Oak Park, MI: Mehring Press, 2016); Deepa Kumar, *Islamophobia and the Politics of Empire: Twenty Years After 9/11* (Chicago: Haymarket Books, 2012); Deepa Kumar, "After 9/11, the US Tried to Force its Will on the World. It Failed," *Jacobin* (September 12, 2021), https://www.jacobinmag.com/2021/09/9-11-us-imperialism-orientalism-neocon-middle-east-intervention-war-foreign-policy-security-islamic-terrorism; Mike Hume, "The New Age of Imperialism," *Living Marxism* (November 1990): 4–7; Frank Füredi, "So Much for the 'Peace Dividend'," *Living Marxism* (October 1990): 14–19.

17. Gershon Shafir, "Opinion: Two Decades after 9/11, Many Questions are Left Unanswered: Moral Panics Leave a Trail of Catastrophic Results," *The San Diego Union-Tribune* (September 9, 2021), https://www.sandiegouniontribune.com/opinion/commentary/story/2021-09-09/911-questions-afghanistan-taliban.

18. "Trump Says He's President of Law and Order, Declares Aggressive Action on Violent Protests," *CBS News*, June 2, 2020, https://www.cbsnews.com/news/trump-protest-president-law-and-order/; Ryan Cooper, "Trump's False Lafayette Square Exoneration," *The Week*, June 11, 2021, https://theweek.com/donald-trump/1001404/lafayette-square-clearing-inspector-general-report. See also Erica Chenoweth and Jeremy Pressman, "Black Lives Matter Protests Were Overwhelmingly Peaceful, Our Research Finds," Harvard Radcliffe Institute (October 20, 2020), https://www.radcliffe.harvard.edu/news-and-ideas/black-lives-matter-protesters-were-overwhelmingly-peaceful-our-research-finds.

19. Wolfe, *Limits of Legitimacy*, 340–341.

20. Gary Teeple, *Globalization and the Decline of Social Reform: Into the Twenty-First Century* (Amherst, NY: Humanity Books, 2000), 149. Cf. Matt Vidal, "Postfordism as a Dysfunctional Accumulation Regime: A Comparative Analysis of the USA, the UK and Germany," *Work, Employment & Society* 27, no. 3 (2013): 451–471.

21. Richard Anderson-Connolly, *A Leftist Critique of the Principles of Identity, Diversity, and Multiculturalism* (Lanham, MD: Lexington Books, 2019), 43.

22. Bastiaan van Apeldoorn, Naná de Graaff and Henk Overbeek, "The Rebound of the Capitalist State: The Rearticulation of the State-Capital Nexus in the Global Crisis," in Bastiaan van Apeldoorn, Naná de Graaff and Henk Overbeek eds, *The State-Capital Nexus in the Global Crisis: Rebound of the Capitalist State* (London: Routledge, 2014), 5–35, on 12.

23. Adam Curtis, *HyperNormalisation* Documentary film (BBC, 2016); Alexei Yurchak, *Everything Was Forever, Until It Was No More: The Last Soviet Generation* (Princeton, NJ: Princeton University Press, 2013).

24. Barbara A. Misztal,"Normality and Trust in Goffman's Theory of Interaction Order," *Sociological Theory* 19, no. 3 (November, 2001): 312–324, on 315.

25. Anthony Giddens, *Modernity and Self-Identity: Self and Society in the Late Modern Age* (Stanford, CA: Stanford University Press, 1991), 42–53, esp. 44; Susie Scott and Charles Thorpe, "The Sociological Imagination of R. D. Laing," *Sociological Theory* 24, no. 4 (2006): 331–352. See also Misztal, "Normality and Trust," 314–315.

26. Anthony Giddens, *The Consequences of Modernity* (Stanford, CA: Stanford University Press, 1990), 92.

27. Harry Collins, *Forms of Life: The Method and Meaning of Sociology* (Cambridge, MA: The MIT Press, 2019), 13.

28. Lefebvre, *Everyday Life in the Modern World;* Gramsci, *Selections*, 277–318.

29. David Garland, *The Culture of Control: Crime and Social Order in Contemporary Society* (Oxford: Oxford University Press, 2001).

30. Wolfe, "New Directions," 154.

31. Robert Brenner, *The Economics of Global Turbulence* (London: Verso, 2006).

32. Office of the Historian, "Milestones, 1969–1976: Nixon and the End of the Bretton Woods System, 1971–1973," https://history.state.gov/milestones/1969-1976/nixon-shock.

33. Nick Beams, "50 Years Since the End of the Bretton Woods Monetary System," *World Socialist Web Site* (August 13, 2021), https://www.wsws.org/en/articles/2021/08/14/wood-a14.html; David North, "The Trump Coup and the Rise of Fascism: Where is America Going?" *World Socialist Web Site* (January 19, 2021), https://www.wsws.org/en/articles/2021/01/19/dnor-j19.html; Nick Beams, "The Rise of Financial Parasitism and the Emergence of Fascism," *World Socialist Web Site* (January 26, 2021), https://www.wsws.org/en/articles/2021/01/26/para-j26.html; David North, "The Capitalist Crisis and the Return of History," *World Socialist Web Site* (March 26, 2009), https://www.wsws.org/en/articles/2009/03/dnor-m26.html.

34. Cf. C. Wright Mills, *The Causes of World War Three* (New York: Simon and Schuster, 1958).

35. Dan Glazebrook, *Divide and Ruin: The West's Imperial Strategy in an Age of Crisis* (San Francisco, CA: Liberation Media, 2013), ix.

36. John Pilger and Alan Lowery, *The War You Don't See* (UK: Dartmouth Films, 2010).

37. Cf. Michael E. Latham, *Modernization as Ideology: American Social Science and "Nation-Building" in the Kennedy Era* (Chapel Hill: University of North Carolina Press, 2000).

38. Neda Atanasoski, *Humanitarian Violence: The U.S. Deployment of Diversity* (Minneapolis: University of Minnesota Press, 2013), 102–127.

39. Quoted in Kevin Liptak, "Biden Defends Pulling US Out of Afghanistan as Taliban Advances: 'We did not go to Afghanistan to nation-build," *CNN*, July 8, 2021, https://www.cnn.com/2021/07/08/politics/biden-afghanistan-speech/index.html.

40. Norbert Elias, *The Germans: Power Struggles and the Development of Habitus in the Nineteenth and Twentieth Centuries* (Cambridge: Cambridge University Press, 1996), 1; Jonathan Fletcher, *Violence and Civilization: An Introduction to the Work of Norbert Elias* (Cambridge: Polity Press, 1997).

41. Kim Sengupta, "Syrian Civil War: The Day I Met the Organ Eating Cannibal Rebel Abu Sakkar's Fearsome Followers," *The Independent* (May 10, 2013), https://www.independent.co.uk/news/world/middle-east/syrian-civil-war-day-i-met-organ-eating-cannibal-rebel-abu-sakkar-s-fearsome-followers-8617828.html; Jay Akbar, "Cannibal 'Moderate' Syrian Rebel Who Cut out and Ate an Assad Soldier's Heart and Liver is Killed 'After his Convoy was Ambushed'," *The Daily Mail*, April 5, 2016, https://www.dailymail.co.uk/news/article-3524976/CANNIBAL-moderate-Syrian-rebel-cut-ate-Assad-soldier-s-heart-liver-killed.html.

42. Medecins Sans Frontieres, "On 3 October 2015, US Airstrikes Destroyed Our Trauma Hospital in Kunduz, Afghanistan, Killing 42 People," Medecins San Frontieres, n.d., https://www.msf.org/kunduz-hospital-attack-depth (accessed July 28, 2021).

43. Ahmad Sultan and Abdul Qadir Sediqi, "U.S. Drone Strike Kills 30 Pine Nut Farm Workers in Afghanistan," *Reuters*, September 19, 2019, https://www.reuters.com/article/us-afghanistan-attack-drones/u-s-drone-strike-kills-30-pine-nut-farm-workers-in-afghanistan-idUSKBN1W40NW.

44. Ehsan Popalzai, Nilly Kohzad and Ivana Kottasová, "A Strike Targeting Taliban Kills 40 Civilians at a Wedding Next Door," *CNN*, September 25, 2019, https://www.cnn.com/2019/09/23/asia/afghanistan-wedding-attack-intl/index.html.

45. Bill Van Auken "Trump's War Crime Pardons: Cultivating a Fascistic Base in the Military," *World Socialist Web Site,* November 27, 2019, https://www.wsws.org/en/articles/2019/11/27/pers-n27.html; Patrick Martin, "Edward Gallagher, Donald Trump and America's Criminal Wars," *World Socialist Web Site*, December 30, 2019, https://www.wsws.org/en/articles/2019/12/30/pers-d30.html.

46. Frederik Federspiel and Mohammad Ali, "The Cholera Outbreak in Yemen: Lessons Learned and Way Forward," *BMC Public Health* 18 (2018): 1138–1146. https://www.ncbi.nlm.nih.gov/pmc/articles/PMC6278080/.

47. Alex Wellerstein, "The Hawaii Alert Was an Accident. The Dread it Inspired Wasn't," *The Washington Post*, January 16, 2018, https://www.washingtonpost.com/news/posteverything/wp/2018/01/16/the-hawaii-alert-was-an-accident-the-dread-it-inspired-wasnt/.

48. Alistair Gee and Dani Anguiano, "Last Day in Paradise: The Untold Story of How a Fire Swallowed a Town," *The Guardian*, December 20, 2018, https://www

.theguardian.com/environment/2018/dec/20/last-day-in-paradise-california-deadliest
-fire-untold-story-survivors.

49. Helen Davidson, "Mallacoota fire: Images of 'Mayhem' and 'Armageddon' as Bushfires Rage," *The Guardian*, December 30, 2019, https://www.theguardian.com/australia-news/2019/dec/31/mallacoota-fire-mayhem-armageddon-bushfires
-rage-victoria-east-gippsland.

50. Aradhana Aravindan and James Mackenzie, "From China to Germany, Floods Expose Climate Vulnerability," *Reuters*, July 22, 2021, https://www.reuters.com/business/environment/china-germany-floods-expose-climate-vulnerability
-2021-07-22/.

51. James K. Galbraith, *The Predator State: How Conservatives Abandoned the Free Market and Why Liberals Should Too* (New York: The Free Press, 2008), 147.

52. G. William Domhoff, *The Corporate Rich and the Power Elite in the Twentieth Century: How They Won, Why Liberals and Labor Lost* (New York: Routledge, 2020), quoting 1. See also Peter Phillips, *Giants: The Global Power Elite* (New York: Seven Stories Press, 2018).

53. *Pace* Daniel Chernilo, "Beyond the Nation? Or Back to It? Current Trends in the Sociology of Nations and Nationalism," *Sociology* 54, no. 6 (2020): 1072–1087, esp. 1080–1083.

54. Jane Mayer, *Dark Money: The Hidden History of the Billionaires Behind the Rise of the Radical Right* (New York: Anchor, 2016); Jane Mayer, "The Reclusive Hedge-Fund Tycoon Behind the Trump Presidency," *The New Yorker*, March 17, 2017, https://www.newyorker.com/magazine/2017/03/27/the-reclusive-hedge-fund
-tycoon-behind-the-trump-presidency.

55. Harold Garfinkel, *Studies in Ethnomethodology* (Cambridge: Polity Press, 1984), 35; Gouldner, "Sociology and the Everyday Life," 422.

56. Marshall Berman, *All That is Solid Melts into Air: The Experience of Modernity* (New York: Simon and Schuster, 1982).

57. Howard Brick, *Transcending Capitalism: Visions of a New Society in American Thought* (Ithaca, NY: Cornell University Press, 2006), 291 note 2.

58. Cf. Raymond Briggs, *When the Wind Blows* (London: S. French, 1983).

59. Sharon Ghamari-Tabrizi, *The Worlds of Herman Kahn: The Intuitive Science of Thermonuclear War* (Cambridge, MA: Harvard University Press, 2005); Charles Thorpe, "Review of The Worlds of Herman Kahn: The Intuitive Science of Thermonuclear War, by Sharon Ghamari-Tabrizi," *Journal of Historical Biography* 3 (Spring, 2008): 134–140; Charles Thorpe, "Review of Daniel Cordle, *States of Suspense: The Nuclear Age, Postmodernism and United States Fiction and Prose*," British Society for Literature and Science, (published online 2009), https://www.bsls.ac.uk/reviews/modern-and-contemporary/daniel-cordle-states-of-suspense/.

60. Elaine Tyler May, *Homeward Bound: American Families in the Cold War Era* (New York: Basic Books, 1999); Daniel Cordle, *States of Suspense: The Nuclear Age, Postmodernism and United States Fiction and Prose* (Manchester: Manchester University Press, 2008).

61. Carole Pateman, *The Problem of Political Obligation: A Critique of Liberal Theory* (Cambridge: Polity Press, 1985).

62. Bauman, *Legislators and Interpreters;* Ernest Gellner, *Nations and Nationalism* (Ithaca, NY: Cornell University Press, 1983).

63. Balibar, *Violence and Civility*, 65.

64. Leon Trotsky, "Once Again on the 'Crisis of Marxism'," in George Breitman ed, *Writings of Leon Trotsky 1938–39* (New York: Pathfinder Press, 1974), 204–206, on 205.

65. Walter J. Oakes, "Toward a Permanent War Economy?" *Politics* (February, 1944): 11–17; Tony Cliff, "Perspectives of the Permanent War Economy," *Socialist Review* 6, no. 8 (May 1957), https://www.marxists.org/archive/cliff/works/1957/05/permwar.htm; Seymour Melman, *Pentagon Capitalism: The Political Economy of War* (New York: McGraw-Hill, 1970).

66. Dominic Boyer and Alexei Yurchak, "American Stiob: Or, What Late-Socialist Aesthetics of Parody Reveal about Contemporary Political Culture in the West," *Cultural Anthropology* 25, no. 2 (2010): 179–221.

67. Boyer and Yurchak, "American Stiob," 183.

68. Guy Debord, *Comments on the Society of the Spectacle* (London: Verso, 2011); Guy Debord, *Society of the Spectacle* (London: Black and Red, 2002). See also Richard Gilman-Opalsky, "Why New Socialist Theory Needs Guy Debord: On the Practice of Radical Philosophy," in Graham Cassano and Richard Dello Buono eds, *Crisis, Politics, and Critical Sociology* (Chicago: Haymarket, 2012), 109–134.

69. Herman and Chomsky. *Manufacturing Consent.*

70. Curtis, *HyperNormalisation*; The Economist, "The Antidote to Civilisational Collapse: An Interview with the Documentary Filmmaker Adam Curtis," *The Economist*, December 6, 2018, https://www.economist.com/open-future/2018/12/06/the-antidote-to-civilisational-collapse.

71. Charlie Lyne, "Hypernormalisation: Adam Curtis Plots a Path from Syria to Trump, via Jane Fonda," *The Guardian*, October 15, 2016, https://www.theguardian.com/tv-and-radio/2016/oct/15/hypernormalisation-adam-curtis-trump-putin-syria.

72. Guy Debord, *Society of the Spectacle* (film, 1974).

73. Herbert Marcuse, *One-Dimensional Man: Studies in the Ideology of Advanced Industrial* Society (Boston: Beacon Press, 1964).

74. Matthew Adams, "Hypernormalised? Heathrow Plan is Proof that we Live in a Catastrophic Fantasyland," *The Ecologist*, October 26, 2016, https://theecologist.org/2016/oct/26/hypernormalised-heathrow-plan-proof-we-exist-catastrophic-fantasyland.

75. Jean Baudrillard, *America* (London: Verso, 1988); Jean Baudrillard, *Simulacra and Simulation* (Ann Arbor: University of Michigan Press, 1994).

76. Daniel Bell, *The End of Ideology: The Exhaustion of Political Ideas in the Fifties* (Glencoe, IL: The Free Press, 1960); Francis Fukuyama, "The End of History?" *The National Interest* 16 (Summer 1989): 3–18. Cf. Alex Hochull, George Hoare, and Philip Cunliffe, *The End of the End of History: Politics in the Twenty-First Century* (London: Zero Books, 2021).

77. Manfred B. Steger and Ravi K. Roy, *Neoliberalism: A Very Short Introduction* (Oxford: Oxford University Press, 2010), 50–75.

78. Frederic Jameson, "Future City," *New Left Review* 21 (May-June 2003): 76–77. See also Slavoj Žižek, *Living in the End Times* (London: Verso, 2011); Mark Fisher, *Capitalist Realism: Is There No Alternative?* (London: Zero Books, 2009).

79. Roy Scranton, *War Porn* (New York: Soho Press, 2016).

80. Scranton, *War Porn*, 31.

81. Roy Scranton, *Learning to Die in the Anthropocene: Reflections on the End of a Civilization* (San Francisco, CA: City Lights Books, 2015).

82. Ingolfür Bluhdorn and Ian Welsh, "Eco-Politics Beyond the Paradigm of Sustainability: A Conceptual Framework and Research Agenda," *Environmental Politics* 16, no. 2 (2007): 185–205; Ingolfür Bluhdorn and Ian Welsh eds, *The Politics of Unsustainability: Eco-Politics in the Post-Ecologist Era* (London: Routledge, 2013).

83. Thomas Singer, "Extinction Anxiety and Collective Madness: Marjorie Taylor Greene, facemasks, extreme sports and Reddit/Gamestock," *Moyers on Democracy*, February 3, 2021, https://billmoyers.com/story/extinction-anxiety-and-collective-madness/.

84. Cf. Ajit Varki and Danny Brower, *Denial: Self-Deception, False Belief and the Origins of the Human Mind* (New York: Twelve, 2013).

85. Elizabeth Stephens, "Post-Normal: Crisis and the End of the Ordinary," *Media International Australia* 177, no. 1 (2020): 92–102.

86. Roy Scranton, "I've Said Goodbye to 'Normal.' You Should Too," *The New York Times*, January 25, 2001, https://www.nytimes.com/2021/01/25/opinion/new-normal-climate-catastrophes.html.

87. Scranton, "I've Said Goodbye to 'Normal'."

88. Bernard E. Harcourt, *The Counterrevolution: How Our Government Went to War Against its Own Citizens* (New York: Basic Books, 2018); "With Whom are Many U.S. Police Departments Training? With a Chronic Human Rights Violator—Israel," Amnesty International, August 25, 2016, https://www.amnestyusa.org/with-whom-are-many-u-s-police-departments-training-with-a-chronic-human-rights-violator-israel/; Benjamin Mateus, "Behind the Epidemic of Police Killings in America: Class, Poverty and Race," *World Socialist Web Site*, December 20, 2018, https://www.wsws.org/en/articles/2018/12/20/kill-d20.html.

89. Deborah Sontag, "Video Is a Window into a Terror Suspect's Isolation," *New York Times*, December 4, 2006, https://www.nytimes.com/2006/12/04/us/04detain.html; Micah Zenko, "Obama Discusses Targeted Killing of U.S. Citizens During Google+ Hangout," Council on Foreign Relations (blog), February 15, 2013, https://www.cfr.org/blog/obama-discusses-targeted-killing-us-citizens-during-google-hangout; Charlie Savage, *Power Wars: Inside Obama's Post-9/11 Presidency* (New York: Little, Brown and Co., 2015).

90. Jeffrey Haynes, *From Huntington to Trump: Thirty Years of the Clash of Civilizations* (Lanham, MD: Lexington Books, 2019), 48–49.

91. Samuel P. Huntington, *The Clash of Civilizations and the Remaking of World Order* (New York: Touchstone, 1996), 251, 252.

92. Leon Trotsky, "War and the Fourth International," trans. Sara Webe (Originally published as a pamphlet by Pioneer Publishers, July 10, 1934, https://www.marxists.org/archive/trotsky/1934/06/warfi.htm.

93. Alfred W. McCoy, *In the Shadows of the American Century: The Rise and Decline of US Global Power* (Chicago: Haymarket, 2017), 37.

94. Quoted in North, *A Quarter Century of War*, 134.

95. David North, *A Quarter Century of War*, xxviii.

96. George H. W. Bush,, State of the Union Address, January 29 1991, Public Papers of the Presidents of the United States, https://www.presidency.ucsb.edu/documents/address-before-joint-session-the-congress-the-state-the-union-1; North, *A Quarter Century of War*, xii.

97. Haynes, *From Huntington to Trump*, 49–50.

98. Ben Watson and Bradley Peniston, "US at war in 7 countries — including Niger; US Army Rebuilds Afghan Firebases; F-35s to India?; and Just a Bit More..." *Defense One*, March 15, 2018, https://www.defenseone.com/news/2018/03/the-d -brief-march-15-2018/146688/.

99. North, *A Quarter Century of War*; Andre, Damon, "Trump vs. the Democrats: Two reactionary factions fight over foreign policy," *World Socialist Web Site*, July 16, 2018, https://www.wsws.org/en/articles/2018/07/16/pers-j16.html.

100. Bill Van Auken, "The US War and Occupation of Iraq—the Murder of a Society," *World Socialist Web Site*, May 19, 2007, https://www.wsws.org/en/articles /2007/05/iraq-m19.html; Bill Van Auken, "The Atrocities of ISIS and the US Wars of Sociocide," *World Socialist Web Site*, August 26, 2015, https://www.wsws.org/en /articles/2015/08/26/pers-a26.html; Keith Doubt, *Sociocide: Reflections on Today's Wars* (Lanham, MD: Rowman and Littlefield, 2021).

101. Blumenthal, *The Management of Savagery*.

102. Peter Dale Scott, *The American Deep State: Wall Street, Big Oil, and the Attack on U.S. Democracy* (Lanham, MD: Rowman and Littlefield, 2015); Graeme MacQueen, *The 2001 Anthrax Deception: The Case for a Domestic Conspiracy* (Atlanta, GA: Clarity Press, 2014).

103. Zachary Laub, "Debating the Legality of the Post-9/11 'Forever War'," *Council on Foreign Relations*, January 12, 2017, https://www.cfr.org/expert-roundup /debating-legality-post-911-forever-war.

104. Gregoire Chamayou, *A Theory of the Drone* (New York: The New Press, 2015); Willie Osterweil, "The Drone of Permanent War," *Dissent*, March 21, 2012, https://www.dissentmagazine.org/blog/the-drone-of-permanent-war.

105. Cf. Jytte Klausen, *War and Welfare: Europe and the United States, 1945 to the Present* (New York: Palgrave Macmillan, 1998).

106. Bernard Rostker, "The Evolution of the All-Volunteer Force," RAND Research Brief, n.d., https://www.rand.org/pubs/research_briefs/RB9195.html; Beth Bailey, "The Army in the Marketplace: Recruiting an All-Volunteer Force," *The Journal of American History* 94, no. 1 (June 2007): 47–74.

107. Tom Engelhardt, *The End of Victory Culture: Cold War America and the Disillusioning of a Generation* (Amherst: University Massachusetts Press, 2007).

108. Hedges, *War is a Force*; Andrew J. Bacevich, *The New American Militarism: How Americans are Seduced by War* (Oxford: Oxford University Press, 2005).

109. Howard F. Stein, *Beneath the Crust of Culture: Psychoanalytic Anthropology and the Cultural Unconscious in American Life* (Amsterdam: Rodopi, 2004); Simon

Clarke and Paul Hoggett, "The Empire of Fear: The American Political Psyche and the Culture of Paranoia," *Psychodynamic Practice* 10, no. 1 (2004): 89–106.

110. Cf. Thorpe, Rebecca U. *The American Warfare State The Domestic Politics of Military Spending* (Chicago: University of Chicago Press, 2014).

111. Galbraith, *Predator State*, 131–132.

112. James M. Cypher, "From Military Keynesianism to Global Neoliberal Militarism," *Monthly Review* (June 1, 2007), https://monthlyreview.org/2007/06/01/from-military-keynesianism-to-global-neoliberal-militarism/.

113. Sabrina Rubin Erdely, "The Rape of Petty Officer Blumer: Inside the Military's Culture of Sex Abuse, Denial and Cover Up," *Rolling Stone*, February 14, 2013, https://www.rollingstone.com/politics/politics-news/the-rape-of-petty-officer-blumer-99154/.

114. Eric Schmitt, "Lloyd Austin Ramps up the Fight against Right-wing Extremism within the Military," *New York Times*, February 3, 2021, https://www.nytimes.com/2021/02/03/us/lloyd-austin-extremism-military.html.

115. "Impeachment Trial Day 3 Highlights: Prosecutors Rest Their Case, Warning Trump 'Can Do This Again' if He Is Not Convicted," *New York Times*, February 22, 2021, https://www.nytimes.com/live/2021/02/11/us/impeachment-trial.

116. Jonathan Fletcher, *Violence and Civilization: An Introduction to the Work of Norbert Elias* (Cambridge: Polity Press, 1997); Norbert Elias, *The Germans* (New York: Columbia University Press, 1996).

117. Todd C. Frankel, "A Majority of the People Arrested for Capitol Riot had a History of Financial Trouble," *The Washington Post*, February 10, 2021, https://www.washingtonpost.com/business/2021/02/10/capitol-insurrectionists-jenna-ryan-financial-problems/.

118. Cf. Lauren Langman and George Lundskow, *God, Guns, Gold and Glory: American Character and its Discontents* (Leiden: Brill, 2016).

119. Lois Beckett, "What the Arrests of Beverly Hills Residents Say about the US Capitol Attack," *The Guardian*, February 25, 2021, https://www.theguardian.com/us-news/2021/feb/25/beverly-hills-arrests-us-capitol-attack; Christian Triebert, Ben Decker, Derek Watkins, Arielle Ray, and Stella Cooper, "First They Guarded Roger Stone. Then they Joined the Capitol Attack," *New York Times*, February 14, 2021, https://www.nytimes.com/interactive/2021/02/14/us/roger-stone-capitol-riot.html; "F.B.I. Finds Contact Between Proud Boys Member and Trump Associate Before Riot," *New York Times*, March 5, 2021, https://www.nytimes.com/2021/03/05/us/politics/trump-proud-boys-capitol-riot.html.

120. Karl Marx, *Capital, Volume 1: A Critique of Political Economy*, trans. Ben Fowkes (New York: Vintage Books, 1977), 381.

121. John McMurty, *Cancer Capitalism: From Crisis to Cure* (London: Verso, 2013).

122. Trotsky, *Death Agony of Capitalism*, 2.

123. V. I. Lenin, *Imperialism: The Highest Stage of Capitalism*, a Popular Outline (New York: International Publishers, 1939).

124. Erich Fromm, *The Anatomy of Human Destructiveness* (New York: Holt, Rinehart and Winston, 1973); Charles Thorpe, *Necroculture* (New York: Palgrave Macmillan, 2016).

125. Thorpe, *Necroculture*, 205–259; Jack Bratich, "'Give me Liberty or Give me Covid!' Anti-Lockdown Protests as Necropopulist Downsurgency," *Cultural Studies* 35, no. 2–3 (2021): 257–265.

126. Tim Boyd quoted in "Texas Snow: Mayor Quits After 'Only Strong Will Survive' Post," *BBC News*, February 17, 2021, https://www.bbc.com/news/world -us-canada-56100743; Elizabeth Findell, "Full Death Toll from Texas Storm could Take Months to Determine," *Wall Street Journal,* February 23, 2021, https://www .wsj.com/articles/full-death-toll-from-texas-storm-could-take-months-to-determine -11614107708?reflink=desktopwebshare_permalink.

127. Cf. Langman and Lundskow, *God, Guns, Gold, and Glory.*

128. Gouldner, *Dialectic of Ideology and Technology*, 102–103; Michelle Barrett and Mary McIntosh, *The Anti-Social Family* (London: Verso, 2015).

129. Henry Giroux, "Racial Injustice and Disposable Youth in the Age of Zero Tolerance," *Qualitative Studies in Education* 16, no. 4 (July-August 2003): 553–565; Brad Evans and Henry A. Giroux, *Disposable Futures: The Seduction of Violence in the Age of Spectacle* (San Francisco, CA: City Lights Books, 2015).

130. Giroux, "Disposable Youth," 557.

131. Stuart Hall, Chas Critcher, Tony Jefferson, John Clarke, and Brian Roberts, *Policing the Crisis: Mugging, the State, and Law and Order* (New York: Holmes and Meier Publishers, 1978).

132. Ruth Wilson Gilmore, *Golden Gulag: Prisons, Surplus, Crisis, and Opposition in Globalizing California* (University of California Press, 2007).

133. Giroux, "Disposable Youth," 563. See also Henry A. Giroux, "Bare Pedagogy and the Scourge of Neoliberalism: Rethinking Higher Education as a Democratic Public Sphere," *The Education Forum* 74, no. 3 (2010): 184–196.

134. Robert B. Westbrook, *John Dewey and American Democracy* (Ithaca, NY: Cornell University Press, 1993); John Patrick Diggins, *The Lost Soul of American Politics: Virtue, Self-Interest and the Foundations of Liberalism* (New York: Basic Books, 1984), 163–167.

135. Aaron Kupchik and Torin Monahan, "The New American School: Preparation for Post-Industrial Discipline," *British Journal of Sociology of Education* 27, no. 5 (2006): 617–631; Henry A. Giroux, "Zero Tolerance, Domestic Militarization, and the War Against Youth," *Social Justice* 30, no. 2 (2003): 59–65; Henry A. Giroux, "Neoliberal's War Against Teachers in Dark Times," *Cultural Studies ←→ Critical Methodologies* 13, no. 6 (2013): 458–468; Henry A. Giroux, "When Schools Become Dead Zones of the Imagination: A Critical Pedagogy Manifesto," *The High School Journal* 99, no. 4 (Summer 2016): 351–359.

136. Henry A. Giroux, *Stormy Weather: Katrina and the Politics of Disposability* (Boulder, CO: Paradigm Publishers, 2006).

137. Jordan Chariton and Jenn Dize, "How a Flurry of Suspicious Phone Calls Sent Investigators on Rick Snyder's Trail," *The Intercept*, January 13, 2021, https:// theintercept.com/2021/01/13/flint-michigan-rick-snyder-legionnaires/. Alex Lantier and Andre Damon, "The Response of the Ruling Class to the Coronavirus Pandemic: Malign Neglect," *World Socialist Web Site* (March 14, 2020), https://www.wsws.org/ en/articles/2020/03/14/pers-m14.html.

138. Gary Teeple, *Globalization and the Decline of Social Reform: Into the Twenty-First Century* (Amherst, NY: Humanity Books, 2000).

139. Vijay Prashad, "We Suffer from an Incurable Disease Called Hope," *TriContinental Newsletter* 48, November 6, 2020, https://www.thetricontinental.org/newsletterissue/48-covid-vaccines/; "Vaccine Apartheid: Marc Lamont Hill, Mitchell Plitnick on Israel's 'Indifference to Palestinian Health,'" *Democracy Now!*, March 4, 2021, https://www.democracynow.org/2021/3/4/vaccine_rollout_palestinian_territories_israel.

140. Alexander Cooley and Daniel Nixon, *Exit from Hegemony: The Unraveling of American Global Order* (Oxford: Oxford University Press, 2020); John L. Campbell, *American Discontent: The Rise of Donald Trump and the Decline of the Golden Age* (Oxford: Oxford University Press, 2018); Chris Hamnett, "A World Turned Upside Down: The Rise of China and the Relative Economic Decline of the West," *Area Development & Policy* 3, no. 2 (2018): 223–240; Florian Böller and Welf Werner eds, *Hegemonic Transition: Global Economic and Security Orders in the Age of Trump* (Cham, Switzerland: Palgrave Macmillan, 2021).

141. See discussion of *ressentiment* in Lauren Langman, "Cycles of Contention: The Rise and Fall of the Tea Party," *Critical Sociology* 38, no. 4 (2011): 469–494.

142. William I. Robinson and Mario Barrera, "Global Capitalism and Twenty-First Century Fascism: A US Case Study," *Race & Class* 53, no. 3 (2012): 4–29; William I. Robinson, "Global Capitalist Crisis and Twenty-First Century Fascism: Beyond the Trump Hype," *Science & Society* 83, no. 2 (April 2019): 155–183.

143. David North, *The Crisis of American Democracy: The Presidential Elections of 2000 and 2004* (Oak Park, MI: Mehring Press, 2004).

144. Glenn Thrush, Mathew Goldstein, and Connor Dogherty, "Eviction Freeze Set to Lapse as Biden Housing Aid Effort Lags," *New York Times*, August 1, 2021, https://www.nytimes.com/2021/07/31/us/politics/eviction-moratorium-biden-housing-aid.html; Trévon Austin, "Democrats Let US Eviction Moratorium Expire, Pushing Millions of Families to the Brink," *World Socialist Web Site*, July 30, 2021, https://www.wsws.org/en/articles/2021/07/31/pers-j31.html; Chase Lawrence, "Eleven Million US Families Face Eviction as CDC Moratorium Expires," *World Socialist Web Site*, July 27, 2021, https://www.wsws.org/en/articles/2021/07/28/evic-j28.html. On Clinton's welfare 'reform' in the context of intellectual attacks on social liberalism, see Daniel T. Rodgers, *Age of Fracture* (Cambridge, MA: The Belknap Press of Harvard University Press), 208–209.

145. Julie Bosman, Sophie Kasakove, and Daniel Victor, "U.S. Life Expectancy Plunged in 2020, Especially for Black and Hispanic Americans," *The New York Times*, July 21, 2021, https://www.nytimes.com/2021/07/21/us/american-life-expectancy-report.html; Sabrina Tavernise and Abby Goodnough, "American Life Expectancy Rises for First Time in Four Years," *New York Times*, January 30, 2020, https://www.nytimes.com/2020/01/30/us/us-life-expectancy.html; Trévon Austin "The US Mortality Crisis: CDC Reports Extraordinary Drop in Life Expectancy," *World Socialist Web Site*, November 30, 2018, https://www.wsws.org/en/articles/2018/11/30/cdcr-n30.html; Kate Randall, "CDC Report: Biggest Drop in US Life Expectancy

Since World War II," *World Socialist Web Site*, February 19, 2021, https://www .wsws.org/en/articles/2021/02/19/pers-f19.html.

146. Alya Ansari and Mitch Hernandez, "Business Always as Usual: Hypernormalization and Pandemic Labor," *Society for the Anthropology of Work* (June 3, 2020). doi: 10.21428/1d6be30e.cc25e869.

147. Trotsky, *Death Agony of Capitalism*. Cf. Owen Worth, *Morbid Symptoms: The Global Rise of the Far-Right* (London: Zed Books, 2019).

148. Cf. Daniel J. Walkowitz, "The Conundrum of the Middle-Class Worker in the Twentieth-Century United States: Professional-Managerial Workers' (Folk) Dance Around Class," in eds A. Ricardo López and Barbara Weinstein eds, *The Making of the Middle-Class: Toward a Transnational History* (New York: Duke University Press, 2012), 121–140; Charles Thorpe, "Death of a Salesman: Petit-Bourgeois Dread in Philip K. Dick's Mainstream Fiction." *Science Fiction Studies* 38, no. 3 (2011): 412–434.

149. Sheri Berman, "Populism Is a Problem. Elitist Technocrats Aren't the Solution," *Foreign Policy*, December 20, 2017, https://foreignpolicy.com/2017/12/20 /populism-is-a-problem-elitist-technocrats-arent-the-solution/.

150. Guardian staff and agencies, "Clinton Lawyer Charged with Lying to FBI During Trump-Russia Inquiry," *The Guardian* (September 16, 2021), https://www .theguardian.com/us-news/2021/sep/16/michael-sussmann-clinton-lawyer-charged -lying-fbi-trump-russia.

151. Chelsea Ritschel, "Ruth Bader Ginsburg Said People Will See This Period in American History as 'an aberration'," *The Independent*, September 19, 2020, https:// www.independent.co.uk/news/world/americas/ruth-bader-ginsburg-rbg-trump-aber- ration-supreme-court-a9143781.html.

152. New York Times Editorial Board, "The C.I.A.'s Reckless Breach of Trust," *New York Times*, July 31, 2014, https://www.nytimes.com/2014/08/01/opinion/The -CIAs-Reckless-Breach-of-Trust.html; Patrice Toddonio, "CIA Director Nominee Supported Destruction of Torture Tapes," *PBS*, May 9, 2018, https://www.pbs.org/ wgbh/frontline/article/cia-director-nominee-supported-destruction-of-torture-tapes/.

153. Glenn Thrush, "Pelosi Playing Defense on Torture," *Politico*, April 27, 2009, https://www.politico.com/story/2009/04/pelosi-playing-defense-on-torture-021724.

154. Charles Thorpe, "The Carnival King of Capital," *Fast Capitalism* 17, no. 1 (2020): 87–108.

155. Jerome R. Ravetz and S. O. Funtowicz, "Science for the Post-Normal Age," *Futures* 25, no. 7 (September 1993): 735–755.

156. Thomas Kuhn, *The Structure of Scientific Revolutions* (Chicago: University of Chicago Press, 1970). Cf. Alvin W. Gouldner, *Against Fragmentation: The Origins of Marxism and the Sociology of Intellectuals* (Oxford: Oxford University Press, 1985), 204.

157. Cf. George A. Reisch, *The Politics of Paradigms: Thomas S. Kuhn, James B. Conant, and the Cold War "Struggle for Men's Minds"* (Albany: State University of New York Press, 2019); Paul Forman, "On the Historical Forms of Knowledge Production and Curation: Modernity Entailed Disciplinarity, Postmodernity Entails Antidisciplinarity." *Osiris* 27, no. 1 (2012): 56–97.

158. Ulrich Beck, *World at Risk*, trans. Ciaran Cronin (Cambridge: Polity Press, 2009); Beck, Giddens, and Lash, *Reflexive Modernization*.

159. Rachel Carson, *Silent Spring* (Boston: Houghton Mifflin, 1962).

160. Kelly Moore, *Disrupting Science: Social Movements, American Science, and the Politics of the Military, 1945-1975* (Princeton: Princeton University Press, 2008).

161. Jane Gregory and Simon Lock, "The Evolution of 'Public Understanding of Science: Public Engagement as a Tool of Science Policy in the UK," *Sociology Compass* 2, no. 4 (July 2008): 1252–1265.

162. Frank Fischer, *Citizens, Experts, and the Environment: The Politics of Local Knowledge* (Durham, NC: Duke University Press, 2000); Thorpe and Jacobson, "Life Politics, Nature, and the State."

163. Silvio O. Funtowicz and Jerome R. Ravetz, "Science for the Post-Normal Age," in Sardar, *The Postnormal Times Reader*, 23–46, on 23.

164. Robert Proctor, *Value-Free Science? Purity and Power in Modern Knowledge* (Cambridge, MA: Harvard University Press, 1991); Clifford D. Conner, *A People's History of Science: Miners, Midwives, and "Low Mechanicks"* (New York: Nation Books, 2005).

165. John Ziman, *Real Science: What it Is and What It Means* (Cambridge: Cambridge University, 2000).

166. Phillip Mirowski, *Science-Mart: Privatizing American Science* (Cambridge, MA: Harvard University Press, 2011).

167. Charles Thorpe, "Science, Technology, and Life Politics Beyond the Market," *Journal of Responsible Innovation* 7, S1 (2020): 553–573.

168. Steve Fuller, *Thomas Kuhn: A Philosophical History for our Times* (Chicago: University of Chicago Press, 2000).

169. Brian Balogh, *Chain Reaction: Expert Debate and Public Participation in American Commercial Nuclear Power 1945–1975* (Cambridge: Cambridge University Press, 1991); Brian Lindseth, *From Radioactive Fallout to Environmental Critique: Ecology and the Politics of Cold War Science* (PhD Dissertation, University of California, San Diego, 2013); Brian Lindseth, "Nuclear War, Radioactive Rats, and the Ecology of Exterminism," in Ryan Hediger ed, *Animals and War* (Leiden: Brill, 2013): 151–174.

170. Ravetz and Funtowicz, "Science for the Post-Normal Age," in Sardar ed, *The Postnormal Times Reader*, 23–46. on 44; S. O. Funtowicz and J. Ravetz, "The Good, the True and the Post-Modern," *Futures* 24, no. 10 (December 1992): 963–976.

171. Funtowicz and Ravetz, "The Good, The True and the Postmodern," 963–964.

172. Funtowicz and Ravetz, "The Good, The True and the Postmodern," 964.

173. Ziauddin Sardar, "Welcome to Postnormal Times," in *The Postnormal Times Reader*, 47–70, on 47.

174. Sardar, "Welcome to Postnormal Times," 50.

175. Naomi Oreskes, "How Earth Science Has Become a Social Science," *Historical Social Research / Historische Sozialforschung*, 40, no. 2 (2015): 246–270, quoting 265–266.

176. Oreskes "How Earth Science," 266.

177. Paul Forman, "On the Historical Forms of Knowledge Production and Curation"; C. P. Snow, *The Two Cultures* (Cambridge: Cambridge University Press, 1993).

178. Collins, *Forms of Life*; see also Richard Biernacki, *Reinventing Evidence in Social Inquiry: Decoding Facts and Variables* (New York: Palgrave Macmillan, 2012).

179. Cf. Fritz Ringer, *The Decline of the German Mandarins: The German Academic Community*, 1890-1933 (Cambridge, MA: Harvard University Press, 1969); Julian Hamann, "Boundary Work between Two Cultures: Demarcating the Modern *Geisteswissenschaften*," *History of the Humanities* 3, no. 1 (Spring 2018): 27–38.

180. On the ambiguities of this, see Jack Douglas, *The Social Meanings of Suicide* (Princeton: Princeton University Press, 1967).

181. On these currents in psychology, see Laurence D. Smith, *Behaviorism and Logical Positivism: A Reassessment of the Alliance* (Stanford, CA: Stanford University Press, 1986).

182. Frederick Engels, "Speech at the Grave of Karl Marx," March 17, 1883, https://www.marxists.org/archive/marx/works/1883/death/burial.htm.

183. Gouldner, *Coming Crisis*, 92–93.

184. Nancy Fraser, interviewed by Martin Mosquera, "Nancy Fraser: Cannibal Capitalism is On Our Horizon," *Jacobin* (September 10, 2021), https://jacobinmag .com/2021/09/nancy-fraser-cannibal-capitalism-interview.

185. Bernard Phillips and Louis C. Johnston, *The Invisible Crisis of Contemporary Society: Reconstructing Sociology's Fundamental Assumptions* (Boulder, CO: Paradigm Publishers, 2007), 52–57.

186. Stephen Turner, *American Sociology: From Pre-Disciplinary to Post-Normal* (New York: Palgrave Macmillan, 2014), 100.

187. Turner, *American Sociology*, 83.

188. Quoted in Schmidt, *Disciplined Minds*, 224.

189. See also Steven Shapin, "Hyper-Professionalism and the Crisis of Readership in the History of Science," *Isis* 96, no. 2 (2005): 238–243.

190. Yurchak, *Everything Was Forever*, 286. On hoaxes as response to hypernormalization, see Boyer and Yurchak, "American Stiob," 189–190.

191. Biernacki, *Reinventing Evidence*, 11–17.

192. John H. Zammito, *A Nice Derangement of Epistemes: Post-Positivism in the Study of Science from Quine to Latour* (Chicago: University of Chicago Press, 2004).

193. Turner, *American Sociology*, 51; Robert K. Merton, "Insiders and Outsiders: A Chapter in the Sociology of Knowledge," *The American Journal of Sociology* 78, no. 1 (1972): 9–47.

194. Yurchak, *Everything Was Forever*, 71–73; Yascha Mounk, "What an Audacious Hoax Reveals About Academia," *The Atlantic*, October 5, 2018, https:// www.theatlantic.com/ideas/archive/2018/10/new-sokal-hoax/572212/.

195. Anthony Giddens, *The Constitution of Society* (Berkeley: University of California Press, 1984), 284; Giddens, *In Defence of Sociology*, 75–77.

196. Michael Rectenwald, *Google Archipelago: The Digital Gulag and the Simulation of Freedom* (Nashville, TN: New English Review Press, 2019); Vivek Ramaswamy, *Woke Inc.: Inside Corporate America's Social Justice Scam* (New York: Center Street, 2021); Liu, *Virtue Hoarders*.

197. Sheila Jeffreys, *Gender Hurts: A Feminist Analysis of the Politics of Transgenderism* (London: Routledge, 2014); Helen Joyce, *Trans: When Ideology Meets Reality* (London: Oneworld, 2021); Kathleen Stock, *Material Girls: Why Reality Matters for Feminism* (London: Fleet, 2021); Silvia Federici. *Beyond the Periphery of the Skin: Rethinking, Remaking, and Reclaiming the Body in Contemporary Capitalism* (Oakland, CA: PM Press, 2020); Women's Liberation Front, "CA Women's Prisons Anticipate Pregnancy After Forcing Women to be Housed with Men," Women's Liberation Front (July 15, 2021); https://www.wom ensliberationfront.org/news/ca-womens-prisons-anticipate-pregnancy-sb123; Haroon Siddique, "Lawful to Imprison Trans Women Sex Offenders in Female Jails, Judge Rules." *The Guardian*, July 2, 2021, https://www.theguardian.com/society/2021/jul /02/trans-women-with-sex-offence-convictions-in-female-jails-lawful-rules-judge.

198. Füredi, *Therapy Culture*; Gouldner, *Future of the Intellectuals*, 82. Cf. Jack C. Bratich, *Conspiracy Panics: Political Rationality and Popular Culture* (Albany: State University of New York Press, 2008); Tarleton Gillespie, *Custodians of the Internet: Platforms, Content Moderation, and the Hidden Decisions that Shape Social Media* (New Haven, CT: Yale University Press, 2021).

199. Yaron Ezrahi, *The Descent of Icarus: Science and the Transformation of Contemporary Democracy* (Cambridge, MA: Harvard University Press, 1990), 127.

200. Schmidt, *Disciplined Minds*, 38, 40, 15–16. Norman Fairclough, *New Labour, New Language?* (London: Routledge, 2000). On the 'Third Way' as New Class ideology, see Lawrence King and Iván Szelényi, *Theories of the New Class: Intellectuals and Power* (Minneapolis: University of Minnesota Press, 2004), 228–229. Cf. Svend Ranulf, *Moral Indignation and Middle Class Psychology: A Sociological Study* (New York: Schocken Books, 1964).

201. Michael Lind, "The New National American Elite," *Tablet*, January 19, 2021, https://www.tabletmag.com/sections/news/articles/new-national-american -elite; Michael Lind, *The New Class War: Saving Democracy from the Managerial Elite* (New York: Portfolio/Penguin, 2020), 80.

202. Turner, *American Sociology*, 103.

203. Turner, *American Sociology*, 92. Stephen Turner, "The Road from 'Vocation': Weber and Veblen on the Purposelessness of Scholarship," *Journal of Classical Sociology* 19, no. 3 (2019): 229–253, esp. 238–242.

204. Cf. Chandra Mukerji, *A Fragile Power: Scientists and the State* (Princeton, NJ: Princeton University Press, 1989).

205. George Caffentzis, "Throwing Away the Ladder: The Universities in the Crisis," *Zerowork* 1 (1975): 128–142.

206. Susan Wright and Cris Shore, *Death of the Public University?: Uncertain Futures for Higher Education in the Knowledge Economy* (Berghahn Books, 2017). Kelly Moore, Daniel Lee Kleinman, David Hess, and Scott Frickel, "Science and Neoliberal Globalization: A Political Sociological Approach, *Theory & Society* 40 (2011): 505–532; Mike Head, "Corporate Blueprint Predicts 'Death' of Higher Education in Australia," *World Socialist Web Site*, August 19, 2021, https://www .wsws.org/en/articles/2021/08/20/unis-a20.html.

207. Cf. National Research Council, *Strategic Engagement in Global S&T: Opportunities for Defense Research* (Washington, DC: The National Academies Press, 2014); Kirsten Bound, Tom Saunders, James Wilsdon, and Jonathan Adams, *China's Absorptive State: Research, Innovation and the Prospects for China-UK Collaboration* (London: NESTA, 2013); James Wilsdon and James Keeley, *China: The Next Science Superpower?* (London: Demos, 2007).

208. Karl Marx, *Grundrisse: Foundations of the Critique of Political Economy*, trans. Martin Nicolaus (Harmondsworth, Penguin: 1973), 694; Nick Dyer-Witheford, *Cyber-Marx: Cycles and Circuits of Struggle In High-Technology Capitalism* (Urbana: University of Illinois Press, 1999).

209. Chris Langley. *Soldiers in the Laboratory: Military Involvement in Science & Technology, and Some Alternatives*, eds, Stuart Parkinson and Philip Webber (Lancaster, UK: Scientists for Global Responsibility, 2005).

210. Susan L. Robinson and Matias Nestore, "Education Cleavages, or Market Society and the Rise of Authoritarian Populism?" *Globalisation, Societies, and Education*, published online, July 19, 2021, doi: 10.1080/14767724.2021.1955662; Liu, *Virtue Hoarders*.

211. Howard Brick, *Age of Contradiction: American Thought and Culture in the 1960s* (Ithaca, NY: Cornell University Press, 2000), 7, 20.

212. King and Szelényi, *Theories of the New Class.*

213. Alvin W. Gouldner, *The Future of Intellectuals and the Rise of the New Class* (New York: Continuum, 1979), 28–43, 58–59.

214. Gouldner, *Future of Intellectuals*, 7.

215. Gouldner, *Future of Intellectuals*, 6–7.

216. King and Szelényi, *Theories of the New Class*, 194.

217. Lisle A. Rose, *Farewell to Prosperity: Wealth, Identity, and Conflict in Postwar America* (Columbia: University of Missouri Press, 2014); Alice O'Connor, *Poverty Knowledge: Social Science, Social Policy, and the Poor in Twentieth-Century U.S. History* (Princeton: Princeton University Press, 2001); G. Calvin Mackenzie and Robert Weisbrot, *The Liberal Hour: Washington and the Politics of Change in the 1960s* (New York: Penguin, 2008); Amity Shlaes, *Great Society: A New History* (New York: Harper, 2019).

218. Rodgers, *Age of Fracture*, 82–83, 86–87, 189–190. Cf. Ehrenreich, *Fear of Falling*, 144–195.

219. Herb Childress, *The Adjunct Underclass: How America's Colleges Betrayed Their Faculty, Their Students, and Their Mission* (Chicago: University of Chicago Press, 2019); Elizabeth Pop Berman, *Creating the Market University: How Academic Science Became an Economic Engine* (Princeton: Princeton University Press, 2012); Sheila Slaughter and Larry Leslie, *Academic Capitalism: Politics, Policies, and the Entrepreneurial University* (Baltimore, MD: Johns Hopkins University Press, 1997); Brendan Cantwell, and Ilkka Kauppinen, *Academic Capitalism in the Age of Globalization* (Baltimore, MD: Johns Hopkins University Press, 2014); Christopher Newfield, *Unmaking the Public University: The Forty-Year Assault on the Middle Class* (Cambridge, MA: Harvard University Press, 2008); Ginsberg, *The Fall of the Faculty*; A. H. Halsey, *Decline of Donnish Dominion: The British Academic*

Professions in the Twentieth Century (Oxford: Clarendon Press, 1995); Steven Shapin, *The Scientific Life: A Moral History of a Late Modern Vocation* (Chicago: University of Chicago Press, 2010); David Tyfield, Rebecca Lave, Samuel Randalls, and Charles Thorpe eds, *The Routledge Handbook of the Political Economy of Science* (London: Routledge, 2017); David Harvie, "Alienation, Class, and Enclosure in UK Universities," *Capital and Class* 24, no. 2 (2000): 103–132; Charles Thorpe, "Capitalism, Audit and the Demise of the Humanistic Academy," *Workplace: A Journal for Academic Labor* 15 (September 2008): 103–125; John Holmwood, "The University, Democracy and the Public Sphere," *British Journal of Sociology of Education* 38, no. 7 (2017): 927–942.

220. Ehrenreich, *Fear of Falling*; Barbara Ehrenreich and John Ehrenreich, *Death of a Yuppie Dream: The Rise and Fall of the Professional-Managerial Class* (New York: The Rosa Luxemburg Stiftung New York Office, 2013); Liu, *Virtue Hoarders*.

221. Boris Kagarlitsky, *The Dialectic of Change,* trans. Rick Simon (London: Verso, 1990), 57–109; Charles Thorpe, "Community and the Market in Michael Polanyi's Philosophy of Science" *Modern Intellectual History* 6, no. 1 (2009): 59–89; Philip Mirowski, *Never Let a Serious Crisis go to Waste: How Neoliberalism Survived the Financial Crisis* (London: Verso, 2014).

222. David Hollinger, "Money and Academic Freedom a Half Century after McCarthyism: Universities amid the Force Fields of Capital," in Peggie Hollingsworth, ed., *Unfettered Expression* (Ann Arbor: University of Michigan Press, 2000): 161–184.

223. Clifford Connor, *The Tragedy of American Science: From Truman to Trump* (Chicago: Haymarket, 2020).

224. Cf. Thorstein Veblen, *The Engineers and the Price System* (New York: B. W. Huebsch, 1921).

Chapter 2

From the Pathology of Normalcy to the Normalcy of Pathology

RISK AND DREAD

Giddens argues that the rationalizing forces of modernity have produced self-undermining unintended consequences. Ravetz's distinction between normal and post-normal science parallels Giddens's distinction between simple and reflexive modernization.[1] Simple modernization is the development of modern societies based on the equation of progress with the linear increase in knowledge and technology. This assumption has been challenged not only by the emergence of devastating ecological risks but also by the release of ethical energies suppressed by modernity. Giddens illuminates how the rationalizing processes of modern societies suppressed existential dilemmas. As the rational systems of modernity replaced tradition in the organization of social life, the traditional patterns of behavior and thought, including religion, that helped to assuage terrors of death, chaos and separateness, were weakened. But modern capitalist societies could not offer new ethical solutions in place of tradition. Instead, the growth of modern rational systems was accompanied by positivist thought which treated ethical questions as meaningless in terms of the rational criteria this thought framework valorized. Positivism stigmatized as arbitrary ethical thought that tried to make sense of human experience in relation to its basic existential realities of death and separateness. It provided no foundations on the basis of which these existential dilemmas could be resolved and which could allow the escape from the uncertainty and chaos that such dilemmas expose. Modernity has created terrifying new dangers, especially nuclear warfare and climate change, while stripping away the cultural narratives and practices by which human beings have rendered mortality meaningful. "This unique conjunction of the banal and the apocalyptic," Giddens exclaims, "this is the world that capitalism has fashioned."[2]

Instead, modern societies remove from everyday life the immediate causes of existential anxiety through what Giddens, drawing on the work of Elias and Foucault, calls "the sequestration of experience."[3] The internal pacification of societies by centralized nation-states, substantially (though of course incompletely, unevenly and unequally) removing violence from everyday experience, combines with the control and removal of illness, death, and madness through medicine and hospitalization. Engineered urban environments accomplish the "smoothing" of everyday experience from the interruptions of natural forces. Modern systems of sanitation, energy production and distribution, infrastructure, and medicine, in other words the instrumental control of nature through scientific, technological, and organizational systems, allow for the practices of daily life to be routinized and predictable. This routinization produces a specifically modern form of everyday banality. This banality is the protection that modernity offers against dread of chaos and death. Modernity's protective banalization of everyday life is fragile precisely because it protects only as long as it works successfully in backgrounding the sources of terror. Once these are exposed and intrude, modernity has no answers because it has degraded all traditional ethico-religious answers as arbitrary and meaningless. The problem of technological risk, therefore, for example, risks of technological accidents or of poisoning from the toxic side effects of the chemicals used to make life modern life clean and convenient, is that these risks expose individuals and society to the suppressed sources of dread. This existential dimension of risk is systematically masked by the ways in which risk is itself subjected to rational calculation. The scientific representatives of these systems of calculation are intolerant of the existential implications. But these existential implications are why it is so important for modernity to suppress such risks and also to explain them away through highly restricted rationalized quantitative sense-making. For modernity has no answers to the existential dilemmas these risks expose.

Existential dilemmas, Giddens argues, arise from the contradictory nature of the human condition. He writes, "Human life is contradictory in the sense that the human being, as *Dasein*, originates and disappears into the world of Being, the world of nature, yet as a conscious, reflective agent is the negation of the inorganic."[4] Giddens's account, while relying more directly on Heidegger, has close affinity with the philosophical anthropology that underlay the psychoanalytic sociology of Fromm.[5] For Fromm also, the human being is an inherently contradictory being, and the existential needs and dilemmas of humanity arise from this contradictory character of human existence. The human being is contradictory by virtue of existing both within and outside nature. The human being is a biological animal and in that sense a material being continuous with the rest of nature. Human beings are also self-conscious beings, aware of the inevitability of their own death, and therefore experience themselves as individuals set apart from the world around them. This separateness is necessarily a source of deep unease because it entails vulnerability and is closely bound up with the possibility of death. It further entails the possibility and necessity of choice and action and, therefore, of making sense of, and dealing with, the seeming chaos of the world. This separateness places the human being in a basic, original condition of negative freedom, to the extent that the human being is *free from* instinctual determinations. Fromm argues that this condition of separateness, and the negative freedom that accompanies it, is a condition of unbearable tension in which the individual cannot rest. The anxiety that necessarily accompanies separateness and freedom spurs the individual to escape from this condition and seek belonging and unity. However, this search for belonging may simply negate and nullify individual separateness and the potentiality that arises from human self-consciousness and freedom. The search for belonging and unity may be regressive and lead even to the rejection of life for the ultimate return to nature in the form of death.[6]

So the problem facing all human beings is to move from negative freedom not into a state of oneness that denies freedom, but toward a higher state in which freedom is compatible with belonging. This is what Fromm calls positive freedom. This higher form of freedom cannot be achieved by the individual alone. It can only be achieved as a social condition, in the form of a society that can cultivate human freedom such that individual freedom is no longer a zero-sum game as in the Hobbesian state of nature and security does not entail the stifling of freedom. It was for this reason that Fromm was a socialist and a humanist Marxist. The condition of positive freedom requires precisely what Marx and Engels called communism when they wrote in *The Manifesto of the Communist Party*, "In place of the old bourgeois society with its classes and class antagonisms, we shall have an association, in which the free development of each is the condition for the free development of all."[7]

Giddens writes that "The mediator of the contradictory character of human existence is society itself."[8] This points to the fact that the problem of finding meaning in the world is not only an individual problem but also a problem for society. The human being was never an individual alone. *Homo sapiens* evolved only as part of a pattern of evolution of ape-like forebears and earlier hominids who were themselves social animals. The solution to the terror of reality as a separate isolated individual was therefore present in the individual's existence within the group. This is in two ways: firstly, the group really protects the individual from death, not ultimately, of course, but temporarily. It is within the group, as a social being, that the human being is able to harness nature to their needs. But the psychological protection of religion is also a social accomplishment, produced and sustained by the group. The only solution to the terror of the individual is the group. And there *is* no self-conscious human individual outside the human group. This is an important dimension of what Marx referred to as the unique existence of the human being as a "species being." It is the universality of the human being that arises from what Harry Collins calls our "socialness" and from the complex language that both develops from and makes possible this socialness.[9]

Language and socialness are co-constitutive, in the sense that they are each dependent on the other. Human language is embedded in socialness and it is this that makes it possible to *understand* a language and a statement in a language. This is the key to meaning. As Wittgenstein said, the meaning of a statement is a feature of a *form of life*, in which that statement is embedded, in which it has meaning. A form of life is a biological species, a collection of living things who are language speakers, and, within that, a social community that uses a particular language. Words have meaning not as an internal formal relation but in their use in particular social contexts.[10]

We are opaque to each other as individuals.[11] What we have sensory access to about the other person is their physical bodily appearance. Expressions and bodily forms of discipline and movement are socially shaped and interpreted as social cues. But the inner mental states of the other are hidden from us. At the same time, it is the other's mental states that are the most accessible to us. This is in the sense that, to the extent that thoughts are constructed and shaped by conceptual frames and these conceptual frames are formulated in language, these concepts, and the thinking with these concepts, are intrinsically shared and social. The form of life is a way of living in the world, a way of being in the world, a way of experiencing the world, a way of making sense of the world. The form of life is a world in itself, in the sense that it is a shared subjectivity that arises in and is reinforced by shared, collective practices. A form of life is a way of living in which certain things exist and other things don't *for those people*. A form of life is in that sense an ontology, *for those people*. It also contains an epistemology——an understanding of what is knowledge and how to go about getting valid knowledge. So a form of life is also a way of acquiring knowledge about the world. A form of life makes knowledge *as such* possible. So forms of life make knowledge possible and create knowledge, and therefore ways of engaging with the real world. But forms of life are also ways of being that construct second "realities," a cultural second nature, which is a socially constructed reality. Human experience of reality is not the whole of reality. The subjective state involved in and shaped by that form of life is something different from reality itself.

Therefore, *being in* a form of life also removes the human being from reality, even as it cognizes reality. The human existence in a cultural world makes us aware of our separateness from the rest of nature and separates us from reality. The human being inhabits a social subjectivity that is a symbolic order by which the human organism's relationship with the reality of nature is socially mediated. Ted R. Vaughan and Gideon Sjoberg write,

> We take the capacity for social reflectivity to be the most essential characteristic of humankind. This capacity, socially shaped and developed within particular institutions and structures, instills the potential to transcend particular settings. It is this capacity, to simultaneously shape and be shaped by social reality, that is the distinguishing feature of humanness—the capacity, problematic though it may be, to be consciously aware of the process of reflectivity.[12]

This conception is closely compatible with Collins's conception of social-ness, emphasizing language as the key to the polimorphic rather than mimeomorphic character of human action.[13] It is an important feature of polimorphic action that it is not a mechanical reproduction. Polimorphic action takes its form from the polis, in other words the collective in which the actor is socially embedded. Socialness is the quality of being capable of being, as Vaughan and Sjoberg put it, "shaped by social reality." And it is also necessarily the capacity to "shape . . . social reality." Socialness is the capacity to exist within a socially constructed reality. It is human to exist within (and therefore participate in) a social second nature, which is only possible by existing within a human collective. Polimorphic action is not a mechanical copy precisely because, by virtue of socialness, by virtue of the actor's existence within a polis, the human actor is able to recognize context and what that context implies for the meaning of the action. Hence human, that is, polimorphic, action is open to change as the human being engages with, and participates in making, new contexts. So it may be said that it is precisely what makes a form of life that makes it possible to change a form of life. Hence, socialness, both expressed in and made possible by language, is what makes it possible to exist within a social reality and to be able to reflexively change that reality.

One could say, instead of human beings *having* language, that human beings *are* language, in that language is essential to the particularly human way of experiencing the world. But it is also true that humans are fire and are cooked food. These are not only things that we have but qualities of our being in the sense both of being in nature, and being in and among other human beings, that make us what we are. What constitutes our separation from nature (and our negative freedom in that sense) is also technology, and in that sense labor, as Engels argued in his essay "The Part Played by Labour in the Transition from Ape to Man" in *Dialectics of Nature*.[14] By their mate-rial engagement with, and transformation of, nature, human beings separate themselves from nature. A separation is created by virtue of the ability to bring nature under control. The human is no longer in nature and at its mercy, but apart from it. The human being creates a more hospitable humanized nature that excludes brute, wild nature and creates a human space, even if this is merely a circle around a fire.

Therefore, both materially and symbolically, the human community is itself the solution to the very problem to which human socialness, or the human community itself, and the existence of the individual as a singularization of that community, gives rise. We wouldn't be terrified of separateness if we weren't social beings. We wouldn't achieve as much separateness if we weren't social beings. We wouldn't be aware of our separateness if we weren't social beings. And in our socialness we are not separate.

The human community holds the individual apart from the world. It creates a world in the world. In this cultural world, the human being's separateness from nature is at the same time unification with the socially constructed world of culture, the world made by human beings. This *social* world has been reflected and represented in religion which, Peter Berger argues, forms a "sacred canopy" enclosing the human world from chaotic reality and creating an orderly symbolic universe which protects individuals from existential terror.[15] If, as Durkheim suggested, religion is the image of society, in its transcendence of the individual, projected as a transcendent super-nature, this fetishization of society is also the cognition of society and at the same time its constitution in the sense of being made cognizable, given a tangible "reality" by its representation. In the form of the sacred canopy, it is society itself that stands between the individual and the brutal chaos of reality.

Negative freedom did not and does not exist *before* society. Rather, the individual's freedom from instinctual determination and from nature arises from the sociality of the individual and this sociality carries *in itself* the solution to the problem of separateness that accompanies individual freedom. One is only separate because one is not separate. One is only separate because one is social and to the extent that one is social one is not negatively free. The individual's actions are not free from external interference because the individual themselves is not free from the influence of society within themselves——the internalization of society. The terror of separateness, therefore, must be the terror *not* of a preexisting existential separateness, but of the loss of preexisting connectedness. Therefore, the terror of separateness is terror of abandonment, banishment, being lost, and being left alone. It is, fundamentally, *separation anxiety.*

Separation anxiety is terror of what the individual is *not*. The human individual is a social being. The human individual is therefore *not* separate. The human individual is not alone before nature but interacts with nature in a socially organized and mediated way. But the individual can be separated from the group and, if so, is then confronted with their extreme vulnerability *as an individual*. To be alone is to be a social being, alone. It is society that has separated one from the rest of the world, that has granted one self-awareness; outside society, this self-awareness is terror. Alone, banished, abandoned, left behind, one is face to face with one's own contradictory being, as a social individual, as a finite infinity, as the only being in the world that can, as Fromm said, feel itself to be homeless. As Fromm put it, the human is "an anomaly, the freak of the universe . . . He is set apart while being a part."[16]

Societies banish as punishment. Groups shun and ostracize deviant members. The United States uses solitary imprisonment routinely as punishment, and it destroys prisoners' minds. Banishment was a way of killing.[17] For human beings, separation is death. While Ernest Becker suggests that the dread of death is at the root of the human condition, and Fromm emphasizes the dread of separateness as the existential anxiety motivating the "escape from freedom," Fromm also connects this to the dread of death, and Becker was profoundly influenced by Fromm. The two things—separateness and death—are inextricably related.[18] Death makes one separate. It separates the individual from the group, which goes on living. The immortal soul in the mortal body is the social mind in the individual body.[19] The individual as finite infinity is an individual body that will die, but what this body was in life was a living embodiment of social relations. Therefore, the individual is both mortal body and immortal "spirit" but this "spirit" is the complex social-ness of the human organism. It would be wrong to think of this socialness as "the mind." It is very much diffused throughout the body in the sense that the body enacts in gesture the sociality of the individual, social mind is material-ized in neural pathways, senses pick up the social cues and communications that others give and, as Goffman said, "give off." The individual brain is engaging in what Edward Hutchins calls "distributed cognition" in the web of human social mind.[20] This brain is the materialization of sociality, in that it has evolved as a social brain and its physical structure reflects that. Of course, the brain is also the materialization of prehuman and pre-social evolution, and Freud's supposition of the conflict between basic instinctual drives and more developed forms of social thought and behavior that involve restraint on primitive compulsions is in its essence compatible with a biological and neuroscientific understanding of the evolution of the brain. The individual is the material instantiation of billions of years of biological evolution out of which the human organism emerged. The individual is the material instantia-tion of hundreds of thousands of years of cultural evolution of *Homo sapiens*, the outcome of which is the technological and complex global culture that exists today and which the individual also embodies. The individual is a finite being, which will die, but also part of wholes that exist beyond them in both space and time. These wholes are in them *as much as* they as individuals are parts of these wholes. The individual *is a part* of the social whole but also embodies that whole *as a whole*.[21] The individual is not a fragment, but an instance of that whole.

But the individual is also a mere mortal fragment. Separated off from the larger web of interactions, the individual does not have the interactions, communications, routines, and collective rituals, that serve not only to give off comforting and exciting warmth of the nearness of human bodies, but also to reinforce the pattern of social illusion, the sacred canopy of culture, which provides a more snug environment than reality. Culture reflects these fears but it renders them manageable in part by symbolizing them, placing them in a narrative, and making sense of them. Culture, and therefore the human being as a cultural being, is a patterning pattern, that is, what Pierre Bourdieu calls a "structuring structure," or Giddens calls structuration.[22] The individual goes out of pattern when they are out of the loop. Being in the loop, in the sense of being plugged into the web of social interaction, keeps you in the loop in the sense that it keeps you repeating the rhymes and rhythms of the continually collectively reproduced social unreality.[23]

In modern societies with a complex economy, division of labor, and cultural pluralism, individuals inhabit many overlapping collectivities.[24] This makes the individual both more and less social ("less" only in the sense of having greater autonomy as an individual). The growing complexity of the social figuration (as Elias put it) that constitutes the individual reflects the increasing geographical reach and intricate interdependence of human relations, which are ultimately rooted in productive relations.[25] It reflects the growth of the productive capacities of labor, the growth of the productive forces, and the growing integration of the human species over the entire planet. The increasing complexity of human social relations is the becoming of the human species as a species being, in other words, a global human species that is intricately interconnected and aware of itself as a species, and able to act as a species.[26]

At the same time, however, the individual is desocialized, rendered less social. Capitalist relations, the relations not only of the workplace but of everyday life in capitalist society, mediated by "cash nexus," break ties of community, place, and tradition. The individual is freed by the weakening of these ties, and by the growing complexity of ties, which enable choice between identities and self-presentations. Identities and roles become less total, less taken-for-granted, and lose much of their power over the individual, who is able, as Goffman showed in micro-interactional detail, to approach them with cynical distance.[27] Identities become role performances. Individuals are freed from the patterns and ties of *Gemeinschaft* and propelled into the impersonal nexus of *Gesellschaft*. This distinction between personal closely knit bonds of community and the more abstract, impersonal connections of modern marketized and bureaucratized society,

and the concern that it implies about the production of an antisocial individualism, goes back to the origins of sociology, especially in Ferdinand
Tönnies and Emile Durkheim.[28] It is one of the core insights of sociology
and foundational for understanding what makes modernity distinctive, and
for appreciating the dialectical tension between the positively liberating and
negatively alienating implications of modern capitalism's transformation of
sociality.[29]

For Fromm, writing in mid-twentieth-century America, the fundamental
problem facing individuals was that the patterns of everyday life of modern
society failed to provide meaningful solutions to the problem of separateness.
The alienated patterns to which bureaucratic corporate-monopoly capitalism
demanded conformity excluded and denied the human need for meaning.
These were patterns adherence to which required, in exchange for the security
offered by its routines, accommodating oneself to a banal order that disconnected one from the existential problems and sources of meaning. In his 1955
book *A Sane Society*, Fromm criticized the lack of sanity of the bureaucratic
and consumer society that demanded conformity to such alienated and alienating patterns. He wrote:

> Many psychiatrists and psychologists refuse to entertain the idea that society as
> a whole may be lacking in sanity. They hold that the problem of mental health
> in a society is only that of the number of "unadjusted" individuals, and not that
> of a possible unadjustment of the culture itself . . . [The] latter problem [is] not
> with individual pathology, but with the *pathology of normalcy*, particularly with
> the pathology of contemporary Western society.[30]

Fromm was a critic of the dominant psychoanalytic and psychiatric conception of normalcy. He opposed the way in which psychoanalysis had been
interpreted and pursued in America, in which mental health was equated with
adjustment to prevailing social norms and expectations.[31] For example, a
"mental hygiene" textbook from 1949 states,

> The conservation of mental health is largely a problem of providing satisfactory
> outlets for the individual's basic urges, providing a balanced or harmonious
> adjustment of the various urges to one another, and adjusting the individual's
> egocentric drives to the cultural demands of the family and the community.[32]

Fromm's criticism of the conceptualization of normal as opposed to
pathological in the understanding of mental health was based on his critical
evaluation of the very forms of behavior and patterns of thought that were
counted as normal. The critique of bourgeois society and of everyday life, as
constructed and reproduced within capitalism was also, necessarily, a critique

of the standards of health and assumptions about how to live that reflected and legitimized this society.[33]

The emphasis of Fromm's critique was on the social psychology of conformity, the "escape from freedom" into the sado-masochistic authoritarianism of fascism and into the passive "automaton conformity" of modern bureaucracies.[34] The pathology of normalcy was the underlying isolation of the individual and condition of estrangement that underlay and was masked by social conformity. Today, the problem facing individuals is different, for the contradictions of capitalism as a global system have reached a point such that they have undermined even the alienated order that this society offered as normalcy. In what Bauman has called "liquid modernity," the problem facing the individual is that there are no stable patterns to which to conform.[35] The psychology of conformity is replaced by the psychology of narcissism, promoted by consumer culture. Narcissism is a psychic defense mechanism, providing protection in a world in which other sources of ontological security are lost. The conformist "marketing character" is superseded by what Lauren Langman and Maureen Ryan have called the "carnival character," who escapes alienation into momentary transgressive hedonism.[36]

WILDING IN POST-NORMAL AND POST-NATIONAL CAPITALISM

While the capitalist cash nexus destroyed preexisting, traditional forms of belongingness, bourgeois society promoted a new locus for belonging in the form of the nation-state. The ideology of nationalism, promoted by the state itself as civil religion, takes on some of the security-giving functions of religion. The reconstitution of solidarity at the level of the nation-state not only serves to legitimize the state institutions by creating emotional attachment to these institutions but also fulfills existential needs of the individual cast adrift from traditional attachments. This individual is able to overcome the terror of separateness by reconceiving their attachment at this more abstract level of the nation-state, which in the ideology of nationalism is given concreteness in such things as the national language, the flag, and through rituals of nationalism. The way in which nationalism draws on solutions to the existential dilemma in its sacralization of the state is continuous with the much longer history of the close relationship between religion and the formation of states, from the divine Pharoah to the divine right of kings. The nation is a secular, not supernatural, idea, but it attaches itself to the cosmos and powers of life and death through war. As Hedges says, "War is a force that gives us meaning." He writes, "Many of us, restless and unfulfilled, see no supreme worth in our lives. We want more out of life. And war, at least, gives a sense that we can rise above our smallness and divisiveness."[37] In this way, the nation forms a secularized sacred canopy, a symbolic order that situates the person and their identity within a meaningful overarching order, providing shelter from chaos and meaninglessness.

War also binds the national people, particularly men, together, making them march to the beat of a single drum in the conscript army, and creating solidarity as a single body protecting each other from death that now comes from outside the boundaries of the nation, from the foreign other. The emergence of the welfare state was historically bound up with the power interests of the nation-state and the dependence of this power on the collective body of the people as nation in the form of the conscript army. It is well known that the first social security provision was the state pension introduced by German chancellor Bismarck. The development of the welfare state attached bodily security to the nation, giving a material reality to the symbolic sacred canopy. The nation-state placed a boundary around everyday life that provided its stable setting. Within these boundaries, and in virtue of the exclusions they entailed (of strange customs, other cultures, and the seeming chaos of the world outside the nation), normalcy could be defined.

The psychological security provided by religion has been supported by the provision of real security, in the form of alms, in the form of the church physically bringing people together and defining the boundaries of a community, and in the social functions performed by churches, such as described by Weber in his essay on the American Protestant sects and their role in vouching for the character of their members.[38] In a similar way, through its welfare and regulatory agencies, as well as through its maintenance of civil order by policing and protection from foreign threats, the nation-state underpinned its symbolic order with real, material forms of security from death. The state creates order through its organization of material resources, construction of infrastructure, and regularization and ordering of economic and social activity, including its "internal pacification" within its territory, as Elias draws attention to.[39] The capitalist state, in particular, has taken over activities that business will not pay for, such as building roads and provision for the elderly that either capital or labor demand, or which the state's own ordering impetus sets within its sights.

While the Western capitalist nation-states carried out the ordering of social relations within its territory, the other side of this was the projection of external violence. Imperialism meant war with other imperialist powers and colonial wars of occupation and pillage that destroyed and uprooted existing communities and patterns of life. Not only through military violence but through financial means of enforced indebtedness and extraction, imperialism ravaged the countries of what was once called the "Third World." In contrast with the devastation caused by imperialism in the global south, within their own borders the Western capitalist nation-states seemed to be havens of orderliness.

Today, under conditions of globalization, the function of the nation-state as gardener is in crisis. Neoliberalism has substantially withdrawn the nation-states from the support of the biological and social life of the population within their territory. At the same time, the integration of private corporations with the state produces the corporatization of the state and the statization of corporations, as seen in the involvement of internet companies in regulating speech. This comes to its logical conclusion in a law passed in Nevada that would allow private corporations to create their own cities with corporate governance. The devolution from national "society" to "communities" as the locus of social organization and social control is seen in community codes of conduct, community standards, principles of community on internet social medial platforms, on campuses, and within privatized zones that operate on the lines of the residential "gated communities" that have proliferated in the United States since the 1990s. Shopping malls, theme parks, themed gated communities are privatized zones of hyperreal hypernormalcy.[40] As Bauman has argued, this means a shift from the nation-state as integrating society within a national community based on citizenship, creating exclusions based on national borders, to forms of privatized belonging and exclusion operating within nation-states. Privatized, privately regulated zones, create new forms of subnational integration and new exclusions around these affluent high-tech zones. Nation-states guard their borders against the flows of people uprooted by imperialist war and economic and political destabilization. Global disorder created by imperialism and, as will be more and more the case, by climate change, creates an impetus to fall back on nationalism as a protective ideology. The disordering effects of capitalist globalization create the conditions not for cosmopolitanism but, rather, for defensive xenophobia.[41] But the spaces demarcated by national borders are themselves, even within the centers of global capitalism, increasingly disordered and fragmented by internal exclusions.

The military de-civilizing process set into motion by American military or intelligence agency activity is overlaid onto economic policies and processes that destroy social bonds and fracture the social order, producing anomie and, as a corollary, crime and violence. Nikos Passas argues that neoliberal assaults on social institutions, public services, infrastructure, and solidarity have unleashed powerful criminogenic tendencies, bringing about global anomie and dysnomie. The explosion of crime in Russia and former Soviet Republics after the collapse of Stalinism and with the imposition of neoliberal structural adjustment policies and rapid predatory privatization is a key example.[42]

Although in the United States and the United Kingdom, rates of violent crime have fallen, since the mid-1990s, this is after steep increases in the postwar period. What criminologist David Garland calls a "solidarity project" reached fruition with the first two decades of Fordist growth after World War II, in and through social democratic welfarist reforms of Western government which reduced social inequality.[43] However, the boom also produced contradictory processes of individualization and consumerism connected with transformations of social character which Marcuse termed (repressive) desublimation, which Christopher Lasch called the "culture of narcissism," and which are related also to individualization, consumerist materialist values, and declining social trust and cohesion.[44] The cultural shifts toward consumerist individualization were reflected in the "crime explosion" of the mid-1960s that lasted through the mid-1990s. On these processes in Great Britain, Rob Reiner writes of the "solidarity project" or "pseudo-pacification" that occurred as "the gradual and uneven spread of social citizenship from the mid-19th century to the 1970s saw a growth of increasingly shared prosperity, security and inclusion." Reiner argues that the development and spread of social citizenship meant "the gradual incorporation of the mass of the population into social as well as civil and political citizenship." The model of social citizenship, Reiner argues, "not only ameliorated crime and disorder, but also underlay a civilising transformation of criminal justice." Reiner argues that, while the growth of crime rates in the UK from the mid-1950s was largely a recording phenomenon, real increase took place from the 1970s to the 1990s and that this was the result of the reversal of the trend toward greater inclusion with the advent of neoliberalism which "generated crime and disorder explosions, and the harsher politics of law and order of recent times."[45]

Reiner's analysis of trends in the UK may be fruitfully brought into dialogue with LaFree's institutional explanation for the postwar increase in criminality in the United States. In his 1998 book *Losing Legitimacy*, LaFree suggests that the very large increases in street crime in the US from historic lows at the end of the World War II to the mid-1990s when street crime rates began to decline, may be understood as caused by the declining legitimacy of US institutions, especially political and economic institutions and the family. In the US, "The *early postwar period*, from 1946 to 1960, is marked by low and stable crime rates; the *middle postwar p*eriod, from 1961 to 1973, is marked by rapidly increasing crime rates, and the *late postwar period*, after 1973, is marked by high but relatively stable crime rates."[46] The 1990s began a period of drastic reductions in rates of street crime.[47] LaFree's analysis suggests that crime began to increase as the social and cultural transformations of the postwar period, which particularly affected African Americans, undermined the legitimacy of the institutional forms that underlay the Fordist-Keynesian postwar compact. LaFree suggested that the crime declines, that were beginning to emerge as he was writing, were "likely due to a combination of institutional changes: stabilization in levels of trust in government, improvement in indicators of economic inequality, and a slowing in the rapidity of family change coupled with growing institutionalization of new family forms."[48] If that is the case, the spike in murders in 2020 may be indicative of a renewed loss of legitimacy, as a result of the exposure of police violence against African Americans, the way in which the Covid-19 pandemic has undermined trust, and perhaps the economic effects of the 2008 great recession.[49] Certainly, to the extent that neoliberalism was able to stabilize itself in the social order in the 1990s, this has been fragile and in tension with the growth of inequality, social fragmentation, and decline in trust that neoliberalism has produced.[50]

Civilizing and de-civilizing processes interact in complex dialectic. While increased rights of women, children, and minorities, and diminishing tolerance for forms of violence like domestic violence, expressed in movements like #MeToo and Black Lives Matter, may be seen as carrying forward the civilizing process, this comes into contradiction with the socially disintegrative effects of neoliberalism as well as the de-civilizing turn to increasing penal punitiveness.[51]

Like development, de-development is combined and uneven. Global anomie and dysnomie are expressed criminologically in social breakdown and extremely high levels of violence in certain areas such as Mexico, as well as in US inner-city areas and politically abandoned de-industrialized cities such as Flint, as well as in illicit practices operating in the hidden grooves of urban life in neoliberal global metropolises, not to mention the forms of social breakdown and associated criminality such as the methamphetamine and heroin trade operating in the seams of the US impoverished rural "heartland" and small deindustrialized towns. A hyper-masculinist, vigilante gun culture has also embedded itself strongly in the culture of deindustrialized rural and small-town America, in significant part as a search for ontological security in a situation in which economic and social supports of identity are evaporating.[52] Since the 1970s, the integration-oriented social welfarist policies of the "solidarity project" have been replaced by exclusion-oriented repressive and coercive law and order practices that have seen the growth of the prison-industrial complex in the United States and implementation of repressive forms of policing, especially zero-tolerance or broken windows policies.[53] The 1970s in both the UK and the US saw a turn to "law and order" politics operating through the scapegoating of ethnic minorities as criminal classes.[54] This is reflected today in Trump's anti-immigrant rhetoric that sets up Mexican and other immigrants as carriers of crime and creates "folk devils" as in, for example, his frequent use of the MS-13 gang to motivate xenophobic fear of crime. As Giroux in particular has traced, this is also reflected in zero-tolerance policies in schools that result in the suspension, expulsion, and stigmatization of large numbers of working class, black and Hispanic youth.[55] The punitive response of the state, and the high level of state violence toward the working class, and especially toward working-class African Americans, that one finds in the United States, with over a thousand people being killed by police annually in recent years should in itself be regarded as an aspect of a de-civilizing process. Also striking is what *World Socialist Web Site* refers to as the "criminalization of the ruling class" that became evident when widespread mortgage fraud and other white-collar crime linked to the finance sector was exposed as part of the 2008 financial crisis, as well as the involvement of high-profile banks such as HSBC in money laundering for Mexican drug cartels.[56] The extent of criminality behind the financial crisis is not as well known as would otherwise be the case, because rather than high-profile court proceedings, the Justice Department and the regulatory agencies such as the SEC under the Obama administration handled the criminal cases with plea bargains and fines for the corporations involved. Senior company executives were shielded by corporate structure of limited liability and were not individually prosecuted. In this way, elite criminality was effectively normalized, with fines being merely a marginal cost of doing business. There was no ritual public "degradation ceremony" in which offenders at J.P. Morgan, Goldman Sachs, Deutsche Bank, and so forth were designated as criminal deviants. But high-profile criminal cases like that of the ponzi scheme developed by Bernie Madoff and the human trafficking network of Jeffrey Epstein have further exposed certain features of what is more endemic and widespread criminality among elites.[57]

Today's criminalized financial ruling class has no interest in the gardening of social order. Rather, they profit from disruption and disorder. Bauman writes that, in order to reproduce, gardens "need design and supervision; without them, garden cultures would be overwhelmed by wilderness."[58] What Charles Derber calls "wilding" should be understood as the inexorable accompaniment of the demise of the modern project of gardening society within the nation-state. Derber uses the term "wilding" and "wilding epidemic" to refer to "America's individualistic culture in an advanced state of disrepair . . . [which] encourages unrestrained and sociopathic self-interest."[59] He writes that

> rugged individualism has merged with free-market capitalism, creating a fertile brew for wilding. A Marxist view of institutionalized wilding—and of political and business elites as carriers of the virus—helps to correct the Durkheimian hint of wilding as deviance. Durkheim, in a major oversight, never recognized that egoism and anomie can themselves be seen as norms, culturally prescribed and accepted.

This is a theoretical key to understanding wilding in America. Wilding partly reflects a weakened community less able to regulate its increasingly individualistic members. In this sense, the American wilder is the product of a declining society that is losing its authority to instill respect for social values and obligations.

But Marx's view of institutionalized wilding . . . suggests not the failure of social authority but the wholesale indoctrination of societal values that can ultimately poison both the individual and society itself. As local communities weaken, giant corporations, including the media, advertising, and communications industries, shape the appetites, morality, and behavior of Americans ever more powerfully. For the rich and powerful, the dream of unlimited wealth and glamour, combined with the Reagan revolution of corporate deregulation and corporate welfare, opens up endless fantasies and opportunities.

A different version of socially prescribed wilding trickles down to everyone else. For those exposed to the same inflated dream of wealth, glamour, and power, but denied the means of achieving it, illegitimate means provide the only strategy to achieve socially approved goals. Whether involving petty or serious wilding, such behavior gradually permeates the population . . . Wilding itself becomes a societal way of life.[60]

In his more recent book *Sociopathic Society*, Derber draws connections between wilding and US foreign policy, wars of aggression, and the rise of fascist politics in America, mass shootings, and climate change. Sociopathy designates "the reign of antisocial social norms."[61] The increasingly sociopathic character of US society is, according to Derber, a product of the growing concentration of wealth and power. This reflects extreme and growing income and wealth inequality. It also reflects the unaccountability of the power elite and the operations of the state, especially the growth of the power of the military and the military-industrial complex and the effects of militarism on the society. Regarding the latter, Derber writes: "Military culture—and its sociopathic ideals—is a root cause of a sociopathic society that places high moral and constitutional value on guns and gun ownership."[62]

It is necessary to think of the notion of a de-civilizing spurt in contrast with civility and civil society. De-civilizing is marked, not by crime rates per se, but rather by the erosion of the possibility and scope for civil interaction, including above all the existence of public spaces in which different ideas and values can be spoken about without the threat of violence. Hence, the January 6 attack on Congress was particularly significant as an attack on a symbolic space of civil deliberation and of the democratic polity. The militias involved are symptomatic of a feature of de-civilizing which is the privatization of violence. In the United States, this is evident in the militia movement which developed in the wake of the Vietnam War and gained initiates and momentum after the Persian Gulf War and subsequent wars in Afghanistan and Iraq. Privatization of violence may also be seen in the growth of private security firms and in mercenaries contracted by the federal government and in the sheer number of guns that make gun violence, targeted or random, an ever-present possibility and fear in the background of everyday life. The relationship between violence and the erosion of the public sphere is an insight of Giroux, whose concern with the school as public sphere led to analyses of the privatization of socialization by mass media, the exclusion and demonization of youth, and the culture of violence that has arisen as part of the War on Terror.[63] The culture of careful critical discourse depends necessarily on civility. Hence, as Weber said, it would be scandalous to use words as weapons in the lecture theatre.[64] But the cultural and physical spaces where civil discourse is possible have been shrunk by neoliberal privatization and by the growth of a fascistic cultural glorification of violence.

A key dimension of the civilizing process, for Elias, was the reduction in power disparities between social superordinates and social subordinates. This ramified throughout social relations, for example, in declining social toleration of physical violence against children by adults. Elias emphasizes the ways in which this equalization of social power followed from the monopolization, and therefore centralization, of violence by kings and ultimately by the nation-state, leading to a progressive long-term decline in the independent, uncontrolled prerogatives of feudal masters over vassals, servants and so on. In a Weberian sense, this process was bound up with rationalization and the development of legal-rational authority as a feature of state building. Also important in the civilizing process was the growing power of subordinate classes in relation to dominant classes as the means of production and the division of labor developed. Urbanization was intrinsically related to the growth of trade, and in towns, outside feudal relations, civic order developed of the kind ultimately described by Goffman with its pacifying rituals of "civil inattention." As Giddens emphasizes, capitalism contributed to the civilizing process by segregating economic life from direct violent coercion.[65] The existence of formally free wage labor legally embodied in the labor contract's formal assumption of equality excluded direct violent plunder as a method of extracting surplus. Concomitant with the rise of capitalism, the means of violence were centralized in the nation-state as a "monopoly of legitimate violence" in Weber's terms. The civilizing process was carried out and made possible by the nation-state. In this way, the nation-state was the guarantor of the space of secular civil society and, therefore, of the culture of critical discourse.[66]

However, everything that Marx said about the violence of primitive accumulation needs to be remembered, and this is an ongoing immensely violent process that is evident in civil wars (with imperialist powers often involved or supplying funding and arms) in which extractive natural resources such as oil, diamonds, and rare earth metals are central to the causes of conflict.[67] Globalization has intensified demand for such resources and intensified conflict, as has the post–Cold War chaos of the US divide and ruin disorganization of the world. Capitalism, therefore, displaces violence to the periphery. It also displaces violence from the direct extraction of surplus to the ongoing repressive and violent actions of the police and military. But also, precisely the way in which capitalism creates a civilizing process is also the way in which it displaces and transforms violence from direct coercion (the feudal taking of surplus at the point of a sword) to structural violence. What is called structural violence in fact follows from an initial immense amount of violence—precisely that involved in primitive accumulation. The free wage labor of capitalism, the proletariat, is established by the massive violence of dispossession, displacement, and disinheritance in order to become "free" in the negative (liberal) sense of capitalist freedom. The extraction of surplus does not require physical coercion because the proletariat never has anything to be taken (in the sense of not having access to commons and not owning any means of production except their own bodies). This renders the proletariat entirely dependent on the capitalist class for its existence. For the proletariat, capitalist freedom is "the freedom to starve to death." Engels explained that what is today called by the left "precarity" or precariousness is the essential, defining condition of the proletariat:

> The proletarian is helpless; left to himself, he cannot live a single day. The bourgeoisie has gained a monopoly of all means of existence in the broadest sense of the word. What the proletarian needs, he can obtain only from this bourgeoisie, which is protected in its monopoly by the power of the State. The proletarian is, therefore, in law and in fact, the slave of the bourgeoisie, which can decree his life or death. It offers him the means of living, but only for an "equivalent" for his work. It even lets him have the appearance of acting from a free choice, of making a contract with free, unconstrained consent, as a responsible agent who has attained his majority.
>
> Fine freedom, where the proletarian has no other choice than that of either accepting the conditions which the bourgeoisie offers him, or of starving, of freezing to death, of sleeping naked among the beasts of the forests! A fine "equivalent" valued at pleasure by the bourgeoisie! And if one proletarian is such a fool as to starve rather than agree to the equitable propositions of the bourgeoisie, his "natural superiors," another is easily found in his place; there are proletarians enough in the world, and not all so insane as to prefer dying to living.[68]

What Marx called the proletariat's "radical chains" are precisely *nothing*. The coercion consists of the threat of nothingness. Marx said in the *Economic and Philosophic Manuscripts* that the worker endures his "filled void" for fear of falling into the "absolute void," that is, death.[69] Power in capitalism is based on that absolute void from which the worker has nothing to protect himself or herself except the resources that are owned and controlled by the capitalist class. Therefore, the primary form of coercion in capitalist society is abandonment.[70] The capitalist does not kill you; he lets you die. Alternatively, he can let you live, on his terms of course, by offering you a job.[71]

Structural violence, then, arises from the very radical dispossession of the worker, their dispossession from the means to live.[72] Structural violence is enacted in interaction in hierarchy and command. The corporation is hierarchical in a way that matches the hierarchical structure of the military (and the two sectors cooperate very successfully in the military-industrial complex). As David Noble notes, the military has a very clear and simple philosophy of management: command.[73] In alienated work under capitalism, command is the thread running through all human relations and human resources and management and labor processes. But this command is abstractified in bureaucracy and, as Giddens emphasizes from Marx, in the labor process, where it is built into the very physical structure of technology. The violence that is displaced into the machine becomes evident in industrial accidents in which thousands of workers die every year, often in horrific ways, being mangled, boiled, and crushed. It is manifest in particularly insidious technologies of the control of labor such as the design by Amazon of a bracelet that the worker wears that vibrates to point the worker's hand in the right direction when they are picking products from shelves: "One of the patents outlines a haptic feedback system that would vibrate against the wearer's skin to point their hand in the right direction."[74] As Marx wrote in the *Grundrisse*, "Thus the appropriation of labour by capital confronts the worker in a coarsely sensuous form."[75]

But as well as abstract form in the market, organization and machinery, command takes personal form in the boss, or in the supervisor. Interpersonal relations at work are shaped by a hierarchy that tacitly presupposes the basic powerlessness of the worker in relation to capital. Due to dispossession, *having* nothing, the worker is in imminent danger of not *being*, that is, no longer being alive. This basic precariousness runs through hierarchy as coercion. This aggression may be more or less sublimated and there is an increasing body of research and commentary suggesting that there is a relationship between neoliberalism and workplace bullying, as a bullying style of management has become normalized in America.[76] Frequent explosions of mass gun violence by disgruntled or fired employees, or without a discernible motive, may reasonably be interpreted as expressions of the abstract violence to which workers are subjected by the very nature of capitalist work, and as intensified insecurity and competition and increasingly harsh and punitive forms of management have ratcheted up the pressure on workers and their

feelings of fear, anxiety, humiliation, and rage.[77] The mass shooting is violence directed against people at large, society at large, the public itself. It is
inchoate violence against society, or against its very absence.

The economy of neoliberal globalization is one of disposability, where
violence is enacted as abandonment. One sees whole cities abandoned. The
era began with the New York City fiscal crisis of 1975 in which the *New York
Daily News* reported the Ford administration's refusal to come to the city's
aid, with the headline "Ford to City: Drop Dead."[78] "Drop Dead" is exactly
what the bourgeoisie says to those human beings who do not accept their
terms or for whom they have no use. It invokes the void that Engels perceived
in the "freedom" offered by bourgeois society and celebrated by liberalism.

The threat of abandonment is the structural violence of capitalism. This
threat of abandonment, and therefore the level of structural violence, was
reduced by the solidarity project of modernity. This project created and
enlarged what Pierre Bourdieu has called "the left hand of the state" (as
opposed to the violently coercive, punitive right hand).[79] The "left hand" is
the welfare state, broadly construed, that takes responsibility for the material
maintenance of the conditions and resources and infrastructures for the reproduction of the life of society for which capital eschews direct responsibility.
The solidarity project of modernity was one side of Karl Polanyi's "double
movement" between laissez-faire and state intervention.[80] Action by the state
is propelled by and, responds to, the growing power of the working class as it
is organized in the socialist movement. The development of the welfare state
was a result both of the working class actively making its interests felt in the
political arena of bourgeois democracy through social democratic parties and
of the ruling class engaging in class compromise, offering concessions to the
working class, via the regulative apparatus of the state. As Jytte Klausen has
argued, the warfare state built up in World War II served as the foundation of
the postwar welfare state.[81] The Russian Revolution is of crucial significance
as historical background to the development of welfare states in the twentieth
century. The welfare state reflected a healthy respect of the ruling class for
the revolutionary potential of the working class. In the "class compromise" of
the first two decades after World War II, the welfare state matured, alongside
the existence of the Soviet Union and other so-called socialist states in which
public provision and social planning were implemented in a far-reaching,
albeit deformed and unsatisfactory, way under Stalinism. The class compromise was a power balance. But it was also made possible by the growth and
profit rates of the advanced capitalist economies, and especially the United
States, which funded the rebuilding of Europe through the Marshall Plan.
With a growing pie, the ruling class was ultimately willing to make certain
concessions and had the resources to do so. Of course, this involved intense
conflicts within national bourgeoisies, such as Domhoff describes between

hardline conservatives and moderates in the US power elite.[82] The key point to make here is that the provision of a certain level of economic (and thereby social) security was an expression of the growing power of the working class in relation to the capitalist class and represented some alleviation of the structural violence projected impersonally through capitalist systems.

The 1960s informalization of society and sexual revolution may, from that angle, be interpreted as a euphoric throwing off of cultural deference and psychic rigidity and various psychological forms of repression. This jettisoning of repression was made possible by what was then called "the affluent society." Ronneberger writes:

> Fordist societalization did indeed produce openings in social space. While the extension of the wage relation functioned as a form of social integration, reductions of labor time and more generous vacation benefits helped liberate subjectivity. Enhanced economic security, prolonged socialization within the family and an extension of cultural activities led—at least for certain social groups—to new, increasingly self-determined ways of life. A new "culture of stimulation" emerged, saturated with commodities and distractions and oriented towards self-realization, pleasure and hedonism. As work discipline was gradually corroded by mass consumption, Fordist societalization became increasingly dysfunctional.[83]

There was also a darker side to desublimation and criminologists regard this cultural transformation in the 1960s as criminogenic and the beginning of a "crime explosion" that carried on until the 1990s. The faltering of the postwar boom in the late 1960s, and the economic recessions of the 1970s, led to the abandonment of Keynesian economics by the ruling class and power elite, and the turn to the monetarist economic policies and punitive social policies of the New Right. From the beginning of the 1980s, Thatcher and Reagan set about concerted class warfare through the powers of government to undo the postwar welfare state, defeat the unions, and create an individualized "entrepreneurial" neoliberal society. This was accompanied by an intensification of state repression and a growth of social inequality. Neoliberalism reasserted the structural violence of capitalism by removing mediating institutions, or protections, thereby exposing workers to the void.

As competition for jobs and for the trappings of material success grew, and as status became rendered a propagandistic demand by advertising, social life took on an increasingly hard and hostile edge. The social world itself increasingly seemed a hostile place in which one was on one's own. The consequent distrust and aggression is what Derber describes as "wilding." Collectivity itself seemed less and less protective and more and more to be pitted against the individual. In this context, it is not so "inexplicable" that mass shootings break out frequently now in which the target is no one in particular but everyone in general. The positivist emphasis on deductive-nomological explanation has deafened social scientists to what these acts are saying. What does the mass shooting mean? What is it communicating? How should we understand the meaning of the act? It is most certainly a communication. But it is inarticulate. It is devoid of culture. The message is the violence. The medium is the message. These outbreaks take place in institutions: churches, schools, workplaces, government buildings. What is being shot down is the collective itself. These are sociopathic, one might say sociophobic, and even sociocidal in intent. The target is abstract. It is alienated society. The attacker is disconnected, methodical sometimes (chillingly so in the case of the Las Vegas shooter who carried out the deadliest mass shooting, killing fifty-eight people). Everything about these acts is abstract and disconnected. The mass shooting is cold violence. Fromm wrote about the nature of power in American society, "Instead of overt authority, 'anonymous' authority reigns . . . [I]n anonymous authority both command and commander have become invisible. It is like being fired at by an invisible enemy. There is nobody and nothing to fight back against."[84] The mass shooter is, wildly, attacking this invisible enemy, that is society.

The weakening of social integration and collapse of social regulation within the United States is associated and intertwined with the US government's eschewing of so-called "nation-building" abroad. As Glazebrook makes clear in his conception of "divide and ruin," the post–Cold War US does not seek to organize the world so much as to disorganize it. As Naomi Klein articulated in *The Shock Doctrine*, neoliberalism thrives on the creation of crisis.[85] In this way, neoliberalism expresses the needs of financial capital. Financialized capital floats free from particular localities and populations and profits through its mobility by responding quickly to market swings. But this is also linked to the declining ability of American imperialism to organize the world, as Glazebrook suggests. The quintessential technology of post-9/11 American military power, the drone, is expressive of this. If military power has become, as Paul Virilio says, "vaporous," this is also in the sense that it has no presence on the ground.[86] It comes out of the blue, from thin air, leaving no trace of itself other than death and destruction. The contradiction of the US post–Cold War unipolar moment was that the very dynamics of globalization that had rendered Stalinist economic isolation no longer sustainable had also generated immense competitive pressures that reduced the economic power of the United States. Hence, its imperial power rested increasingly on powers of destruction rather than production.

The protests and riots that have followed in the wake of the police murder of George Floyd represent an outpouring of revulsion against racism and police violence. The demonstrations have been a powerful manifestation of working-class unity against the violence of the bourgeois state apparatus. The video footage of the demonstrations shows millions of people united across so-called racial lines and shows police across America attacking demonstrators of all skin colors. The demonstrations are manifestations of the progressive development of egalitarian social consciousness that necessarily comes into conflict with social inequality and its necessary injustices, and with the violent hierarchical power of the bourgeois state, which operates to preserve these inequalities. As protests against state violence, these necessarily enter into conflict with the apparatus of class rule of which the capitalist state is a central component. The response of what Lenin called the state's "special bodies of armed men" has exposed the systematic brutality that underpins class rule.[87] Instead of being a few racist police officers, it is clear that the immense brutality of policing in the United States is systemic, built into the organization and its relationship to society, but also, crucially, arising from the nature of this society as a class society.

Capital is no longer capable of organizing society; nor does the ruling class care to. Globalization has extinguished the need of capital to organize society at the level of the nation-state and the bourgeoisie is incapable of organizing society at any higher level. The historical development of capitalism was interwoven with the creation of nation-states, which were the means by which capital expanded markets and the bourgeoisie institutionalized and exercised its political power. The nation-state system that resulted entered into crisis at the end of the nineteenth century with the development of imperialism, which expresses the contradiction between the nation-state and capital's development of a global economy. Imperialism is the only solution to this contradiction of which capital is capable: the most powerful capitalist nation-states seeking political domination of the world in the interests of their banks and big businesses. These derive various forms of protection from this nation-state in the context of global competition and also pursue their interests through the political apparatuses. World War I was the first explosion of the imperialist system in all its irrationality and destructiveness, followed twenty years after by another even more global descent into hell. Imperialism is, as Lenin put it, the "highest stage of capitalism," and marks the period of the decline of capitalism.[88]

Lenin's analysis of imperialism as the highest, and final, stage of capitalism, was borne out by the history of the twentieth century as a century of revolution and war and the completion of the transformation, begun in 1848, of the bourgeoisie from a historically progressive to a reactionary force. The significance of these conditions for revolutionary strategy was cognized and expressed in Trotsky's theory of permanent revolution. The Russian Revolution of 1917, the practical confirmation of permanent revolution, demonstrated the revolutionary power of the working class as the necessary historical agent of the overthrow of capitalism. Stalinism and fascism were the means by which this initial revolutionary upsurge of the working class was suppressed.

The history of the twentieth century is the history of its betrayed and crushed revolutions, drowned in blood by Stalinist and imperialist violence, beginning with the imperialist intervention in the Russian Civil War and continuing with the genocidal crimes of the Nazis and ongoing genocidal counterinsurgency warfare against Third World revolutions and national-liberation movements.[89] But even though betrayed and murdered, these revolutions and attempted revolutions that swept every continent of the planet, were realizations of the coming into being of an international proletariat and demonstrations of the revolutionary power and potential of the global working class.

The objective power of the working class as a global class is immense, even while the power of the working class organized (or today, disorganized) within the nation-state has massively declined. The working class exists objectively, and has its objective power, at the level at which cooperative social labor is organized. The working class in every country, in its very productivity, is connected in a cooperative chain of human activity with workers all over the world. To say that "the economy" is global is to say that the cooperative connections of human activity that sustain human life are global networks of interconnected labor that span the planet. The manufacture of an automobile involves the assembly in one country of parts manufactured in a number of other companies. Commodities often move across national borders not only in distribution but in the very process of production. Capital draws on the productive powers of human labor as the labor of a global species and in so doing globally interconnects the working class in complex chains of socialized labor. Our sustenance and species survival is totally dependent on a global complex division of labor, a metabolic relationship with nature that is now systematically interconnected on a planetary level. But, of course, these global interrelationships have no conscious organization at the planetary level.

Capital is incapable of organizing the world. Imperialism more and more destructively disorganizes the world, and this is evident in the sociocide perpetrated by the United States in Afghanistan, Iraq, and Libya, and attempted in other countries such as Iran and Venezuela through its economic warfare in the form of "sanctions."[90] The sociocide perpetrated by the US government and military against other countries is reflected by, and connected through myriad threads with, the sociocidal abandonment of the American working class, the withdrawal of the state from any positive responsibility for the reproduction of human populations and the conditions for social life. In its stead, in the destroyed communities that were once productive and solidaristic but which are ground down by poverty, hardship, self-destructive despair, and undirected anger, capital places the police and tells them, in Trump's words, not to be "too nice." Trump only made explicit what is in their training and physically manifested in the array of arms and armor that they bring to the streets. The revolt against policing is objectively a revolt against the capitalist state which has left itself only the mechanism of the police as the means of its relationship with society. "Governing through crime," or governing through policing, is what the relation between the working class and the state has been reduced to as capital has lost interest in maintaining the condition of any national working class and so the capitalist state has withdrawn.[91] Governing through policing also means profiting through policing, as the private prison industry has grown and as commercial enterprises have developed providing the police with weapons, surveillance technologies, and so on. But governing through policing makes the police the primary representation of government. To oppose police violence is to oppose the capitalist state. The revolt against policing is a revolt against the capitalist nation-state. The repressive apparatus of capital expresses capital's relationship to the working class: it is abandoned and beaten down. The knee on the neck is the capitalist nation-state on the working class, which cannot breathe. To live, it has to find the power to throw that knee off, and that power lies in its global collectivity.

The latent power of the working class as global collective rises in direct proportion to the also very real powerlessness and despair that the working class endures in its undefended condition as the former organizers of its power on the national level have turned against it and implemented the dictates of globally empowered capital. Globalization of production has allowed capital to escape the limitations of the national economy and to abandon the burden of maintaining the conditions of life of the national population. Neoliberal austerity policies are the political method of the abandonment of the national working-class population by globalized capital. What takes the form of the abandonment of the national working class by the nation-state to which, they are told, they "belong" is also, in essence, and today more and more in form also (only thinly masked by the national organization of bourgeois politics), part of the global assault on the working class by global capital. In the early to mid-twentieth century, capital temporarily escaped its own crisis by drawing on the solidaristic energies of the working class, channeled through the mediating institutions of social democracy, the welfare state, and the trade unions to socially organize the advanced national economies so as to temporarily stabilize itself through "class compromise." This compromise took place on the national level and the conditions of its existence have disappeared.

The social conflicts of the 1960s represented the coming apart of this so-called Keynesian-Fordist solution, and the economic crisis and upsurge of working-class militancy in the 1970s brought this period to a close. Driving this socioeconomic shift was the growth of international competition and the decline of the rate of profit manifesting structural crisis, arising from the fundamental contradictions of the capitalist system between socialized production and private appropriation.[92] Since the 1970s, capital has sought to escape from these contradictions through the growth of the transnational corporation, the globalization of production, and financialization. These efforts have only intensified its crisis and amplified the importance in this crisis of the contradiction between nation-state and global economy.

The contradiction between nation-state and global economy has fundamental implications for the legitimacy of the capitalist state, if by legitimacy we mean the state's ability to secure social order and the social relations of class rule without recourse to violence, in the sense of physical force against human bodies. The concessions won historically by the working class through social democracy and trade union struggles were secured and organized at the level of the nation-state and, in this process, transferred legitimacy, in the sense of voluntary attachment, to the nation-state. Today, the political elites are defunding and privatizing in line with the dictates of global capital. So the legitimacy of the state is the legitimacy of policing. To oppose police violence is to oppose the way the capitalist state works. In the midst of economic disaster, there is the daylight robbery of the state in the channeling of the trillions of dollars to the corporations while the working class is abandoned to the ravages of the Covid-19 virus. The virus has brought to an acute condition the position of the American working class living on the edge of physical survival. The contradiction is fundamental between a state that demands heartfelt allegiance but leaves people to die with antiquated and underfunded systems of temporary assistance to the working class. What is called neoliberalism are capital's combined policies of abandoning and beating down the working class: "free market, strong state."[93] The working class is abandoned and murdered: in confrontations like that in which George Floyd died but also in the conscious and intentional lead poisoning of Flint, Michigan, and in the ruling class's back-to-school and back-to-work policies, which the *BMJ* (*British Medical Journal*) has called, echoing Engels, "social murder."[94]

THE NORMALCY OF PATHOLOGY

Normalcy was the calm in the eye of the storm. The storm has now shifted and the hurricane winds are tearing apart what once was the center. Today, there is no center, as capital has been released from attachment to any geographical population and set free to seize any opportunity around the world and to dump any bad assets, whether people's houses or people's lives. The disembedding of capital from the nation-state severs the connection that once existed between nation and state. As capital is able to float free from any population, the state as "executive committee of the ruling class" abandons its responsibility for the reproduction of any population. The state takes the form of what James Galbraith calls "the predator state." The predator state roams the world with its predator drones, opening and closing temporary "kill boxes" into which it unleashes Hellfire missiles, striking as if out of thin air and disappearing.[95] The unnecessary population, especially the elderly and infirm, can die of Covid-19. It is of no concern. The state is the means by which capital opens up the world for exploitation, eliminates barriers to the extraction of surplus value, and keeps unneeded, surplus populations under control. Just as there has been an erosion in the universality and reciprocity of law, a similar change has occurred in taxation.[96] As a result of their ability to float free from taxation regimes, the economic, social, and political logic of the amassment of wealth by the superrich is toward the entrenchment of a new aristocracy, but radically different from feudalism because not tied to land and, therefore, having no need for even the reciprocity built into feudal obligations. The interest of billionaires Richard Branson, Jeff Bezos, and Elon Musk in space travel symbolically expresses their aristocratic transcendence of the realm of necessity in which their workers dwell. The ability of populations to exert political pressure through democracy in order to have the executive committee of the powerful, the state, recognize their collective needs has been drastically eroded by the mobility of capital and the concomitant decline of the viability of unions and mass political parties as a vehicle for influencing the state.[97]

The nation is the bourgeois solution to the problem of social order. The boundaries of the nation-state are the confines within which the bourgeoisie has been able to create society. The nation-state form that emerged out of the absolutist state was reconfigured under the pressures of the modern capitalist configuration of class conflict, and historical and technological conditions of warfare.[98] The nation-state is the geographical structure within which the bourgeoisie has been able to secure control of populations and manufacture the consent of the governed. Giddens argues that apparatuses of rule have, throughout history, secured power not only through violence but also through the construction of symbolic order, offering solutions to the existential dilemma. For this reason, Giddens argues that the state is a way in which the existential contradiction is "externalized," in the sense of being projected out from day-to-day life governed by ritual, magic, and myth and taking shape in transcendent form in attachment to something higher.[99] This has enabled states to secure the cooperation of populations through its place in the symbolic order as transcending mortality, and through its authoritative and organizing role in securing the symbolic order.[100] The state becomes a constitutive part of the solution to the problem of separateness and of chaos, symbolically as well as materially.

In modernity, it was the idea of the nation that became the basis of this attachment and that made the nation-state the focus of belonging and protection, both real and imagined, against chaos. In the modern world in which quotidian life, purged of its relationship to nature and its traditional rituals, is rendered as "everyday life" in its complete banality, the nation and the state institutions that symbolically embody its unity, became particularly important as the shared basis for ontological security. This was the function of nationalism as a secular religion. This is the service that nationalism provides to the state. This is also the service that nationalism provides to the individual; belonging to the nation makes the world less chaotic and provides a sense of having a place in the universe and not being a mere particle in the void.[101] Today, however, it is easy to allow the upsurge of nationalism to disguise how fundamentally anachronistic nationalism has become in relation to the material conditions of life. The cruelty of the predator state is how it continues to use an attachment grown ever more desperate in the face of abandonment. This cannot but further erode the ability of the myth of the nation to provide a basis for ontological security.

The bourgeois ideology of the unattached, autonomous, negatively free individual makes it hard to find the language in which to understand and express the feelings of loss and terror that accompany the growing social disintegration and social dislocation that the forces of capital are wreaking. In the United States, negative freedom has been deeply engrained, paradoxically, as the basis for collective national attachment. This is expressed today in emphatic and threatening form, emblazoned in nature's warning colors of yellow and black, with a coiled rattlesnake, and the slogan "Don't Tread on Me." In the United States, national identity is particularly associated with the value of negative freedom and the myth of the individual.[102] Therefore, the sense of abandonment by the state is expressed in paradoxical ways—it ideologically becomes right that the state should abandon the population because to stand on one's own is to be a true American. Hence, Texas, not long after leaving its population freezing without power, lifted restrictions on wearing masks, even as a new strain of Covid-19 was rampaging through the country and hospitals were overrun.[103]

The social crisis of the United States is the crisis of the solution to the problem of social and political order that combined the sovereignty of the individual with the sovereignty of the nation-state. The contradictions in that political model are exposed as the contradiction between the socialization of production and private appropriation grows ever more explosive, especially as it takes the form of the contradiction between the global economy and the nation-state. The contradiction is between the globality of the networks through which the productive activity of the producers is organized and the nation-state which increasingly clearly shows its form as an association of appropriators. The entropy of the organized society within the nation-state, and the consequent condition of social disorder, breakdown, and conflict—*the normalcy of pathology*—has only one solution for the human species. This is to realize the political implications of the global economy and to form a new political society at the level of the globe. The bourgeois class cannot achieve this because of the competitive nature of private appropriation and because to do so would unite as one political unit the already materially united associated producers, that is, the global working class. The realization of society at the level of global humanity, a human species capable of regulating itself as a global species, can only be achieved by the action of the global working class, realizing its global universality and commonality of interest as a class. The crisis of the nation-state as society is the undercutting of the social underpinnings of the institutions of the state. This is the undermining of the legitimacy of the state. The state, as nation-state, less and less corresponds to the actuality of social relations within globalized late capitalism. Most importantly, the forces and relations of industrial production are completely global in scope, uniting the globe as a single productive process which sustains humanity as global species. There is now an interdependent global humanity. And there is, correspondingly, a global human productive force, a global proletariat. This global working class consists of the vast mass of humanity. Ecologically, its work is the metabolism of the human species with nature. In this way, humanity is materially unified, globally, as a single human organism. This inhabitation of a global human species body was made evident by the Covid-19 pandemic. The response was divided into mutually hostile nation-states. The response to the pandemic has illuminated the vast gulf separating the organization of global human society under capitalism and the needs of humanity. It has shown the chasm between what is possible, given the level of development of the productive forces, and what actually gets done with those productive forces. Imperialism has also so far blocked all attempts at a coordinated global response to climate change, which is now upon us in producing catastrophic weather patterns such as hurricanes, floods, droughts, and wildfires. The predictability of life is breaking down because the material conditions for predictability are undercut by the dysfunctions of the capitalist organization of the global productive force of humanity. Society is organized under the nation-state but the notion of a national "society" is more and more fictitious. This fiction is often held to with increasing desperation and is mobilized more aggressively as it becomes increasingly at odds with reality.

The contradiction of the nation-state with the globality of social relations is acutely expressed in the contradiction between the university as a nation-state institution and the globality of science. The research university as a secular institution arose within the nation-state and continues to depend on the nation-state even while the knowledge it organizes is more and more in practice, and not only in ideal, universally human. The university tethers knowledge to the interests of the nation-state. But the university itself is increasingly intertwined in global social relations. These global relations of the "entrepreneurial university" are relations that are directly involved in the global productive forces. Therefore, the contradiction between global economy and nation-state is acute within the university.

The university is a mediating institution that functions to support, and is supported by, the nation-state. The legitimacy of the university and that of the nation-state are intertwined.[104] The crisis of the congruence between nation-state and society has undermined the legitimacy of the traditional humanities, which were deeply interconnected with the idea of national culture and with the project of constructing national culture. The crisis of the nation-state is expressed in those parts of the university whose existence is tied to the mediation of social relations within the framework of the nation-state, that is, the humanities and social sciences. The crisis of the nation-state in its function in organizing society on a national basis is expressed particularly acutely in the declining conditions for the legitimacy of sociology. This is the source of the crisis of sociology of which Gouldner marked the beginning.

NOTES

1. Ulrich Beck, Anthony Giddens, and Scott Lash, *Reflexive Modernization* (Stanford, CA: Stanford University Press, 1994).

2. Anthony Giddens, *A Contemporary Critique of Historical Materialism, Volume 1: Power, Property and the State* (London: Macmillan, 1981), 252.

3. Giddens, *Modernity and Self-Identity*, 149–169.

4. Giddens, *A Contemporary Critique*, 236.

5. Charles Thorpe, "Escape from Reflexivity: Fromm and Giddens on Individualism, Anxiety, and Authoritarianism," in Durkin and Braune eds, *Erich Fromm's Critical Theory*, 166–193; Giddens, *Modernity and Self-Identity*, 190–191.

6. Erich Fromm, *Escape from Freedom* (New York: Henry Holt and Co., 1969); Erich Fromm, *The Heart of Man: Its Genius for Good and Evil* (New York: Harper and Row, 1964).

7. Karl Marx and Frederick Engels, *Manifesto of the Communist Party* (Moscow: Progress Publishers, 1986), 54. Cf. Finn Bowring, "Negative and Positive Freedom: Lessons from, and to, Sociology," *Sociology* 49, no. 1 (2015): 156–171.

8. Giddens, *Contemporary Critique*, 236.

9. Harry M. Collins, "Socialness and the Undersocialized Conception of Society," *Science, Technology and Human Values* 23, no. 4 (Autumn 1998): 494–516; Thorpe, "Toward Species Being."

10. Peter Winch, *The Idea of a Social Science and Its Relation to Philosophy* (London: Routledge & Kegan Paul, 1958); Collins, *Forms of Life.*

11. R. D. Laing, *Knots* (London: Tavistock, 1970).

12. Ted R. Vaughan and Gideon Sjoberg, "Human Rights Theory and the Classical Sociological Tradition," in Mark Wardell and Stephen P. Turner eds, *Sociological Theory in Transition* (London: Routledge, 1986), 127–141, on 138.

13. Harry Collins and Martin Kusch, *The Shape of Actions: What Humans and Machines Can Do* (Cambridge, MA: MIT Press, 1998); Harry Collins, *Artifictional Intelligence: Against Humanity's Surrender to Computers* (Cambridge, UK: Polity Press, 2018).

14. Frederick Engels, *Dialectics of Nature*, trans. Clemens Dutt (New York: International Publishers, 1940), 279–296.

15. Peter Berger, *The Sacred Canopy: Elements of a Sociological Theory of Religion* (New York: Anchor, 1990).

16. Erich Fromm, *The Anatomy of Human Destructiveness* (New York: Holt, Rinehart and Winston, 1973), 225.

17. Giorgio Agamben, *State of Exception*, trans. Kevin Attell (Chicago: University of Chicago Press, 2005).

18. Ernest Becker, *The Denial of Death* (New York: The Free Press, 1997).

19. Emile Durkheim, "The Dualism of Human Nature and its Social Conditions," (reprinted in) *Durkheimian Studies* 11 (2005): 35–45.

20. Edward Hutchins, *Cognition in the Wild* (Cambridge, MA: The MIT Press, 1995).

21. Collins, *Forms of Life*; Collins, "Socialness."

22. Pierre Bourdieu, *Outline of a Theory of Practice* (Cambridge: Cambridge University Press, 1977), 90; Giddens, *Constitution of Society.*

23. Cf. Tom Bunyard, *Debord, Time and Spectacle: Hegelian Marxism and Situationist Theory* (Chicago, IL: Haymarket Books, 2018).

24. Georg Simmel, *Conflict; The Web of Group-Affiliations* (New York: Free Press, 1964); Robert K. Merton, "The Role-Set: Problems in Sociological Theory." *The British Journal of Sociology* 8, no. 2 (1957): 106–120; Collins, *Forms of Life*, 5–11.

25. Norbert Elias, *What is Sociology?* trans. Stephen Mennell (New York: Columbia University Press, 1978); Zygmunt Bauman, "The Phenomenon of Norbert Elias," *Sociology* 13 (1977): 117–135.

26. Nick Dyer-Witheford, "Digital Labour, Species-Becoming, and the Global Worker," *Ephemera: Theory & Politics in Organization* 10, no. 3/4 (2010): 484–503; Charles Thorpe, "Toward Species Being," *Logos: A Journal of Modern Society & Culture* (Summer 2021), http://logosjournal.com/2021/toward-species-being/.

27. Erving Goffman, *Encounters: Two Studies in the Sociology of Interaction* (Indianapolis: Bobbs Merrill, 1961); Peter Fleming and Andre Spicer, "Working at a Cynical Distance: Implications for Power, Subjectivity and Resistance," *Organization* 18, no. 1 (2003): 157–179.

28. Ferdinand Tönnies, *Community and Society (Gemeinschaft und Gesellschaft)* (New Brunswick, NJ: Transaction Publishers, 1993).

29. Fromm, *Escape from Freedom.*

30. Erich Fromm, *The Sane Society* (New York: Holt, Rinehart and Winston, 1955), 6 (emphasis in original). See also Carl Ratner, "Pathological Normalcy: A Construct for Comprehending and Overcoming Psychological Aspects of Alienation," *The Humanistic Psychologist* 42, no. 3 (2014): 298–303; Snell Putney and Gail J. Putney, *The Adjusted American: Normal Neuroses in Individual and Society* (New York: Harper Colophon Books, 1964).

31. Jack D. Pressman, "Human Salvage: Why Psychosurgery Worked in 1949 (and Not Now)," in Jack D. Pressman ed., *Last Resort: Psychosurgery and the Limits of Medicine* (Cambridge: Cambridge University Press, 1998), 207–208. Psychoanalysis, in the first two decades after World War Two, formed a conceptual bridge between the mental health fields and sociology. Andrew Scull writes that "The commanding heights of psychiatry in the years between 1945 and 1970 were occupied by those espousing a psychodynamic account of the aetiology of mental disturbances, and a psycho-therapeutic approach to their treatment": Scull, "The Mental Health Sector and the Social Sciences in post-World War II USA, Part 2: The Impact of Federal Research Funding and the Drugs Revolution," *History of Psychiatry* 22, no. 3 (2011): 268–284, on 269. George Cavalletto and Catherine Silver quote Howard Kaye: "In the 1950s and 1960s, Freudian theory was deemed to be a vital part of the sociological tradition": George Cavalletto and Catherine Silver, "Opening/Closing the Sociological Mind to Psychoanalysis," in Lynn Chancer and John Andrews, *The Unhappy Divorce of Sociology and Psychoanalysis: Diverse Perspectives on the Psychosocial* (New York: Palgrave Macmillan, 2014), 17–53, on 17.

32. J. E. Wallace Wallin, *Personality Maladjustments and Mental Hygiene: A Textbook for Students of Mental Hygiene Psychology, Education, Sociology, and Counseling* (New York: McGraw-Hill Book Company Inc., 1949), 30. Cf. Theresa R. Richardson, *The Century of the Child: The Mental Hygiene Movement & Social Policy in the United States & Canada* (Albany: State University of New York Press, 1989).

33. Fromm, *The Sane Society*. See also Donald Ipperciel, "The Paradox of Normalcy in the Frankfurt School," *Symposium: Canadian Journal of Continental Philosophy* II, no. 1 (1998): 37–59.

34. Fromm, *Escape from Freedom*, 183–204.

35. Zygmunt Bauman, *Liquid Modernity* (Cambridge: Polity Press, 2000); Zygmunt Bauman, *Liquid Life* (Cambridge: Polity Press, 2005); Zygmunt Bauman, *Liquid Times: Living in an Age of Uncertainty* (Cambridge: Polity Press, 2006).

36. Lauren Langman and Maureen Ryan, "Capitalism and the Carnival Character: The Escape from Reality," *Critical Sociology* 35, no. 4 (2009): 471–492; Thorpe, "The Carnival King of Capital."

37. Chris Hedges, *War is a Force that Gives us Meaning* (New York: Public Affairs, 2014), 7.

38. Weber, "The Protestant Sects and the Spirit of Capitalism," in Hans Gerth and C. Wright Mills eds, *From Max Weber: Essays in Sociology* (New York: Oxford University Press, 1958), 302–322.

39. Norbert Elias, *The Civilizing Process* (Oxford: Wiley-Blackwell, 1994); see also Patrick Carroll, *Science, Culture, and Modern State-Formation* (Berkeley: University of California Press, 2006).

40. Mike Davis, *City of Quartz: Excavating the Future in Los Angeles* (New York: Vintage Books, 1992); Mike Davis and Daniel Bertram Monk eds, *Evil Paradises: Dreamworlds of Neoliberalism.* (New York: New Press, 2007); Michael Sorkin, *Variations on a Theme Park: The New American City and the End of Public Space* (New York: Hill and Wang, 1992).

41. Catarina Kinnvall, "Globalization and Religious Nationalism: Self, Identity, and the Search for Ontological Security," *Political Psychology* 25, no. 5 (2004): 741–767.

42. Nikos Passas, "Global Anomie, Dysnomie, and Economic Crime: Hidden Consequences of Neoliberalism in Russia and Around the World," *Social Justice* 27, no. 2 (Summer 2000): 16–44.

43. Garland, *Culture of Control.*

44. Marcuse, *One-Dimensional Man*; Christopher Lasch, *The Culture of Narcissism: American Life in an Age of Diminishing Expectations* (New York: Norton, 1978).

45. Robert Reiner, "What's Left? The Prospects for Social Democratic Criminology," *Crime, Media, Culture* 8, no. 2 (2012): 135–150, on 141.For cultural sources of violent crime and effects of migration in the US, see Barry Latzer, *The Rise and Fall of Violent Crime in America* (New York: Encounter, 2017). See also John Clegg and Adaner Usmani, "The Economic Origins of Mass Incarceration," *Catalyst* 3, no. 3 (Fall 2019), https://catalyst-journal.com/2019/12/the-economic-origins-of -mass-incarceration.

46. Gary LaFree, *Losing Legitimacy: Street Crime and the Decline of Social Institutions in America* (Boulder, CO: Westview, 1998), 27 (emphasis in original).

47. John Gramlich, "What the Data Says (and Doesn't Say) about Crime in the United States," Pew Research Center, December 20, 2020, https://www.pewresearch .org/fact-tank/2020/11/20/facts-about-crime-in-the-u-s/.

48. LaFree, *Losing Legitimacy*, 172. See also Gary LaFree, Karise Curtis, and David McDowall, "How Effective are our 'Better Angels'? Assessing Country-level Declines in Homicide since 1950," *European Journal of Criminology* 12, no. 4 (2015): 482–504. Cf. Anthony Ellis, "A De-civilizing Reversal or System Normal? Rising Lethal Violence in Post-Recession Austerity United Kingdom," *British Journal of Criminology* 59 (2019): 862–878.

49. Cf. German Lopez, "2020's historic surge in murders, explained," *Vox*, March 25, 2021, https://www.vox.com/22344713/murder-violent-crime-spike-surge -2020-covid-19-coronavirus.

50. Cf. Wendy M. Rahn and John E. Transue, "Social Trust and Value Change: The Decline of Social Capital in American Youth, 1976–1995," *Political Psychology* 19, no. 3 (September 1998): 545–565.

51. Cf. John Pratt, "Towards the Decivilizing of Punishment?" *Social and Legal Studies* 7, no. 4 (December 1998): 487–515.

52. Jennifer Carlson, *Citizen Protectors: The Everyday Politics of Guns in an Age of Decline* (New York: Oxford University Press, 2015); Luigi Esposito and

Laura L. Finley, "Beyond Gun Control: Examining Neoliberalism, Pro-gun Politics and Gun Violence in the United States," *Theory in Action* 7, no. 2 (April 2014): 74–103. Cf. Christa Buschendorf, Astrid Franke, and Johannes Voels, *Civilizing and Decivilizing Processes: Figurational Approaches to American Culture* (Newcastle, UK: Cambridge Scholars Publishing, 2001). On the disintegrative effects of jobless-ness and the low-wage economy, see William Julius Wilson, *When Work Disappears: The World of the New Urban Poor* (New York: Vintage, 1997). See also David G. Blanchflower, *Not Working: Where Have all the Good Jobs Gone* (Princeton: Princeton University Press, 2019).

53. Michael Parenti, *Lockdown America: Police and Prisons in the Age of Crisis* (London: Verso, 2008); Ruth Wilson Gilmore, *Golden Gulag: Prisons, Surplus, Crisis, and Opposition in Globalizing California* (University of California Press, 2007). Elizabeth Hinton, *From the War on Poverty to the War on Crime: The Making of Mass Incarceration in America* (Cambridge, MA: Harvard University Press, 2016); Katherine Beckett and Steve Herbert, *Banished: The New Social Control in Urban America* (Oxford: Oxford University Press, 2011).

54. Stuart Hall, Chas Critcher, Tony Jefferson, John Clarke, and Brian Roberts, *Policing the Crisis: Mugging, the State, and Law and Order* (New York: Holmes and Meier Publishers, 1978).

55. Giroux, "Racial Injustice and Disposable Youth."

56. Thorpe, *Necroculture*, 8; Barry Grey, "Senate Report on Wall Street Crash: The Criminalization of the American Ruling Class," *World Socialist Web Site*, April 18, 2011, https://www.wsws.org/en/articles/2011/04/pers-a18.html; Doug Henwood, "Take Me to Your Leader: The Rot of the American Ruling Class," *Jacobin*, April 27, 2021, https://jacobinmag.com/2021/04/take-me-to-your-leader-the-rot-of-the-ameri-can-ruling-class.

57. Cf. Eileen Leonard, *Crime, Inequality, and Power* (New York: Routledge, 2015).

58. Zygmunt Bauman, *Legislators and Interpreters: On Modernity, Post-Modernity and Intellectuals* (Cambridge: Polity Press, 1987), 51.

59. Charles Derber, *The Wilding of America: Money, Mayhem, and the New American Dream* (New York: Worth Publishers, 2004): 10–11.

60. Derber, *Wilding of America*, 19–20.

61. Derber, *Sociopathic Society* (New York: Routledge, 2015), 4.

62. Derber, *Sociopathic Society*, 62.

63. Henry Giroux, *Beyond the Spectacle of Terrorism: Global Uncertainty and the Challenge of the New Media* (New York: Routledge, 2006); Henry Giroux, *Terror of Neoliberalism: Authoritarianism and the Eclipse of Democracy* (New York: Routledge, 2018); Henry Giroux, *The University in Chains: Confronting the Military-Industrial-Academic Complex* (New York: Routledge, 2015) Henry Giroux, *Twilight of the Social: Resurgent Politics in an Age of Disposability* (New York: Routledge, 2015); Henry Giroux, *The Mouse that Roared: Disney and the End of Innocence* (Lanham, MD: Rowman and Littlefield, 2010); Henry Giroux, *Teachers as Intellectuals: Toward a Critical Pedagogy of Learning* (Praeger, 1988); Henry Giroux, *Theory and Resistance in Education: Pedagogy for the Opposition* (Praeger, 1983).

64. Charles Thorpe, "Violence and the Scientific Vocation," *Theory, Culture and Society* 21, no. 3 (2004): 59–84.

65. Anthony Giddens, *The Nation-State and Violence: Volume II of A Contemporary Critique of Historical Materialism* (Berkeley: University of California Press, 1987).

66. Cf. Alvin W. Gouldner, *The Dialectic of Ideology and Technology: The Origins, Grammar, and Future of Ideology* (New York: The Seabury Press, 1976), 179–209.

67. Saskia Sassen, *Expulsions: Brutality and Complexity in the Global Economy* (Cambridge, MA: The Belknap Press of Harvard University Press, 2014); Philippe Le Billon ed., *The Geopolitics of Resource Wars: Resource Dependence, Governance and Violence* (Abingdon, Oxon: Routledge, 2015).

68. Friedrich Engels, *The Condition of the Working Class in England*, ed. David McLellan (Oxford: Oxford University Press, 1993), 88.

69. Karl Marx, *The Economic and Philosophic Manuscripts of 1844*, ed. Dirk Struik, trans. Martin Milligan (New York: International Publishers, 1964), 122; Thorpe, *Necroculture*, 19.

70. Zygmunt Bauman, *Wasted Lives: Modernity and its Outcasts* (Cambridge: Polity Press, 2004); Giroux, *Stormy Weather*; Thorpe, *Necroculture*, 1–37.

71. Cf. Étienne Balibar, *Violence and Civility: On the Limits of Political Philosophy*, trans. G. M. Goshgarian (New York: Columbia University Press, 2016), 53–54; Remy Yi Siang Low, "Education as/against Cruelty: On Étienne Balibar's Violence and Civility," *Educational Philosophy and Theory* 51, no. 6 (2019): 640–649, on 642.

72. Galtung, Johan. "Violence, Peace, and Peace Research." *Journal of Peace Research* 6, no. 3 (1969): 167–191; Sassen, *Expulsions*.

73. David Noble, "Command Performance: A Perspective on the Social and Economic Consequences of Military Enterprise," in Merritt Roe Smith ed, *Military Enterprise and Technological Change* (Cambridge, MA: MIT Press, 1985), 329–346.

74. Solon, Olivia, "Amazon Patents Wristband that Tracks Warehouse Workers' Movements," *The Guardian,* January 31, 2018, https://www.theguardian.com/technology/2018/jan/31/amazon-warehouse-wristband-tracking.

75. Marx, *Grundrisse*, 704.

76. Charles Derber and Yale R. Magrass, *Bully Nation: How the American Establishment Creates a Bullying Society* (Lawerence, Kansas: 2017); Roddey Reid, "Bullying in US Public Culture, Or, Gothic Terror in the Full Light of Day," *TOPIA: Canadian Journal of Cultural Studies* 20 (Fall 2008): 129–150. Reid, Roddey, 2017. *Confronting Political Intimidation and Public Bullying: A Citizen's Handbook for the Trump Era and Beyond* (Santa Barbara: Amazon Self-Publishing, 2017).

77. Mark Ames, *Going Postal: Rage, Murder and Rebellion* (New York: Soft Skull, 2005); Michael Perelman, *Manufacturing Discontent: The Trap of Individualism in Corporate Society* (London: Pluto Press, 2005).

78. Ryan Moore, *Sells Like Teen Spirit: Music, Youth Culture, and Social Crisis* (New York: New York University press, 2010), 5–6.

79. Pierre Bourdieu, *Acts of Resistance: Against the New Myths of Our Time* (Cambridge: Polity Press, 1998), 1–2; Pierre Bourdieu, "The Invisible Hand of the Powerful," in Pierre Bourdieu ed., *Firing Back: Against the Tyranny of the Market 2*, trans. Loic Wacquant (London: Verso, 2003), 26–37, on 34–35; Thorpe, *Necroculture*, 239–240.

80. Karl Polanyi, *The Great Transformation: The Political and Economic Origins of Our Time* (Boston, MA: Beacon Press, 1957), 139–150.

81. Klausen, *War and Welfare*.

82. Domhoff, *The Corporate Rich*.

83. Klaus Ronneberger,"Contours and Convolutions of Everydayness: On the Reception of Henri Lefebvre in the Federal Republic of Germany," *Capitalism Nature Socialism*, 13, no. 2 (2002): 42–57, on 45.

84. Fromm, *Escape from Freedom*, 166.

85. Naomi Klein, *The Shock Doctrine: The Rise of Disaster Capitalism* (New York: Picador, 2008).

86. Paul Virilio, *Popular Defense and Ecological Struggles* (New York: Semiotexte, 1990), 72.

87. Lenin, V. I. "The State and Revolution," in Robert C. Tucker ed., *The Lenin Anthology* (New York: W. W. Norton and Co., 1975), 311–398, on 316.

88. Lenin, *Imperialism*.

89. Vadim Rogovin, *Stalin's Terror of 1937-1938: Political Genocide in the USSR* (Oak Park, MI: Mehring Books, 2009); Vincent Bevins, *The Jakarta Method: Washington's Anticommunist Crusade and the Mass Murder Program that Shaped Our World* (New York: PublicAffairs, 2020).

90. Bill van Auken, "The US War and Occupation of Iraq—the Murder of a Society," *World Socialist Web Site*, May 19, 2007, https://www.wsws.org/en/articles /2007/05/iraq-m19.html; Bill Van Auken, "The Atrocities of ISIS and the US Wars of Sociocide," *World Socialist Web Site*, August 26, 2015, https://www.wsws.org/en /articles/2015/08/26/pers-a26.html; Keith Doubt, *Sociocide: Reflections on Today's Wars* (Lanham, MD: Rowman and Littlefield, 2021).

91. Jonathan Simon, *Governing Through Crime: How the War on Crime Transformed American Democracy and Created a Culture of Fear* (Oxford: Oxford University Press, 2007).

92. Vidal, "Postfordism as a Dysfunctional Accumulation Regime"; Brenner, *Economics of Global Turbulence*; Chris Harman, *Zombie Capitalism: Global Crisis and the Relevance of Marx* (Chicago, IL: Haymarket Books, 2010).

93. Andrew Gamble, *The Free Economy and the Strong State: The Politics of Thatcherism* (Basingstoke, UK: Macmillan Education, 1988).

94. Editorial, "Covid-19: Social Murder, they Wrote—Elected, Unaccountable, and Unrepentant," *BMJ* (February 4, 2021): 372.

95. Grégoire Chamayou, *Theory of the Drone*, trans. Janet Lloyd (New York: New Press, 2015).

96. Chuck Collins, *The Wealth Hoarders: How Billionaires Pay Millions to Hide Trillions* (Cambridge: Polity Press, 2021).

97. Teeple, *Globalization and the Decline of Social Reform*; Nick Beams, "The Significance and Implications of Globalisation: A Marxist Assessment," *World*

Socialist Web Site, January 4, 1998, https://www.wsws.org/en/articles/1998/01/glob -j04.html.

98. Giddens, *Nation-State and Violence*.

99. Giddens, *A Contemporary Critique*, 236–238.

100. See also Becker, *Denial of Death*; Berger, *Sacred Canopy*; Langman, "From Subject to Citizen to Consumer."

101. Robert H. Wiebe, *Who We Are: A History of Popular Nationalism* (Princeton: Princeton University Press, 2002); Frank Furedi, *Why Borders Matter: Why Humanity Must Relearn the Art of Drawing Boundaries* (London: Routledge, 2020).

102. Thorpe, *Necroculture*, 205–259; Langman and Lundskow, *Gold, Guns, Gold, & Glory*.

103. Eileen Sullivan, Dave Montgomery and Brian Pietsch, "Texas is Ending its Mask Mandate and Will Allow All Businesses to Fully Re-Open," *New York Times*, March 2, 2021, https://www.nytimes.com/2021/03/02/world/greg-abbott -texas-masks-reopening.html.

104. Mukerji, *A Fragile Power*.

Chapter 3

Reason of State in a Global Age

SCIENCE, MARKET, STATE

The fate of sociology is the fate of the research university. If, as Michael Mulkay argued, the Mertonian sociology of science replicated the dominant ideology of the scientific elite, this was because the dominant ideology in the first two postwar decades was, broadly speaking, sociological, correspond-ing with the period of Keynesian economic and social regulation. Sociology provided a secular justification for why the state should fund the research university and why, despite that, the state should not infringe on scientific autonomy. The justification for funding science as a public good depended on some conceptualization of "the public" and this was necessarily the public of a nation-state, corresponding with sociological "society." At the same time, Mertonian sociology of science meshed with broader intellectual currents constituting what David Hollinger has called an ideology of "laissez-faire communitarianism."[1] Sociology provided the ideology that gave a coherent worldview allowing for the self-conscious direction of the institution of the university under conditions of the professionalization of science. Sociology gave the rationale for the university under conditions in which the ideology of pure science needed to be reformulated to take into account the socializa-tion of science, a process which was interconnected with the socialization of labor. The fates of both sociology and the university were tied to that of the nation-state and, in particular, to the scope for social reform within the nation-state.

In the postwar period, sociology provided the intellectual foundation for the core ideology of the university as a relatively autonomous institution that was the seat of power of a relatively autonomous professional-managerial class (the degree of autonomy of which depended on the degree of autonomy

of the university).² The ideology of sociology was the consciousness emanating from this relatively autonomous PMC. The collapse of sociology as
ideology has left science without an ideology and has, accordingly, left the
research university as the core institution of science without an ideology to
justify its occupying this central position. Without an ideology, science is
unable to articulate itself, is assimilated by capital, and is rendered impotent
to address anything like a totality.³

The decline of sociology is, therefore, linked to the decline of what Michel
Foucault called the "universal intellectual" and the rise of the "specific intellectual."⁴ The measurement and understanding of the process of climate
change exemplifies the technical accomplishment of specific intellectuals.
The inability to stop or slow the process exemplifies the impotence of the specific intellectual to address and influence the totality.⁵ Different aspects of the
same process are indicated by Bauman's contrast between the legislator intellectual and the "interpreter." The role of legislator was, as Bauman argued,
inextricably tied to the nation-state and especially to what Bauman called the
"gardening" character of the nation-state. The nation-state as gardener was
also the nation-state as designer, that is, social planner. The garden that was
being produced was society, within the boundaries of the nation-state.

Reformism and mediation have been particularly attached to the image of
scientific objectivity, since this suggests the possibility of reform as a project
that is neutral with respect to the interests of capital and labor. The image of
objectivity, therefore, gives the reformer political room to maneuver as well as
legitimizing their interventions. However, the very neutrality of science potentially threatens the substantive rationality that science promises for reformers.
This point was made perhaps most forcefully by Weber, in his insistence
in "Science as a Vocation" that the application of science is not necessarily
benevolent for humankind and that the true, the good, and the beautiful are
entirely different and separate value-spheres.⁶ Weber was a staunch defender
of the market. A negative evaluation, not only of socialism, but of any kind
of economic planning followed from Weber's accounts of both science and
bureaucracy. According to Weber, the bureaucracy is in itself incapable of
setting ends, which must come from external charismatic sources essentially
antithetical to the rationality of bureaucracy. Weber stood against the reformist project with its distortion of the individualistic rationality that Weber
ascribed to the entrepreneur. Weber's thought tends in the same pessimistic
conservative direction as that, later, of Joseph Schumpeter, both seeing the
development of modern societies as closing down the dynamism that initially
propelled capitalism. Wolfe suggests that it was a feature of imperialism, or
what he calls the "Expansionist State," that saw "the transformation of liberalism from an optimistic to a pessimistic outlook."⁷ Weber's pessimism was an
expression of the turn to conservatism and reaction by liberalism that could

not fulfill its promises to democracy, and that found itself threatened by the democratic forces of the working class that capitalism had unleashed and by the expansion of the state which was its only recourse.

For technocratic progressive reformers, objectivity itself constituted a substantive ethical orientation which connected into and oriented scientifically rational reform toward the common good. The disinterested application of rationality to social problems carried with it an ethos which provided the basis for trust in the ability of the reformer to mediate conflicting interests and to serve the general interest. In this sense, technocratic reformism assumed (explicitly, or, most often, tacitly) a conception of the individual or collective virtue of scientists and professionals.[8] This virtue, expressed in objectivity, provided the seemingly mechanical connection between the formal and substantive rationalities of the governmental-policy-planning system.

Weber, however, refused to accept any logical connection from objectivity to general interest. Rather than the scientist as planner constructing, or working within, a substantively rational system tending toward rational outcomes, Weber proposed a contractor-client model of the engagement of the scientist with social goals. Weber put forward a model of the scientist as being moral in their very amorality: passionately devoted to truth but responsible only to the facts of the matter, not to moral values in any broader sense.[9] Weber's contractor-client model of the scientific vocation significantly fit with the rationality of the market, including its potential irrationality with respect to outcomes when judged by ethical or moral standards, for example, of human well-being, rather than simply by their internal rationality.

Technocratic social reformism, promising a (substantively) rational society, depends for this promise on a tacit or explicit claim to virtue by the bearers of rationality, the scientists or experts. It also has historically depended on an implicit or explicit framework of values and has drawn in the twentieth century on both humanism and nationalism. That is, it has involved the claim that the production of scientific knowledge and its application to human beings and society benefits human beings and increases the level of organization and general material comfort provided by society. The neoliberal version of this claim, shorn of broader humanistic values and detached from the substantive goals of social reformism, is that science contributes to economic growth.

Jan Rehmann argues that Weber was a strategist of bourgeois hegemony under Fordist conditions of which Weber was an early sociological theorist.[10] Weber sought to assert bourgeois hegemony for, and through, the imperialist, military power of the nation-state. For the purposes of imperialism, the working class should be integrated into the polity.[11] Weber absolutely resisted the connection between Fordism and social democracy. Wolfgang Mommsen writes that although Weber moved closer to Social Democratic views toward the end of 1918,

In truth, Weber did not in any way believe in the socialization of the economy either in the near or the distant future . . . To be sure, he believed that, as a result of the present economic emergency, centralist direction of the economy was necessary for the foreseeable future; he saw, with a certain fatalism, that the future would bring a further expansion of bureaucracy and therefore a more strongly "socialized" economy in which entrepreneurial initiative would be more severely confined than in the past. By no means did he see even the glimmer of an ideal in this state of affairs. He remained as loyal as ever to the principle of a *voluntarist* organization of the economic system as far as this was possible. In no way did he share the "belief" in the future of socialism as a new and better social order that was then common among wide sections of the intelligentsia including, among others, Weber's own "students" Schumpeter and Lukács.[12]

Weber opposed the extension of the planning principle beyond the firm to the activities of the left hand of the state in providing for the planning of social good. He was much more favorable to the right-hand power-political necessities of the nation-state. Weber in particular sought to shield science from the implications of its "state capitalist" organizing, preserving its autonomy through discipline and method, while denying its attachment to any values that might make science the bearer of visions of social change.

The technocratic liberalism with which the discipline of sociology has historically been closely enmeshed is torn between an instrumental and value-rational orientation. The promise of liberal reform is bound up with a value-rational orientation derived from humanism and from a conception of "society" as a whole with a common interest (as in "for the benefit of mankind" and "for the good of society"). Yet, the claim to technocratic authority relies on a conception of scientific neutrality that equally has the implications Weber drew out of an entirely amoral science. The sociologists' dilemma between instrumental and value-rationality reflects the existential dilemmas that reemerge in the form of what Giddens calls "life politics." This concept is formulated in reference to Weber's invocation in "Science as a Vocation" of Tolstoy's critique of the meaninglessness of science. Weber concurred with Tolstoy's statement that "Science is meaningless because it gives no answer to our question, the only question important for us: 'What shall we do and how shall we live?' "[13] This provides the basis for Giddens's account of modernity's use of science and technology to suppress the existential dilemma, and for his conception of "life politics" as the politicization of the question "How shall we live?" now released from its containment by modernity.[14]

Weber had looked to the charismatic leader as the vehicle for the introduction of new values that would move the switches of history. The counterpoint to "Science as a Vocation" was his lecture on "Politics as a Vocation" in which he set out the characteristics of the political hero as a man with "his hand on the wheel of history."[15] Weber's belief in the potential of charisma to redeem modernity was linked to his belief in the redemptive power of nationalism. Weber's overarching concern was with how the German bourgeoisie could gain the willpower and perspective necessary to successfully assume state power, which they had hitherto allowed to remain in the hands of the Junker landed aristocracy.[16] For Weber, nationalism offered the key to bourgeois ideological leadership and the source of values in the modern world otherwise excluded by market and bureaucratic relations. The rationalized relations in which the bourgeoisie were embedded in capitalism could not provide them with the spirit of leadership required for political power. Weber's historical study of world religions resolved itself into an assumption of nationalism as the secular religion of the modern bourgeoisie.

In his essay "Beauty: A Study in Bourgeois Aesthetics," Caudwell addresses the claim of the incommensurability of value-spheres, of the kind that Weber asserted, analyzing this idea as a bourgeois assumption arising from the character of market relations, taken for granted by the bourgeois intellectual "reared on the anarchy of the social process." In market relations, values are occluded within "social relations masquerading as laws of supply and demand." The ideology of bourgeois political economy pervades bourgeois thought: "Thus any attempt at social consciousness which necessarily involves the manipulation of desires, i.e. of 'the laws' of supply and demand, seems to him outrageous."[17] Classically, liberal bourgeois thought assumes an atomization of consciousness, rather than social consciousness. Liberalism assumes a natural individualistic anarchy of values which are only rationalized and reconciled by the operations of supply and demand.

Weber was convinced that, in the economic sphere, formal rationality depended on the value-free procedures of the market. Weber's scientific methodology and conception of the scientific vocation are epistemological reflections of the abstract, formal, and alienated relations of the market. That is, Weber's theory of knowledge reflects the appearances of market relations, through the occlusive lens of commodity fetishism, or what Caudwell calls "the ravages of bourgeois unconsciousness." Caudwell observes that through the market, "Labour now becomes, not labour to achieve a goal and attain the desirable, but labour for the market and for cash."[18] The social formation of the buyer and the social formation of the producer, both embodiments of the evolution of human culture, is obscured by the market's substitution of money for the desiring consumer and commodity for the laboring producer. Hence labor appears to be for no purpose. Desires appear to be entirely nonrational, like those of Weber's student who comes to him for advice, but must bring his own *Weltanschauung*, which Weber prohibits himself from challenging, except to put forward " 'inconvenient' facts," certainly not by advocating an alternative worldview or a different purpose.[19] Weber characterized this marketized exchange relationship as that of the American student who thinks buying an education no different from buying a cabbage.[20] This petit-bourgeois Babbitt image sits uneasily, however, alongside Weber's statement that the university has become a "state capitalist" enterprise.[21] The latter would suggest a monopsony buyer, not a marketplace of ideas but state direction of the value-directions in which research is applied.

Weber gave his "Science as a Vocation" lecture on November 7, 1917. It was on this very night that the Bolsheviks stormed the Winter Palace in the October (by the Julian calendar) Revolution in Russia.[22] This was also World War I, in which Fritz Haber's poison gas was killing thousands on the battlefield. Weber's contractor-client model of social science and his rigid separation of science from politics exclude revolutionary fervor that Weber treats as entirely irrational. But it is clear that the "state capitalist" apparatus in which this value-free science was carried out was the German imperialist war machine. And it was the absence of any nonarbitrary standard by which to judge it which was entailed in Weber's advice to the new kind of charismatic political leader he hoped to tutor.

In his 1961 essay "Anti-Minotaur," analyzing the doctrine of value-neutrality, Gouldner emphasizes Weber's nationalism and ideal of science in service to the state. Gouldner writes: "Weber aimed not at curtailing but at strengthening the powers of the German state, and at making it a more efficient instrument of German nationalism."[23] Weber's contradictory conception of the scientist mirrors the contradictory character of his entire conception of reason, as Marcuse points out when he says that Weber's conception of reason "ends in irrational charisma."[24] These epistemological and sociological contradictions, however, are overdetermined by the deeper contradiction between socialized production and private appropriation. Weber was working in, and writing about, the German research university which materially embodied the high level of socialization of the productive forces in the relationships cultivated between university science and Germany's monopoly "state capitalist" cartels. But at the same time, the German university carried an institutional ideology of "pure science," meaning separation from social goals and political power, thereby institutionally obscuring the mutual interdependence of science and the productive forces that these academic institutions embodied. This institutional occlusion of production also reflected the division between intellectual and manual labor under capitalism and the subordination, and indeed effacement or de-conscientization, of manual labor. The academic ethos, standing in sharp contradiction with the reality of its material conditions, reflected the subordination of manual to intellectual labor, the relationship of power which enabled the mind to float free from the constraints of the body and the world, and hence gave rise to the seeming autonomy of science. Existing forms of academic and intellectual autonomy are, therefore, dialectically related to the unfreedom of manual labor.[25]

The very autonomy of science from particular or local interests was highly dependent on the nation-state and bound up with the state's own claim, on which its legitimacy depends, to transcend the conflicting particular interests of the society that it arises from, stands above, and oversees. The notion that science is neutral with respect to values and interests makes science a useful resource for the state. Value-neutrality of science provides legitimation for what Marx called the "idealism of the state," that is, the state's appearance as transcending the competing material interests of civil society.[26] It is axiomatic for the liberal state that its administrative functions should be neutral between the competing parties of civil society.[27] Science is state knowledge in the sense that it coincides with the interest of the state in presenting itself as universal and insofar as it is sponsored by, financially underwritten by, and used by the state. The state appropriates what Chandra Mukerji calls "the voice of science," with its aura of neutrality and objectivity.[28] At the same time, the state reciprocally grants legitimacy to science by giving scientific institutions the imprimatur of official knowledge. States, for example, not only fund but charter universities. Universities have manifold connections with the organs of state power, and to a significant extent are repositories of expertise for use by the state. In that way, Mukerji calls scientists "an elite reserve labor force."[29] Universities cultivate ties to officialdom for economic and political reasons. For this reason, the crisis of scientific authority is also a crisis of nation-state authority.

Ezrahi argues in *The Descent of Icarus* that science played a crucial role in the legitimation of the liberal democratic nation-state because science provided a template for the impersonality of the actions of the bureaucratic state and ensured the neutrality of the knowledge at its disposal.[30] What Ezrahi treats as a cultural shift, beginning in the 1960s, undermining belief in the ideals of impersonality and neutrality has, he argues, eroded the cultural conditions for trust in science. This also produced a legitimation crisis of the nation-state, which could no longer legitimize its programs in terms of norms of universalism and neutrality associated with science. The interconnectedness of the crisis of science with the crisis of the nation-state sheds light on the transformation of the research university. The institutional crisis of the research university, manifested in the breaking down of its humanistic legitimation and in the erosion of institutional boundaries by commercialization, is integrally related with globalization.

In "On the Jewish Question," Marx explained that the separation of state from church constituted an incomplete emancipation from religiosity. This was exemplified by the United States, in which a secular state coincided with the thriving of religion in private life and in civil society. As Tocqueville had noted, outside of public institutions America was "pre-eminently the land of religiosity." Therefore, Marx argued, political emancipation from religion was only the emancipation of the state, not of the human being: "The *state* can thus emancipate itself from religion even though the *overwhelming majority* is still religious. And the overwhelming majority does not cease being religious by being religious *in private*."[31] This goes to show that human emancipation must be understood as broader than a merely political form of freedom. Fully human emancipation, Marx argued, entailed overcoming the separations embodied in the divisions of the world and the human being between civil society and state:

> Only when the actual, individual man has taken back into himself the abstract citizen and in his everyday life, his individual work, and his individual relationships has become a *species-being*, only when he has recognized and organized his own powers as *social* powers so that social force is no longer separated from him as *political* power, only then is human emancipation complete.[32]

What Marx argued about political freedom and the state applies also to intellectual freedom and the university.

The ideology of value-free science, and the closely linked idea of academic freedom, ideas central to the self-legitimation of the modern research university, represent just this kind of partial emancipation, creating a set of demarcations around the activity of knowledge production and marking institutional boundaries and divisions within the self. Academic freedom is generally understood as protecting knowledge production and expression within the university from external influences and pressures, especially from politics and religion. This is closely aligned with and supported by the idea of value-free science, the idea that scientific knowledge of fact is properly demarcated from value-considerations of what ought to be. Preserving value-freedom is understood to be part of the function of the demarcation of the university as a bounded institution committed to secular knowledge production. Value-freedom also assumes boundaries within the self of the knowledge producer. It means that a scientist's personal commitments, especially moral, religious, and political, must be psychologically walled off from their attention to facts of the matter. Value-freedom, therefore, assumes a demarcation of the self into distinct roles, above all, a separation of the professional from the personal. It calls for the individual themselves to be split along the lines of dualisms of reason versus emotion, mind versus body, and fact versus value. Hence Gouldner presented Weber as the embodiment of the dualistic consciousness of value-freedom: "a magnificent minotaur named Max—Max Weber, to be exact."[33]

The form of emancipation represented by academic freedom and value-free science corresponds to that embodied in the kind of political emancipation criticized by Marx. There is a close historical relationship: the "freedom" of science from religion embodied in the secular university is historically intertwined with the development of the modern secular state and the growing involvement of the state in education and science. In America, the secular character of public research universities follows from the separation of church and state. In the same way that public institutions in America coincide with a highly religious civil society and the significant role of religion in private life, the secular university exists in America in an uneasy relationship with the influence of religion in the broader society and culture. The state makes possible and protects the existence of institutions of science in separation from competing values, and value-neutrality of science supports the "idealism of the state."[34] The objective view from nowhere of science makes possible the state's eye view of society.[35] For this to be possible, of course, the state must be seen as supporting but not influencing science.[36]

Marx argued that political emancipation was not only partial, but also illusory: the state is under the sway of the ruling powers in civil society. The state therefore is an expression of alienated power.[37] It is evident that partial freedom similarly negates itself in intellectual life. To the extent that the emancipation of knowledge takes place in separation from human emancipation, and a more general articulation of human needs, it is experienced as a compulsive development: in terms such as the technological imperative, autonomous technique, or technics-out-of-control.[38] Further, the very separation of science from social needs that is mandated by the ideology of value-freedom facilitates the appropriation and shaping of science by capital.[39] If detached from a broader emancipation of human individuals as fully social beings, intellectual freedom represents the unfettering of *estranged* human capacities. Hence, technical progress, detached from human emancipation, is experienced as a form of compulsiveness.[40]

"SCIENCE AS A VOCATION" AND THE PARADOXES OF CAPITALIST RATIONALIZATION

Weber articulated what was the dominant self-conception of the sciences and the dominant ideology of the modern university: a rigorously instrumentalized conception of knowledge. "Science as a Vocation" is about demarcations and boundaries between incommensurable value-spheres, between institutions representing these different value-spheres, and within the self a set of boundaries that reflect these conceptual and institutional divisions. This meant strict demarcations within the self of professional from personal, intellectual from moral, and emotion from reason. Weber's advice to the scientist was to "put on blinders."[41] Science is constructed as a distinct role, demarcated *within* the living individual.

However, these demarcations were accompanied by Weber's contradictory urge precisely to link science with the individual, to reconnect knowing with being. So even as he established boundaries between the scientist's professional role and all other commitments, he also insisted that pursuing science as a vocation was not merely "cold calculation" but instead meant "passionate devotion" to the task. Weber's contradictory position of disconnecting and then attempting to reconnect knowing with being expressed contradictions endemic to his broader project of setting out the historical tasks of the German bourgeoisie. "Science as a Vocation" must be understood alongside the lecture on "Politics as a Vocation" that he gave a year later. In the latter, Weber set out his vision of political leadership that corresponded with his notion of the historical mission of the bourgeoisie through a form of liberal imperialism. In "Science as a Vocation," Weber presents rationality as operating only within a domain—the choice between value commitments is an irrational leap of faith. Science can never justify itself—to choose any value-orientation, including that toward science constitutes a nonrational leap of faith. In "Politics a Vocation," Weber insisted on the essentially irrational character of politics, as an activity inseparable from violence and beset with unintended consequences of violence. Whereas Weber insisted that charismatic leadership had no place in science or the university, political leadership was par excellence the realm of charisma. Weber's ideal political leader was a charismatic decider.

In line with his political project, Weber tried to hold together an insistence on the preservation of the formal rationality that he saw perfectly expressed in the "free market" and the maintenance of barriers to any extension of rationalization that would undermine the political vocation of the bourgeoisie. The success of the bourgeoisie would be indicated by the class's ability to give rise to charismatic leaders capable of exerting a will to power with world-historical consequences. The class vocation of the bourgeoisie translated into, firstly, the replacement of Junker control over the state with liberal democracy and, secondly, the struggle against socialism. Weber embraced democracy just to the extent that it furthered this vocation. As Lukács put it, "he regarded democracy as the form most suited to the imperialist expansion of a major modern power."[42] These twin aspects of the mission of bourgeoisie corresponded to Weber's interest in (a) the formulation and defense of the formal rationality of the market and closely related to this, the instrumental rationality of science and (b) the shaping of the self through the calling and the emergence of the charismatic leader in politics.[43] Weber needed to assert the demarcation between, and preserve the purity of, these domains: he presented politics as a realm of will and violence in contrast with the marketplace and science as the realms of reason. The charismatic political leader and nationalism go together as Weber's solution to meaning and emotional bonds, filling in the lacunae left by rationalization, as sources of spirit in a spiritless world.

Weber's conception of science as a vocation was expressive both of market relations and alienated labor. Weber regarded the market as a paradigmatic system of formal rationality which excluded and was opposed to frameworks of value-rationality. In support of his conception of capitalism as the historical apex of rationality, Weber drew on the anti-Marxist marginal utility theory of Eugen Böhm-Bawerk. Kieran Allen writes:

> In *Economy and Society*, Weber explicitly supported Bohm-Bawerk and made the concept of "utility" the cornerstone of his theory of economic action . . . Behind this rather abstract theorizing, there was a notion that society was a collection of individual interests who were connected through the market . . . Bohm-Bawerk and Weber . . . took the ideological image of man in a market society as an isolated, selfish soul and generalised it throughout all history.[44]

Weber wrote in *Economy and Society*, "From a purely technical point of view, money is the most 'perfect' means of economic calculation. That is, it is formally the most rational means of orienting economic activity."[45] Weber argued that, in contrast, planning epitomized substantive rationality in the economic field, and therefore planning threatened to introduce distortions in the economy: "Where a planned economy is radically carried out, it must further accept the inevitable reduction in formal, calculatory rationality which would result from the elimination of money and capital accounting." The more value-oriented economic activity becomes, the less formally rational. As Guenther Roth has shown, Weber was committed to the "free market," a commitment that reflected and expressed his social position within what Roth calls the "cosmopolitan bourgeoisie." At the University of Vienna in 1918, Weber argued against what he saw as the obvious temptation for Germany to print paper money to wipe out war debts and foreign loans by means of inflation. Basing money on precious metals was necessary to maintain monetary stability. Roth writes,

> Weber acknowledged that paper (or administrative) money was the most suitable means to pursue substantive (*material*) social ideals, which included Communist and Fascist ones, whereas the formal rationality of the market economy was oriented primarily to profitability, currency stability, and exchange parity.[46]

To allow political control over the economy would, as John Patrick Diggins puts Weber's view, "deny capitalism an accounting of its own rationality."[47]

The tension between market and state has deep roots in Weber's thought: it was a tension endemic to Weber's outlook of liberalism and German nationalism. Weber was attached politically to liberal ideals of the free market and liberal democracy (both expressing formal rationality) and to a value-framework of German nationalism. The tension between rationality and irrational blind commitment at the heart of Weber's essays on vocation was also inherent in Weber's liberal nationalism. Weber exemplifies how free market liberalism and nationalism, as the two central components of bourgeois social thought, find their bourgeois resolution in imperialism, that is, in the integration of the interests of capital with the power-political interests of the nation-state.[48]

While he defended the formal rationality of the market, the exclusion of noneconomic values from the calculus of the market was a source of concern to Weber from the perspective of political attachment to the nation-state. As Diggins argues, in Weber's early work on rural economics, he suggested the incompatibility between market-oriented values and duty to the state. The Junker aristocracy, now increasingly taking on capitalist attitudes, had proven themselves unfit as bearers of national interest by their hiring of Polish workers. Weber saw the influx of foreign workers as a threat to Germany's national territorial integrity and indicative of the decline of the patriotism of the Junker class in favor of their own developing capitalist interests. His conception of the threat to national interests was also a racialized understanding of the nation. He argued that, as patrimonial bonds of responsibility and duty broke down in the countryside with the shift toward capitalist agriculture, German peasants were "abandoning their homeland to a race which stands on a lower level."[49]

Weber's concern with calling and the shaping of self has to be seen in the context of his liberal imperialism. Harvey Goldman situates Weber in relation to the crisis of bourgeois culture:

> Although class practices and cultural ideals had helped hold the increasingly bourgeois social order together and guide individual life choices, these were now threatened by social and cultural changes: rising social mobility and the sharpening of class conflict, the intensification of capitalist competition, the pace of developments in science and technology, the advances of technique and rationalization into every sector of life, the imperatives of specialization in a period of mass education, and the pressures of the market in every form.[50]

The older bourgeois cultural ideals and moral codes were not suited to providing the bourgeois class with the inner strength and commitment required to be a ruling class. To do this meant to assume responsibility over the state and the demands of carrying Germany's imperialist interests in military competition with other imperialist powers. The individual problem of self (and therefore the existentialist dimension of Weber's writing) was, for Weber, at the same time the problem of bourgeois class power and the imperial strength of the German nation.[51]

The discrediting of the Junker class made both possible and necessary the political calling of the middle class. The bourgeois class had to emerge as ruling class. But Weber's model for the ruling class was aristocratic. Hence, his essays on vocation were a clearing of the way for a new quasi-aristocratic Machiavellianism of the middle class by discrediting and disavowing the moralistic cultural orientation of the nineteenth-century middle class.[52] Weber rejected the German Enlightenment concept of *Bildung*, or individual self-cultivation through education. In "the struggle of the 'specialist type of man' against the older type of 'cultivated man'," Weber took the side of the specialist.[53] "Science as a Vocation," with its call to "put on blinders," advocated a new mode of self-formation that was more compulsive, less contemplative, and also depleted of substantive morality, while moralizing narrow commitment itself.[54]

Weber's rationalism as an advocate of value-free science was complementary with his glorification of war as a source of human meaning and a source of identity of the German nation:

> The American who is now fighting in the West knows actually nothing wherefore he dies. But *our* soldiers *know it*, and that is the majestic thing, that the German war has this emotion, to fight and bleed for the native country and the security of the land.[55]

This is Weber's reactionary resolution of the contradiction between capitalist organization and disorganization. The advance of capitalist organization, leading to bureaucratization, was undermining the autonomous individual bourgeois character. At the same time, meaning could be found in the submersion of the individual in the collective in nationalism and in war—in collective emotion, melee, and blood. Nationalism served Weber as a reservoir for those values and emotions excluded from the formal rationality of the market and the instrumental rationality of science. War was the necrophilic version of the anti-rationalist, Dionysian values that Weber found fascinating among the middle-class anarchists, libertines, and utopians in the retreat of Asconsa, Switzerland.[56]

Nationalism was the overall framework of meaning for Weber's prescriptions for the self. His notions of character, will, self-discipline, and maturity had to do with shaping a middle class that had the capacity for rule. In his emphasis on qualities of hardness, strength, and discipline, Weber was in the mainstream of the Wilhelmine bourgeoisie. He followed the trajectory of the

German bourgeoisie in his rejection of the moralism and the apolitical attachment to culture that characterized bourgeois thought and outlook under the influence of the German Enlightenment. Instead, Weber, like the mainstream of the German bourgeoisie after 1871, assimilated and adopted much of the habitus or orientation of the aristocracy. Elias described the shift as follows: "parts of the German middle class were assimilated into the higher-ranking stratum and made its warrior ethos their own. But in the course of being adapted, this aristocratic code was transformed. To put it briefly, it became 'bourgeoisified.' " The bourgeoisie intellectualized the aristocratic code of honor and violence: "Seldom before had so much been said and written in praise of power, even of the violent sort." Nietzsche, an important influence on Weber's irrationalist conception of politics, was, Elias argues, chief philosophical proponent of this bourgeois "romanticization of power."[57] In "Politics as a Vocation," Weber cathected this intellectualized romanticization of violence, the capacity for which is equated with masculine maturity and resoluteness.

In opposition to the earlier middle-class code of "virtue" rather than "honor," Weber followed the merger of middle-class and aristocratic norms by moralizing violence as responsibility, presenting the capacity for violence as the ethical duty of the mature man: "He who seeks the salvation of the soul, of his own and others, should not seek it along the avenue of politics, for the quite different tasks of politics can only be solved by violence." Irrational conviction, backed up by responsible violence was, for Weber, "immensely moving . . . something genuinely human and moving."[58] "Politics as a Vocation" was an exercise in tutoring the middle class, particularly middle-class youth, on what it was to act as a ruling class. What was wrong with the attitude of the German middle class, according to Weber, was its failure to adequately follow the aristocratic model. Since unification, the middle class had acquiesced in Junker leadership. With Junker domination of the state bureaucracy and the military, the middle class had in Weber's view become passive and directionless. The middle class's failure to constitute itself as a leadership group had become a crisis now that the old aristocratic elite was proving itself no longer adequate as a ruling class. Goldman writes:

"Politics as a Vocation" is his version of *The Prince*, an attempt to persuade the German nation of the need for a leader with an ascetic and empowered self, independent and autonomous, capable of giving energy and direction to the nation in its political struggles. Indeed, despite the tendency to see Weber as a power-political Machiavellian, Weber actually reconnects "statecraft" and "soulcraft" and is thus more reminiscent of Plato and Christian thinkers before Machiavelli. Weber wants to shape persons and institutions for "domination," given the realities of mass politics and imperial competition.[59]

The bourgeois prince is the embodiment and concentrated expression of bourgeois freedom—the autonomous individual. Bourgeois freedom is now expressed not only on the market but in the organized and directed form of state power. Weber's longed-for charismatic political leader is the embodiment of the bourgeois nation-state and the personalization of bourgeois hegemony. This figure carries bourgeois freedom out of and beyond the trap of the iron cage. "Politics as a Vocation" adopts a conception of politics that resonates with the aristocratic conception of state activity. It is characterized by Machiavellianism, or so-called realism, regarding power relations but also, as Goldman argues, an argument for how the realistic exercise of political power can carry existential meaning for individuals in service of the nation.

Politics, Weber insists, is the use of violence. The figure for whom Weber is writing is the head of state, the prince, who has warrior virtues as a wielder of violence. This figure is the locus of agency or decision-making. Weber's argument against the ethic of absolute values can be read as an argument against the moralism and self-distancing from power that characterized classical German bourgeois thought. His argument for an ethic of responsibility can be read as addressing the problem of how to balance the demands of power with classical bourgeois values. The major thrust of Weber's argument is to urge the middle class to accept the necessity of wielding violence and hence a role as bearers and defenders of the national interest. Responsibility means the necessity of viewing oneself as the agent of politics—in other words, not relying on another class to take over such difficult decisions.

The argument of "Science as a Vocation" intersects with, and complements, that of "Politics as a Vocation." A key feature of both essays is a denigration of moralism as a form of immaturity and a failure to take responsibility. Weber's prescription for value-free science can be seen as instrumentalizing cultural values. It preserves the nineteenth-century associations that pitted culture against politics, in the sense that science is preserved as a cultural sphere external to politics and political intrusions in science are vigorously resisted. In politics, words are "swords against the enemies: such words are weapons."[60] It would be an outrage to use words in this way in the lecture theatre. Yet, Weber's conception of science was an instrumentalization of cultural values that rendered knowledge and culture as tools that could be used by the political leader or the state. By purifying the realms of politics and intellectual life, he suggested how the latter could more fruitfully come to serve the former.

Concern for the bourgeoisie's self-assertiveness and sense of purpose as a class—the molding of bourgeois political will—was the essential meaning of Weber's attention to the calling. The splitting of knowing from being, and attempts at reconnection in "Science as a Vocation" follow from this. The distinction between science and politics was aimed at preserving not only the purity of science as a realm of objectivity, but also the purity of politics as a realm of charismatic will. Marcuse quotes Weber's exclamation that "I cannot bear problems of world-shaking importance . . . being turned into a technical 'question of productivity.' "[61] Confusion between politics as a vocation and science as a vocation would dilute political will between these domains, detracting from the concentration of will in the leader. It would also result in the corruption of science as instrumental expertise. On the other hand, Weber recognized the importance of science to the state and to the bourgeois project. He resisted the kind of political corruption of academia that he saw in the "Althoff system," with the Prussian Minister of Culture determining university appointments, and that he also saw manifested in political disruption of the lecture theatre by students.[62] It was important to preserve the integrity of science so that it could serve the state as instrumental expertise.

A corrupt science was for Weber a kind of corruption of the self. Science, if pursued with integrity, could also be an activity that expressed the mission of the bourgeoisie, the inner-worldly asceticism of the calling. The power of the bourgeoisie was in the world. Work was a means of transcending the banality of everyday life, within everyday life. Weber wrote, "one may also see the fabulous capacity of work, the superbness and matter-of-factness, the capacity—not the attainment—of beautifying everyday life, in contrast to the beauty of ecstasy or of the gestures of other nations."[63] In contrast to the mystical contemplative appreciation of nature, the bourgeois project beautified everyday life, the second nature of society. The calling was a vehicle for transcendence, or group charisma, for the bourgeoisie.[64] The calling was a means through which to dominate the world.[65] The emotional hardness of hard science was the perfect complement to the charismatic will of the politician. And indeed, political will required rational technique for its actualization. Hence, Weber was concerned to preserve the integrity of science as an orientation to the world that was complementary to power.

Weber's insistence on the separation of science from other value-spheres rested not only on the logical separation of fact from value, but also on a sociological description of the character of the university. The university was empirically the sort of environment appropriate to the pursuit of disenchanted, instrumental knowledge, not the formation of charismatic insight: "Science today is a 'vocation' organized in special disciplines in the service of self-clarification and knowledge of interrelated facts. It is not the gift of grace of seers and prophets dispensing sacred values and revelations, nor does it partake of the contemplation of sages and philosophers about the meaning of the universe."[66] The university was increasingly "Americanized," that is, bureaucratized. And it was axiomatic in Weber's thinking that bureaucracy and pure charisma were mutually exclusive opposites. So Weber says: "The large institutes of medicine or natural sciences are 'state capitalist' enterprises, which cannot be managed without very considerable funds." In these institutes, the worker is separated "from his means of production." And the relationship between the assistant and the head of the institute replicates the dependence of "the employee in a factory upon the management."[67] This indicates, Shapin argues, that "at the beginning of the twentieth century the identity of the scientist was radically unstable. To be a scientist was *still* something of a calling but it was *becoming* something of a job."[68] Weber's use of "state capitalism" was particularly relevant to the context of World War I. State capitalism was arguably epitomized by the German wartime economy.[69] Weber's reference to the institutes of medicine and natural science also seems particularly apt given the wartime context of the connections between Fritz Haber's Kaiser-Wilhelm Institute for Physical Chemistry, the IG Farben chemical cartel, and the military demand for wartime products such as chemical weapons. Weber was writing at the time of the formation of the prototypical "military-industrial-academic complex."[70]

Weber's attitude toward state capitalist organization in academia fit both with his pessimism about the march of bureaucratization and with his commitment to market capitalism. Weber's concern for the autonomy of the scientist paralleled opposition to state interventionism by German employers who saw wartime controls as carrying the danger of creeping "state socialism."[71] Roth notes that, after the end of the war, Weber

[o]n various occasions . . . opposed the moves toward *Gemeinwirtschaft*, that is, socialized or collectivized economy. He objected to the efforts to socialize key industries . . . He wanted to see the war economy end quickly and the currency stabilized as soon as possible.[72]

The contradiction was that, while imperialist war made state control of the economy necessary, the capitalist foundations of imperialism depended on market exchange. Weber had no way out of this contradiction except to wish for wartime measures to be short-lived.[73] Weber's concern for the autonomy of the academic calling was bound up with his broader political opposition to state encroachment. Weber associated the state capitalist organization of academia with potential for political intervention in academic life as under the Althoff system.[74]

Alongside his image of the "state capitalist enterprise," Weber puts forward a different conception of the social role of the academic—exemplified by an American attitude: In "Science as a Vocation," Weber presents the student as a "client" and the teacher (of politics or sociology) as being like a small businessman selling his services on the market. This is, to Weber, the grain of truth in the Americans' idea that the teacher sells me his knowledge and his methods for my father's money, just as the greengrocer sells my mother cabbage . . . And no young American would think of having the teacher sell him a *Weltanschauung* or a code of conduct.[75]

Rehmann argues that Weber's 1904 to 1905 visit to America left him with the impression of "an 'Americanist' formation of capitalism that seem[ed] to [him] superior to the German condition" and from which he sought to draw lessons.[76] Weber discusses what the teacher can do when someone comes to them with a value-choice—the teacher can aid in clarification:

If you take such and such a stand, then, according to scientific experience, you have to use such and such a *means* . . . Does the end "justify" the means? Or does it not? The teacher can confront you with the necessity of this choice. He cannot do more.[77]

"Science as a Vocation" puts forward a conception of professionalism that is in tension between a definition of the academic in the role of civil servant as a "privileged hireling of the state" and the American conception of the academic as a petty retailer of knowledge directly selling expertise to clients on the market. The "greengrocer" image operates for Weber both as an attack on the pretensions of academics who sought to put forward a worldview, and also as an image of formal market rationality counteracting the specter of direct political interference in the academic role. The image of the greengrocer is a model of the formal rationality of the market, in which instrumental expertise is available to a multiplicity of ends. In that sense, it counteracts the monopolization of expertise by the state in which the dominance of a narrower framework of ends could penetrate the academic calling in the form of political interference.

The American student's insistence on treating the professor as a petit-bourgeois retailer is crucial to the way in which Weber holds back the specter of planning that is an unstated implication of state capitalism for the intellectual role. As Marcuse argues, Weber's conception of scientific neutrality was closely aligned with his ideal image of the formal rationality of the market. This connection is further explored by King and Szelényi who argue that the ideology of professionalism (of which the Weberian notion of value-free expertise is the core) expresses a *market* contractual relationship between the professional and the client. Here they contrast the manager as an expert/professional in a market economy and the bureaucrat as planner in a state socialist economy. The job of the planner, unlike the manager, is not just to allocate surplus as investment, but to

decide on the direction of the extended reproduction of the system . . . While, under market capitalism, the expert/professional manager knows how to sail when the wind blows, under state socialism, at least in principle, it is the scientific planner who blows the sail![78]

The overcoming of purely formal rationality is, the authors argue, the motivation for the planned economy since it represents an attempt to replace the anarchy of the market with an orientation toward rational goals. Planning attempts to overcome the market's prioritization of exchange value and to distribute effort on the basis of, to use Marx's words, "social need, that is the use-value on a social scale."[79]

Primary attention to use-values in planning necessarily brings value-orientation to the fore: what are legitimate and good uses? A planned economy is supposed "to overcome the domination of techne over telos and create a society in which rationally selected goals would guide the economy."[80] In practice, this has rarely been the case. Since existing planned economies operate within a world system of economic and military competition, economic and technological growth and military-technological force become ends in themselves and planning tends to be reduced to guidance of a process of forced industrialization. The anarchy of the market is overcome but the despotism in the workshop extends throughout society, with society conceived of by technocrats as, to quote Boris Kagarlitsky, " 'one big factory' in which all questions are resolved through administrative-technical means."[81] Nevertheless, planning at least muddies the distinction between techne and telos and this was at the root of Weber's dislike for planning as a distortion of formal rationality.

King and Szelényi argue that the status and legitimacy of the professional in a market society is tied to "the domination of techne over telos." Therefore, under market capitalism, "the central ideology of the intellectual stratum is professionalism . . . [which] emphasizes knowhow, is based on 'formal rationality,' and expresses the spirit of legal/rational authority and rules that regulate market economies."[82] Deliberation over ends is outside the purview of the professional precisely because the professional stands in a market relationship with a client. The client contracts the professional to solve a problem: the client sets the goal, the professional provides the technical solution. As King and Szelényi note, this relationship is expressed in Weber's formulations of social scientific objectivity as value-neutrality. The job of the social scientist is to tell people what they *can* do, not what they *ought* to do.[83] The image of a market relationship between professional and client is fundamental to Weber's conception of the relationship between science and values. However, this market relationship produces exactly the type of "specialists without spirit" the modern prevalence of which Weber lamented, because the professional must sell expertise detached from any worldview or spirit.[84]

Weber's account of science is informed by an extreme individualism, valorization of metaphysically undetermined individual will, and a corresponding negative conception of freedom (as freedom from external interference). Weber's conception of value-judgments is highly individualistic. The individual must choose what for him is a god and what a devil.[85] As Lukács put it, Weber "raised the consciousness of the solitary individual to the status of an inappellable arbitrator."[86] The assumption of the individual will as radically free in the sense of being undetermined is intimately related to the way in which social relations are mediated by the market. This has been explored by Caudwell, who argues that bourgeois thought is characterized by a radical split between subject and object as a split between freedom and necessity. This division corresponds to the relationship between desire and production as mediated by the market. Caudwell writes:

> Man is the subject; Nature is the object. Therefore in bourgeois society, the object appears solely as "things" over which man has rights, and whose laws or "necessity" he discovers in order to satisfy his desires. These desires appear arbitrarily proposing an end for Nature to satisfy, and by exploring the necessity of Nature, they are satisfied.
>
> Notice that these desires for products appear spontaneously, and the products, having been formed, disappear. The desires come out of the blind market, and vanish into it. And yet the market veils the desires of Man, his whole active relation to Nature, as a conative creature, and veils also the satisfaction of those desires, which take place behind the same screen.[87]

Nature—the object of production and the object of science—appears as the realm of necessity, subject to causal law. Human desire appears, in contrast, as uncaused and spontaneous. As Caudwell puts it: "man's desires emerge from the night of the market and are realized through the machine as products, which vanish again into the night."[88] This description perfectly corresponds to Weber's conception of the relationship between human goals or desires and science. Value-oriented questions arise spontaneously in the individual who brings the scientist a problem. The scientist provides an objective answer, which then is taken away, disappearing again into the night as a "use" of science. Human goals, desires, demands appear purely spontaneously and arbitrarily. These are walled off from scientific inquiry as to their causes, and science is walled off from their influence. The origin of these goals, desires, demands remains obscure.

It is significant that Weber stands out in classical sociological theory as insisting on a subject-object split in the sense of demarcation between ideas and material forces. Indeed, the adoption of Weber in American sociology as an antidote to Marxist materialism is precisely with reference to his insistence on treating ideas as causally efficacious in history, combined with his opposition to treating ideas as themselves caused. Hence in his analogy, if material interests power the train of history—ideas are the switchmen that may change the direction of that train. To ask why ideas emerge to throw the switch one way rather than another is beyond the scope of Weberian sociology.[89] And indeed, this is the place in Weber's sociology for the charismatic leader. The charismatic leader is the concentrated expression of the individual agencies of the followers, who in their submission give up their agency to the leader, who becomes the individual personification and fulfillment of the bourgeois ideal of the metaphysically free agent.[90] Human desire appears in the form of the mysterious charismatic leader—and scientific objectivity is there not to question his desires but to serve them. Caudwell argues:

> In fact man's desires are also subject to necessity. They change with history, with the change of methods of production and corresponding alterations in the superstructure of society. Yesterday a Roman glutton; to-day an Egyptian hermit. But all this causation of desire in society is hidden by the basic form of modern society, in which desires emerge from the blind market.[91]

Desires are not spontaneous but are themselves socially caused.

Weber's analogy with the "greengrocer" ties the scientist as professional to the petty bourgeois retailer selling on the market. But his image of state capitalism indicates the erosion of the market as a result of the concentration of capital in advanced conditions. There is an important difference between the image of the scientist as an employee of a state capitalist enterprise and the image of the scientist as a retailer of knowledge in a market relationship with a client. The difference corresponds to the dual aspects of capitalism as described by Marx: "anarchy in the social division of labour and despotism in the manufacturing division of labour."[92] Both of these facets of capitalism militate against the ability to make judgments of ends. The anarchy of the market means that the selection of ends is impersonal and abstract. Bauman observes, "Intellectuals (like anybody else) have no control over market forces and cannot realistically expect to acquire any."[93] In the case of the employee, ends are imposed within a hierarchical relationship of command. Hence, the scientist as employee experiences a loss of autonomy. The petit-bourgeois image of the greengrocer is, therefore, important since it implies the maintenance of bourgeois autonomy within an abstract set of relations. But in comparison with state capitalism, the greengrocer appears as a nostalgic image. The sense that bourgeois autonomy is doomed to disappear is the recurrent nightmare that leaves residues throughout Weber's thought. The famous image of the iron cage expresses the way in which Weber is defensive against the very Western rationalism that he champions.

Weber's treatment of rationality is paradoxical.[94] On the one hand, rational capitalism must be defended against its socialist challengers who are, almost by definition for Weber, at odds with reason: Karl Leibknecht belonged in a "madhouse" and Rosa Luxemburg in a "zoo."[95] As Marcuse put it, for Weber, "Socialism contradicted the idea of Western Reason and the idea of the Nation-State—therefore it was a world-historical error, if not a world-historical crime."[96] The cultivation of the political vocation of the bourgeoisie was necessary for the defense of Western Reason and the Nation-State. On the other hand, the vocation of the bourgeoisie required limiting rationalization—maintaining politics as a realm for the exercise of will. As Marcuse put it, "Weber's concept of reason ends in irrational charisma."[97] Weber maintains politics as the sphere of the nonrational, focused ultimately on the power interests of the state that are posited a priori as the ultimate value.

Reason of state is the point of convergence of instrumental value-free science and nonrational politics. Politics provides science a priori with the ultimate values which it serves within the research university. Hence, Weber wrote in "The National State and Economic Policy," "For us in this national state the ultimate standard of value even for reflection on political economy is *Staatsraison*."[98] Goldman writes that Weber was putting forward "the elevation of the nation into a holy cause."[99]

Hence, nationalism provides Weber with a channel for the religious value of the calling, but in secular form. Goldman writes that "In Weber's analysis of the nature of empowered leaders, the calling and 'charisma' are inextricably linked."[100] The charismatic leader is the concentrated embodiment of the calling, which is the source of the strength of the bourgeois class, the charisma of the bourgeoisie. Nationalism provided a channel through which charisma and calling could reenter the modern world. But this went along with a tragic view of the fate of charisma, since the advance of rationalization undercuts its conditions for existence. Since charisma "serves him as a metaphysical vehicle of man's freedom in history," rationalization is cast by Weber in tragic terms and associated with the loss of autonomy.[101] The preservation of the bourgeois individual as an autonomous, choosing subject is bound up with the rationality of the market but threatened by the advance of rationality beyond a narrow domain. This reflects the self-defeating nature of market freedom in which the "autonomous" petit-bourgeois greengrocer is inevitably replaced by the monopoly (or "state capitalist") enterprise. As George Orwell said, "the trouble with competitions is that somebody wins."[102]

This paradoxical defense of, and against, rationalization also conditions Weber's views about science. Weber's language is shot through with ambivalence: intellectualism is the "worst devil" but "one has to see the devil's ways to the end."[103] So what Weber gives us is a strictly limited conception of reason: narrow specialization that requires putting "blinders" on and an instrumental conception of knowledge that requires that ends be set externally and that human wants, needs, and desires mysteriously appear before science and, once satisfied, disappear from it just as mysteriously.

THE SELF-NEGATION OF AUTONOMOUS SCIENCE

Marcuse's critique of the illusory character of Weber's insistence on value-free science mirrors Marx's attack on the partial character of political emancipation. The modern liberation of knowledge that is celebrated by liberal thinkers as freeing intellectual life from political constraints and from distortions imposed by religion, preconceived morality, and so on establishes a form of intellectual activity that is inherently unable to question the ends that it serves. These ends must be set from outside. Hence this science becomes the victim and assistant of the dominant social powers. The very evacuation of (explicit) values and interests from science creates a disembedded form of intellectual activity that is less able to resist, and is more useful to, the dominant powers of capital and the state. The very insistence on the separation between reason and values generates a form of rational intellectual life that is timid of overt political involvement for fear of contaminating its own domain-specific rationality. This is a compulsory neutrality motivated by the fear of losing professional authority.

Weber's lecture on "Science as a Vocation" articulated what has become the dominant ideology of the research university. This is a dimension of Alasdair MacIntyre's observation that "The present age and its presentation of itself is dominantly Weberian."[104] The dominant academic ideology is an idea of the neutrality of technology as a set of value-neutral tools, from which it follows that the accumulation and advancement of technology is inherently beneficial—the more and better tools we have the better we can realize our goals. Hence technological progress is equated with human progress. The dominant discourse of the contemporary research university is, therefore, a breathless enthusiasm for technology.[105]

The technological orientation of the university accompanies a denial of responsibility for ends and a detachment of intellectual life from the shaping of the goals and values of the broader society. A particular expression of this detachment is the United States, in which the secular character of the university coexists with the influence of religion in civil society and in the shaping of social consciousness and molding of subjectivities. Conceptualizing their intellectual life as a role demarcated off from the other aspects of the self, academics may manage a distinction between a secularized professional life and a privatized religiosity. Looking at American culture as a whole, one observes the curious phenomenon of a highly developed technoscientific capacity, centered in secularized higher education and research institutions and government and commercial laboratories, at the same time as widespread public rejection of this secular scientific knowledge. In the age of Covid-19, this takes the form of the anti-vaccination movement. A technical reason that has detached itself from a responsibility to articulate public meaning is treated with suspicion by a vast mass of the population.

A defensive posture of the secular intellectual within the university, facing a broader culture that the intellectual perceives as hostile, leads to attention to maintaining institutional and cultural boundaries and demarcations around the space of secular reason. The self-conception of academics, the reward structures and the habits of intellectual judgment all militate against any kind of public intellectual role. Instead, one finds the tendency toward hyper-professionalism in fields such as academic philosophy and sociology. Shapin writes:

> "Doing philosophy," as it is currently practiced, is often more about dexterity in manipulating the disciplinary literature than it is about knowledge, mind, or morals. "Doing sociology," similarly, is in large part a display of methodological virtuosity and of knowing familiarity with the discipline's currently fashionable "models." You can tell a self-referential discipline by the fact that no one reads its products who doesn't have to. Disciplinary members have to, or at least they acknowledge a moral responsibility to do so. Beyond those boundaries readership drops off like a cliff face.[106]

The hypertrophy of narrowly technical reason accompanies the atrophy of reason in public.

In America, one finds the ongoing barbarization of public discourse: the prevalence of anti-scientific discourses such as creationism, the systematic distortion of public understanding by corporate propaganda as in the case of climate change denial, and, now, with Covid, the loss of hundreds of thousands of human lives caused by a president with a poison tongue—a demonstration of the sheer power of propaganda in a time of legitimation crisis. When all institutions have ceased to be trusted, the path is clear for the irrationality of charisma.[107] Disregard for truth in public speech has been evident for years in falsehoods about weapons of mass destruction that led America into the war in Iraq, denial of climate change, "black helicopter" conspiracy theories about the United Nations put forward by right-wing radio jockeys, palpably false assertions about "death panels," and the complete disregard for truth in the Trump administration's "alternative facts," which culminated in the lie of the stolen election that has now become a "stab in the back" myth for the Republican Party. The lack of purchase of truth in public discourse is observed uneasily from within the university.[108]

However, the academic role is constructed in such a way that increases the division between a technicized academic discourse and the broader realm of public discourse. The instrumentalization of the university and the demise of reasonable public discourse are locked together in a self-perpetuating downward spiral. The self-insulation of academic discourse contributes to the reigning irrationalism of public discourse. Insularity also produces a mode of thought that cannot be enriched by engagement with human action and struggles—in other words, the active unfolding of human history—and so becomes increasingly desiccated. It is a form of knowing that is detached from being: *knowingness*.

The university, of course, relies on external support and so—despite the insularity of much of its discourse—can never actually insulate itself. The detachment of intellectual life from human struggles and public action, the preservation of the university as a space of knowledge evacuated of human interests and passions, creates a vacuum that is immediately filled by dominant interests of the state and capital. An interest in technical proficiency for its own sake becomes united with the interest in power for its own sake and the interest in accumulation for its sake. Virilio points to the way in which the science of the "limit performance" oriented toward pushing back limits of what is technically feasible articulates with the military state interest in the maximization of technical power.[109] Noble argues that technical experts align themselves with the holders of power because "it is the access to that power, with its huge resources, that allows them to dream . . . and the reality of that power that brings their dreams to life."[110] Bill Readings suggests how the detachment of intellectual value from other frameworks of value leads to the primacy of the empty language of "excellence" as the directionless goal of academic life. "Excellence," Readings suggests, is the core discourse of the commercialized university: it signifies of knowledge and education as commodities.[111]

Technically proficient experts, who have eschewed concern for values other than the augmentation of proficient technique, have no way of setting their own goals; they rely de facto on goals set externally. Hence Marcuse's argument against Weber's valorization of the value-free science:

> Your "neutrality" is as *compulsory* as it is *illusory*. For neutrality is only real where you have the power to repel interference: if you do not, you become the victim and assistant of any power that chooses to use you.[112]

Neutrality is compulsory because the expert must have themselves available to external interests: to state and corporate funders—to do so is the precondition of survival—having the resources to continue. And, in the so-called entrepreneurial university, having the resources is itself, increasingly, the measure of value. It is in this way that the doctrine of "pure science" based on value-freedom, dialectically transforms into its opposite, science as commodity.[113] Gouldner wrote in "Anti-Minotaur" that

> the value-free doctrine is useful both to those who want to escape *from* the world and to those who want to escape *into* it . . . . The belief that it is not the business of a sociologist to make value-judgments is taken, by some, to mean that the market on which they can vend their skills is unlimited . . . In brief, the value-free doctrine of social science was sometimes used to justify the sale of one's talents to the highest bidder and is, far from being new, a contemporary version of the most ancient sophistry.[114]

Schmidt has described the ways in which professional and scientific training cultivates "assignable curiosity"—the ability to be intrigued by, and dedicated to solving, those puzzles one's organization or funder needs solved. This is less obvious in the university than in research jobs in industry or government. University researchers tend to be "directed in ways that allow them to see themselves as self-directed." Schmidt describes how this subtle direction operates through the "unsolicited proposal" in which the researcher proposes a topic to a government funding agency. Due to their dependence on these agencies for their ability to carry out their work, and the intense competition for grants, "professors who want money to do research inevitably have funding agencies' interests in mind as they plan their work and write their proposals. Consciously or unconsciously, they tailor their own interests to match those of the sponsors."[115] Apparently unsolicited proposals are often framed in a process of consultation with the funding agencies allowing agencies' interests to be integrated into the researcher's own apparently autonomous plans. Schmidt notes that the unsolicited proposal allows the researcher to believe that they are self-directed even when their work is funded by, for example, the Department of Defense.[116] Being a successful researcher means being skilled at anticipating and internalizing funding agencies interests and in the art of representing those interests back to the agencies.

Accompanying the way in which the power of external interests is obfuscated through this cultivation of "assignable curiosity" is what Schmidt calls the "social significance concealment game." The importance of notions of autonomy and neutrality in the self-image of scientists makes the externally directed character of much research difficult and problematic to acknowledge, so technical language often fulfills the function of masking social interests. Schmidt writes:

> The way research is described, funded and carried out conceals its social origins. The titles that scientists give their research projects (and publications) usually

make their work look very abstract and esoteric. These titles, and the technical descriptions that accompany them, make no mention of underlying technological work. This practice lends prestige to the work by making it look more basic and more like a pursuit of truth for its own sake.[117]

For illustration, Schmidt contrasts a series of examples of University of California Irvine physics researchers' descriptions of their projects with funding agencies' descriptions of those same projects. The physicists' language abstracts the technical content "the interactions of electromagnetic radiation, particularly in the infrared, with matter." By contrast, the air force funders foreground the technological goals: "Aerospace communications surveillance and detection systems require electro-optical devices which exploit the special properties and interactions of infrared radiation with solid state materials."[118] Scientific curiosity is a kind of sublimation of social interests that expresses but occludes those interests. The concealment of interests allows researchers to present themselves *qua* professionals as apolitical. But that overtly apolitical orientation also prevents conscious attention to, and discursive-political contestation over, the interests to which science is subject. Assignable curiosity is facilitated by an institutional culture that discourages researchers from raising questions about political values of research programs.

The usefully "apolitical" scientist and the professionalized insular scholar are involved in a similar kind of self-defeat. This was described eloquently by C. Wright Mills in his 1950 critique of the transformation of the intellectual into white-collar worker, an account that Schmidt can be seen as updating and developing. Mills argued that the detachment from political action had its corollary in a pervasive sense of powerlessness among intellectuals.[119] While their professional identity was justified by the "academic cult" of "Objectivity or scientism," which eschewed responsibility for goals or the state of the world, this had its "personal counterpart in the development of a tragic sense of life."[120]

In "Science as a Vocation," Weber articulated the cult of objectivity and embraced its accompanying tragic disposition. Both objectivity and tragedy involve the denial of responsibility. The tragic sense of the impossibility of responsibility is expressed in Weber's language of "fate" and "destiny" and in his language of submission to gods, devils, and demons, wherein "the answer is plain and simple if each finds and obeys the demon who holds the fibers of his very life."[121] Weber's conception of autonomy is self-defeating. The autonomy of intellectual life from other value-spheres produces scientists who, Weber says, are "privileged hirelings of the state."[122] One chooses which god or demon to obey, in other words to which set of fundamental values one commits oneself—but having chosen one is utterly committed.

But in consequence, Weber's tragic resignation in the face of the inexorable rationalization and bureaucratization of the world is itself indicative of the *self-defeating* character of his conceptions of freedom and reason. Freedom is submission to some set of fundamental values that one accepts as transcendent. Reason is acceptance of the ultimate primacy of irrational forces. Lukács writes: "So Max Weber banished irrationalism from his methodology and analysis of isolated facts only in order to introduce it as the philosophical basis of his world-picture."[123]

Weber's irrationalism follows from his fragmentation of human capacities into rigidly separated value-spheres with no connection or coherence. His language of gods and demons is a function of this *alienation* of human capacities. Science and politics as alienated human capacities appear as alien forces or gods to which human beings must pledge allegiance. History then becomes a tragic unfolding of the domination of human beings by these forces: the "iron cage" or "a polar night of icy darkness and hardness" are Weber's visions of the human future.[124] Weber was attracted to the irrationalism of charisma and he conceptualized a commitment to scientific rationality in terms of a philosophy of hardness and callousness about its own consequences, which were defined as beyond its concern. These ways of accepting and even embracing irrationality go along with Weber's pessimistic resignation in the face of what he presents as an ultimately stultifying and entrapping rationality. These elements of romanticism in Weber symptomatize and express the contradiction in the individualism that pervaded Weber's sociological thought and that is at the core of bourgeois ideology. This is precisely the self-negation of bourgeois freedom within bourgeois social relations. The underlying dynamic that produces this self-negation is the self-negation of bourgeois "free trade," since the atomized buyer and seller in the "perfect market" provides the model for the freedom of the bourgeois individual. Free trade and small enterprise are destroyed by monopoly capital. Weber's self-contradictory greengrocer of knowledge under state capitalism is the expression of his bourgeois bewilderment in the face of the inexorable process by which, as Marx and Engels wrote, "the priest, the poet, the man of science" become the bourgeoisie's "paid wage labourers."[125] The strain of pessimism is that of the German mandarin intellectuals marginalized by the rise of science and industrial capitalism.[126]

Weber's conception of the iron cage symbolizes rationality itself as a form of unfreedom together with the vulgar economic materialism of capitalism that turned vocation into a "forced" pursuit of material gain.[127] But this materialism for Weber is understood as an outcome of the calculatively rational spirit of capitalism. Materialism is dematerialized in Weber and subsumed by rational spirit. This conception of oppressive rationalism, accompanied by a romantic and nostalgic structure of feeling and a tragic view of history, is a central motif in bourgeois thought. It runs alongside the bourgeois culture of utilitarianism and the related assertion of the rationality of the market and quantitative scientific knowledge as the only legitimate basis for thought (as in rational choice theory) and the liberal-utilitarian belief in the market and science as the basis for human progress. Weber embodied this split in bourgeois culture between rationalism and irrationalism, the inextricably intertwined but opposing impulses of the Enlightenment and Romanticism.[128]

As the bourgeoisie contained society within the nation-state, the nation-state became the vehicle for the social scientific projects for the rational ordering of society. Science became linked to the nation-state as the institutional support of secular culture. However, this embroiled science in the contradictions of the capitalist nation-state with capitalist global economy. The universality of science is the universality of global economy. This is science conceptualized as emerging as a product of social life, what Marx called in *The Grundrisse* "general scientific labor," "general intellect," "the social intellect," "society's science," and "the general productive forces of the social brain."[129] These productive forces clearly extend far beyond the nation-state. The "social brain" is increasingly a global brain. However, the institutional support for science ties it to the nation-state, which ties science to the irrational, conflictual relationship between nation-states, that is, to the political economy of war. The tethering of science to the irrational structure of the nation-state renders the value-framework in which science operates ultimately irrational. Weber's rational science leads not only to irrational charisma, but relatedly, to irrational nationalism which glorifies war. Sam Whimster writes of Weber's response to the outbreak of World War I, "Weber's patriotism and cultural nationalism were aroused by the war."[130] Romantic nationalism is the anti-rationalist value-framework to which the bourgeois rationalist must cling precisely because science is caught up in the contradiction between the nation-state and global economy and, therefore, sucked into the violent vortex of imperialism.

WAR IS A FORCE THAT GIVES SOCIOLOGISTS MEANING

The contradictions of liberal nationalist universalism are shown by Wolfe's liberal imperialist project for a "return to greatness" for America in his 2005 book of that title. Wolfe praised George W. Bush's invasion of Afghanistan and assertion of American global power while making superficial critiques of Bush's irresponsible excesses. The book may be treated as an instantiation of what Hedges calls "the death of the liberal class" and Wolfe's trajectory from the New Left to Clinton-Obama-Biden Democratic Party liberalism, entailing support for American imperialism, represents the broader shift of middle-class radicalism toward accommodation and integration with imperialism.[131] This process of integration was aided by the fact that, as Jeremy Scahill writes, "The war on terror, launched under a Republican administration, was ultimately legitimized and expanded by a popular Democratic president." Former expert adviser on counterterrorism for the Obama administration, Michael Boyle observes that President Obama "has routinized and normalized extrajudicial killing from the Oval Office."[132] As Hedges argues,

> Dick Cheney and George W. Bush may be palpably evil while Obama is merely weak, but to those who seek to keep us in a state of permanent war, such distinctions do not matter. They get what they want. The liberal class, like Dostoyevsky's Underground Man, can no longer influence a society in a state of permanent war and retreats into its sheltered enclaves, where its members can continue to worship themselves. The corridors of liberal institutions are filled with Underground men and women. They decry the social chaos for which they bear responsibility, but do nothing. They nurse an internal bitterness and mounting distaste for the wider society. And because of their self-righteousness, elitism, and hypocrisy, they are despised.[133]

In contrast to the post–World War II period when scientists had a critical public voice in opposing the nuclear arms race, there is no significant public critical voice of science questioning today's drone wars. Scientists have become the silent technicians of the War on Terror.

Carl Boggs's *Fascism Old and New* makes the case that American fascism is not a sudden efflorescence of irrationalism propelled from below and embodied charismatically by Trump but, rather, is something that has for many decades been solidifying within the political-economic structures and shaping the culture.[134] It is above all a creation of what Mills called the power elite.[135] Boggs traces the development of an authoritarian corporate state capitalism in the United States back to World War II. The institutional roots of fascism are in the increasingly tight integration between, and concentration of power in, the federal government, the corporate elite, and the military.[136] Boggs emphasizes the growth of the military and its increasing preponderance within the state apparatus. The permanent warfare state, he insightfully observes, shapes a warfare culture, to some extent directly through the close integration of Hollywood with the Pentagon propaganda machine, but also through war mobilization and through the real violence of war which comes home in television news, in the bodies and minds of soldiers and in the practices of militarized police. This violence must be rationalized and rendered acceptable. So there develops a culture both of denial and celebration of violence.

Boggs points out the cultivation of nationalistic group narcissism in America, which grew out of America's position at the end of World War II as the world's most powerful nation, with its initial monopoly of the atomic bomb. Hiroshima and Nagasaki had to be denied and rationalized and the vast military expenditures justified by xenophobic anti-communism, which also functioned to suppress the organized left and thereby tame the unions and purge the nation's educational and cultural institutions, enforcing a constricted public discourse through anti-communism as civil religion, a taboo which is now breaking down among youth. As historian Gary Wills shows in his book *Bomb Power*, the atomic bomb also concentrated power in the presidency, who holds the power of life and death over the entire planet.[137] Lewis Mumford had seen just such a convergence of technological power and authoritarianism in the atomic bomb which he called the epitome of the modern "megamachine" combining scientific-technological power over nature with the bureaucratic organization of human beings: "Overnight, the civilian and military leaders of the United States were endowed with powers that hitherto had been claimed only by Bronze Age gods." Trump drew on bomb power in his own self-aggrandizement and perhaps libidinal gratification in his power. He used in Afghanistan the MOAB, the largest nonnuclear weapon in existence, and repeatedly threatened to obliterate other countries, including North Korea, Syria, and Afghanistan. American global power has been heavily reliant on, and underpinned by, technology from the atomic bomb to satellite surveillance. The binding of science to the war machine has been a key feature of the postwar power of United States and has since World War II shaped its universities. Mumford noted the way in which a discourse of professional value-neutrality, based on science, permeated the authoritarian power structure: "every part of the megamachine was made over in consonance with the peculiarly limited type of knowledge, deliberately sterilized of other human values and purposes, that their refined mathematical analysis and exact methods had been designed to further."[138] Marcuse, quite similarly, stressed the way in which science and technology functioned for destructive and repressive purposes, legitimated by positivistic thought. The atomic bomb epitomized the irrational destructive purposes that were masked by the superficial positivistic rationality of the scientists at Los Alamos and Livermore and the defense intellectuals at the RAND Corporation. "We are again confronted," Marcuse wrote, "with one of the most vexing aspects of advanced industrial civilization: the rational character of its irrationality."[139] The rational systems and professional roles that America's technocratic liberals present themselves as upholding against Trump's irrationalist populist fascism are themselves the supporting structures of the growth of authoritarianism in the American state. The drones that Trump inherited from Obama, with which Trump murdered at will, feeding his irrational destructive narcissism, are the products of America's technical intelligentsia in the laboratories of universities and testing facilities of arms companies. The technical intellectuals put forward drones as a depoliticized, instrumental solution to geopolitics. Today's use of drones by US imperialism recalls Wolfe's description, in *Limits of Legitimacy*, of the Kennedy administration's consideration of air strikes against Cuba during the missile crisis: "A surgical strike became a wish fulfillment for these men, a fantasy that what irritated them could be swatted out of sight and out of mind."[140]

For Weber, the meaninglessness of a scientifically disenchanted world was assuaged by an alternative source of meaning in nationalism and German imperialism. For Wolfe, three decades after *Limits of Legitimacy*, American imperialism similarly provided a source of meaning through identification with national "greatness" asserted in war:

> I discovered that my country was one I could admire and respect, and before long, it also became one I loved. When it was attacked, I took to the podium, defending George W. Bush's decision to fight back against the Taliban in Afghanistan and letting my students at Boston College know, in no uncertain terms, that Noam Chomsky and Michael Moore were not going to help them live in a country capable of defending itself against its enemies.[141]

In 1914–1918, there were professors who similarly exhorted their students toward the meatgrinder of trench warfare.

Wolfe's statement that the invasion of Afghanistan was to "fight back against the Taliban" asserts an extremely oversimplified account of the 9/11 attacks even within the parameters of the official 9/11 Commission Report. While the Taliban was effectively allied with al-Qaeda and provided harbor to the terrorist group, it was not directly involved in carrying out the 9/11 attacks, whereas fifteen of the nineteen hijackers were Saudi Arabian.[142] The elision and vagueness of the enemy was a key aspect of the "War on Terror" rhetoric by which Bush justified the invasions of Afghanistan and Iraq and that continues to allow the United States to pursue military operations in countries like Somalia, recently bombed by the Biden administration.[143] Wolfe justified Bush's invasion of Afghanistan, while seeking to distance himself from what he calls the "ill-considered . . . ill thought-out" "military debacle" in Iraq. This splitting of the "good" war on terror from the bad became a feature of Obama's masquerade as an "anti-war" candidate.[144] Wolfe's readiness to support the Bush administration's murderous war in Afghanistan displays at the very least a monumental lack of curiosity, particularly for a sociologist and political scientist, regarding the geopolitical motivations underlying the US military involvement in the Middle East.[145]

Daniel Golden describes a new generation of academics who have no qualms about serving the US military and intelligence agencies and find a sense of patriotic gratification in doing so:

> A generational shift also underlies the increasing ties between the intelligence community and academia. Baby boomer professors who grew up protesting the CIA-funded misadventures of the 1960s, from the Bay of Pigs to the Vietnam War, began to retire, replaced by those shaped by the Soviet invasion of Afghanistan, the first Gulf War, and 9/11. Younger faculty are more likely to regard the collecting and sifting of intelligence as a vital tool for a nation under threat and a patriotic duty compatible with—even desirable for—academic research.[146]

Golden's account points to a significant historical transformation of the professoriate, but also of the broader liberal, especially professional, upper-middle-class milieu within which the professoriate exists.

The CIA social media campaign titled "Humans of CIA," released in the spring of 2021, although usually reported on as being a campaign to attract millennials, was also reflective of the trajectory of middle-class radicalism. The superficial use of "woke" politics to cover for assassination and torture suggests the superficiality of that "radicalism" associated with that politics.[147] Golden is right that the baby boom generation's opposition to the Vietnam War did leave lasting anti-military sentiments in the university and that was rooted in a generation. But it is also the case that there has been a growing accommodation to imperialism within this layer, including, very significantly, within the generation of middle-class students radicalized in the 1960s.[148] The change in orientation reflected the demise of the national social reform model. The crisis of bourgeois thought that this produced was described by Wolfe in 1977:

> Something peculiar seems to have happened to the politics of advanced industrial societies. Twenty years ago a select group of social scientists praised Western societies for having achieved the Platonic Good; class conflict, disharmony, and disruptive ideas had withered away in paradise of permanent perfection. Yet, fads being what they are, it is currently fashionable to argue exactly the opposite. The world of Pangloss has become that of Céline, and in a strikingly effortless manner. Societies once praised for having solved their problems are now viewed as overwhelmed to the point of paralysis by those very same problems. The key terms are no longer harmony, growth, and reconciliation, but stagnation, *immobilisme*, limited options, closed circles, steady states, *la société bloquée*. The shift in emphasis from iridescent optimism to a militant, aggressive pessimism can be seen in almost every area of life, from social conflict to the consequences of technology.[149]

The liberal-left resolution of its ideological crisis arising from the collapse of social reform and the rise of neoliberal globalization is bound up with, and reflected in, the transformation of the Democratic Party, away from its New Deal history and into a neoliberal party.

With the presidency of Bill Clinton, the Democratic Party engaged in what James Galbraith calls "a new and historic compromise, between the leadership of the Democratic Party and the very rich."[150] Liu writes that "It was after 1968 that the PMC gradually shifted its allegiance from workers to capital."[151] This relationship was consummated in the Obama admin-istration with the continuation and expansion of Bush's TARP program to maintain the inflation of asset prices, leading to a government-fueled stock market surge that, together with the abandonment of millions of homeowners to go bankrupt and lose their homes to the banks, greatly increased wealth inequality. At the same time, the organizations of the anti-war movement dissolved themselves and sections of the left began to advocate for the United States, Israel, and the Gulf monarchies' proxy war for regime change in Syria, presenting this as a revolution. The election of Obama was the occasion for the integration of the more affluent sections of the middle class, with the rear brought up by the middle-class radicals in a long, and accelerating, retreat from radicalism.This retreat was concluded with Obama's election. North writes that in the early 2000s, culminating with the election of Obama,

> a profound shift took place in the political orientation of the remnants of the old middle-class protest movements that had emerged out of the mass movements of the 1960s.
>
> In the weeks leading up to the outbreak of the Iraq War, there were mass protest demonstrations around the world. But they ended once the war began and never resumed. The nomination and election of Obama, the first African-American president, served as political justification for the integration of the petty-bour-geois left into mainstream American politics. Substantial sections of the old protest movements—especially those whose members were part of the affluent middle-class milieu—completed the long and protracted process of their break with left political radicalism and their transformation into an anti-socialist and pro-imperialist pseudo-left.[152]

It is possible to see this shift in the political trajectory of Wolfe who, while involved with Marxist academics theorizing the state in the 1970s, by the end of that decade has, as he puts it, had the opportunity "to rethink my radi-calism and emerge as more of a liberal than a leftist."[153] By the turn of the millennium, he was fully in support of the Bush administration's invasion of Afghanistan.[154]

Wolfe bemoans that Americans' "mature patriotism" has since given way to an "immature" politics of "petulance."[155] But the title of his 2005 book suggests that the "mature patriotism" he advocates may not be so easily held apart from the more extreme Trumpist forms of nationalism. Years of war, extended and supported by the liberals in and around the Democrat Party, have eroded democratic rights and democratic political culture and cultivated jingoistic, xenophobic, and authoritarian tendencies that manifested themselves in support for Trump. Wolfe's support for the American assault on the Middle East is reminiscent of the support for the US entry into World War I by such liberal luminaries as John Dewey. Of the latter, John Tipple wrote, "What Dewey and the pragmatic proponents of war failed to perceive was that war was the supreme tragedy of a modern mechanized society for, as Mumford has pointed out, war sanctioned savagery and deified the machine."[156] And indeed, the United States brought Afghanistan "kill teams" and drones.

Whereas Dewey's militarism was in the context of America's rise as a world power, Wolfe's comes after protracted decline, as his nostalgic 2005 title suggests. Wolfe's support for war in the Middle East was under conditions in which any link between nationalism and liberal universal values has long been broken. Wolfe's support is for a declining world power seeking to maintain its global hegemony by means of military power through disorganizing the world.[157] Wolfe's support for war is in a context in which the modern relationship between war and citizenship no longer operates.

Wolfe applies the language of universalistic liberalism to support the violence of the "predator state." Wolfe's growing national chauvinism was a response to the breakdown of the welfare state and rising living standards as the basis for the legitimacy of the capitalist state. In his 1998 panegyric to the simple, everyday "modest virtues" of the American middle class, *One Nation, After All*, Wolfe acknowledged this decline but put forward the idealist tonic that America was knit together by values: "For all the wealth generated in America in recent years, economic security, once the very definition of the middle-class way of life is unlikely to return to our shores. Yet the very insecurity that has come to characterize middle-class life may make us more of one nation than ever before." Since middle-class values and identity transcend middle-class living standards and since there are few "middle managers of impeccable middle-class income who have not felt at least some of the uncertainty once experienced by primarily blue-collar workers," this shared experience of insecurity could, he suggested, even more strongly knit Americans together, not in any oppositional way but in such a way to support the stability of American society and state.[158]

Wolfe's Marxist analysis of the state in the 1970s was the Marxism of reformist social democracy. In a 1974 article, Wolfe put forward a revision of

Marx such that the false universality of the capitalist state (its class character masquerading as universality) could attain a certain extent of true universality. He wrote:

> Yet it is possible to suggest a much less condescending alternative: that the universality of the state is only *partially* false. The welfare state is more easily denounced by intellectuals than by workers. Compared to what existed previously, it does move in the direction of universality, though with all deliberate speed, to use its own expression. In short, the welfare state is the positive symbol of the fluidity of the modern class state, its position both in and above the class struggle.[159]

This is a version of the argument for the "relative autonomy" of the state from the interests of the ruling class, and that the state can instead be itself an arena of struggle and come to represent the interests of society more universally, including the interests of the working class. This argument was both a justification and an explanation of the welfare state. Wolfe was explicit that the defense of the welfare state was the essential core of his Marxist political sociology: "The whole point of this exercise in definition and historical application is to stress the point that the contemporary capitalist state is very much a contradictory phenomenon. This is especially true of its welfare character." It is in "the nature of the capitalist state," Wolfe argued, that

> any government, especially in liberal democratic society, can at one time be both part of a capitalist state *and* a partial reappropriation by people of their common power . . . [A]t any given point in time, *the capitalist state can appear as both itself and its potential opposite.*[160]

Writing in the period of the 1970s "fiscal crisis of the state," but before the neoliberal onslaught had fully taken shape, with the Reagan administration, Wolfe made this argument that the "left hand" of the state manifested its relative autonomy, prior to the massive assault by the ruling class against the gains that had been made within the post-New Deal, Keynesian state. This assault was a reassertion of the essential class character of the state and there has not been a return to the welfare state and social democracy. Wolfe's own rightward political trajectory was an example of the more general abandonment of the welfare state by the upper middle-class liberals. The ideas of "civil society" and "communitarianism" as an alternative to the state, that Wolfe made as part of his rightward trajectory, were part of the discursive world of the Third Way, of the Clinton Democrats in the United States and New Labour in Britain. Wolfe's rightward movement, like that of much of the middle-class liberal-left, may be seen as deriving not from the collapse of the Soviet Union, but from the processes of globalization that were the underlying cause of this collapse. These global processes were destabilizing all projects of constructing society with the bounds of the nation-state, shielded from the forces of the global economy. Globalization freed the ruling class from the compromises into which it had entered earlier in the century under pressure of a revolutionary global working class. Globalization not only arose from the growth of the productive forces, but was also actively pursued as a strategy by the ruling class in order to get out of those national compromises.

Wolfe's turn to civil society may be understood as the search for new legitimations for the capitalist state as the welfare state was being rolled back and this process was threatening state legitimacy. He turned from analyzing the contradiction between liberalism and democracy to seeking social resources to mediate that contradiction. The Trumpist attempted coup of January 6 was a manifestation of precisely this contradiction and the growing tendency of the ruling class to seek authoritarian solutions. In *Limits of Legitimacy*, Wolfe identified an early manifestation of this tendency in the Trilateral Commission Report on the Governability of Democracies. Wolfe recognized this as a likely path the ruling class would take in seeking to preserve its power in the face of crisis.[161] Globalization exacerbated the contradiction between liberalism and democracy and produced crisis in what Wolfe called the "dual state" showing "two faces, one responsible for preserving the prerogatives of those in power and the other for winning consent for those prerogatives."[162] "Transnational political and economic activity has pushed the historic contradictions of the capitalist state to new heights," Wolfe wrote.[163] The declining legitimacy of American political institutions today should be understood as a result of the former "face" of the state displacing the latter, in other words, the task of maintaining the power and wealth of the ruling class undermining the legitimacy of the state and of all mediating institutions. The authoritarian turn indicated, Wolfe then wrote, that "the dominant forces within late capitalism are losing their ability to rule."[164] Wolfe's turn to explicitly seeking to mediate these contradictions follows from his original reformism and also the idealist utopianism that was evident in *Limits of Legitimacy* in his talk of "democratic dreams":

> Democratic dreams have come and gone, sometimes appearing as visions of what a humane world would be like and sometimes turning into perverse nightmares as people become desperate in the search for answers to the pressures in their lives. But even though they may be suppressed momentarily, their existence can never be discounted, for the desire to be part of a meaningful community is a human urge that no historical event has yet completely overcome.[165]

If democratic goals arise from the urge for "meaningful community," then through theories of civil society and the growing nationalism of Wolfe's thought, constructing that meaningful community could be the task of mediating the contradictions of the capitalist state.

The primary form of "meaningful community" on offer in capitalist society is the nation-state. In his 1998 book, Wolfe excoriated the identity politics "left" for the fact that it "has persistently denied this moral ideal of one nation." Identity politics go against "the middle-class belief in one nation." The left was most successful when it "could claim to speak for the one nation we ought to be."[166] But why is the higher unity above particularistic identity-political categories of race and sexual preference the nation? The nation is a particularism. And the violent implications of this particularism were expressed in Wolfe's attraction to war a few years later. The nation as basis for meaningful community is continually being undercut by the growth of the productive forces, which are inexorably binding humanity together as a unified whole. In the face of these contradictions, but unable to break from the bourgeois ideology of nationalism, Wolfe retreated into American chauvinism. There is a definite logic that leads from national reformism to national chauvinism. In seeking to construct a moralized social basis for the state, Wolfe was following in the footsteps of earlier twentieth-century social reformers who framed their arguments in Christian or utopian language. But ultimately Wolfe's reformism was entirely wedded to the nation-state, even while that nation-state less and less incorporated the concessions to the working class that he had earlier argued constituted its latent universality.

Return to Greatness exemplified how, with the decline of American hegemony, the liberal sociologist must become less abstract in their framing of society as nation and so the underlying nationalism to which bourgeois sociology, and the much-weakened project of social reform, remain attached, must become explicit. Like the moralist reformers, Christian socialists, Fabians, and social democrats of the early twentieth century who supported their countries in World War I, the political logic of Wolfe's sociological and reformist project attaches it to the nation-state and, therefore, to support for the right-hand of the state and the violence of imperialism. Bourgeois thought is incapable of escaping the irrationality of nationalism because the nation-state is the bourgeoisie's central, and ultimately its only, solution to the problem of social order.

In *The Limits of Legitimacy*, Wolfe had argued that liberal democracy was the expression of the contradictory character of the capitalist state. The legitimacy of the capitalist state after World War II rested on "the great compromise that has . . . come to be called liberal democracy."[167] This compromise was made possible by functions of the state that mediated between its capitalist character, and, at the same time, its embodiment, in its welfarist functions, of the interests of the working class. In the realm of political participation, parties mediated the contradiction between rule by power elites on behalf of the ruling class and universal suffrage. The class compromise of the postwar period, however, was inherently contradictory and unstable. It depended on the mediation of the inherent contradiction of liberal democracy, between liberalism (which was rooted in market relations and the defense of the property rights of the bourgeois class) and democracy (which was an ideal of universal participation). The form of liberal democracy mediated this contradiction. But the form is breaking down. It has become rote and ritualistic, in the sense of Yurchak's hypernormality, and its fragility is more and more exposed beneath the façade. The contradiction between liberalism and democracy is tied to contradictions between individual and society, market and state, and public and private. It has, at its root, the contradiction between private appropriation and socialized production. This is further expressed in the contradiction between global economy and the nation-state. Globalization has unglued the compromise between liberalism and democracy and undermined the mediating institutions. Sociology, as the bourgeois science of mediation, cannot recover its equilibrium.

NOTES

1. Michael J. Mulkay, "Norms and Ideology in Science," *Social Science Information* 15, no. 4/5 (1976): 637–656; David A. Hollinger, *Science, Jews, and Secular Culture: Studies in Mid-Twentieth-Century American Intellectual History* (Princeton: Princeton University Press, 1996); Charles Thorpe, "Community and the Market in Michael Polanyi's Philosophy of Science" *Modern Intellectual History* 6, no. 1 (2009): 59–89; Audra J. Wolfe, *Freedom's Laboratory: The Cold War Struggle for the Soul of Science* (Baltimore, MD: Johns Hopkins University Press, 2018); David J. Hess "Neoliberalism and the History of STS Theory: Toward a Reflexive Sociology." *Social Epistemology* 27, no. 2 (2013): 177–193. See also discussion of the "national professional" in J. E. Elliott, "Insourcing Dissent: Brand English in the Entrepreneurial University," *Telos* 187 (Summer 2019): 129–155, on 140–142.

2. David Hollinger, *Science, Jews, and Secular Culture.* Cf. Christopher Jencks and David Riesman, *The Academic Revolution* (Chicago: University of Chicago Press, 1977).

3. Gouldner, *Dialectic of Ideology and Technology*, 184.

4. Michel Foucault, "Truth and Power," in Colin Gordon ed, *Power/Knowledge: Selected Interviews and Writings, 1972–1977* (New York: Pantheon, 1980), 109–133; Thorpe, "Violence and the Scientific Vocation," 60. See also Frank Furedi, *Where Have All the Intellectuals Gone?* (London: Continuum, 2005), 43–49.

5. Guy Debord, *A Sick Planet*, trans. by D. Nicholson-Smith (London: Seagull Books, 2008), 79; Charles Thorpe and Brynna Jacobson, "Abstract Life, Abstract Labor, Abstract Mind," in Brett Clark and Tamar Diana Wilson eds, *The Capitalist*

Commodification of Animals (Bingley, UK: Emerald Publishing Limited, 2020), 59–105, on 72.

6. Max Weber, "Science as a Vocation," in H.H. Gerth and C. Wright Mills eds, *From Max Weber: Essays in Sociology* (New York: Oxford University Press, 1958), 129–56.

7. Alan Wolfe, *The Limits of Legitimacy: Political Contradictions of Contemporary Capitalism* (New York: The Free Press, 1977), 103.

8. Cf. Steven Shapin, *The Scientific Life: A Moral History of a Late Modern Vocation* (Chicago: University of Chicago Press, 2010); Thomas L. Haskell, "Professionalism *versus* Capitalism: R. H. Tawney, Emile Durkheim, and C. S. Peirce on the Disinterestedness of Professional Communities," in Thomas L. Haskell ed., *The Authority of Experts: Studies in History and Theory* (Bloomington: Indiana University Press, 1984), 180–225; Thorpe, "Community and the Market."

9. Steven Shapin, "Weber's *Science as a Vocation*: A Moment in the History of 'Is' and 'Ought'," *Journal of Classical Sociology* 19, no. 3 (August 2019), 290–307; Shapin, *The Scientific Life*. 47–92.

10. Jan Rehmann, *Max Weber: Modernisation as Passive Revolution* (Chicago: Haymarket Books, 2015). See also Michael Bittman, "A Bourgeois Marx? Max Weber's Theory of Capitalist Society: Reflections on Utility, Rationality, and Class Formation," *Thesis Eleven* 15 (1986): 81–91.

11. Harvey Goldman, *Politics, Death, and the Devil: Self and Power in Max Weber and Thomas Mann* (Berkeley: University of California Press, 1992), 185–187, 189.

12. Wolfgang Mommsen, *Max Weber and German Politics, 1890-1920* (Chicago: University of Chicago Press, 1984), 298–299 (emphasis in original).

13. Max Weber, "Politics as a Vocation," in Gerth and Mills eds, *From Max Weber*, 77–128, on 115. See also Shapin, *The Scientific Life*, 11, 40; Nicholas Gane, *Max Weber and Postmodern Theory: Rationalization versus Re-enchantment* (Houdmills, Basingstoke: Palgrave Macmillan, 2004), 55–59.

14. Anthony Giddens, *Beyond Left and Right: The Future of Radical Politics* (Stanford: Stanford University Press, 1994), 212; Charles Thorpe and Brynna Jacobson, "Life Politics, Nature and the State: Giddens' Sociological Theory and The Politics of Climate Change," *The British Journal of Sociology* 64, no. 1 (2013): 99–122.

15. Weber, Politics as a Vocation," 115.

16. Goldman, *Politics, Death, and the Devil*, 159; Mommsen, *Max Weber and German Politics*, 271.

17. Christopher Caudwell, *The Concept of Freedom* (London: Lawrence and Wishart, 1965), 100.

18. Caudwell, *The Concept of Freedom*, 101.

19. Weber, "Science as a Vocation," 147.

20. Weber, "Science as a Vocation," 149.

21. Weber, "Science as a Vocation," 131.

22. On the coincidence of Weber's lecture with the Bolshevik seizure of power, see Keith Tribe, "Max Weber's 'Science as a Vocation': Context, Genesis, Structure," *Sociologica* 12, no. 1 (2018): 125–136, on 127. For further context, see Max Weber, *The*

Vocation Lectures, eds David Owen and Tracy Strong (New York: Hackett, 2004), xix; Shapin, "Weber's *Science as a Vocation*"; Jason Ãnanda Josephson Storm, "A Note on the Dating of Max Weber's 'Science as a Vocation'," *Absolute Disruption: Theory After Postmodernism* (blog), October 24, 2017, https://absolute-disruption.com/2017 /10/24/a-note-on-the-dating-of-max-webers-science-as-a-vocation/#_ednref3. See also Howard Amos, "Hermitage Re-Starts Clocks Stopped at the Moment Bolsheviks Seized Power," *The Calvert Journal*, October 26, 2017, https://www.calvertjournal.com/ articles/show/9170/hermitage-re-starts-clocks-stopped-russian-revolution.

23. Alvin W. Gouldner, "Anti-Minotaur: The Myth of a Value-Free Sociology," in Alvin W. Gouldner ed., *For Sociology: Renewal and Critique in Sociology Today* (New York: Basic Books, Inc., 1973), 3–26, on 9. See also Kieran Allen, *Weber: Sociologist of Empire* (London: Pluto Press, 2017), 7–8; Istvám Mészáros, *The Power of Ideology* (London: Zed Books, 2005), 145–154.

24. Herbert Marcuse, "Industrialization and Capitalism," *New Left Review* 30 (March–April 1965): 3–17, on 13. See also Gouldner, *Dialectic of Ideology and Technology*, 241–242.

25. Alfred Sohn-Rethel, *Intellectual and Manual Labour: A Critique of Epistemology* (London: Macmillan, 1978); Charles Derber, William A. Schwartz and Yale Magrass, *Power in the Highest Degree: Professionals and the Rise of a New Mandarin Order* (Oxford: Oxford University Press, 1990), 82; Cf. Zygmunt Bauman, *Freedom* (Milton Keynes, UK: Open University Press, 1988); Steven Shapin, and Barry Barnes, "Head and Hand: Rhetorical Resources in British Pedagogical Writing, 1770–1850," *Oxford Review of Education* 2, no. 3 (1976): 231–254; Simon Schaffer, Simon, "Babbage's Intelligence: Calculating Engines and the Factory System." *Critical Inquiry* 21, no. 1 (1994): 203–227.

26. Karl Marx, "On the Jewish Question," in ed. and trans. Lloyd D. Easton and Kurt Guddat, *Writings of the Young Marx on Philosophy and Society* (Garden City, NY: Anchor Books, 1967), 216–248, on 239.

27. Yaron Ezrahi, *The Descent of Icarus: Science and the Transformation of Contemporary Democracy* (Cambridge, MA: Harvard University Press, 1990); Theodore M. Porter, *Trust in Numbers: The Pursuit of Objectivity in Science and Public Life* (Princeton: Princeton University Press, 1995).

28. Chandra Mukerji, *A Fragile Power: Scientists and the State* (Princeton: Princeton University Press, 1989), 190–203.

29. Mukerji, *Fragile Power*, 3–21.

30. Ezrahi, *Descent of Icarus*.

31. Karl Marx, "On the Jewish Question," in ed. and trans. Lloyd D. Easton and Kurt Guddat, *Writings of the Young Marx on Philosophy and Society* (Garden City, NY: Anchor Books, 1967), 216–248, on 223–224 (emphases in original).

32. Marx, "On the Jewish Question," 241 (emphases in original).

33. Gouldner, "Anti-Minotaur," 3.

34. Ezrahi, *Descent of Icarus*; Porter, *Trust in Numbers*.

35. Cf. Thomas Nagel, *The View from Nowhere* (Oxford: Oxford University Press, 1986); James C. Scott, *Seeing Like a State : How Certain Schemes to Improve the Human Condition Have Failed* (New Haven, CT: Yale University Press, 1998).

36. Mukerji, *Fragile Power*.

37. Wolfe, *Limits of Legitimacy*, 288–321.

38. Langdon Winner, *Autonomous Technology: Technics-Out-of-Control as a Theme in Political Thought* (Cambridge, MA: MIT Press, 1977).

39. Marcuse, "Industrialization and Capitalism."

40. Cf. Merritt Roe Smith and Leo Marx, *Does Technology Drive History?: The Dilemma of Technological Determinism* (Cambridge, MA: MIT Press, 1994).

41. Weber, "Science as a Vocation," 135.

42. György Lukács, *The Destruction of Reason* (London: Merlin, 1980), 609.

43. R. B. J. Walker, "Violence, Modernity, Silence: From Max Weber to International Relations," in David Campbell and Michael Dillon eds, *The Political Subject of Violence* (Manchester: Manchester University Press, 1993), 137–160.

44. Allen, *Weber*, 136. For Marxist responses to Böhm-Bawerk, see Moishe Postone, *Time, Labor, and Social Domination: A Reinterpretation of Marx's Critical Theory* (Cambridge: Cambridge University Press, 1993), 133–134; Andrew Kliman, *Reclaiming Marx's "Capital": A Refutation of the Myth of Inconsistency* (Lanham, MD: Lexington Books, 2007), 144–146.

45. Max Weber, *Economy and Society: An Outline of Interpretive Sociology*, Volume 1, ed. Guether Roth and Claus Wittich (Berkeley: University of California Press, 1978), 86, 111.

46. Guenther Roth, "The Near-Death of Liberal Capitalism: Perceptions from Weber to the Polanyi Brothers," *Politics and Society* 31, no. 2 (June 2003): 263–282, on 272 (emphasis in original).

47. John Patrick Diggins, *Max Weber: Politics and the Spirit of Tragedy* (New York: Basic Books, 1996), 80.

48. István Mészáros, *The Necessity of Social Control* (New York: Monthly Review Press, 2015), 259.

49. Weber, quoted in Diggins, *Max Weber*, 60. See also Andrew Zimmerman, "German Sociology and Empire: From Internal Colonization to Overseas Colonization and Back Again," in George Steinmetz ed, *Sociology & Empire: The Imperial Entanglements of a Discipline* (Durham, NC: Duke University Press, 2013), 166–187.

50. Goldman, *Politics, Death, and the Devil*, 3.

51. Cf. Gershon Shafir. "The Incongruity Between Destiny and Merit: Max Weber on Meaningful Existence and Modernity." *The British Journal of Sociology* 36, no. 4 (1985): 516–530.

52. Charles Thorpe, "Science and Political Power," *Metascience* 19, 3 (2010): 433–439; Goldman, *Politics, Death, and the Devil*, 3. Cf. Norbert Elias, *The Germans: Power Struggles and the Development of Habitus in the Nineteenth and Twentieth Centuries* (Cambridge: Cambridge University Press, 1996); George L. Mosse, *German Jews Beyond Judaism* (Bloomington: Indiana University Press, 1985).

53. Max Weber, "Bureaucracy," in Max Weber ed., *From Max Weber*, 196–244, on 243.

54. Weber, "Science as a Vocation," 135. See also Thorpe, "Violence and the Scientific Vocation"; Charles Thorpe, "Science Against Modernism: The Relevance of the Social Theory of Michael Polanyi," *British Journal of Sociology* 52, no. 1 (March 2001): 19–35.

55. Quoted in Diggins, *Max Weber*, 192 (emphasis in original).

56. Sam Whimster ed., *Max Weber and the Culture of Anarchy* (Houndmills, Basingstoke, UK: Mamillan, 1999); Klaus Theweleit, *Male Fantasies, Volume 1: Women, Floods, Bodies, History*, trans. Stephen Conway, Erica Carter, and Chris Turner (Cambridge: Polity Press, 1987).

57. Norbert Elias, *The Germans*, 180–181.

58. Weber, "Politics as a Vocation," 126–127.

59. Goldman, *Politics, Death, and the Devil*, 163.

60. Weber, "Science as a Vocation," 145.

61. Weber, quoted in Marcuse, "Industrialization and Capitalism," 4.

62. Joseph Ben-David, "Review of Edward Shils ed., *Max Weber on Universities: The Power of the State and the Dignity of the Academic Calling in Imperial Germany*," *American Journal of Sociology* 80, no. 6 (May, 1975): 1463–1468, on 1464; Diggins, *Max Weber*, 228.

63. Quoted in Hans Gerth and C. Wright Mills, "Introduction: The Man and his Work," in Weber, *From Max Weber*, 1–74, on 30.

64. Harvey Goldman, *Max Weber and Thomas Mann: Calling and the Shaping of the Self* (Berkeley: University of California Press, 1988).

65. Goldman, *Politics, Death, and the Devil*.

66. Weber, "Science as a Vocation," 152.

67. Weber, "Science as a Vocation," 131. Cf. Clyde W. Barrow, *Universities and the Capitalist State: Corporate Liberalism and the Reconstruction of American Higher Education, 1894–1928* (Madison: The University of Wisconsin Press, 1990).

68. Shapin, *The Scientific Life*, 46.

69. Jürgen Kocka, *Facing Total War: German Society 1914–1918* (Leamington Spa: Berg Publishers, 1984), 34.

70. Daniel Charles, *Master Mind: The Rise and Fall of Fritz Haber, the Nobel Laureate Who Launched the Age of Chemical Warfare* (New York: HarperCollins, 2005); Werner Plumpe, "Carl Duisberg, the End of World War I, and the Birth of Social Partnership from the Spirit of Defeat," in Werner Plumpe ed., *German Economic and Business History in the Nineteenth and Twentieth Centuries* (Houndmills, Basingstoke, UK: Palgrave MacMillan, 2016), 305–332; Theo Emery, *Hellfire Boys: The Birth of the U.S. Chemical Warfare Service and the Race for the World's Deadliest Weapons* (New York: Little, Brown and Co., 2017), 15–16.

71. Kocka, *Facing Total War*, 138–139.

72. Roth, "The Near-Death of Liberal Capitalism," 270.

73. Roth, "The Near-Death of Liberal Capitalism," 274.

74. Diggins, *Max Weber*, 141. See also Robert Proctor, *Value-Free Science? Purity and Power in Modern Knowledge* (Cambridge, MA: Harvard University Press, 1991), 106–107; Keith Tribe, "Commerce, Science and the Modern University," in Larry J. Ray and Michael Reed eds, *Organizing Modernity: New Weberian Perspectives on Work, Organization and Society* (London: Routledge, 1994), 141–157, esp. 144–145.

75. Weber, "Science as a Vocation," 149–150.

76. Rehmann, *Max Weber*, 20.

77. Weber, "Science as a Vocation," 151 (emphasis in original).

78. Lawrence King and Iván Szelényi, *Theories of the New Class: Intellectuals and Power* (Minneapolis: University of Minnesota Press, 2004), 195.

79. Marx, *Capital* Volume 3, extracted in Robert Freedman, *Marx on Economics* (Harmondsworth, Penguin, 1961), 43.

80. King and Szelényi, *Theories of the New Class*, 195–196.

81. Boris Kagarlitsky, *The Dialectic of Change,* trans. Rick Simon (London: Verso, 1990), quoting 78, and see also 339–342.

82. King and Szelényi, *Theories of the New Class*, 196.

83. King and Szelényi, *Theories of the New Class*, 198.

84. Quoting Max Weber, *The Protestant Ethic and the Spirit of Capitalism* (London: Routledge, 1992), 182. Cf. Gane, *Max Weber and Postmodern Theory*, 62.

85. István Mészáros, *The Challenge and Burden of Historical Time: Socialism in the Twenty-First Century* (New York: Monthly Review Press, 2009), 40, 441 note 7.

86. Lukács, *Destruction of Reason*, 617.

87. Caudwell, *The Concept of Freedom*, 205.

88. Caudwell, *Concept of Freedom*, 207.

89. Albert Dragstedt and Cliff Slaughter, *State, Power and Bureaucracy: A Marxist Critique of Sociological Theories* (London: New Park Publications, 1981), 33–39.

90. Goldman, *Politics, Death, and the Devil*, 201.

91. Caudwell, *Concept of Freedom*, 204–205.

92. Karl Marx, *Capital: A Critique of Political Economy,* Volume 1, trans. Ben Fowkes (New York: Vintage Books, 1977), 477.

93. Bauman, *Legislators and Interpreters*, 167.

94. Cf. Michael Symonds and Jason Pudsey, "The Concept of 'Paradox' in the Work of Max Weber," *Theory, Culture, and Society* 42, no. 2 (2008): 223–241.

95. Quoted in Diggins, *Weber*, 228.

96. Marcuse, "Industrialization and Capitalism," 3.

97. Marcuse, "Industrialization and Capitalism," 13.

98. Quoted in Goldman, *Politics, Death, and the Devil*, 188.

99. Goldman, *Politics, Death, and the Devil*, 191.

100. Goldman, *Politics, Death, and the Devil*, 174.

101. Gerth and Mills, "Introduction," 72.

102. George Orwell, "Review of *The Road to Serfdom* by F. A. Hayek, *The Mirror of the Past* by K. Zilliacus," in *As I Please, 1943-1946* (Jaffrey, NH: David R. Godine, 2000), 117–119; Charles Thorpe, *Necroculture* (New York: Palgrave Macmillan, 2016), 234–235.

103. Weber, "Science as a Vocation," 152.

104. Macintyre, quoted in Allen, *Weber*, 173.

105. Paul Forman, "The Primacy of Science in Modernity, of Technology in Postmodernity, and of Ideology in the History of Technology," *History and Technology* 23, no. 1–2 (2007): 1–152. Cf. Andrew Feenberg, *Critical Theory of Technology* (Oxford: Oxford University Press, 1991), 5–7.

106. Steven Shapin, "Hyper-Professionalism and the Crisis of Readership in the History of Science," *Isis* 96, no. 2 (2005): 238–43, 239.

107. Thorpe, "Carnival King."

108. David Geoffrey Smith, *Trying to Teach in a Season of Great Untruth: Globalization, Empire and the Crises of Pedagogy* (Rotterdam, The Netherlands: Sense Publishers, 2006).

109. Paul Virilio, *The Information Bomb*, trans. Chris Turner (London: Verso, 2006), 2.

110. David Noble, *Forces of Production: A Social History of Industrial Automation* (New York: Knopf, 1984), 44.

111. Bill Readings, *The University in Ruins* (Cambridge, MA: Harvard University Press, 1996).

112. Marcuse, "Industrialization and Capitalism," 11 (emphases in original).

113. Philip Mirowski, *Science-Mart Privatizing American Science* (Cambridge, MA: Harvard University Press, 2011).

114. Gouldner, "Anti-Minotaur," 12 (emphases in original).

115. Jeff Schmidt, *Disciplined Minds: Salaried Professionals and the Soul-Battering System that Shapes their Lives* (Lanham, MD: Rowman and Littlefield, 2001), 61.

116. Schmidt, *Disciplined Minds*, 62.

117. Schmidt, *Disciplined Minds*, 72.

118. Schmidt, *Disciplined Minds*, 73–74.

119. See also Carl Boggs, *Intellectuals and the Crisis of Modernity* (Albany: State University of New York Press, 1993), 111–115; Stanley Aronowitz, *Science as Power: Discourse and Ideology in Modern Society* (Minneapolis: University of Minnesota Press, 1988).

120. C. Wright Mills, *White Collar: the American Middle Classes* (New York: Oxford University Press, 1951), 158, 160. Cf. Charles Thorpe, *Oppenheimer: The Tragic Intellect* (Chicago: University of Chicago Pres, 2006).

121. Weber, "Science as a Vocation," 156.

122. Weber, "Science as a Vocation," 152–153.

123. Lukács, *The Destruction of Reason*, 619.

124. Weber, *The Protestant Ethic*, 181–182; Weber, "Politics as a Vocation," 128.

125. Marx and Engels, *The Communist Manifesto*, 37.

126. Fritz K. Ringer, *The Decline of the German Mandarins: the German Academic Community, 1890-1933* (Middletown, CN: Wesleyan University Press, 1990).

127. Weber, *Protestant Ethic*, 181.

128. Whimster, *Max Weber and the Culture of Anarchy*; Caudwell, *Crisis in Physics*; Christopher Caudwell, *Romance and Realism: A Study in English Bourgeois Literature*. ed. Samuel Hynes (Princeton: Princeton University Press, 1970); Gane, *Max Weber and Postmodern Theory*.

129. Marx, *Grundrisse*, trans. Martin Nicolaus (New York: Penguin Books, 1973), 694, 699, 700, 706, 709.

130. Whimster, "Introduction to Weber, Ascona and Anarchism," in Max Weber ed., *Max Weber and the Culture of Anarchy*, 1–40, on 31. See also Karl-Ludwig Ay,

"Max Weber: A German Intellectual and the Question of War Guilt after the Great War," in Whimster, op. cit., 110–128 and Carl Levy, "Max Weber, Anarchism and Libertarian Culture: Personality and Power Politics," in Whimster, op cit, 83–109. See also Mommsen, *Max Weber and German Politics, 1890-1920.*

131. David North, *The Frankfurt School, Postmodernism and the Politics of the Pseudo-Left: a Marxist Critique* (Oak Park, MI: Mehring Books, 2015), viii–ix, 197–198, 212–215, 219; Boris Kagarlitsky, *Between Class and Discourse: Left Intellectuals in Defense of Capitalism* (London: Routledge, 2021), 26, 136–138. See also Catherine Liu, *Virtue Hoarders: The Case Against the Professional Managerial Class* (Minneapolis: University of Minnesota Press, 2021).

132. Jeremy Scahill, *Dirty Wars: The World is a Battlefield* (New York: Nation Books, 2013), 516, quoting Michael Boyle on 517.

133. Chris Hedges, *Death of the Liberal Class* (New York: Nation Books, 2010), 21.

134. Carl Boggs, *Fascism Old and New: American Politics at the Crossroads* (New York: Routledge, 2018).

135. C. Wright Mills, *The Power Elite* (Oxford: Oxford University Press, 1957).

136. Boggs, *Fascism Old and New*, 158–167.

137. Gary Wills, *Bomb Power: The Modern Presidency and the National Security State* (New York: Penguin, 2010).

138. Lewis Mumford, *The Pentagon of Power: The Myth of the Machine Volume II* (New York: Harcourt, Brace, Jovanovich, 1970), 255.

139. Marcuse, *One-Dimensional Man*, 9.

140. Wolfe, *The Limits of Legitimacy*, 260.

141. Alan Wolfe, *Return to Greatness: How America Lost its Sense of Purpose and What It Needs to Do to Recover It* (Princeton: Princeton University Press, 2005), xi.

142. National Commission on Terrorist Attacks Upon the United States, *9/11 Commission Report* (New York: Barnes and Noble, 2006), 65–66, 250–252; BBC News, "9/11 attacks: US to reveal key name in Saudi lawsuit," September 13, 2019, https://www.bbc.com/news/world-us-canada-49686128; Rory McCarthy, "New Offer on Bin Laden," *The Guardian*, October 16, 2001, https://www.theguardian.com/world/2001/oct/17/afghanistan.terrorism11?fb=optOut; Rory McCarthy, "Taliban Order Bin Laden to Leave," *The Guardian*, September 27, 2001, https://www.theguardian.com/world/2001/sep/28/afghanistan.terrorism1?INTCMP=ILCNETTXT3487.

143. Gordon C. Chang and Hugh Mehan, "Why We Must Attack Iraq: Bush's Reasoning Practices and Argumentation System," *Discourse & Society* 19, no. 4 (2008): 453–482; Alexander Ward, "Welcome to Joe Biden's Somalia War," Politico, July 21, 2021, https://www.politico.com/newsletters/national-security-daily/2021/07/21/welcome-to-joe-bidens-somalia-war-493679.

144. Wolfe, *Return to Greatness*, xi, 50. Cf. Greg Shupak, "Afghanistan Was Never a Good War," *Jacobin* (September 11, 2021), https://www.jacobinmag.com/2021/09/afghanistan-war-united-states-taliban-civilian-deaths.

145. Cf. McCoy, *Shadows of the American Century*; Alex Callinicos, *The New Mandarins of American Power* (Cambridge: Polity Press, 2003), 54–98. John

Bellamy Foster, *Naked Imperialism: The US Pursuit of Global Dominance* (New York: Monthly Review Press, 2006). See also Seymour Hersch, *The Killing of Osama bin Laden* (London: Verso, 2017).

146. Daniel Golden, *Spy Schools: How the CIA, FBI, and Foreign Intelligence Secretly Exploit America's Universities* (New York: Henry Holt and Co., 2017), 184.

147. Julian Borger, "CIA Forges Unity in Diversity: Everybody Hates Their 'Woke' Recruitment Ad," *The Guardian*, May 4, 2021, https://www.theguardian.com /us-news/2021/may/04/cia-woke-recruitment-ad.

148. North, *The Frankfurt School,* 219. Cf. James W. Russell, "A Left Weberian Road to Identity Politics in the United States," in Graham Cassano and Richard Dello Buono eds, *Crisis, Politics, and Critical Sociology* (Chicago: Haymarket, 2012), 37–44; Shadia Drury, "The Postmodern Face of American Exceptionalism," in Gregory Smulewicz-Zucker and Michael J. Thompson eds, *Radical Intellectuals and the Subversion of Progressive Politics: The Betrayal of Politics* (New York: Palgrave Macmillan, 2015), 15–32; John Sanbonmatsu, "Postmodernism and the Corruption of the Critical Intelligentsia," in Smulewicz-Zucker and Thompson eds, *Radical Intellectuals*, 33–68; Michael J. Thompson, *The Domestication of Critical Theory* (London: Rowman and Littlefield, 2016).

149. Wolfe, *Limits of Legitimacy*, 1.

150. Galbraith, *The Predator State*, 100–101. See also Lawrence Selfa, *The Democrats: A Critical History* (Chicago: Haymarket, 2012).

151. Catherine Liu, *Virtue Hoarders: The Case against the Professional Managerial Class* (Minneapolis: University of Minnesota Press, 2021), 3.

152. North, *The Frankfurt School*, ix. See also Liu, *Virtue Hoarders*, 2–3.

153. Alan Wolfe, "So Right Together," *The New Republic* (February 11, 2016), https://newrepublic.com/article/129013/right-together-exit-right-oppenheimer.

154. Wolfe, *Return to Greatness*, x–xi.

155. Alan Wolfe, *The Politics of Petulance: America in an Age of Immaturity* (Chicago, IL: University of Chicago Press, 2018).

156. John Tipple, *The Capitalist Revolution: A History of American Social Thought, 1890-1919* (New York: Pegasus, 1970), 345.

157. James Petras, *The End of the Republic and the Delusion of Empire* (Atlanta, GA: Clarity Press, 2016).

158. Alan Wolfe, *One Nation, After All: What Middle-Class Americans Really Think About* (New York: Penguin Books, 1998), 320.

159. Alan Wolfe, "New Directions in the Marxist Theory of Politics," *Politics & Society* (Winter 1974): 131–159, 143–144 (emphasis in original).

160. Wolfe, "New Directions," 154–155 (emphasis in original).

161. Cf. Nancy MacLean, *Democracy in Chains: The Deep History of the Radical Right's Stealth Plan for America* (New York: Viking, 2017); Wendy Brown, *Undoing the Demos: Neoliberalism's Stealth Revolution* (New York: Zone Books, 2015); Wendy Brown, *In the Ruins of Neoliberalism: The Rise of Antidemocratic Politics in the West* (New York: Columbia University Press, 2019); Robert Kuttner, *Can Democracy Survive Global Capitalism?* (New York: W. W. Norton and Co.,

2018); Chalmers Johnson, *The Sorrows of Empire: Militarism, Secrecy, and the End of the Republic* (New York: Owl Books, 2004); Peter Dale Scott, *The American Deep State: Wall Street, Big Oil, and the Attack on U.S. Democracy* (Lanham, MD: Rowman and Littlefield, 2015); Herman Schwendinger and Julia Schwendinger, *Homeland Fascism: Corporatist Government in the New American Century* (Surrey, BC, Canada: Thought Crimes, 2016); North, *The Crisis of American Democracy*; Peter Hudis, "The Attack on Voting Rights—a Test for Everyone on the Left," *International Marxist-Humanist*, June 28, 2021, https://imhojournal.org/articles/the-attack-on-voting-rights-a-test-for-everyone-on-the-left/.

   162. Wolfe, *Limits of Legitimacy*, 187.
   163. Wolfe, *Limits of Legitimacy*, 241.
   164. Wolfe, *Limits of Legitimacy*, 340.
   165. Wolfe, *Limits of Legitimacy*, 341–342.
   166. Wolfe, *One Nation, After All*, 321.
   167. Wolfe, *Limits of Legitimacy*, 8.

Chapter 4

The Sociological Moment

NORMALCY AND NORMAL SOCIOLOGY

"There is a sense of precarious artificiality in every garden," writes Bauman.[1] Normalcy was a garden, managed within the borders of the nation-state. It was within the nation-state, as what Giddens calls a "bordered power-container" that the processes of the sequestration of experience and internal pacification produced the distinctively modern sense of "everyday life" which Giddens describes as "routinised day-to-day activities in which the routinisation of those activities is not strongly embedded normatively in frameworks of tradition." The processes of the production of everyday life also, Giddens writes, "go together with the creation of generalized deviance," as a necessary corollary of the creation of generalized normalcy.[2] Deviance is also the quintessential object of sociological expertise allied with, and supporting, the nation-state's gardening functions.[3] Bauman points to the way in which American sociology, in its origins, expressed the idea that modern societies required "conscious management of the human condition." Sociology was, therefore, strongly informed by the "modern tendency for social engineering." The discipline "was hoped to be reformatory, and groomed to be managerial." Sociology was, therefore, a project *for* the social production of normalcy, a project of routinizing social activity in a modern capitalist world uprooted from tradition. Such a world was exemplified by America, perhaps especially the mid-west where American sociology was born.[4]

Sociology was a project actively involved in the production of modern everyday life. And yet, through its epistemology and methods, it worked to occlude this very produced (and therefore precariously contingent) makeup of everyday life. Gouldner's 1975 essay "Sociology and the Everyday Life" adds this important insight to his critique of normal sociology. The everyday life, Gouldner writes,

> is the pedestrian and mundane life that is so commonly recurrent that its participants scarcely notice it. EDL [the everyday life] is the seen-but-unnoticed life. It is the everyday, the mundane, the secular, the deserted-by-the-sacred, the god-emptied life . . . It is precisely the EDL of the group and its common background assumptions that constitute its standard of the normal and, thereby, of the more-than-normal, or extraordinary, which is history.[5]

Gouldner argues that everyday life is also the "unnoticed" background and grounding of sociological theory. It is the assumed ordinary against which theoretical awareness of the historical and extraordinary is constructed, but also the source of the theorist's taken-for-granted domain assumptions, which are rooted in their "everyday" social world.[6] This rootedness of sociology in everyday life is both necessarily the case and a trap and limitation on sociology. It is a trap to the extent that it prevents sociology from carrying out its quintessential task, which is precisely to take the everyday from the tacit and unnoticed to the explicit and remarkable. Gouldner writes that

> Sociology's task, then, is to transform the common perspective on the common and . . . to heighten the stable accessibility of the common: to make it visible. Sociology's task is thus to liberate subjugated reality, to emancipate underprivileged reality.[7]

The liberation of subjugated reality requires a *reflexive sociology*.[8] According to Gouldner,

> sociology is a study of everyday life whose object is not so much to discover but to *recover* the nature of that EDL—to help the "object" to become less of an object and more of a subject, to become more fully aware of and hence more fully in control of his EDL.[9]

In contrast, "normal sociology" stymies precisely this quintessential sociological function. Far from making everyday life accessible to reflexive intelligence, normal sociology contributes to its invisibility.

The occlusive consequences of normal sociology lie precisely in the taken-for-granted "common perspective" of normal sociologists that their task is the discovery of a social reality that exists "out there," apart from the sociologist. Gouldner writes,

> The common perspective speaks of sociology as "discovering" reality, as finding or constructing new social laws or regularities, whereas our emphasis here

is not on the discovery of the new *but on the display of the already known*. That is, sociology's task here is *re*covery, not *dis*covery.[10]

The task of reflexive sociology is to recover the social knowledge that is constitutive of, and embedded in, social life. To say this is to reject the idea that its task is to "discover" a social reality that is projected as existing unknown, as a mute and inert object, while the "normal" professional sociologist rhetorically asserts their own monopoly of knowledge as if from a position outside this discovered reality. As Habermas states, with irony, about technocratic ideology: "It is a singular achievement of this ideology to detach society's self-understanding from the frame of reference of communicative action and from the concepts of symbolic interaction and replace it with a scientific model."[11] Normal sociology systematically obscures its own embeddedness in the everyday life, and it is this very occlusion that more tightly binds normal sociology to everyday life, and renders it fettered by the assumptions and limitations of the everyday "natural attitude" or the "seen but unnoticed" character of the world of everyday life, limiting reflexivity.[12] Normal sociology's reification of norms, institutions, and structures is also the reification of human beings by turning them, as Garfinkel put it, into "cultural dopes."[13]

Normal sociology creates its much-cherished objectivity by transforming the people it studies from people into objects. But the study of people is quite unlike the study of objects in that people are necessarily subjects as actors and interpreters of the action. Such interpretations are not extraneous to the action but constitutive of it as social action. Gouldner makes the point that the relationship of sociology to its "object" is unlike that of the physicist to the object-world physicists study and more like an encounter between two groups of scientists, in which one group aims to understand the work of the other:[14]

The "object" of knowledge here, men, is unlike other objects of knowledge, in that they can participate in, have, and share the knowledge developed. They not only provide "data," in whose interpretation they play no part, but are themselves interpreters of their own and of one another's behavior. Sociology is that special study that is about those who investigate their own behavior, who have their own theories about their own collective being and have substantial knowledge of this life of theirs. Sociology is the study of human beings who can construct and achieve a sociology and who continually do so as part of their own seen-but-unnoticed construction of EDL.[15]

By recovering awareness of the quotidian and its active, but hidden, making by people in the course of their everyday lives, reflexive sociology empowers people to remake their ordinary world. Normal sociology, in contrast, hinders the recovery of the ordinary, obscures the tacit knowledge that people have of their everyday lives, and shores up the "seen-but-unnoticed" character of everyday life. It blocks the recovery of the pervasive knowledgeability of ordinary people in ordinary life precisely in order to assert a professional monopoly over societal knowledge. Normal sociology is, therefore, an obstacle to the essential task of sociology.

The professional, normal sociologist is driven by their status-interest to deny and obscure the knowledgeability of ordinary people in society, precisely in order to hide the sociologist's own ordinariness and the rootedness of their own professional knowledge in the everyday life that they share with others. Gouldner writes that the theorist obscures their own ordinariness by "working hard at being different from, and superior to, the ordinary member."[16] Normal sociology operates with a subject-object split, constituting the ordinary member of society as object in order to constitute the sociologist as knowing subject, as if removed from the social realities that they cognize. In so doing, through its claimed professional monopoly of social knowledge, normal sociology undermines the task of sociology by denying the knowledge of ordinary members and preventing their recovery of their social knowledge. Normal sociology is, therefore, an obstacle to the development of society's reflexive knowledgeability.[17]

Normal sociology is tied to the everyday life and prevents its recovery precisely by treating social life and people in society as objects. Normal sociology reinforces the veil of ordinariness that prevents the recovery of everyday life. Gouldner writes, "In a secured world, one need take no notice."[18] The world is "secured" by being assumed, and therefore by being seen-but-unnoticed. Normal sociology constructs a "secured world," a world in which objects have their place, and the right place of objects is known by people in the right place, the experts. It militates against questioning the givenness or objectivity of the social world, which would call into question the role of the sociologist in making a social world of objects, a social world in which people are administered as objects and must accept the world as it confronts them because they are powerless to change it. The sociologist feels secure in a world of objects and feels secure in their own special place as professional knower of this object-world. According to Gouldner:

> To construct the social world as real, reality must be constructed in a special way; it must be constructed as a given and not be infused with problematicity; it must be constituted as something that can be finished rather than being established as a continuing construction, or as an unending work. In sociology, this means that society must be presented as an object-thing and as separate from the process of "making" it. Being external, or taken to be external, objects are used as points of orientation and hence constitute terms and frames in which the self

may be defined. Both sociologists and the men to whom they make reference are object-making; and in part they both make objects for much the same reason: to constitute terms of reference that are security-enhancing.[19]

Normal sociology is, in that way, normalizing. Rather than problematizing the everyday social world, sociology participates in shoring up the "objective" reality of the everyday world, thereby securing existing relations against being called into question. Objectivism supports the epistemic authority of the professionalized expert which, in turn, supports the prevailing authority-structures, institutions and roles which provide the professionalized experts with their institutional position and their warrant to pronounce on objective reality, simultaneously denying epistemic authority and agency to the people whom they study as objects. However, contrary to the ideological appearance of scientificity as different from and superior to ordinary knowing, it is precisely the objectivism of normal sociology that binds it to everyday consciousness. Gouldner writes:

> The normal sociologist's reification of "culture" and of "society" as object-things is essentially the same kind of construction as the ordinary person's construction of an object-centered social world. Both defocalize the extent to which these objects are of their own making.[20]

Normal sociology is joined with the natural attitude, the ordinary everyday perspective, in the reification of the social world. Sociologists' ideas of social structure, institutions, norms, and operationalized variables, Gouldner suggested, were ways of seeing the world without noticing it.[21]

Paradoxically, it is precisely the way in which sociology imagines itself to be apart from the everyday life that roots it most strongly in it. Sociology's methodological "scientificity" is itself what makes sociological consciousness continuous with the ordinary "seen-but-unnoticed" occlusion structured into everyday life.[22] Occlusion derives not from any particular method per se, but from the model of relationship between the knowing subject and the known object. It derives from the assumption of the known as object, which is also the making of the known into an object. In this, sociology participates in reifications of capital and bureaucracy. The interweaving of sociology with these forms of domination, and the interweaving of these with patriarchy, is elaborated Dorothy E. Smith. She writes,

> Established sociology has objectified a consciousness of society and social relations that "knows" them from the standpoint of their ruling and from the standpoint of men who do that ruling. To learn how to know society from sociology . . . is to look at it from these standpoints. It is to take on the view of ruling.[23]

The ways of seeing and discussing in sociology are, Smith argues, homologous with those of the array of professionals who administer society within the framework of the nation-state. Hence, sociology is a form of knowledge that views the social world from the standpoint of the institutions of rule that make up the nation-state. Vaughan argues that "Sociologists have been hesitant, even resistant, to examine the discipline's growing incorporation into the nation-state apparatus and into the process of bureaucratic rationalization more generally." Vaughan suggests that the "natural science model" is the core commitment that prevents such reflexivity and thereby accommodates sociology to the objectifying abstractions of the state: "The natural science model, which assumes the existence of fixed and immutable laws of nature, calls on sociologists to conceive of existing social relationships as 'legitimate'."[24] By constructing a stable world of objects, the sociologist joins with the assumptions of everyday life in providing ontological security. For, as Gouldner writes, "Ordinariness and stability are the ontological requirements of security. Or, more properly, of the sense of security, and of passivity and acquiescence."[25] Sociology is not just observing an external reality but, by its very interpretations of the world and its claim to epistemic authority for those interpretations, is involved in making the social world, in the sense of the collectively inhabited social reality. Sociology imagines the collective it inhabits to be nation and nation-state; it has constructed society as nation-state. It recovers life in such a way as to render it as society and to render society as nation-state.[26] Its natural science model authorizes sociology to assert the reality of this entity, society. If successful, sociology makes "society" into a category through which human beings collectively interpret reality, in this case the reality of themselves. Society thus becomes part of the social ontology of the collectively inhabited social world. But the grounds by which sociology claims authority, its scientificity, its objectivity, are the means by which sociology does something that model of scientific objectivity excludes, it makes its object through its very acts of interpretation. Gouldner argues,

> Sociology has the problem of constituting the social world's reality, of constituting society as real, without making pointed affirmation of this and thereby speaking ambiguously about that reality. To do so, it speaks of society as an out-there world, as externalized and externally situated. To intimate the reality of society, sociologists defocalize the manner in which they along with other, non-sociologists, participate in the construction of that world and have not merely discovered it. It is thus that the social world is made solid, secured, ordinary.[27]

This passage suggests that what objectivism masks is precisely that it is sociology's *task* to *create* society as ontologically real, to make society, and to make a particular kind of society, a modern industrial bourgeois society that is stable and can be taken for granted. In other words, sociology has been tasked with constructing bourgeois hegemony. As such, sociology's positivistic affirmation of the actual is involved in a legitimizing project. The task of sociology is to constitute bourgeois relations as society, as real and stable and lasting, and to legitimize them as such. Gouldner writes that to make the world ordinary and, therefore,

> solid is to quiet doubts and anxieties, to relax and tranquilize; it is to create a world in which one can be at home, or rather, at Home. Normal sociology's task, then, is to put men at their ease and to make the world homey.[28]

Sociology's task is to replace the religious sacred canopy with a secular, scientific canopy appropriate to an industrial society. But any such canopy makes what is under it appear more resilient than it truly is and hides what is beyond the canopy. A further sense that could be attached to Dennis Wrong's concept of the "over-socialized conception of man" is that sociology's imagination of the sacred canopy of society occludes the natural world beyond it, out of which this social canopy is ultimately constructed.[29] That is especially true of the canopy of modernity, which is a profane canopy built out of technologies that control nature and keep it at bay. It is true of the quasi-sacred canopy of the commodity fetish, which occludes both labor and nature.

There is a particular kind of reification of social life that takes place in capitalist society. Sohn-Rethel argues that the scientific worldview arises from commodity fetishism bound up with the abstract nature of the social synthesis, achieved through the market. This real abstraction is the foundation on which bourgeois social relations are made and the basis on which sociology's abstract "society" is intellectually constructed. Sohn-Rethel's argument implies that the routinization of daily life in capitalist society expresses a more radical reification due to the way in which social relations are abstractified by the market.[30]

Quotidian life in capitalist societies is organized around and oriented to commodities. Marx opened *Capital Volume 1* with the statement that capitalism presents itself most immediately as an "immense accumulation of commodities."[31] Normalcy in capitalist society depends on the availability of commodities, a balance of availability and scarcity that shapes a class way of life. But what was distinctive about the mid-twentieth century, and especially mid-century-American modernity, was the suppression of class differences in consumption, as a feature of mass consumerism and the achievement of relative equality in comparison with what went before and what has come after. Normalcy evoked a middle-class way of life, and its generalization as an ideal that was broadly achievable, making possible the idea of a middle-class society as a classless society, something that America at this time seemed to model. Klaus Ronneberger writes that "consumption was established as the dominant form of culture under Fordism and became a motor of social development."[32]

According to George Steinmetz, "The integration of sociology into the Fordist domestic and foreign policy scientific infrastructure" was bound up with the way in which sociological assumptions meshed with, reinforced, and derived plausibility from, the patterns of life under postwar Fordism and Keynesianism. A key aspect of this was the rising living standards that underpinned the sense of structuredness and stability, and therefore the reification, of the social world. Steinmetz writes,

> Wage earners in general, including the better-paid sectors of the working class, were able for the first time in the history of capitalism to develop a horizon of stable expectations concerning their own future, enhanced by relatively generous protection against the risks of unemployment, sickness, and poverty in old age. The social ontology of the Fordist subject was aligned with *security*.[33]

The image of normalcy was associated with consumerism, or the emergence of a mass consumer society. This implies a connection between normalcy and commodity fetishism. The seeming homogeneity of life in a middle-class society of consumers depended on the occlusion of the social antagonism inherent in commodity production, that is, the conflict between capital and labor. The taken-for-grantedness of everyday life in capitalist society reflected the finished, objectified form of the things with which, and in orientation to which, everyday life was conducted.[34] Wolfe wrote, in 1974,

> increasingly the process of alienation becomes reproduced in all aspects of society. It is one of the great contributions of writers like Ronald Barthes and Jean Baudrillard to see authority relationships in the symbols of everyday activity: furniture arrangements, wrestling matches, and gadgets.

Hence, Wolfe wrote, "A narrowly political or economic critique of capitalism makes less sense than a full-scale critique of its culture."[35]

"SOCIETY" AS COMMODITY FETISHISM AND NATIONALISM

Everyday life under capitalism is conducted in a world that presents itself as finished. The disparate human activities that manifest the division of labor are united and coordinated invisibly through the operations of the market.

What Sohn-Rethel calls the "social synthesis" is therefore accomplished blindly, unconsciously, and abstractly. Sohn-Rethel argues that this abstract ordering of human activity, through the impersonal operations of the market, historically enabled the conceptualization of the physical universe as an abstract system operating according to impersonal laws. This impersonal Newtonian universe provided the ontological model and scientific ideal for the emergence in the nineteenth century of sociology, the term coined by Auguste Comte for what he initially conceptualized as "social physics." The rise of capitalism was the creation of social relations of the kind that could be conceptualized as impersonal laws, not acts of men or even a deity. Hence, the religious representation of the social whole could no longer be sustained and a new scientific representation was called for, a representation of a social world existing sui generis, operating according to its own immanent rules and mechanisms.[36]

Under capitalism, the synthesis of the division of labor is accomplished not by the laborers themselves and not within the laboring activity, but is removed from this activity by the abstract operations of the market. In the capitalist factory, the organization and coordination of working activity is achieved through a plan embodied in the technological specifications of the machinery. At both these levels, then, the synthesis takes place behind the backs of the producers, rather than according to their conscious will. Intelligence and decision are removed from the working activity itself, that is, the labor process. The synthesis of working activity takes place outside, and removed from, the work. Intelligence is removed from the physical activity of work and this physical activity is denied the ability to organize and coordinate itself—this is done from above. The division between intellectual and manual labor, therefore, arises from the alienation of intelligence from the worker. Intelligence appears outside the labor process itself.[37]

Society, as the social synthesis of the division of labor, appears in reified form as a thing in itself, a mysterious abstract thing, the cognition of which requires a special position that is also outside of the working activity that produces this abstract thing. The contemplation of society as a whole, as if from the outside of this whole, is the work of intellectuals, specifically sociologists. The sociologist appears, therefore, to exist somehow apart from the thing.

Comte's fashioning of the sociologist on the model of the priest and the construction of a new religion illustrates how it was necessary to conceive of the sociological knower as separate from and, as a priest, superior to, or transcending, the known. The Comtean image of the sociologist was dropped as an explicit part of sociological positivism, though it remained, implicitly, at the core of Durkheim's project. The construction of a new religion, as such, was no longer necessary to provide an institutional support for the claim of the sociologist to exist above society once sociology became institutionalized as a discipline within the university. The university, by its institutional boundaries, positions the sociologist as separate from the known and supports the sociologist's claim to scientific objectivity as a "view from nowhere."

However, for Comte, sociology was necessarily reconnected with its object through the aspiration to provide conscious direction to society, through reform and planning. Sociology came into being as a project to contemplate the social world *in order to intervene* on, guide, and manage the social order. While it was the market and the monetary exchange abstraction that made possible the abstract and reified conception of social order as amenable to scientific study, sociology developed as a response to the failure, and impossibility, of securing social order on the basis of market relations left to themselves.[38]

The emergence of sociology represented a shift in bourgeois ideology, away from classical liberal doctrine based on the ontological assumption and ethic of individualism and the political economy of the unfettered self-ordering market, toward the recognition of the ontological reality of the social.[39] According to Leon Bramson, "sociology's most important historical source [was] 19th century European conservatism."[40] Sociology represented the incorporation of conservatism into liberalism.[41] While maintaining a liberal belief in progress, led by the advance of science and industry, Comte's philosophy was a turn away from liberalism toward a holist ontology of the social. Liberal social contract theory entailed an ontology of individuals, the state, and civil society (as an economic market combined with a "free market of ideas"). Comte's organismic conception of society, and therefore holist ontology, contrasted markedly with the liberal conception of civil society. Against the liberal conception of civil society as composed of competitive relations between individuals, Comte put forward a cooperative and holistic account of the social organism.

The resistance that Comte faced in his time reflected the inherent difficulty surrounding sociology within bourgeois culture and the bourgeois university. The fundamental ontology of bourgeois social thought is atomism, in the sense of taking the individual as the basic unit and agent. Social contract theory, Benthamite utilitarianism, and rational choice theory are expressions of the default ontological assumption of bourgeois thought, in other words its original classical liberal form. This individualist ontology is basic to bourgeois social thought, precisely because it reflects "homo economicus," or the type of individual the bourgeois is required to be by the conditions of the market. It is the basic ontology of the market, from which bourgeois thought emanates.

Comte's explicit rejection of the utilitarian model of the social represents in itself a significant turn in bourgeois thought away from classical liberal and Enlightenment republican assumptions on the basis of which the bourgeoisie staked its claims as a rising and revolutionary class and toward terms that reflect the maturing of capitalism and the growing problem of controlling the working class. Comte's greatest influence was Henri Comte de Saint Simon, for whom Comte was secretary as a young man. Gouldner emphasizes the position of Saint Simon as the founder of positivism. Durkheim said that in Saint Simon "we encounter the seeds already developed of all the ideas which have fed the thinking of our time."[42] The importance of Saint Simon means also the emanation of sociology's conception of the social from utopian socialism. In this way, sociology co-opted the solidaristic ideology of the growing political consciousness of the working class, transforming socialism's "social" from a negative to a positive principle, in the sense that it was no longer counterposed to the prevailing order but became enlisted in its maintenance.

Comte, a student of the Ecole Polytechnic, was concerned with the creation of a social order for a modern technological society. The interest expressed in and by Comte was in the creation of the social conditions for reason, put into practice in industrial engineering. The functionalism that derived from Comte took as its task the identification of social forms functioning optimally for a modern, industrial social order. In sociology, reason, now operating scientifically rather than metaphysically, discerns its purpose, not in abstract thought but positively in what exists. Comte was fond of De Maistre's aphorism, "Whatever is necessary exists." According to Gertrud Lenzer, Comte thought that "To move the social and political crisis toward a permanent end, therefore, we must bring human ideas and sentiments into harmony with the necessary course of development." This meant "universal submission to the necessity embodied in the predominant and rising social and economic forces—more specifically, the new industrial-economic order."[43] Comte, therefore, presented the emergence of a post-capitalist cooperative industrial society as an evolutionary development operating within the present order rather than requiring a radical revolutionary break with the present order. Lenzer explains that Comte crafted a new type of conservatism: "[W]ith Comte conservativism entered a qualitatively new phase. Indeed, he is the originator of a new conservativism that does not remain in the realm of mere reaction—it might be called anticipatory conservativism."[44] Anticipatory conservatism, or sociology, arises as a conservative response to the new organized forms of opposition to bourgeois society in the working class. But this is a doctrine of maintaining order through managing change.

The departure from classical liberalism is made evident by Herbert Spencer's laissez-faire critique of the technocratic statist implications of Comte. Spencer characterized Comte's social ideal as "one in which government is developed to the greatest extent . . . [and] the individual life shall be subordinated in the greatest degree to the social life."[45] Spencer's critique is indicative of the difficult place that the ontology of the social occupies in bourgeois thought and, as a result, the difficult position of sociology as a discipline within the bourgeois university and bourgeois culture, precisely because of the conflict between the sociological idea of "society" and the liberal assumption of an individualist ontology.

Sociology's combination of liberalism with utopian socialism and conservatism may be understood as a reaction against the emergence of the working class as a political force as manifested in the growth of socialist movements, and the ideological significance of Marxism from the 1848 Manifesto of the Communist Party onward as the antithesis of bourgeois liberalism. Göran Therborn argues that

> Sociology . . . developed and became decisively established as an attempt to deal with the social, moral and cultural problems of the capitalist economic order, under the shadow of a militant working-class movement and a more or less immediate threat of revolutionary socialism.[46]

The incorporation of sociology into the university as a social scientific discipline has to be understood against the background of the challenge that the working class posed to the stability of bourgeois relations and the need of the bourgeoisie to utilize the nation-state for the task of making order, not just by the negative means of coercion but by the positive means of social amelioration and reform. In the United States, the emergence of sociology was bound up with middle-class social reformism, often expressed in liberal Protestantism but also drawing its philosophical perspective from pragmatism, as well as a broadly pragmatic orientation in the sense of regarding the state as an instrument for achieving social purposes. Hence, Tipple writes,

> Nearly all men of pragmatic persuasion, whether conservative or liberal, regarded the state as the most desirable instrument of social control. From Theodore Roosevelt and Brook Adams to Walter Lippmann and Edward Ross, their dream envisaged a kind of modified state capitalism, run along the lines of a big modern corporation, with a trained administrative elite firmly in control, a powerful but disciplined industry, and an orderly, informed, forward-looking public.[47]

Wolfe similarly describes the American apostles of a new social order, shaped by the national state, mobilizing the wisdom of experts:

> One of the key theorists of the new order in the United States was economist Richard Ely, founder of the American Economic Association, teacher of Woodrow Wilson, Edward Ross, John R. Commons, Frederick Howe, Frederick

Jackson Turner, and (indirectly) Robert LaFollette, and sworn enemy of both
socialism and laissez-faire liberalism. To Ely the state was, literally, to be
worshipped. It is "religious in essence." Further, "God works through the State
in carrying out His purposes more universally than through any other institution." With God on their side, reformers like Ely were convinced that the future
belonged to them. It did.[48]

These reformist thinkers promoted and helped to solidify, Wolfe writes, the
"principle of using the power of the government to preserve the capitalist
order."[49]

The nation-state is the bourgeois solution to the problem of social order,
and the contradiction of this with the individualist commitments of bourgeois
thought constitutes the fundamental problem of liberalism: in philosophy
what political theorists call the problem of "political obligation," that is,
the need to justify in abstract moral-philosophical terms why the individual
is obligated to obey the state, and in practice the continual tension around
attempts to limit the state by "civil rights." The abstract insolubility of the
contradiction, generated by social contract theory, between the supposi-
tions of the sovereignty of the individual and the sovereignty of the state,
represents the theoretical and practical insolubility of the problem of social
order within the framework of classical liberalism. If the nation-state is the
institutional solution to the problem of order, nationalism is the bourgeoisie's
cultural solution. It is through nationalism that Edmund Burke's insistence
on the nonrational emotional bond to institutions and to the past in the form
of tradition occupies its position in bourgeois thought as a counterbalance
to the individualizing and disembedding tendencies of the market and social
contract theory. What Eric Hobsbawm calls the "invented traditions" of
nationalism are a crucial conservative element mobilized in the bourgeois
solution to the problem of social order that is characteristic of, and chronic
to, modernity.[50]

Nationalist and statist themes were at the heart of the concerns of the
Verein für Sozialpolitik (Social Policy Association) of which Weber was an
active member. Andrew Zimmerman writes:

> The approach taken by economists in the Verein für Sozialpolitik represented
> a venerable academic mainstream in Germany, a direction associated with the
> economist Friedrich List, whose 1841 *National System of Political Economy*
> criticized followers of Adam Smith for ignoring the distinct positions of nations
> in international economies in their pell-mell endorsement of free trade.[51]

What Zimmerman calls the "state socialism" of the *Verein für Sozialpolitik*
in the form of advocating a "paternalistic" welfare state together with their

calls for regulation against classical liberal laissez-faire was the basis for the label *Kathedersozialisten*, or socialists of the chair or lectern, which was applied to the *Verein*. The "state socialist" element of the outlook of the German economists and sociologists was, Zimmerman writes, "formed in reaction to the social democracy of the workers' movement."[52]

Weber's bourgeois liberal commitment to the free market was tempered by his concern for the maintenance of bourgeois social order, tied to the nation-state, national identity, and the nation-state's capacity for empire. Weber's anxieties over the racial characteristics of the German nation combined with his concerns with labor discipline and with his historical-comparative sociological preoccupation with the shaping of the self. The market could not, by its own action, produce the kinds of human beings psychologically constituted in such a way as to sustain it. Bourgeois society, therefore, required more than the market in order to maintain the bourgeois class in control. Capitalism required the production of workers suited to industrial discipline and members of the bourgeoisie suited to the tasks that confronted the class beyond commercial activity, that is, in the sciences (and professions more generally) and as politicians.

As Goldman has shown, Weber's interest in the idea and historical practice of the calling or vocation was fundamentally a concern with self-discipline and the self as a source or channel of social power.[53] The making of disciplined subjects required the action of the state in the role of what Bauman calls the gardener. The securing of the spatial boundaries of the nation, which Weber emphasized in his very definition of the state as a monopoly of violence within a "territory," and securing the ethno-racial-cultural boundaries of the population, were essential for securing social order and bourgeois rule. Since market relations were insufficient to generate solidarity and affective legitimacy for the bourgeois state, and since solidarity in the production process is potentially in direct contradiction with bourgeois class rule, the bourgeoisie depended on pre-capitalist traditions, or their ersatz nationalist reconstruction, as sources of social order. Traditional solidarities destroyed by the development of capitalism were reconstituted at the level of the nation.[54] These forms of folkish solidarity based on national identity, which constitute the bourgeois solution to the problem of social order, are by their very nature exclusive to the population groups that they define. These forms of mechanical solidarity or *Gemeinschaft*, precisely by the solidarity that they create on the basis of sameness, imply boundedness and difference. The way they create inclusion is also the way they exclude. Weber's nationalism indicates the way in which sociology as a project was tied to the nation-state as the bourgeois solution to the problem of order. In the face of the growth of the working class and its political consciousness and power, sociology represented a current of bourgeois thought that sought to respond to this by shoring up the nonmarket sources of social order that supported market relations.

As well as being a middle-class response to the growth of the working class, sociology also reflected the transformation of capitalism itself and the transformations of social life wrought by capitalism. The inherently contradictory sociological attempt to combine a conservative conception of collective life with liberal individualism reflected the fundamental contradiction in capitalism, identified by Engels, as the contradiction between socialized production and private appropriation. Classical liberalism was the ideological manifestation of private capitalist appropriation. But classical liberalism was conceptually and politically unable to handle the ideological and political tasks posed by capitalism's development of the socialization of labor and production. Liberal individualism as a reflection of the atomizing anti-social sociality of the market was unable to provide solutions to the problems of coordination and control posed by the increasingly complex chains of cooperation involved in the process of production, an increasing complexity for which mechanization was both a cause and an effect. This social complexity of production, involved in the increasing scale and complex organization of the workplace and in the multiplying furcation of the division of labor, was manifested in the growth of the industrial working class. The contradiction between private appropriation and socialized production also manifested itself in the problem of control within the factory, and therefore in the contradiction, as Marx put it, between "anarchy in the social division of labor and despotism in the manufacturing division of labor." Hence, the contradiction between private appropriation and socialized production is expressed in the tension between liberal freedom modeled on the freedom of atomized buyers and sellers on the market and the political requirements of class rule.[55]

The abstract political individual, abstract rights, impersonal reason and legalism of classical liberalism reflected the impersonal abstractness of the "cash nexus" which, as Marx and Engels said, doused all social life with the "icy water of egotistical calculation."[56] But the bourgeoisie faced the heat of the densely packed, seething urban masses into which it continually flung individuals. Conservatives argued that there could be no order without the warmth of emotion, passion, and personal fealty. How could capitalism prevent these emotional currents coursing through the great collectivities that it produced from eroding its icy edifices? The relationship between impersonal rules and more personal and human forms of belonging and attachment has been a central philosophical problem of the sociological endeavor.

The socialization of production required the societalization of capitalism, in other words the creation of a capitalist social order. This, it was increasingly evident, could not consist only of contractual relations emanating from the market and could not be the (inherently competitive and conflictual) social relations of the bourgeois class itself but must incorporate the "whole" of society, in particular the growing and increasingly restive working class. It could not be the spontaneous equilibrium of buyers and sellers on the market but had to become a conscious project of building a society within which these market relations could be stabilized. Abstract market relations between things (money and commodities) were necessarily embedded in concrete relationships between human beings. These were not merely relations of exchange but increasingly complex cooperative coordination of labor within the production process.

Further, the growth of the working class and its political power demanded attention to social relations extending beyond the immediate process of production to life outside the workplace required for the biological and social reproduction of labor and the control of the working class. Religious charitable institutions and the poor house were the bourgeoisie's favored means. But they extended further to the development of penitentiaries, police forces, asylums, clinics, and schools, as Foucault is most known for delineating. Despite his hostility to a Marxist explanation, the most valuable historical documentation and insights of his *Discipline and Punish* are not only compatible with a class explanation but require it.[57] But while Foucault emphasizes the individualizing effects of the forms of surveillance imposed by these institutions, it is equally the case that the development and imposition of these forms of discipline were responses to the growing socialization of production with which the growth of the working class and its threat to the ruling order was entangled. It is evident, even from Foucault's account, that new institutions of social control reflected and extended capital's despotism in the workshop, with its factory discipline and scientific-technological rationalization of production and the time-discipline that was an accompaniment not only of the "time is money" spirit of capitalism but also the reduction of the worker to what Marx called "time's carcase" in the wage relationship.[58] The demand for bodily and mental self-control and punctuality in the school and in the new forms of control operating via surveillance was amenable to the new forms of work discipline and economic rationality required and imposed by capitalist production. The whole history of middle-class reformism in the nineteenth century, from the treatment of the mentally ill to the limitation of the working day and restrictions on child labor, should be understood in terms of the project of constructing a stable bourgeois social order. This meant embedding capitalism in social relations in which the working class would be accommodated, regulated, and controlled and within the prevailing structures of class power.[59]

Societalization of capital, as the construction of a social order capable of sustaining capitalist production, has been to a large extent a project carried out by middle-class reformers. It has been historically interwoven with philanthropy, religiously motivated moralism, utopian socialism (and, later, social democracy), and the development of the human sciences and the social sciences. Sociology was necessarily caught in the broader currents of the "double movement" whereby the rise of capitalism rips apart preexisting social bonds, while the demands and needs of the working class, mediated by this kind of reformism often directly enacted by members of the middle class, reconstruct social bonds in new forms within the context of capitalist relations.[60] It is the history of the modern nation-state, with its coercive but also regulative, protective, and organizing administrative functions, which Pierre Bourdieu calls, respectively, the right hand and the left hand of the state.[61]

However, the project of stabilizing capitalism as a social order stood in contradiction with the internal dynamics of capitalism itself: the anarchy of the market and the power and economic interests of the owners of capital. In opposition to the long-term stabilization of a capitalist social order stands the capitalists' own short-term interests and outlook: *Après moi le déluge!*[62] This introduces a tension between the reformist efforts spurred by middle-class layers and the more direct interest of the owners of the means of production in exploitation. There is a related tension between the right hand and the left hand of the state, and between capitalist interests and the left hand in particular.[63] Capital continually undermines, or threatens to undermine and renders precarious, its own societalization, that is, the project of embedding capitalist relations in a stable and lasting capitalist social order.

This contradiction is expressed in the notion that "the ruling class does not rule."[64] Since the direct rule of capital would be disastrous to society, and thereby to the stability of its own foundations, social democracy has played a crucial historical role in the stabilization of capitalist relations. It has done so as the mediator of class struggle, introducing forms that both rationalize capitalism and rationalize the social order for capitalism.[65] This has become a conscious project of social democracy as it has historically accommodated itself to the prevailing structure of class power and come to serve it. Hence, today it is not unusual to hear social democrats repeat the mantra that they must "save capitalism from itself." This formulation expresses exactly the contradictions in the process of the societalization of capital that have been sketched above.

The contradictory nature of the societalization of capital is evident in the role of the working class, pursuing its needs and interests through political mobilization. The accommodation of the interests and demands of the working class through political reform and the institutions of the nation-state, most often against the opposition of the bourgeois class, played a fundamental role in establishing institutions and practices that came to be associated with the very idea of a modern society and that reciprocally acted to integrate the working class into a modern way of living which was embourgeoisiefied, in the sense of an atomized, individualized, and nucleated (in the family), consumerist way of life. At the same time, the increasingly complex sociality generated by the socialization of labor was expressed in the political power of the working class and integrated into the structures of the capitalist state and also projected, as idea, onto the state in the form of nationalism. This was the ideological corollary, with its saturation of everyday life in what Michael Billig calls "banal nationalism," of the growing organizing power of the nation-state over everyday life.[66] Nationalism, even while ideology, reflected the reality of the organization of solidarity around, and attachment of solidarity to, the nation-state.

The routinization and emerging taken-for-grantedness of modern everyday life provided the infrastructure and background assumptions that yielded "tacit consent" and stabilized capitalism as a form not only of economy but of society, colonizing and incorporating quotidian life. This process (an aspect of Polanyi's "double movement") may be regarded as the self-domestication, self-pacification, and self-integration of the working class within capitalism. The working class, thereby, reciprocally civilized the ruling class, demanding restrictions on the cruelest manifestations of the exploitation relationship. This process of self-integration of the working class was a central part of the building of the modern nation-state. The double movement, then, consisted of capitalism's destruction of pre-capitalist social bonds and social identities, located at the geographical level or range of the village or region or organized through pre-capitalist occupational structures such as guilds, and the reconstruction of social solidarity now symbolically and materially attached to the nation-state with its warfare and welfare Janus face.

Capitalism creates a destabilized world in which, as Marx said, "all that is solid melts into air." But, at the same time, capitalist society is a world in which everyday life becomes routinized and banalized and the reproduction of capitalism takes place through the mundane and taken-for-granted activities of everyday life.[67] Capitalism creates chaos, disruption, and perpetual change. But living in capitalism can be so often banal, routine, repetitive, and emptied of meaning. The societalization of capital is the embedding of capitalist relations in a capitalist everyday life that can be accepted as given. Lefebvre wrote that "The quotidian is what is humble and solid, what is taken for granted and that of which all the parts follow each other in such a regular, unvarying succession that those concerned have no call to question their sequence."[68] It is the construction of an orderly, routinized, and prosaic world, which is also a world in which it is possible to feel a sense of security, predictability, graspability, familiarity, and habituality. The times and places in which this societalization was accomplished constitute the reference of the notion of normalcy, for which there is now nostalgia.

Caudwell observed that capitalism "presents the unique picture of disorganization amid organization."[69] Today it increasingly seems to be organization amid a more overarching disorganization. Capitalism is both of these things:

the anarchy of the market and the despotism of the workshop. Everyday life contains in it the anxious awareness that behind it is the chaos of the market, which disturbs the everyday. Sometimes everyday life is entirely drawn into this vortex, as with unemployment and other related calamities. But normal everyday life is also organized into certain standard rhythms, routines, patterns, utterances, and behaviors.[70] Work is a central organizing force in shaping these rhythms and patterns. The factory and the corporation have been central institutions in which the lived time of everyday life is experienced, and in which it has become organized and patterned. Work time has its reproductive corollary in the activity of commodity consumption, which becomes, correspondingly, increasingly monopolistically organized, with the increasing liquidation (dissolution and social dispersal) of the traditional petit-bourgeoisie. Lefebvre called this monopolistic organization of everyday life through commodity consumption "the bureaucratic society of controlled consumption."[71]

SOCIOLOGY AS TECHNOCRATIC UTOPIANISM

As J. K. Galbraith pointed out in *The New Industrial State*, published in 1967, the organization of the firm itself, increasing in scale over the course of the twentieth century, incorporated within itself the principle of planning.[72] The corporation also incorporated science within itself, in the form of industrial research laboratories. Corporate planning represents an attempt to control not merely an organization of human bodies and actions extending in spatial scope, but also to colonize the future. The corporation, therefore, represents not merely a formal system, not a blind mechanism as in the market, but a consciously directed system of planning. It seeks to organize the future and thereby produce outcomes that accord with the conscious objectives of a plan. Technocratic social reformism within capitalism has been motivated by the conception that the socially disorganizing tendencies of the free market could be regulated and tempered by the substantively rational potential of capitalist planning, if only this principle of conscious direction could be extended from within the factory or firm to the social organization of consumption and the ordering of reproduction and leisure.

Howard Brick's *Transcending Capitalism: Visions of a New Society in American Thought* traces the rise and development, from the Progressive Era to the 1970s, of a continuous strand of American "social liberalism" which presented the social as a sphere that could regulate and harmonize the competitive relations of capitalist society and as the locus of technocratic social reform in which this conscious regulation of society would gradually replace the market as the primary organizing mechanism of industrial society.[73] The idea of science as being, in and of itself, the antidote to the chaotic tendencies of capitalist society has appealed to intellectuals (both humanistic and scientific-technical), for it gives intellectuals, as the carriers of knowledge, reason, and scientific culture, the vanguard role in shaping the human destiny and, therefore, a leading position in the institutions and power structures of modern society.[74] This idea has been particularly attractive to social democracy in its reformist orientation and to broader reformist tendencies within the middle class, especially among professionals. The notion of science as an autonomous force of modernity, operating independently of the market and capable of restraining or even overcoming capitalist self-interest, greed, and conflict, is also inherently appealing to the professional middle class and to intellectuals as members of the middle class, because it seems to obviate the need for violent class struggle and relegates the working class to a passive position in the background. It suggests the possibility of orderly change, carried out rationally, from above, by intellectual and professional elites. It suggests the possibility of technocratic reform of capitalism or, beyond that, of the possibility of transcending capitalism through a process of (elite-guided or managed) evolution, toward a technocratically organized industrial or post-industrial society.[75]

Technocratic thinking, therefore, appeals to middle-class layers who, due to their class position, experience themselves as in between the opposing class forces of capitalism and conceive of themselves as capable of mediating between capital and labor, while also understanding their own status as deriving from their autonomy or independence from these classes.[76] Gouldner identified the position of sociology within this broader middle-class culture of utilitarianism:

> In fine, the newly emerging sociology did not reject the utilitarian premises of the new middle-class culture, but rather sought to broaden and extend them. It became concerned with *collective* utility in contrast to individual utility, with the needs of *society* for stability and progress, and with what was useful for this. In particular, it stressed the importance of other, "social" utilities, as opposed to an exclusive focus on the production of economic utilities.[77]

Sociology arose from the contradiction in bourgeois culture between economic and social utilitarianism. This contradiction is derived from, and is an intellectual expression of, the contradiction between exchange value and use value. Sociology pushed the implications of conceiving utility as applying socially, above the level of the individual, to the limits possible within the framework of bourgeois thought. It, therefore, corresponded with the efforts of middle-class reformists to, in practice, push collective responsibility to the limits allowable within bourgeois culture and politics. The construction of the nation-state as locus and machinery of reform corresponded with, and was reflected in, sociology's nation-based conceptualization of the social whole, that is "society."

Sociology and middle-class social reform shared a common technocratic epistemology and social basis. The social basis was the professional-managerial class that was growing in response to working-class struggle (as a feature of what Fred Block points to as the rationalization of capitalism from below[78]) and the technological and organizational transformations of capital resulting from automation and Taylorism and the growth of the welfare state. What the growth of this stratum reflected was the rationalization and societalization (and in a certain way, bound up with this, the nationalization) of capitalism as the problem of order posed itself in the form of the emergence of the working class as a political force.[79] This meant the development of an ideology of the social through which to conceptualize the "society" that was the object of administration. It, therefore, meant the emergence of sociology as a form of bourgeois ideology that ran counter to the individualism of classical liberalism. What Gouldner argues it retained from classical liberalism was its utilitarianism. Sociology and social reform drew on the implication of substantive rationality in utilitarianism that stood in contradiction with the formal rationality of the market. This may be discerned in Bentham's utilitarian philosophy precisely in the fact that this philosophy is *consequentialist*. In other words, it is concerned with the evaluation of outcomes. It *morally* evaluates actions on the basis of the happiness, or lack thereof, to which they lead. Jeremy Bentham, as moral philosopher and social reformer, was explicitly articulating the moral implications of utilitarianism. Such moral outcomes were not necessarily achievable through the formally rational system of the market. Hence, the nonmarket substantive implications of utilitarianism, manifesting the contradiction between use value and exchange value, formed the language of the bourgeois social reformer. Further, this language of utility, combined with science and technology, was institutionalized in the welfare state.

The growth of the welfare state and of associated professional roles institutionalized utilitarianism in these paid managerial, administrative, and professional positions. It was precisely this "New Class" of middle-class professionals and managers that carried the norm of utilitarianism with its anti-market and reformist implications. This gains a certain independent economic existence that is particularly related to the growth of the functions of the state and public sector, but also is not highly distinguishable from the growth of corporate bureaucracy and management. The neoliberal and neoconservative fear was that this "New Class" had gained too much power, reflecting a sense of the challenge that it posed to business interests. Universities were of course central to this and the conflicts of the 1960s and

1970s between Governor Ronald Reagan and the University of California reflected this politically.[80]

Prior to the 1970s, the PMC had legitimized itself based on its knowledge, and especially with a discourse of science that presented science as socially and politically neutral. The legitimation of social reform in terms of its scientifically based objectivity and neutrality was, therefore, related to the problem of the discipline of sociology in justifying its own claim to authoritative knowledge about the social. Functionalist sociology of science presented the objectivity and neutrality as achieved through the socialization of professionals into these values as norms of a community. It thereby provided justification for universities, for the academic education of professionals, and for state support for science including social science. Gouldner argues that sociology and social reform were legitimized by "the extrusion of the economic from the social" so that sociology would deal with what was left over from economics, just as reformers would deal with what was left over from the market.[81] In contrast with Marxist analysis, technocratic post-capitalism displaces the concept of capitalism as the central organizing concept for understanding modernity. In that way, such ideas have fit with the displacement of class struggle in non-Marxist sociology. It suggests that modern society is something other than capitalist, that while the market is a sector, science gives industrial society a rationality not just of mechanism or means but, if applied properly, of outcomes.

If modern society was, in essence, rational, rather than capitalist, and if science was integral to that rationality, this suggested that modernity was evolving in a progressive way, as science does, and that this social evolution was due to science. It further implied that the forms of social organization, orientation, and occupational role that underpinned and socially carried scientific rationality also provided the basis for the broader organization of society. Hence, it ascribed to scientists, scientific communities, intellectuals, professionals and professional groups a status independent from the class structure of capitalism and from the interests that follow from class position. Notions of objectivity and disinterestedness attaching to science and professions, therefore, have been important to technocratic claims that science is neutral with respect to competing social interests and that science can be applied neutrally so as to serve general rather than particular interests. Gouldner suggests that, for Parsons, the professionals, their institutionalized motives transcending the profit-motive, provided a way to redeem modernity.[82]

Sociology is the utopia of the professionals and the professionalization of utopia. The utopia of the professionals is normalcy. Comte transformed Saint Simonian utopianism into a utopia of normalcy. Presenting modernity as a babel upon which positivism would impose intellectual order, Comte wrote:

While stability in fundamental maxims is the first condition of genuine social order, we are suffering under an utter disagreement that may be called universal. Till a certain number of general ideas can be acknowledged as a rallying point of social doctrine, the nations will remain in a revolutionary state . . . and their institutions can be only provisional. But whenever the necessary agreement on first principles can be obtained, appropriate institutions will issue from them, without shock or resistance; for the causes of disorder will have been arrested by the mere fact of the agreement. It is in this direction that those must look who desire a natural and regular, a normal, state of society.[83]

So the goal of sociology, according to Comte, was social "stability," "regularity," and "a normal state of society." This normal state of society is here contrasted with society in a "revolutionary state." In an anticipation of the functionalist view that social systems tend toward equilibrium, Comte presented *normal* regularity and stability as the *natural* condition of society.

Sociology may be regarded as the ideology of normalcy. The fate of sociology is, therefore, tied to the fate of normalcy. Sociology arose with, and is inextricably connected with, the social production of normalcy. Sociology provided ideological and scientific support and, in this way, conscious theorization, for the professional project of producing normalcy. Sociology was the self-consciousness of the professional strata, or the new middle class. Despite its aspirations to be the consciousness of society (a phenomenon it was involved in creating) it was a one-sided and partial consciousness of society because it was not conscious of itself, or at most only dimly so. The project of reflexive sociology was always an unwelcome one. Despite, or rather because of, its lack of reflexivity, sociology may be understood as the self-conscious awareness of the professional project of producing normalcy, in other words, the ideology of the professionals. It was flawed, precisely because it was the ideology of this particular class fraction, necessarily obscuring its own partiality. It was the ideological emanation and fullest intellectual expression of the professional project of managing society (in order to produce normalcy). It was the most abstract of professional ideologies in the sense of being the highest level of synthesis of the activities and ideas of this stratum. Therefore, the fate of sociology was tied to the relatively autonomous agency of the professional stratum. This, in turn, was tied to the scope for planning through the nation-state.[84]

It was especially the planning apparatus and functions of the nation-state that corresponded with the level of abstraction of sociology—its highest level of abstraction corresponding to the highest level of development of social relations possible within the framework of capitalism and bourgeois class rule, this highest level being the nation-state. Therefore, the autonomy of the professional stratum from other sectional interests, in particular from the interests of, or the "forcefield" of, capital, depended on carving out a sphere of the social which made for the possibility of a consensual common interest that the professional could neutrally represent. Herman and Julia Schwendinger, in their study of the social ideology of early American sociology, that positioned sociology within the culture of technocratic corporate liberalism, showed in much greater historical specificity than Gouldner the close relationship between the ideology of sociology and the limited reformism of the professional-managerial stratum, which at that time served the interests of capital.[85] Sociology is the utopia of the professionals in the sense that it derives from utopian socialism but represents the routinization, professionalization, and bureaucratization of utopia.

Gouldner's view of Saint Simon as the originator of sociology puts this relationship between sociology and utopian socialism squarely in view. The multifaceted growth of proto-social-scientific techniques for measuring and tracking populations combined with the growing capacities of engineering that accompanied the consolidation of state power in absolutism, as well as the growth of capitalism and science, and the rationalistic ambitions of the Enlightenment and French Revolution. There was an increasing number of scientifically and technically trained personnel working for the state and industry. Saint Simon may be understood as formulating an ideology for this emerging technical stratum, enabling and calling upon them to be self-conscious as a social layer. In other words, Saint Simon's utopianism was an ideology through which this emerging technical and bureaucratic stratum could potentially become a "class for itself." Saint Simon gave expression to the potential for the various technical apparatuses and personnel of the modern nation-state, the professions, and capitalist industry to cohere into an autonomous group with its own ambitions but also representing the most progressive development of humanity, and therefore as a universal class. Through Comte's positivism, Saint Simon's technocratic-producerist socialism was transformed into a project whereby the idea of society became established as the field upon which the cultural supremacy and authority of science could be given a sphere of action. Science, in the form of sociology, would manage and regulate modern society, with the creation of a new priest caste.

In positivism, utopia ceased to be an ideal projected into the future but is constituted in the present. This collapse of utopia into the management of the present is in fact a tendency in all utopianism, as in Robert Owen's creation of model communities. Utopia is in such projects no longer "news from nowhere" but a somewhere in the here and now and this kind of utopian socialism lies in the background of the planning of communities (such as Ebenezer Howard's garden cities in the south of England). As Marcuse observed in *Reason and Revolution*, positivism dissolves the dialectical tension between ideal and actuality.[86] In positivism, the actual becomes the ideal, in the sense that modern society realizes itself as utopia. Professionals and scientists become the agency for realizing utopia that is immanent in the present. In that sense, Saint Simon's utopian socialism and positivism represented the consciousness of the technical and professional strata of their potential for an autonomous role. Hence its intertwining with new class theory. Gouldner's own iteration of new class theory, set out in his 1979 book, *The Future of the Intellectuals and the Rise of the New Class*, was the owl of Minerva with regard to the powerful role that the PMC had had within the institutions of the Keynesian national welfare state. But the PMC was about to lose under the assault of capital in the form of neoliberalism. The PMC would soon set about reorienting itself to these new conditions and seeking ways to carve out its role within them as the gap opened up between capitalization and proletarianization of the roles contained within the PMC.[87]

The positivist project of constructing a managed technocratic utopia in the present—a utopia of the well-regulated, stable, and integrated modernity—reached its fruition in Fordism, with the construction of the Fordist society as what Negri has called "the social factory" or "the factory society."[88] It was in the context of Fordism that sociology achieved the apogee of its influence. Doug McAdam notes that "in the quarter century following World War II, sociology enjoyed a public presence and policy resonance that far exceeds its influence in society today."[89] The peak of sociology's influence was in the 1960s when, as Turner writes, the sociological outlook meshed with the Keynesian programs of the Kennedy and Johnson administrations:

> Sociology had greatly enhanced its public importance, in part by sociologists serving as public interpreters of events, and in part by acceptance into the world of Presidential policy-making, especially with the measures that implemented Lyndon Johnson's idea of the Great Society. The brand "sociology" was associated with the Great Society Programs. Sociologists were involved in formulating these programs, justifying them publicly, and in the research that supported them. The basic reasoning was this: if there was social variation in some outcome, such as disease, the variation had a social cause and was a social problem, which could be corrected by a social program.[90]

The ambitions of sociology came closest to realization in the mid-twentieth-century utopia of Fordist normalcy, and in America, where Fordism was ideologically projected as an immanent capitalist utopia that was pitted in ideological battle against communist utopia.[91] Positivist utopia became Fordist utopia.

Steinmetz argues for the close relationship after World War II between Fordism and positivism in sociology:

> Fordism helped to render positivist approaches to social explanation more plausible both to sociologists and to other people exposed and attentive to the new logics governing activity in the advanced capitalist world . . . After the war . . . social reality appeared increasingly to fit the positivist expectation that social practices could be subsumed under covering laws, that is, fall into patterns that were the same everywhere and always. Social actors now seemed atomized, rational, and interchangeable, lacking any distinctive cultural peculiarities; social practice was more predictable and controllable. In sharp contrast to the crisis conditions of the interwar years, orderly postwar Fordist societalization resonated with positivist notions of repetition.[92]

Sociological explanation meshed with the patterns of life of postwar Fordist mass consumer society. Science in general was accorded value and supported by the state due to "the greatly enhanced role of science (including social science) in the Fordist form of governmentality."[93] This moment of peak sociological influence, in the sense of confluence between sociology and the outlook of the broader managerial-professional class and direction of state policy, might be called the sociological moment.

The sociological moment in America (and more broadly in Western societies) coincided with the period that Ian Welsh refers to as "the nuclear moment" and, equivalently, as "peak modernity," in his study of British nuclear power. What characterized peak modernity, Welsh argues, was the belief held broadly among elites in science and in the state apparatus that society could be rationally organized by applying scientific knowledge. Welsh shows how peak modernity was expressed in the British government's pursuit of civilian nuclear power, and the same could be said of the Atomic Energy Commission in the United States in this period.[94] Welsh's analysis draws attention to the energy infrastructure upon which Fordism depended, even though the dream of solving the energy problem by replacing coal and oil with nuclear power proved elusive, the failure of this dream marking the end of peak modernity. Peak modernity was powered by fossil fuels. As historian Bob Johnson shows, fossil fuels are the suppressed ontology of modernity, the foundation on which the culture of modernity rests, but also the truth hidden in "modernity's basement."[95] America's mid-twentieth-century Fordist utopian normalcy was dependent on cheap energy. Elizabeth Shove has explored how the physical organization of normalcy, its "comfort, cleanliness and convenience," was marketed as a way of life along with the consumer appliances that made it possible. This entailed the energy-intensiveness, and therefore carbon intensiveness, of that everyday normalcy.[96]

THE MANUFACTURE OF NORMALCY
AND ITS MATERIAL FOUNDATIONS

Attention to the biophysical foundations of normalcy shows that the creation of social normalcy was in fact the destruction of the biophysical foundations for the continuity of life-as-we-have-known-it, which was the geological period of the Holocene. The creation of social normalcy has brought to an end the conditions that were normal for humanity during the period when complex human civilizations developed, that is, the last 10,000 years. So the post-normal was contained within normalcy. Normalcy inevitably gave birth to the post-normal. Peak modernity was marked by the creation and use of the atomic bomb in 1945, an event that geologists have used as the indicator of the end of the Holocene and the beginning of a new era, that of the Anthropocene, since the radioisotopes spread by atomic bomb tests establish a clear geological marker. The beginning of the Anthropocene—the era in which human beings are the greatest impact on the Earth's climate and ecology—is characterized by the fear that, by these very impacts, human beings are hastening their own extinction. The Anthropocene is not a humanization of the world but an inhumanization, the erasure of the natural conditions for human flourishing. Normalcy was created at the expense of the immense entropic disruption of the natural basis for the development of complex, civilized human life. As the creation of industrial capitalist civilization, normalcy was undermining its ecological basis from the beginning.

What counts as normalcy in the modern world is an everyday life that is contained within the second nature of urban technological society. As Jacques Ellul characterized it, technology rather than nature becomes the milieu for human life.[97] Modern urban life is, as Giddens said, "smoothed of those interruptions that once provided the very marrow of the experience of temporality in the relations between human beings and nature."[98] It is this technological milieu into which the routines of modern life are woven, which provides the basis for ontological security in the modern world. The rhythms of modern life are not those of the natural world. Modern everyday life is abstracted from the timescapes of nature and instead transforms nature according to standardized measures of time as money, as Barbara Adam has illuminated.[99] In so doing, it has undermined the predictability of nature based on these natural rhythms of seasonality. But the ecological crisis has shown that the notion that nature could be kept at bay through technology was illusory. The depletion and disruption of nature to construct a technological normalcy has transformed the natural world into an even greater force of unpredictability and risk. Normalcy is, therefore, revealed to have been fundamentally illusory. Whereas religion provided what Berger called the "sacred canopy," modernity instead created a profane canopy. In modernity, everyday life itself became the primary protective shield against the chaos of reality.

In modernity, with the weakening of tradition and of religion as providing the taken-for-granted background to life, normalcy takes on significance in itself in such a way that it is ungrounded in anything else. Normalcy becomes its own support and justification. Normalcy becomes the opium of the masses. In the film *The Matrix*, the virtual reality that masks the "desert of the real" is everyday life itself.[100] Lefebvre wrote that "Everyday life, a compound of insignificances united in this concept, responds and corresponds to modernity, a compound of signs by which our society expresses and justifies itself and which forms part of its ideology."[101] Everyday life legitimizes itself and, in so doing, legitimizes capitalist society. This is usually subtle but it was more explicitly evident in the so-called Kitchen Debate when Nixon (as vice president) extolled capitalism in a replica American house, showing off its home appliances. As the spectacle is woven into and integrated into everyday life, everyday life becomes spectacle. The film *Koyaanisqatsi*, released in 1982, depicts the vast disjunction between capitalist civilization and its ecological basis, the cityscape reveals a neon sign with the words "Grand Illusion."[102] It is as if the entire world of consumer capitalist everyday life is an illusion.

The first two postwar decades marked the fruition of the process that Giddens calls "simple modernization." The high point of simple modernization, which Welsh calls "peak modernity," corresponded with Fordism. Normalcy, as a particular organization and existential significance of everyday life, corresponded with Fordism. Normalcy was the societalization of capitalism under Fordism. Roger Keil writes: This "factory society" is equivalent to Lefebvre's "bureaucratic society of controlled consumption." He also writes,

> Lefebvre's concept of the everyday is a reflection of the Fordist "societalization" of European societies after World War II. Lefebvre captured the very technologies of power that late twentieth-century capitalist states and societies had at their disposal through the channels of mass production, culture, and consumption.[103]

Fordism, as the real subsumption of society by capital, stands in contrast with, but also provided a historical pathway toward, the de-socializing tendency of the real subsumption of social relations under neoliberalism. In a variety of ways, Fordist real subsumption provided a basis upon which the de-socializing trajectory of neoliberalism could be pursued. Mass production and the aggregate demand-supporting policies of Keynesianism fostered a consumerist everyday life. The commodification of everyday life undermined preexisting forms of solidarity rooted in tradition, including traditions of solidarity in the working class. This was traced in Britain by Richard Hoggart in *The Uses of Literacy*, which showed the ways in which mass print and electronic consumer culture were subsuming and transforming the culture of the British working class.[104] The welfare state and associated forms of urban planning broke up the solidarities of the slums while providing estate housing that was given form by the broader culture of Fordism, with its emphasis on mass production and standardization, and also its technocratic administrative culture. The very real improvements in the standard of living of the working class, and real gains, that the welfare state represented were, nevertheless, given form by the needs of capital, within the context of Fordism and technocratic Keynesianism. The welfare state represented the subsumption by the nation-state of the oppositional solidarity of the working class, replacing local working-class cultures with the abstract administrative solidarity of the national welfare state. This was an indirect real subsumption of social solidarity by capital in the sense that the welfare state was embedded in and shaped by the character of the nation-state as a capitalist state, dependent on and representing the interests of capital.

The culture of the industrial working class was born out of the need to survive in the face of the tendency of capital to destroy preexisting means of survival, including social bonds, communities and forms of solidarity, and to degrade the standard of life of the working class. Working-class cultures developed as a solution to the problem of social reproduction which was at the same time, necessarily, a defensive response to the destructive short-termism of *Après moi le déluge*! The extent to which these working-class cultures and the solidarities which they expressed, and in which they were embedded, were sources of social power also meant that they facilitated, organized, and fostered opposition to, and thereby counterbalanced, capital's "despotism" in the workplace.[105] Capital was, therefore, locked into struggle with, and continually seeking to undermine, these solidarities. When Marx wrote that mechanization was the forging of "weapons against [the] working class," he was pointing, in part, to the use of automation to destroy existing cultures of solidarity in the workplace and in the broader working class. Taylorism and Fordism smashed existing forms of working-class solidarity in the workplace. This was exemplified by the prohibition of talk between workers on Henry Ford's assembly line. Taylorist management sought to suppress the social factory in the sense of the spontaneous solidarity of workers within the factory. In white-collar work, there was an equivalent managerial campaign against the "social office."[106] In the capitalist workplace, the micro-sociality of workers' spontaneous solidarity, and traditional solidarities that supported it, was suppressed but replaced with "the factory society" in the sense of the macro-organization of "society" as nation for the purposes of efficient production and consumption.

In the United States of America, while management sought to exploit ethnic divisions and differences of national origin within the working class and to foster and encourage racism, Fordism was also in conflict with the pre-industrial cultures and solidarities that immigrant workers brought from the agrarian and preindustrial contexts from which they emigrated (whether the Eastern European shtetl or the southern Italian village). Ford's "Sociological Department" pursued the Americanization of the immigrant workforce.[107] Mid-twentieth-century American Fordist culture with its national homogeneity of consumer taste was both the outcome of, and itself produced a further impetus toward, the suppression of ethno-national differences among European immigrants and their homogenization within the category of American "whiteness."[108] This homogenization of a national mass culture was facilitated by the two world wars which carried with them patriotic pressure for nationalistic, xenophobic, and anti-communist conformity, while also spurring the development of homogeneous mass commodities and tastes.[109]

The template of normalcy, the postwar "affluent society" critiqued by John Kenneth Galbraith, rested on profoundly abnormal conditions that arose from World War II itself and postwar reconstruction under US hegemony.[110] Postwar normalcy was achieved not only by repressing but also by sublimating, channeling, routinizing, and incorporating the energies of class conflict. From its revolutionary origins, social democracy followed a Bernsteinian reformist path which led to its self-destructive nationalist stances in World War I. Social democracy played both a repressive and stabilizing role. Above all, this was evident in the central role of social democratic governments in Europe in managing capitalism after World War II. In the British Labour Party and in European social democracies, the socialization of the means of production became "nationalization." The American New Deal incorporated class conflict by establishing a bureaucratic institutional framework for collective bargaining and by granting limited welfare concessions to the working class.[111] In this way, reformism became tied to the Keynesian project, not of overthrowing and replacing capitalism, but of enlisting the state in its management and incorporating the working class as consumer demand.

The postwar compact between capital and labor was administered through unions, large bureaucratic corporations, and by Keynesian interventionist state policy. State intervention appeared to have displaced the classic Marxist contradiction between the forces and relations of production, as Habermas suggested his 1968 essay "Technology and Science as 'Ideology.' "[112] The normalcy of capitalism after World War II, the taken-for-grantedness of capitalist society as the way of things, depended on state intervention that managed and suppressed the "spontaneous" tendencies of the market. Hillel Ticktin argues that underlying the apparent success of capitalism in the post–World War II period was the fact that "capitalism has not solved its problems at all but made huge concessions to the working class such that it has negated the very essence of capitalism."[113]

Massimo de Angelis writes of the coming apart of the "social micro-foundations of Keynesianism." He shows how the crisis of Keynesianism was produced by the undermining of the social order in which it was embedded. De Angelis draws on Michael Kalecki's 1943 paper, "Political Aspects of Full Employment."[114] Here, Kalecki argues that a stable full employment economy depends on a political settlement which operates to restrain workers' wage demands. Since full employment removes fear of being laid off, it removes anxiety about going on strike and, therefore, is extremely empowering for workers. But higher wages threaten to undermine the full employment Keynesian regime by producing inflation.

The transformation of the nineteenth-century craft-skilled factory worker into the relatively de-skilled, by Taylorism and automation, Fordist mass worker of the twentieth-century represented an increase in the real subsumption of labor by capital and an increase in the alienation of the worker from their work. Deprived of pride in their working activity, the mass worker was not oriented to a politics of workers' control of industry. Rather, through increasingly bureaucratic unions, wage struggles became the primary expression of class struggle.[115] Unions played a mediating role in these struggles. While organizing and mobilizing the workers and voicing their demands, unions also framed and regulated those demands. Unions provided a means through which class struggle was regulated within the framework of Keynesianism. Unions were, therefore, an important component of the micro-foundations of Keynesianism. With the incorporation of unions into the regulatory apparatus, the aspirations of the working class could be managed and met in and through the overall strategy of economic growth. While wage struggles provided real material advances in workers' conditions and in the social power of the working class, they were also a means by which working-class demands and aspirations were co-opted into and harnessed for the Keynesian strategy of economic growth. Rising wages and working-class spending on mass consumer products translated into increasing aggregate demand, absorbing the surplus produced by the growth of production. This function of the unions corresponded with the political-ideological convergence within "consensus capitalism," a "consensus" that the repression of war and the political repression of McCarthyism served to artificially carve out.[116] The social liberalism of mid-century sociology was also very much Cold War liberalism. This was evident in the sociology of science, in which the Mertonian image of scientific freedom was entirely aligned with the image of science promoted in the CIA-funded Congress for Cultural Freedom and which, as Audra Wolfe has shown, formed part of the US propagandistic contrast between the "free world" and the "Iron Curtain."[117]

The micro-foundations of Keynesianism, therefore, involved not only bureaucratic unions but also the broader culture of social conformity and patriotism that was fostered by World War II and the political culture of the Cold War. Forms of normalcy such as suburban living, automobiles, and mass consumerism functioned ideologically as images of the immanent utopia of capitalism, thereby organizing consent. The interconnected normalcy and political conformity were made possible by the postwar boom. Normalcy *was* "the social micro-foundations of Keynesianism." In this way, normalcy underpinned, but was in turn sustained by, the social, cultural, economic, and political hegemony of the period.

Kalecki identified wage restraint as a political precondition for Keynesianism and wage struggles as a crucial political problem that would accompany Keynesian full employment. This draws attention to the way in which Keynesianism operated within a broader social-political-cultural regime. Keynesianism was a form of power that relied intrinsically on the active cooperation of the governed, through the ways in which they were collectively organized.

The social micro-foundations of Keynesianism were constructed within boundaries that entailed social exclusions, but Keynesianism itself served to undermine the legitimacy of these exclusions by raising expectations of progress and of its support by government action. The Civil Rights Movement was a movement of a population, southern blacks in what were then still primarily rural states, who were excluded from the Keynesian compact. When Martin Luther King, Jr. joined the struggle to organize sanitation workers in Memphis, which is when he was killed, he was aligning the civil rights struggle with economic struggle by sections of the urban working class who were not included in the Keynesian regime of collective bargaining.[118] The Civil Rights movement arose from and reinforced the struggles of workers. It gained momentum in the 1930s, during the New Deal, despite the limits imposed by the Roosevelt administration for fear of antagonizing the southern segregationist democrats.[119] The apparatus for managing wage growth, collective bargaining through the AFL-CIO, was one that served urban industrial workers. African Americans became involved in union struggles as they emigrated out of the South during the 1930s and 1940s. The Communist Party and the radicalization of the 1930s provided impetus to civil rights. So the social struggles of the working class earlier in the twentieth century, to which Keynesianism was a response, and the revolutionary potential of which was to a certain extent neutralized by Keynesianism, prepared the basis for new struggles both within and from without the Keynesian regime. As historian Mary Dudziak has traced, the existence of the Soviet Union, and the ideological contest of the Cold War, also situated the civil rights struggles as potentially destabilizing the ideological dimension of international US hegemony. Images of southern cops brutalizing blacks, picked up around the world including in the Soviet Union, tended to undermine the image of the United States as leader of the free world.[120]

There was also a close connection between the civil rights and global decolonization struggles.[121] These struggles took inspiration from the Russian Revolution, which represented a massive breach in the power structure of imperialism and which opened up a new range of political possibility for oppressed people globally. This was in addition to the role of the Soviet Union in funding and supporting many of these third-world anti-colonial movements and the regimes to which they gave rise. The revolutionary struggles by third world peoples against the European colonial powers and the successes of these struggles inspired blacks in the United States just as the civil rights struggle was recognized by these movements as a cause with affinity to their own. King's opposition to the Vietnam War again made these global affinities of the civil rights movement clear. Keynesianism-Fordism and Bretton Woods were means of containing and channeling the conflicts and aspirations opened up by the Russian Revolution and the global crisis of capitalism to which it gave political expression. The bourgeois compromises and concessions represented human progress, driven by this pressure from below, in contrast with the barbarity of simultaneous bourgeois repression. Therefore, these temporary solutions themselves stimulated hopes that the structures could not indefinitely contain.

The fate of the United States was to emerge as a global power, in World War I, simultaneously with the Russian Revolution and the establishment of the first workers' state in the Soviet Union. The US emergence as the dominant imperialist power at the end of World War II coincided with the upsurge of anti-colonial struggles against the attempts by former European empires to hold onto their colonies after the defeat of Germany and Japan. While it suited the United States to distinguish itself from its old imperialist rivals as anti-colonialist, the United States sought to hold onto its own colonies, acquired during the Spanish-American War, and ruthlessly assert the Monroe doctrine by crushing democratic, socialist, communist, and national liberation movements in Latin America as well as around the world from Iran to Indonesia. The period of Keynesian consensus capitalism in the United States was also a period in which the United States was engaging in brutal destabilization campaigns and wars against the peoples of the third world.

The US government sought to manage domestic class conflict through Keynesian class compromise, integrating the working class through politics of growth, full employment, and welfare in the United States (which imposed a certain level of political and cultural oppression, as in the Smith Act and McCarthyism). This depended on supporting Bretton Woods worldwide through the carrots and sticks of the Marshall Plan and military intervention or covert destabilization.[122] The costs of these projects of maintaining the conditions for capitalism domestically and internationally became unsustainable in the context of the rise of international competition from the very states defeated in World War II, the capitalist stabilization and development of which the United States had financially underwritten. The stability of the Bretton Woods regime was riven with destabilizing contradictions. These contradictions manifested themselves in the form of fiscal crisis at the beginning of the 1970s. The United States was, by the end of the 1960s, borrowing too much to support its warfare-welfare spending in the Vietnam War and the Great Society welfare programs and this, combined with the worsening balance of payments, was undermining the value of the dollar, and with that further undermining the US ability to service its debts. In response to the crisis, President Nixon floated the dollar on international exchange rates on August 15, 1971. This event inaugurated the current period of globalization, characterized by the globalization of production (the pressures toward which, in the form of global competition, were manifesting themselves already by the mid-1960s). The Nixon shock may be used to pinpoint the end of the postwar boom, and the Keynesian compact, and the stable capitalist order that constituted normalcy and that lasted for no more than a quarter of a century.

The present political crisis, vividly enacted in the Trump coup attempt of January 6, 2021, has its roots in the end of the postwar boom and of the period of class compromise. North has argued that this can be dated to Nixon's suspension of the dollar's convertibility into gold:

> In historical retrospect, this action marked a turning point in not only the global economic position of the United States, but also in the fate of American democracy. As long as the United States was a rising global power, whose military component was secondary to the country's economic strength and dominance, the basic thrust of American politics was of a broadly progressive character.[123]

The floating of the dollar was followed by growing illegality of ruling-class operations and increasing attacks on democracy. The Nixon administration ended in the ignominy of Watergate. Since then, there has been the Iran-Contra Affair, the Supreme Court's halting of the vote count which handed the 2000 election to George W. Bush, the Patriot Act and illegal NSA surveillance after 9/11, and the Trump administration's coup attempt on January 6, 2021. The growing illegality by the US state since the 1970s has accompanied the turn by the state away from integration and toward coercive exclusion. North writes, "The abandonment of social reform required a turn toward increasing social repression. The trajectory of American democracy followed the trajectory of American capitalism—that is, downward."[124]

The financialization of the economy was accompanied by the undermining of the social conditions of the working class and the undermining of democracy. The series of global economic crises between the 1980s and the beginning of the new millennium manifested the growing instability of a financialized capitalism not only in which money circulated almost instantaneously around the world but in which profit was increasingly divorced from the real economy, in the Marxist sense of the extraction of surplus value from labor. Nick Beams writes that financialization is "the expression of a deepening malaise flowing from the relentless accumulation of profit through financial activities completely divorced from the underlying real economy and the production of real value."[125] Since 2008, the global capitalist economy has been dependent on the actions of the US Federal Reserve in propping up the United States, and global, economy via the maintenance of ultra-low interest rates and the injection of bailout money, most recently with the CARES Act designed to make sure that the financial markets were protected prior to the US government alerting the public to the danger of the Covid-19 virus.[126] Financialization has produced a massively unstable economy based on speculation, which rests on and requires governmental support in the form of low interest rates and periodic bailouts.

The transformation of the state into what James Galbraith calls the "Predator State," combines this largesse for corporations with the dispossession of the population. This dynamic was exemplified after 2008 by courts streamlining and speeding up the process of foreclosing on people's homes and evicting them so that the banks could take possession of the houses for which they had in many cases underwritten fraudulent loans. Largesse for the corporate oligarchy in the 2020 CARES Act cynically used the Covid-19 pandemic as an opportunity to inject more money into the propping up of corporations and asset prices while providing insultingly inadequate relief for the American population. Giroux's paradigm of disposability and Galbraith's Predator State are two sides of the same regime.

THE END OF SOCIOLOGY'S "SOCIETY"

The publication in 1970 of Gouldner's *The Coming Crisis of Western Sociology* marks the end of the postwar boom and the end of the period of social reform.[127] What Gouldner regarded as the result of the incorporation of sociology into the welfare state was, with the benefit of hindsight, also the result of the crisis and neoliberal dismantling of the welfare state, in which sociology was embedded. Giddens insightfully observed in 1982 that the crisis of structural-functionalist sociology had political-economic roots. He wrote:

> Today, the orthodox consensus is no more . . . But its demise is certainly not something to be explained solely in terms of intellectual critique. The changes that have swept through the social sciences reflected transmutations in the social world itself, as the period of stable Western economic growth was interrupted by fresh reversals, crises and conflicts. The seemingly secure domain staked out by the theorists of industrial society proved fragile indeed.[128]

Richard Lee Deaton makes the important point that the demise of consensus in American sociology was crucially related to the decline of American global power (which the Nixon shock recognized and exacerbated). Deaton writes that

> in the nearly thirty years since Gouldner's death we have gone from the crisis of American sociology to the decline of the American empire and the two issues are integrally related. Structural functionalism in U.S. academic sociology closely parallels the consolidation and dominance of *Pax Americana*, especially in the post-World War II period, in the same way that Spencer, Kipling, and Spengler are associated with the ascendancy of the British Empire.
>
> The converse is equally true. Given the mounting problems in the United States, and the advanced industrialized world more generally, ranging from pollution, unemployment, the debt crisis, economic instability, and military adventurism, to mention a few, suggests that we now live in an increasingly unstable world—one that is characterized by disequilibrium, not self-adjusting stability.[129]

The crisis of sociology is that it cannot overcome what Irving Louis Horowitz called its post-Parsonian theoretical "decomposition," because bourgeois society cannot prevent its own ongoing decomposition, under the impact of the contradiction between global economy and the nation-state.[130]

While a variety of agency-based approaches within sociology marked the transformation of sociology so as to align with the tenets and framework of neoliberalism, these could, almost by definition, not provide an integrating perspective giving sociology coherence as a discipline. Agency approaches could not provide a coherent sociological ideology, justifying sociology as a project sui generis.[131] Neither could these approaches provide justification for a role for intellectuals/professionals as autonomous from the market. Indeed, agency perspectives provided the basis for skepticism about the very possibility of such autonomy. For public choice theorists, if activities were insulated from the market they would be inefficient. Agency approaches tended to involve a hermeneutics of suspicion, due to the positing of the universal pursuit of particular self-interest. This liberal individualist acid dissolved the fabric of the social. Socially atomistic, micro-reductionist agency approaches exacerbated rather than resolved the crisis of sociology.

"Mainstream" American sociology is hyper-normal science in post-normal conditions. The crisis in sociology arising at the end of 1960s represented the collapse of sociology as ideology and, at the same time, the breakdown of the conditions for sociology as normal science, precisely because normal science required a consensus ideology. The crisis of sociology was inextricably intertwined with the broader crisis and collapse of the postwar ideological consensus and of the postwar boom that sustained this ideology. The postwar ideology was normalcy (and therefore the end of ideology) and sociology played a central role in the production of this ideology.

And yet, even while postwar sociology valorized normalcy, it itself contributed to undermining it. A sociological account of values as "norms" strips values of any transcendent reality and special ontological status. The sociological account of the "sacred canopy" necessarily profanes it, renders it open for question, and therefore triggers the anxiety that it may not exist at all other than in our collective imagination. To give an account of values as societal norms necessarily relativizes these values to a particular society, undermines their claim to universality, and thereby potentially calls them into question. Harry Collins and Graham Cox, providing a sociological interpretation of Leon Festinger et al.'s famous study of an apocalyptic UFO cult in their book *When Prophecy Fails*, argue that the sociologist should treat Mrs. Keech and her followers' belief in the UFOs not as inherently irrational, but simply as abnormal, where normalcy is just what has *contingently* come to be taken for granted as the parameters of reality. Collins and Cox write:

> Normalcy is the expression of the sum of historical contingencies to date. It expresses the fact that we do not all see flying saucers, and cannot all wake up tomorrow to see them: it expresses the fact that the creative individual has to work hard to persuade us to see the world in a different way.[132]

Sociology not only normalizes but undermines the norm, by subjecting normativity to the culture of critical discourse. This may be seen in the history of the sociology of deviance. The notion of deviance, a central category of modern sociology, was undermined by cultural changes involved in the counterculture and the rise of post-Fordist consumerism since the 1960s.

These shifts were themselves not only reflected in, but reinforced by, socio-logical reflexivity. So the sociology of deviance, as Colin Sumner argues in his "obituary" for the subfield, effectively dissolved, under the glare of critical scrutiny, its own object. Sumner writes:

> Insanity seemed sane and sanity seemed lunatic. Deviance was being seen as at least as normal as normality, and the latter looked very deviant indeed. The signifiers were becoming unhooked. They were being rendered as parodies of themselves. Reality was mocked up, and mock-ups became reality. Deviance became politics, politics became deviant. Connections between images of deviance and actual social practices became less coherent, less clear, less persuasive. The media spectacle was taking over at the expense of any dialectic with reality. What was deviance became less clear. Who were the deviants became less clear—was it the corporate rich, with their corruptions, client genocides, tax evasions and environmental destruction, or the kinky transvestites and swingers, with their creative play on the corpses of disappearing sexual norms. By the time of the de-regulated eighties and the enterprise culture, deviance had gone. Drowned in a sea of amoralism. Cut loose from its moorings in polarized but coherent opposed moralities, . . . it became . . . daily, de-regulated, diversity divorced from any deep dalliance with deity and diabolism.[133]

Hence, the modern sociological project of banishing ambivalence with a scientifically defined secular moral order gave way to the postmodern play of difference.[134]

Gouldner identified, as a key part of the crisis of sociology, the incompatibility of the conservative normalizing tendencies of Parsonian functionalism with the antinomianism of the 1960s counterculture. The integration of the baby-boomer youth into the professoriate would, Gouldner predicted, necessitate theoretical change.[135] Gouldner saw the counterculture as the manifestation of

> increasing pressure for some total redefinition of the traditional moral code, a pressure which may take the form of a new, mass social movement for "cultural relativization." This last is already in evidence with the emergence of the new psychedelic and communitarian counter-cultures.[136]

The transformation of middle-class habitus, away from the valuing of restraint and toward the valorization of transgression of norms, of which the counterculture was a concentrated expression and a herald, would feed into and reinforce the emergence of new "disorganized" globalized forms of capitalism.[137]

The breakdown of consensus within sociology was centrally important to (it both reflected and was an element of) the fragmentation of culture, politics, and ideology that characterized the 1970s and that has persisted ever since. In his intellectual history of the fragmentation of American thought since the 1960s, Daniel T. Rodgers emphasizes that intellectual fragmentation reflected at its heart "the fracture of the social." "The recession of the social," he writes, "echoed the shrinking prestige of sociology, which had ridden the crest of the social movements of the 1960s." At least, says Rodgers, "What society conjured up now was something smaller, more voluntaristic, fractured, easier to exit, and more guarded from others."[138] Sociology was the lynchpin of the postwar consensus to the extent that it was the most abstract synthesis of this consensus and exerted a high degree of influence on broader intellectual and public culture. The breakdown of consensus within sociology was, therefore, in an important way, causative of the more widespread fragmentation of intellectual life and the collapse of public culture. The 1970s was a hinge between two periods of American intellectual history, just as in social and economic history. It was the collapse of the idea of the social as an organizing and unifying concept underlying a reformist vision of American society as nation-state.

The crisis of Keynesianism produced crisis in sociology (from which sociology never recovered theoretical integration around an ontology of the social). This was for the reason that the crisis of Keynesianism was a crisis of bourgeois social order for which the bourgeoisie had no social solution. Clara Elisabetta Mattei writes, in an analysis of Geoff Mann's book *In the Long Run We Are All Dead: Keynesianism, Political Economy, and Revolution*, that

> Mann stresses that Keynesianism is much more than the mere perception of the endogenous instability of the economy. Its kernel is deeply tragic and political: it represents an existential anxiety, a real terror for the collapse of the bourgeois social order. In the author's poignant definition, Keynesian reason "is a scientific form of a political anxiety endemic to modernity."[139]

For Keynes, the action of the state in preserving the stability of the market economy was tantamount to the defense of civilization against barbarism. He said in 1938, "Civilization is a thin and precarious crust, erected by the personality and will of a very few, and only maintained by rules and conventions skillfully put across and guilefully preserved." Mann writes, "As Keynes's theory of civilization makes clear, because the bourgeoisie cannot imagine a nonbourgeois society, it cannot conceive of its own end as anything other than the end of the world."[140] It is the corollary of this that sociology has not been able to imagine "society" beyond the image of the nation-state order maintained in the postwar period through Keynesianism.

MEDIATION AND ITS CRISIS

In his essay "Keynes and the Capitalist Theory of the State Post-1929," Antonio Negri writes that "the science of capital," by which he means economics but more broadly bourgeois self-consciousness, "mystifies as much as it reveals." Bourgeois science is faced with the problem of simultaneously accomplishing the tasks of mystifying and revealing. It must reveal because it must understand the dangers that capital, and the bourgeoisie as personification of capital, faces. But its motivation is the goal of self-preservation, the maintenance of capitalist social relations and bourgeois class power. Negri writes,

> Ultimately the only possible solution to this contradiction is to place one's faith in an independent political will; a sort of "political miracle" capable of reuniting the various necessary but opposing elements of the capitalist system—socialisation of the mode of production and socialisation of exploitation; organisation and violence; organisation of society for the exploitation of the working class.[141]

This paragraph would serve as an encapsulation of the outlook and project of Weber and the source of the splits that *necessarily* ran through his thought and personality. Again, Weber is the embodiment of the contradictions and dualities of bourgeois culture.

Weber indeed put his faith in an independent political will. "Politics as a Vocation" was a statement of Weber's conception of the requirements of this will, in order to be truly independent, and above all the requirement to be able to apply violence realistically and with responsibility in an ethically irrational world.[142] The *independent* will that Weber sought to call into being was a politically independent bourgeoisie, one capable of exercising hegemony as a class. Weber's preoccupation with violence concerned state power and war and the ability of the bourgeois class in Germany to assert itself politically against the control of the state by the Junker aristocracy and to take responsibility for the suppression of the working-class. To take responsibility for wielding violence was to take responsibility, and therefore power, over the state.

Railing against the short-sightedness of the Allied Powers in imposing punitive reparations on the defeated Central Powers in the Versailles Treaty, Keynes predicted "Nothing can then delay for very long that final civil war between the forces of reaction and the despairing convulsions of revolution," a conflict which would destroy "the civilisation and the progress of our generation."[143] Weber's political project was, in the fraught context of Germany, the political development of the bourgeois class as an independent and emerging hegemonic class, acting apart from and wielding power against both the aristocratic forces of reaction and the proletarian impetus to revolution.[144] Upon Weber's death in 1920, this project had been through the experiences of Germany's wartime defeat, revolution, and the founding of the Weimar Republic. The signing into law of the Weimar Constitution in August 1919 was in these circumstances a symbol of the coming to fruition of this independent bourgeois class hegemony but also of its precariousness and its potential destructiveness.[145]

Weber's sociological writing revolved around the fissures at the center of bourgeois thought. Weber's neo-Kantianism framed the dualistic character of his thought: divisions between fact and value, necessity and freedom, neutrality and commitment, other-worldliness and this-worldliness.[146] His political sociology revolved around the opposition between charisma and its routinization and between charisma and bureaucracy. This was an opposition between nonrational, and, as unruled, free, forces of change and institutional frameworks of order and stability. His two lectures on vocation expressed either side of this split between organization and violence, as well as the way in which Weber shaped his prescriptions on each sphere in relation to the other.[147]

In order to become the ruling class politically, the bourgeoisie needed to generate a new worldview different from, and in many ways opposite to, the humanistic culture that had characterized German thought and the university in the early to mid-nineteenth century. Weber gave explicit articulation to a shift that was already underway and that found more implicit articulation in the so-called *Methodenstreit*, or conflict over social scientific methodology between humanism and the example of the natural sciences.[148] The power of the bourgeoisie rested on its conquest of reality. This meant science, but it also meant the power-political realism that had hitherto been carried by the aristocracy as a class that emerged from war. But whereas the Junker class was decadent and unfit, the bourgeoisie had as their charisma the calling and indeed its routinization into an instrumental orientation to life. Wolfe suggests that, for Weber,

> the bourgeois politician, for all his lack of principles, has a certain virtue after all. The fragility of democratic societies can be preserved only if politics as a vocation is reserved for the political brokers who seek power rather than the salvation of men's souls.[149]

And yet, it was in the charismatic political leader and the value-orientation of nationalism that Weber sought the salvation of the bourgeois soul and the real source of strength of the nation.[150]

Weber may in this way be regarded as an embodiment of the tensions and contradictions that arose from the process, beginning with the defeat of the revolutions of 1848, of the bourgeoisie transforming from a rising and revolutionary class into a hegemonic ruling class and, necessarily in this process, into a reactionary class. This, as Negri argues in more general terms, was responsive to developments over the course of the nineteenth century, marked by the 1848 revolutions and the Paris Commune of 1871, and culminating in the Bolsheviks' October Revolution in 1917. This was the development of the proletariat as an independent force in history. "1917 is a crucial point of rupture," Negri argues. From then on, the bourgeoisie "would have to come to terms with a working class that had achieved political identity, and had become a historical protagonist in its own right."[151] It was between 1848 and 1917 that liberalism turned from optimism toward pessimism and this was, as Wolfe argues, bound up with imperialism: "the Expansionist State, in spite of its aggressiveness, marked the transformation of liberalism from an optimistic to a pessimistic outlook."[152] "Science as a Vocation" was the culmination of this process.

Talcott Parsons was responsible for bringing Weber's work into American sociology. For example, Parsons provided the first English-language translation of *The Protestant Ethic and the Spirit of Capitalism*.[153] Parsons's student, Robert K. Merton, founded the subdiscipline of the sociology of science along Weberian lines. Merton's doctoral dissertation on science and Protestantism in seventeenth-century England supports with historical research Weber's note in *The Protestant Ethic* that Protestantism was a spur to the development of scientific empiricism.[154] The relationship between science and values remained the central concern of his sociology of science. Merton's argument was that the value-freedom of science, for which Weber called, was itself the product of value-commitment. Historically, Protestantism was an important source of this value-commitment both to the discovery of truth through the study of nature and to science as a calling. Weber's problem in "Science as a Vocation" was how to retain that sense of the calling in the secular context of twentieth-century modernity and, specifically, the research university. Weber's solution was an existential leap of faith by the individual—"I stand here, I can do no other." It was, therefore, a lonely position maintained by the inner-direction of *character*. Merton provided a much more communitarian account, in which value-commitment was in and through belonging within the social collective, rather than a deeply individualistic existential act.[155] Merton's account of scientific community as a moral order combined Durkheimian functionalism with American pragmatism. The individual commitment to value-neutrality was a feature of the normative regulation of individuals by the community of scientists.

Merton's account of science provided a much less bleak vision of modern rationalization than that put forward by Weber. Secularization did not leave values foundationless, the individual alone to find meaning in an ethically irrational world. Rather, secularization institutionalized and routinized values in their form while stripping them of their religious content. Hence, the development of the university in America from the Protestant liberal arts college to the research university was not de-moralization but rather the institutionalization of a more abstract, and universal, framework of values in the form of an ethos of an academic community. Weber's worries about value-pluralism were solved by Merton in the division of labor, expressed in the differentiated institutional structures of modern societies. Value-neutrality was protected by the specific normative structure of science as a specific set of institutions and roles within modern society. Merton rewrote "Science as a Vocation" for what David Riesman called the "other-directed" character of bureaucratic society, as opposed to Weber's innerly directed ascetic.[156]

Merton's account of the self-regulation of the scientific community fit with the more general "ideology," as Mulkay put it, of American science, which provided legitimacy for their claim to government support. It was support from the nation-state that ultimately protected Merton's enclave of disinterestedness. Bourgeois market relations require a neutral body outside the competition of interests to regulate this competition. The neutrality of the state with respect to social interests has been, as Ezrahi argues, essential to the liberal justification of state power.[157] It is only as neutral that the state is able to exercise power in such a way as to protect negative freedom, even while doing so requires coercion and therefore infringement upon the free will of individuals. The liberal justification of the state depends on the state's neutrality between freedoms. Ezrahi argues that science was a key symbolic resource for the state's self-representation as a neutral apparatus. Science provides the model for instrumental action and, therefore, for the instrumental rationality that, Weber argues, typifies bureaucratic action. Therefore, science and the nation-state (the quintessentially bourgeois form of state) were mutually justifying.

Indeed, Merton was writing in a period in which science was increasingly nationalized, in the sense of being financially supported and, to a certain extent, organized, by the nation-state. David Paul Haney writes that "The social sciences' participation in such New Deal programs as Social Security, the Works Progress Administration, and the Department of Agriculture, together with President Roosevelt's enthusiasm for policy-oriented social science research, lent them new professional credibility."[158] Stephen Turner and Jonathan Turner write that in the wake of the 1957 Sputnik launch, prompting a surge of federal money into education and research, "The end result was for the nature of funding for the social sciences in general and sociology in particular to move decisively away from private foundations to public agencies, primarily in the federal government."[159] The nationalization of science funding was an aspect of the increase in the size and scope of the federal government that emerged with World War I, New Deal and the World War II. Another aspect of this was the nationalization of welfare provision and regulation of society. It is in connection with the strengthening of the nation-state as the locus of social regulation, and the orientation of sociology therefore to the nation-state as its patron and its audience, that there took place in sociology a decisive shift from reformism to disciplinarity as a value-neutral science.

The growing predominance of a conception of sociology as value-neutral science and the exclusion or marginalization of social work and active reformism from the discipline reflected the shift of reform itself to a higher level, from local initiatives and philanthropic foundations to the nation-state itself. This transformation of sociology's value-orientation to value-neutrality was a feature of its adaptation to the nation-state, even while asserting its autonomy, but also actively distinguishing itself from ideology in the stigmatized form of Communism.[160] The doctrine of value-neutrality took hold from the 1920s and grew in strength in the conservative 1950s, a consensus against which Mills fought. But the ideal of a value-neutral social science had deeper roots. The Schwendingers discuss the influence of the German so-called socialists of the chair, or theorists of the imperialist state who stressed the importance of social and economic integration and the role of the state in preserving these as well as the importance of doing so for state power itself. The emergence of sociology in America was part of the process that Robert Wiebe has called "the search for order" which was an aspect of the forging of post-Civil War America into a unified industrial nation. Nevertheless, during the Progressive Era, in which sociology emerged as a discipline in America, while there was the beginning of the modern regulatory role of the federal government, social reform was still largely the local effort of charities and philanthropic agencies. It was not until the New Deal that the federal government, representing the US as national society, became the central and primary organizer of these functions. Sociology self-transformed from local observational studies of the Chicago school to the hegemony of Parsons's grand theory as a reflection of the shift from the local to the national level as the locus of conscious intervention in society.[161] Brick writes that Parsons was "decisive" in establishing a conception of the social as separate from the sphere of the economic. He writes:

The move to distinguish conceptually the sphere of society from that of the economy was evident in the maturation and self-conscious independence of fields such as sociology, anthropology, and social psychology from the methods of academic economics. These Parsons championed as the "new social sciences," whose growing stature marked "a shift of emphasis away from economics" or the debut of a "social relations" concept that defined society in noneconomic terms, constituted by family, neighborhood, community, solidarity, voluntary association, and nonprofit service institutions.[162]

Brick argues that Parsons, therefore, did not represent the abandonment of reform, but rather was "an intellectual product of those interwar reformist milieus that nurtured the emerging postcapitalist vision."[163] Parsons' politics were the reformist-welfarist social liberalism that was hegemonic in the period, as, according to David Hess, were Merton's.[164] This was, however, the Keynesian liberalism of the post-New Deal and particularly post–World War II period. The politics of functionalism were the politics of social reform on a higher level than the local, that is, on the level of the nation-state. Particularist value advocacy correspondingly gave way to the value-neutral positivist language of functionalism and of the statistical studies by Paul Lazarsfeld at Columbia. This value-neutral ideology aligned with the neutrality of the state as bureaucracy. What Horowitz calls the "decomposition of sociology" is bound up with the end of postwar national reformism and the legitimation crisis of value-neutral expertise.

The movements of the 1960s were the product of the stabilization of capitalism in the postwar boom and the degree of rising living standards, social welfare, and mass "affluence" with the growth of a "middle class." The middle-class student movement in which the "New Left" was embedded expressed the rejection of the older middle-class habitus by baby-boomer youth, as the conditions of the postwar boom allowed a release from what Marcuse called "surplus repression" among the middle class. The student movement gave political expression to a change in middle-class social character away from authoritarianism. What Langman called the "Dionysian" message of the youth counterculture was the herald of far-reaching transformations of social character toward greater flexibility and less internalized repression.[165]

The civil rights and black liberation movements expressed the contradiction between what the Keynesian-Fordist regime made possible and promised as universal—a mass homogeneous society of consumers—and the caste system of the south as well as the caste-like ghettoization of blacks in impoverished inner-cities, which exploded into flames in the riots of the mid- to late 1960s. The incompatibility between caste and "mass society" made the contradiction between caste and democracy even more intolerable, materially and ideologically, in a society in which reform had proved possible and which accepted the principle that society itself was malleable and subject to progressive change and conscious improvement. The nonviolence of the civil rights movement was closely related to reformism, since it assumed the ability to nonviolently, through moral force, ameliorate social conditions.[166] It also assumed the employment by the nation-state of its monopoly of legitimate violence against the local perpetrators of violence. Hence, it was conditioned on the supremacy of the nation-state and the reformist character of the nation-state.

The New Left, internationally, assumed the long-term stabilization of capitalism, in the sense of the stabilization of the economic base. The theory allowed for new contradictions to emerge in the political and cultural super-structure. This assumption of the suppression of contradiction due to the economic stabilization of capitalism underpinned Marcuse's notion of the "one-dimensional society."

However, the bureaucratic society of controlled consumption gave rise to individuals who felt incompatible with bureaucracy and control. In *The Coming Crisis*, Gouldner argued that sociology was entering crisis because it had become the intellectual handmaiden of the welfare state and was threat-ened with loss of intellectual autonomy and critical edge as it became increas-ingly absorbed and directed by the policy needs of the welfare state. At the same time, he identified a contradiction between the Protestant conservative-liberalism of the sociological establishment, personified by Parsons, and the values and sensibilities of the counterculture. The new sensibilities carried by counterculture youth were, Gouldner thought, already producing their own ramifications in sociology, and such was his characterization of ethnometh-odology. These would undermine the domain assumptions of the discipline, especially the discipline's central positivist epistemology which connected it with the technocratic orientation of the welfare state and the bureaucratic society. Gouldner correctly diagnosed the crisis, from which the discipline has never recovered, but misdiagnosed its cause. This was not the stability and power of the welfare state, but its weakness and temporariness. Gouldner was astute in observing that the epistemic crisis of functionalism was signifi-cant because Parsonian functionalism represented the unification of academic sociology within a conception of the social as totality. The breakdown of the functionalist consensus was highly significant for the coherence, and the very legitimacy of the notion, of a unified discipline of sociology. Gouldner saw in the counterculture the herald of the emergence of structures of feeling antithetical to the structures of feeling and worldview of functionalism. This heralded a generational value-shift that would pose a fundamental challenge to the theoretical, moral, and political tenets that organized and animated sociology as a discipline. These counterculture values were also the herald of the crisis of the so-called welfare state (an institutional corollary and com-ponent of the Keynesian solution to the crisis of capitalism and the Bretton Woods international political and financial order).

Gouldner's *Coming Crisis*, followed a year later by the "Nixon shock," marked the entanglement of the crisis of sociology with the crisis of the Bretton Woods and Keynesian political-economic order and the crisis of Fordist societalization. In the later political-economic context of fully blown neoliberalism, Horowitz's 1993 book *The Decomposition of Sociology* railed futilely against the breakup of sociology by its splintering into identity categories. Horowitz's rage was due to the reflection in the decomposition of sociology of the decay of American national consensus and the crisis of national identity. His orientation to sociological thought is distinctly nationalistic. He attacks ideas as "un-American," he seeks to return American sociology to the American pragmatist empirical tradition, and he thinks sociology is properly applied to national policy representing a unified response of America as a nation to its domestic and international relations. He conceives of sociology as a science *for* the nation-state, for a "a truly national policy" which will "serve the interests of the American people as a whole." He laments the "fragmentation of society into polarized interest groups" and the contribution made to this by the fragmentation of sociology into particularistic fields such as black studies, Hispanic studies, and feminist studies.[167] As well as the dissolution of sociology into identitarian parcels catering to "special interest groups within academic life," the discipline had also fragmented into specializations with no coherent center. Horowitz writes:

> Methodological precision and moral purity became polarized expressions of the collapse of the scientific "middle." Sociology dissolved into its parts: criminology, urban studies, demography, policy analysis, social history, decision theory, and hospital and medical administration. Sociology as such was left with "pure theory": sections of itself on Marxism, feminism, and Third Worldism. It became, in short, a strident "interest group," a husk instead of a professional society.
>
> The themes covered in the new sociology—the study of the media, administration, development, family organization, crime, and race relations—have hardly dissolved over the past thirty years. What has dissolved is the ability of sociology as such to serve as a unifying intellectual framework.[168]

Horowitz acknowledges globalization and the fact that "The entire post-World War II environment to which we have grown accustomed is now under intense scrutiny." But he retains a fundamentally nationalist orientation, interpreting globalization as giving rise to the need for "the globalization of policy" in the sense of the globalization of the perspective of national policy.[169] His orientation is always to the nation-state. He rails against the fragmentation of society, and of sociology, without a clear sense of its cause. Hence, he swipes blindly at "anti-Americanism," "anti-Semitism," tenured radicals, the moralism of the discipline which made it susceptible to the moralizing politics of identity, and a cultural and moral drift away from the foundational liberal principles of America and the Weberian ethics of value-neutrality.

Horowitz has one foot on either side of the chasm between sociology and the neoliberal transformation of the nation-state under the pressure of the pre-eminence of the global economy. He put forward an uncomfortable mixture of welfarist liberal Keynesian national commitments and neo-conservative attachment to American imperialism, Zionism, and capitalism. The "free market" was guarantor of freedom against the tyranny of socialist planning. The task of sociology is to defend that space for individual freedom between the "behemoths" of the Big Society and the Big State. Except that Horowitz was attached to both sides of his dichotomy. His perspective is that of the middle-class individual of the state petty-bourgeoisie. This is a middle class that depends on the patronage of the state apparatus, of which they are a part through the academic system, and yet has been able to carve out a degree of autonomous agency while protected within the state apparatus (i.e., university funding). This autonomy is continually under threat from the State Behemoth of which they are a part, even while that Behemoth protects them from the Society Behemoth, of which they are also a part, but from which they remain apart, aloofness possible thanks to support from the State Behemoth. This Weberian position of the scholar, formulated and defended in terms of value-neutrality, depends on a state-society compact which sets the terms of, and makes possible, this middle ground, this median position and mediating function. It is the existence of a degree of societal consensus that makes possible the neutral position occupied by this bureaucratic section of the middle class. Sociology exists at the cutting edge of this contradiction for the reason that its cognitive authority depends not only on the protection of a sphere of discourse accepted as value-free and, therefore, neutral between social interests, but also on the very existence of consensus itself, for which sociology speaks. Sociology speaks for consensus in that it speaks for the conditions of possibility of such a consensus. Sociology gives voice to the problem of social order and the reality of social order, the ontological reality of society, and therefore the possibility of transcending value and interest conflict within society. That is, sociology speaks for society, *qua* that level of reality in which all conflicts are subsumed and that is the condition for the existence of any conflict.

Sociology in this way derives its cognitive authority not only from a claim to neutrality, but also, directly, from solidarity, recognized as a *good*, a value for which sociology speaks. Sociology speaks for solidarity by virtue of the very fact that solidarity is what makes social life, sociology's topic, possible. Therefore sociology requires a degree of societal consensus that is both product and effect of solidarity and it depends on the broader societal recognition of solidarity as a value. Sociology as a discipline is, therefore, intrinsically bound up in the solidarity project of modernity. It is the academic, intellectual, and scientific voice of this solidarity project. Therefore, the break-up in the 1970s of the postwar social consensus, reflected in the collapse of the functionalist consensus in sociology, and the consequent intellectual fragmentation of the field of sociology, represented a deep undermining of the conditions of intellectual authority of sociology. Horowitz was unable to grasp the depth of the crisis of sociology and lashed out against its symptoms without comprehending its cause. His new ideal of sociology as a value-neutral administrative science in service of the nation-state expressed his attachment to the defunct postwar compact. He praised public choice theory or rational choice theory for its ambition of scientific sociology while rejecting its scientism. This attraction to public choice theory and antipathy to planning reflected Horowitz's alignment with the very political forces of neoliberalism that had attacked the foundations of the postwar welfare state Keynesian consensus which earlier supported sociology and which made possible sociology's claim to neutrality. Sociology has responded to its own crisis by producing the idea of the "mainstream" of the discipline based on quantitative methodology. The dominant paradigm, as it has developed from the 1970s onward, rests not on any substantive theory about the social world and its ontology but, rather, on what Vaughan calls "methodological hegemony."[170] This may be regarded as a means of achieving ideological hegemony in a post-ideological age, or after the decline of sociology as ideology.

This technically legitimated and cartel-organized "consensus" around quantitative methodology is what is meant by referring to sociology as a hyper-normal science. It stands in tension with sizeable currents in sociology that Stephen Turner has identified as "post-normal" due to the fact that they do not present themselves as value-free science, but present themselves as aligned with particular movements and identities, for example, feminist sociology and critical race theory. These latter "post-normal" forms of sociology reflect and are fragments of the shattering of the postwar consensus that was expressed in consensus sociology. The collapse of the value-framework around which postwar normalcy was constructed and which was legitimized by the functionalist consensus in postwar sociology allowed the proliferation of particular value-frameworks. Unlike functionalism, these did not construct an image of the social totality and did not present themselves in universalistic terms as either neutral science or "for the benefit of humanity," but rather specifically attacked the claims to universality and neutrality and the very possibility of such universality and neutrality. In this way, the trajectory of sociology was part of the transformation of American liberalism from social universalism to multicultural particularism and difference.

Gouldner identified the origins of this "post-normal sociology" in Howard Becker's presidential address to the Society for the Study of Social Problems, and article published in 1967 in *Social Problems*, titled "Whose Side Are We On?" Becker argued for a partisan sociology that would take the side of the "underdog." Gouldner devastatingly exposed the class politics of this avant-garde radicalism. Gouldner argued that the sociologist of deviance, taking the side of the underdog, was in fact identifying with, and giving expression to, the welfare state at a higher, more abstract managerial level than the street bureaucrats that usually represent the state to the underdog. Gouldner wrote:

> The new underdog sociology propounded by Becker is, then, a standpoint that possesses a remarkably convenient combination of properties: it enables the sociologist to befriend the very small underdogs in local settings, to reject the standpoint of the "middle dog" respectables and notables who manage local caretaking establishments, while, at the same time, to make and remain friends with the really top dogs in Washington agencies or New York foundations.[171]

If sociology is on anyone's side, Gouldner was saying, it was the welfare state apparatus that it intellectually represented. Goulder identified Becker's partisan sociology with "state liberalism."[172] Chriss writes: "Becker and his group, then, by professing a new, seemingly compassionate underdog sociology, are doing little more than developing a new establishment sociology . . . compatible with the new character of social reform in the United States."[173] The underdog perspective was in fact that of the higher levels of the state apparatus of mediating institutions. Today, underdog sociology is decoupled from the tattered remnants of the welfare state. Underdog sociology is part of the capitalist state's mediating apparatus that, eschewing redistribution, centers on the therapeutic management of feelings and expectations. It operates in the space created by the bureaucratic mediation of command, the space of plausible deniability. So the corporate-financial ruling class and its aligned power elites can express compassion for the underdog and opprobrium against the raw violence of their own street enforcers, from whose crude "excesses" they seek to distance themselves. Sympathy for the underdog becomes part of the organization and social hierarchies and symbolic and cultural forms of distinction whereby the upper echelons retain aloofnees from their lower-middle-class enforcers.

Gouldner provided an early and important analysis of currents that have emerged and grown in importance, operating outside the self-declared mainstream, and that have only grown in significance within sociology, but also have overspilled the boundaries of sociology, creating new academic departments and fields often defined by particular identity characteristics (ethnicity, gender) separate from the project of the study of society as a whole. In many ways, such post-normal forms of social science coexist with hyper-normal sociology—cognitive territory is willingly and disdainfully abandoned and ceded by sociology's professional exclusions. A technicized sociology that itself has no way of articulating a concept of social whole does not stand in any substantive theoretical contradiction with identity-based particularism and often supports it. The politicized fragmentation that Horowitz bemoans is paralleled and compounded by the fragmentation wrought by technicized specialization. Hence, Arlene Stein writes,

> As sociology became more professionalized, and more committed to a positivist model that discouraged interdisciplinarity and policed professional boundaries, it became more complex, leading to a proliferation of subfields lacking a central "core" or identity. The rapid growth of the discipline during the postwar era meant that it became impossible for any one person or persons to master the whole field. A growing proliferation of a wide array of different subspecialities is reflected in the proliferation of sections of the American Sociological Association—of which there are forty-three today, encompassing such subfields as "Theory," "Sex and Gender," and "Alcohol and Drugs." When new fields and subfields develop, they quickly breed their own technical languages. The consequence of this is that many people experience their professional identities in relation to their participation in subfields rather than in the discipline as a whole. Sociology, once seen as offering a "general understanding of society," has come to focus instead on a series of smaller, relatively disconnected problems.[174]

The coexistence of technocracy and identity politics is in fact characteristic of contemporary American liberal politics as represented by the Democratic Party.[175] It remains the case that, as Gouldner said, "liberalism is also an operating code that links academic life to the political machinery of the Democratic Party."[176]

Sociology reflects and contributes to the transformation of American liberalism into an ideology without a sense of the social whole (post-ideological ideology) in contrast with mid-twentieth century social liberalism. The sociology that speaks in a partisan way for the underdog today speaks in fact for the official multiculturalism of post-social liberalism. In this post-social liberalism, the project of constructing homogeneous mass consumer citizenship within the nation-state is replaced by the positing of homogeneous communities below and between nation-states.

In *Multiculturalism and Its Discontents*, Kenan Malik makes the important observation that multiculturalism assumes homogeneity within bounded cultural groups. This assumption of shared values within a cultural group then legitimizes the claims of leaders who represent homogeneous cultural values, often highly conservative and religious as in the case of Muslim communities in the United Kingdom. In its administrative division of society into supposedly homogeneous cultural blocks, the state seeks ways of then addressing these rather artificial blocks, and brings forward these "cultural leaders." Malik writes:

Multicultural policies, in other words, have not responded to the needs of communities but, to a large degree, have helped *create* those communities by imposing identities on people and by ignoring internal conflicts arising out of class,
gender and intra-religious differences.[177]

The term "community," in multiculturalism, has romantic *gemeinschaftlich*
connotations of a cozier world than modern rational capitalism. There was
a similar orientalist romanticism in Foucault's attraction to Iranian Islamic
fundamentalism.[178] Gouldner suggested a romantic orientation in Becker's
"underdog" sociology of deviance:

> [T]heir pull to the underdog is sometimes part of a titillated attraction to the
> underdog's exotic difference and easily takes the form of "essays on quaintness"
> . . . [S]uch an identification with the underdog becomes the urban sociologist's
> equivalent of the anthropologist's (one-time) romantic appreciation of the noble
> savage.[179]

Gouldner's early critique of partisan sociology was prescient in light of
the close relationship between post-normal sociology and identity politics
and the close relationship between universities and the pseudo-left. What
has emerged out of the collapse of the functionalist consensus is the shaping of sociology and the broader "critical" social science fields by, and their
accommodation to, neoliberalism. The retreat and fragmentation of sociology
is central to the dynamic of fragmentation that overtook social thought in
general from the 1970s. The crisis within sociology was an important factor
in this broader fragmentation precisely because of the integration of what
Gouldner called the "domain assumptions" of sociology with the underlying
tenets of mid-twentieth-century social liberalism. The crisis of sociology that
Gouldner identified in 1970 should be understood as being at the center of
the crisis of social liberalism and at the root of the intellectual and cultural
fragmentation that has occurred as a result of the collapse of social liberalism.
The split between hyper-normal and post-normal sociology expresses the
contradiction, insoluble within bourgeois culture, between the Enlightenment
and Romanticism, or between Apollonian and Dionysian values.[180]

MEDIATION THROUGH FRAGMENTATION

Liu writes,

> The PMC is deeply hostile to simple redistributive policies . . . [I]t is against
> the idea of building solidarity among the oppressed. It prefers obscurantism,

balkanization, and management of interest groups to a transformative reimagination of the social order.[181]

Post-social liberalism has abandoned the universalistic grand narrative of social liberalism and the failed project of a universalistic nationalism. Instead, it engages in small-scale, clientelist, paternalistic, means-tested, "targeted assistance."[182] The PMC is highly invested in the image of meritocracy, since this is the basis for its own legitimacy. Meritocracy is a legitimation of inequality. In a time of deeply entrenched economic inequality with low social mobility, the ideology of meritocracy is weak and contradictory. Affirmative action and other forms of targeted assistance involved in the "diversity, equity and inclusion" paradigm are attempts to touch up the veneer of meritocracy over a system of deeply entrenched inequality. Affirmative action and "diversity" are the pretense that equality and opportunity can be created within capitalism by a few tweaks to institutional systems. The result is not to undo inequality but to camouflage it in so-called visible diversity. These measures are most fundamentally ways of protecting the legitimacy of the PMC within, and thereby maintaining, the capitalist structure of inequality. Whereas real social equality requires socialism, the PMC opposes and seeks to undermine any politics that would mobilize the working class and threaten its position as the clerks of capital.[183] It is because of the importance of diversity for repairing the tattered image of meritocracy and protecting the weak legitimacy of the PMC that universities, as core PMC organizations, require strict ideological discipline among faculty and staff in the maintenance of this facade.[184]

The PMC substitutes therefore recognition, *qua* therapy, for redistribution.[185] Its therapeutic discourse corresponds to, and masks, the political economy of what Arlie Hochschild calls the "commercialization of feeling." Post-normal sociology is positioned in a legitimizing relationship with the corporate and public bureaucracies of human feeling (post-Weberian, post-positivist bureaucracy).[186] The therapeutic orientation of post-normal sociology meshes with that of the growing ascendancy of managerial positions in the university. Wolfe writes, "The old class may have managed things; the new class managed people."[187] Post-positivist sociology, especially when combined with an identitarian ethos, resonates with the therapeutic new methods of management. A typical example of the university's bureaucratic therapy, and its intersection with the American power elite's ideology of "woke" liberal imperialism, is the public statement by the Chancellor Pradeep Khosla of the University of California, San Diego—an engineer whose curriculum vitae includes membership of the Pentagon's Defense Advanced Research Projects Agency (DARPA) Senior Advisory Group for Joint Unmanned Combat Air Systems, that is, drones—during the "Black

Lives Matter" protests of the summer of 2020 against police violence. Khosla made the public statement that

> we deeply regret the trauma this turmoil inflicts upon you, the collective trauma
> experienced by our Black community, and the trauma endured by genera-
> tions past . . . To our faculty: We acknowledge your pain and know that it is
> intensified.[188]

The unctuous compassion of academics, foundations, and corporations is made possible by the bureaucratic mediation of command.[189] Liu writes, "Despite its veneer of detached sophistication, the PMC embraces melodrama and sentimentality when dealing with inequality, imagining powerless people as innocent victims who it alone is uniquely able to 'help.' "[190] The PMC's mediation work links with, and culturally underwrites, JP Morgan Chase CEO Jamie Dimon "taking a knee" in front of his bank vault to signify sympathy with "black lives."[191] Stanley Aronowitz has observed, "Compassion may itself be a substitute for justice . . . . [C]ompassion . . . signifies inequality."[192] Post-normal sociology supports the paternalism of postmodern bureaucracy, that is, bureaucracy informed by what Frank Furedi calls the "prevailing therapeutic ethos."[193] In other words, post-normal sociology is sociology for cooling out the marks.[194]

Bauman argues that the transformation of the intellectual role from leg-islator to interpreter followed from, and accompanied, the breaking of the connection between culture and the nation-state. In a 1980 essay, "Research Note on the State and Society," Nicos Poulantzas predicted, alongside the growing insulation of the nation-state from democratic politics, an increase in state secrecy, and an increase in the scope of the state's authoritarian-repressive apparatuses (reconfigured through "unofficial state networks"), "a massive shift in hegemony towards monopolistic capital." This meant a shift in legitimation or consensus-building processes "away from ideologi-cal apparatuses such as schools and universities" and toward the media.[195] Poulantzas identified the emergence of phenomena whose fruition is evident today, for example, in the intersection of private tech corporations such as Amazon and Google with state surveillance and secrecy, the privatization of prisons, the integration of mercenary private contractors with the military, and the deregulation of media allowing direct corporate political propaganda in the form of Fox News. Poutlantzas wrote of "a decisive 'de-institutional-ization' of the ideologico-repressive machinery." It is also notable that the publication of Poulantzas's essay was in the same year as the Bayh-Dole Act which, allowing the patenting and commercialization of federal research, was a key moment in the development of the so-called entrepreneurial university

directly engaged in capital accumulation and increasingly internally structured along business lines.

Whereas Poulantzas saw a shift in the function of legitimation from state
ideological apparatuses to corporate commercial media, Bauman argues that
legitimation itself has become surplus to requirements. Bauman suggests that
consumer capitalism involves a far-reaching destruction of people's ability to
reproduce their own lives or engage with each other, rendering them entirely
dependent on the consumption of commodities for every aspect of their lives.
In this context, seduction through the consumer spectacle operates to entice
people into transferring more of their needs to commodities. Hence consumerism creates a need for itself. It does not require legitimation. Consumerism
sells itself. It does not need intellectuals, only advertisers. A problem arises
with those who cannot consume through the allowed channels. For them,
there is the apparatus of repression, violence by the state's bodies of armed
men, backed up by an immense surveillance and incarceration apparatus.

Hyper-normal sociology reflects the technocratic orientation of American
social liberalism, no longer with a connection to social reform. Post-normal
sociology derives an anti-technocratic neo-romantic ethos from the 1960s
counterculture and associated middle-class radical movements.[196] It draws
upon this to fashion a post-reform liberalism focusing on questions of culture
and identity rather than economic distribution. Foucault provided intellectual resources to justify the PMC's growing hostility to the solidarism and
universalism embodied in the welfare state.[197] Both hyper-normal sociology
(today's "mainstream" of the discipline) and post-normal sociology (with
its post-positivist epistemology and identitarian foci) are expressions of the
impotence of sociology in the wake of the demise of the gardening project
of the nation-state. While hyper-normal sociology presents itself with the
authority of a legislator, it has nobody to legislate for. It has no power over
the variables it correlates. It is technocratic consciousness without technocracy. Its epistemic power is increasingly eclipsed by the big data and artificial
intelligence capacities of private corporations involved in what Shoshana
Zuboff calls "surveillance capitalism."[198] This is a post-sociological form of
knowledge in the sense that it aims not to order society but to strategically
extract value from disorganized complexity. Zuboff writes:

> In another decisive break with capitalism's past, surveillance capitalists abandon
> the organic reciprocities with people that have long been a mark of capitalism's
> endurance and adaptability. Symbolized in the twentieth century by Ford's
> five-dollar day, these reciprocities hearken back to Adam Smith's original
> insights into the productive social relations of capitalism, in which firms rely on
> people as employees and customers . . . The shareholder–value movement and

globalization went a long way toward destroying this centuries-old social contract between capitalism and its communities, substituting formal indifference for reciprocity. Surveillance capitalism goes further. It not only jettisons Smith, but it also formally rescinds any remaining reciprocities with its societies.[199]

The attraction of computational power as a way to escape the impotence of hyper-normal sociology is likely to lead positivistically inclined sociologists into allegiance with surveillance capitalism at the intersection between corporate power, the university, and the repressive and war-making powers of the state. Instead of sociology linked to integration and order within the nation-state, it would then be aligned with the DARPA-funded scientists, engineers, and "new mandarins" of the sociocidal divide and ruin strategies of the "war on terror."[200] Big data is the vehicle through which sociological positivism will pass from serving the atrophied left hand of the state to the hypertrophied right hand.

Post-normal sociology, or what Bauman equivalently calls "postmodern sociology," instantiates and embraces the role of intellectual as "interpreter." Bauman writes:

> As interpreters, sociologists are no longer concerned with ascertaining the "truth" of the experience they interpret—and thus the principle of "ethno-methodological indifference" may well turn from the shocking heresy it once was into a new orthodoxy. The only concern which distinguishes sociologists-turned-interpreters as professionals is the correctness of interpretation; it is here that their professional credentials as experts (i.e., holders of skills inaccessible to the lay and untrained public) are re-established.[201]

However, this is a weak basis for professional authority since, if the fundamental assumption is that "the world is irreducibly pluralist" then a plurality of interpretations is also possible; that of the professional sociologist is just one among many.[202] So Bauman's observation aligns with Gouldner's sense of ethnomethodology as the herald of post-crisis sociology.[203] But post-normal sociology uses "scholar-activism" to establish by moral crusade the correctness of interpretation that cannot be maintained value-neutrally.[204]

Gouldner observed that the PMC-legitimizing concept of professional morality promoted by Parsons also worked to legitimize the business class by assimilating business to the professions. The concept suggested the rationality and reformability of capitalism. Gouldner argued that "Parsons provides a new legitimation for the old business class by intimating their impending moral revival."[205] Post-normal sociology does a similar service by suggesting that all voices can be heard and all can gain recognition, within the marketplace.[206]

The fracturing of the worldview of the bourgeois humanities and social sciences reflected the decline of the bourgeoisie's willingness to tolerate the compromises into which they had been forced by the organized power of the working class. Wolfe wrote in 1977:

> Contrary to assertions that businessmen supported the welfare state in order to buy off discontent, most corporate executives accepted government spending for social welfare only with extreme reluctance. Now that capitalist economies are in the midst of stagflation, these antidemocratic attitudes, always latent, are shooting to the surface.[207]

In the context of increased global competition and diminished profit margins, the ruling class sought to increase exploitation and drive down wages. As the wave of reform that followed the Watts riots of 1965 and other urban rioting receded, a different, more targeted, mediation strategy was developed under the Nixon administration. The Nixon administration promoted "black capitalism" as a way to develop a black upper middle class to act as buffer between the majority of impoverished blacks and the establishment. Affirmative action policies do not oppose neoliberalism but rather are historically connected to the rise of neoliberalism and the decline of universalistic social democratic welfare measures. John Skretny has traced how the impetus for affirmative action policies came not from below but from members of the power elite. For example, he writes: "By 1967 and 1968, business elites were increasingly advocating racial hiring, usually articulated in the available discourse of crisis management," in response to the urban riots of that decade.[208]

The civil rights movement and the urban struggles of the 1960s came together with other sources of contradiction, destabilizing the Keynesian-Fordist compact of the first two postwar decades. The racial exclusions of the postwar national Keynesian solution to crisis were exploded by mass revolt of the civil rights movement and black liberation movements, the urban struggles and revolt of the black working class in the 1960s, which themselves took place in an international context of working-class upsurge and anti-imperialist struggles around the world. In the universities, the crisis of the national compact was reflected in the coming apart of the nationalist cultural and social syntheses that were reflected in the worldview and outlook of the humanities and the social sciences, including especially sociology. The crisis was at the same time brought to bear on campus in the form of the New Left student movements, as Gouldner emphasized. Of particular importance here was the student movement for the remaking of the curriculum toward what was at the time widely called "relevance." But there was also considerable elite support for the creation of departments of Black Studies and Ethnic Studies, in particular from the Ford Foundation, even while these elites, as

Fabio Rojas writes, "actively tried to moderate black studies' more radical tendencies."[209]

As the attempt to manage class contradictions within the framework of the Keynesian state came undone in the mid- to late 1960s and the postwar boom came to an end with the economic crises of the 1970s, hope faded in the social-liberal dream of creating a stable, integrated, technocratically managed advanced industrial or "post-industrial" society under the guiding hand of the state. The crisis of both the humanities and the social sciences, in their declining state support, status and position in the hierarchy, and increasing marginality in relation to the expressed goals of the contemporary university, has to do with the crisis of the nation-state under conditions of globalization. The therapeutic ethos of post-normal sociology reflects the post-social liberalism of the professional-managerial stratum which has abandoned its earlier more universalistic conceptions, as part of the process of abandoning any vestiges of social democracy and attachment to the politics of the working class.[210]

The humanities, especially the study of literature, as Readings among others has argued, were understood as giving expression to, preserving, continuing, and socializing the young into a national culture.[211] It was in this way that they articulated with the power interest of the nation-state in organizing a national culture within its territory, and in defining legitimate, semiofficial, culture. The attachment of humanistic values to science was central to the construction of a secular culture, a project that united the sciences and humanities with the nation-state. A humanistic discourse of the sciences was part of the language in which natural and social scientists formulated their conflict with religious culture and institutions, and their demand for autonomy. It also marked continuity with religion to the extent that humanism was a secularization of Judeo-Christian theology. Humanism provided a formulation of a moral mission of the university, and thereby proclaimed the unity between knowledge and morality, a unity which had previously been formulated in religious terms, for example, through natural theology. The decline of the humanities was bound up with the decline of what Robert Westman calls "scientific humanism."[212] The construction of a humanistic secular culture ideologically connected the university with the nation-state.[213]

The shift of the 1970s toward the conceptualization of the university as an economic engine, or the rise of what Ziman calls "post-academic science" obviated the value of autonomy. Instead, the value-framework shifted to "university-industry links" based on technology transfer. This transformation toward a neoliberal conception and basis for legitimacy of the university severed the connection between natural science and humanism, and rendered humanism, if anything, a counter-discourse against the commercialization of knowledge. Postmodernism, as Lyotard specifically and explicitly argued, was a response to these transformations.[214] His rejection of grand narratives arose from an analysis of the commodification of knowledge in the university. This rendered the grand narrative defunct. Lyotard's main target of criticism was Marxism, but the elimination of grand narratives was also the decline of the unifying narrative of nation-state identity that had underpinned the humanities.

The de-moralization of science under neoliberalism, and its entirely instrumental conceptualization as an economic engine, developed as the humanities were marginalized and the university redefined its mission in terms of entrepreneurial technoscience.[215] The decline of the humanities represents the decline of a centripetal force holding the university together as an institution around a central set of values or goals. Instead, the university is subject to the centrifugal force of capital, which pulls out beyond it, in university-industry links and the evaluation of research by its economic "impact." The decline of the humanities is central to the transformation of the university into a mode that Ziman terms "post-academic." It is a decline that is nevertheless taking place as the university becomes ever more central to modern societies and ever more interlinked with other institutions and processes and ever more involved in shaping the broader culture and society.[216] The globalized entrepreneurial university has no interest in the project of defining a specifically national culture.

The decline of the humanities, and of humanism within the university, also represents and carries with it the decline of liberal secular nationalism, a nationalism that sought to justify itself in universal terms. This was the contradictory unity between nationalism and humanism, that while humanism pointed toward values that were universal to humanity as a species, and therefore contained within it a critique of nationalism, nationalism also drew on and sought to cloak itself in the language of human values. Post-normal sociology and identity politics are combined expressions of a new form of the mediating role of the professional-managerial class. They involve the reorganization of the ideological structures of the humanities and social sciences, and also of the university as an institution. In contrast with the solidarity project of social democracy, this pursues, as Kagarlitsky says, an "anti-solidary logic." He argues that this is the logic of multiculturalism and identity politics and the institutional apparatuses such as affirmative action and "diversity" that this new form of liberal mediation has produced. Kagarlitsky writes:

> The principal narrative of the "rights of minorities" . . . opens up the possibility of evading common civic obligations. In other words, these are not rights, but privileges. As a result, civil society, in which the totality of groups and organisations should ideally make up a unified expanse of participation and discussion, is gradually destroyed.[217]

The emergence of identity politics was bound up with the processes producing the giving way of welfare state reformism to an exclusionary politics
of law and order. These were features of the collapse of Keynesianism and
welfarist social reformism and the intellectual crisis of what Rodgers calls
the "age of fracture" and the rise of its political corollary, which Kagarlitsky
calls the "logic of fragmentation." There is a way in which post-normal
sociology is normalizing: it naturalizes and celebrates as the play of difference the "fragmentation of society . . . [that] was born of the social logic of
neoliberalism."[218]

David L. Eng, Judith Halberstam, and José Esteban Muñoz open their 2005
essay, "What's Queer About Queer Studies Now," by saying:

> Around 1990 *queer* emerged into public consciousness. It was a term that chal-
> lenged the normalizing mechanisms of state power to name its sexual subjects:
> male or female, married or single, heterosexual or homosexual, natural or
> perverse. Given its commitment to interrogating the social processes that not
> only produced and recognized but also normalized and sustained identity, the
> political promise of the term resided specifically in its broad critique of multiple
> social antagonisms, including race, gender, class, nationality, and religion, in
> addition to sexuality.[219]

The context of the end of the Cold War and the destabilizing of national identity by globalization lies in the background of this rejection of the gardening
role of the state by the cultural studies avant-garde, urging the destabilization
of all social identities and the proliferation of difference. In opposition to the
gardening state, Halberstam puts forward a "strategy of wildness."[220]

The antinomian romanticism (and what Liu calls "transgressive antiprofes-
sionalism") adopted by the avant-garde of the PMC has assisted in legitimizing this upper middle-class stratum's retreat from the decayed universalism of
the welfare state.[221] The romantic individualistic desire for liberation through
transgression expressed in post-normal sociology complements the hypernormalized social science of multivariate analysis, rational choice theory and
big data, forming a contradictory unity. Post-normal sociology appeals to the
idealism of unfettered subjectivity that is the accompaniment of the bourgeoisie's mechanical materialism, positivism, objectivism, technocratism,
foreign policy "realism" and Mammonism. Post-normal and mainstream
sociology are expressions of the competing urges of bourgeois culture, a cultural dualism which is related to the ways in which the bourgeoisie has split
up the world into soft and hard, feminine and masculine, private and public,
intimate and detached, value and fact, emotion and reason, freedom and
necessity, subjective and objective. The conflict between subject and object

in capitalism is the conflictual unity between the humanities and sciences in the university. The contradictory unity is between Weber's Asconsa and his iron cage.[222]

Hyper-subjective romanticism accompanies hyper-objectifying science. Post-normal and hyper-normal sociology reflect the antagonistic dualisms of bourgeois society. At the same time, both are expressions of the PMC's turn away from the gardening project of nation-state toward reconstituting their mediating role as being through the overseeing of fragmentation. They combine with the surveillance capitalists in managing the chaos of the unstable, fractured, and temporary forms of social life that have followed from the decline of social ordering by the nation-state.

The most important service that post-normal sociology provides to the bourgeoisie is in being anti-Marxist, in its burying of class in a haystack of identity categories. Its latent function is the promotion of crosscutting antagonisms in order to undermine class solidarity and class consciousness, prevent the development of the political independence of the working class and block the subjective development of the working class's global unity by losing it in the labyrinth of unfettered subjectivity.[223] Yet, this unity continues to be made as a material fact. It is the global productive force that is the working class that carries the new post-national global society, or species being. The birth pangs began in 1917.

NOTES

1. Zygmunt Bauman, *Legislators and Interpreters: On Modernity, Post-Modernity and Intellectuals* (Cambridge: Polity Press, 1987), 51.

2. Anthony Giddens, *The Nation-State and Violence: Volume II of A Contemporary Critique of Historical Materialism* (Berkeley: University of California Press, 1987), 120; Anthony Giddens, *A Contemporary Critique of Historical Materialism, Volume 1: Power, Property and the State* (London: Macmillan, 1981), 154.

3. Cf. Colin Sumner, *The Sociology of Deviance: An Obituary* (New York: Continuum, 1994).

4. Zygmunt Bauman, *Intimations of Post-Modernity: On Modernity, Post-Modernity and Intellectuals* (London: Routledge, 1992), 76, 78. Cf. Julius Weinberg, *Edward Alsworth Ross and the Sociology of Progressivism* (Madison: The State Historical Society of Wisconsin, 1972).

5. Alvin W. Gouldner, "Sociology and the Everyday Life," in Lewis A. Coser ed, *The Idea of Social Structure: Papers in Honor of Robert K. Merton* (New York: Harcourt Brace Jovanovich, 1975), 417–432, quoting 422–423.

6. Gouldner, "Sociology and the Everyday Life," 424–425.

7. Gouldner, "Sociology and the Everyday Life," 425.

8. Gouldner, "Sociology and the Everyday Life," 425.

9. Gouldner, "Sociology and the Everyday Life," 427 (emphasis in original).

10. Gouldner, "Sociology and the Everyday Life," 425 (emphasis in original).

11. Habermas, "Technology and Science as 'Ideology'," 105.

12. D. Lawrence Wieder, "Ethnomethodology and Ethnosociology," *Mid-American Review of Sociology* 2, no. 1 (1977): 1–18, esp. 7. See also Dorothy E. Smith, *The Everyday World as Problematic: A Feminist Sociology* (Milton Keynes, UK: Open University Press, 1987), 6.

13. Harold Garfinkel, *Studies in Ethnomethodology* (Cambridge: Polity Press, 1984), 68.

14. Harry Collins, *Forms of Life: The Method and Meaning of Sociology* (Cambridge, MA: The MIT Press, 2019); Peter Winch, *The Idea of a Social Science and Its Relation to Philosophy* (London: Routledge & Kegan Paul, 1958. See also Joe R. Feagin and Hernàn Vera, *Liberation Sociology* (Cambridge, MA: Westview Press, 2001), 117–118.

15. Gouldner, "Sociology and the Everyday Life," 425–426.

16. Gouldner, "Sociology and the Everyday Life," 429.

17. See also the critique of "instrumental positivism" in Feagin and Vera, *Liberation Sociology*, 59–137.

18. Gouldner, "Sociology and the Everyday Life," 429.

19. Gouldner, "Sociology and the Everyday Life," 429.

20. Gouldner, "Sociology and the Everyday Life, 430.

21. See also Hugh Mehan and Houston Wood, *The Reality of Ethnomethodology* (New York: John Wiley and Sons, 1975), 44–63; Richard Biernacki, *Reinventing Evidence in Social Inquiry: Decoding Facts and Variables* (New York: Palgrave Macmillan, 2012).

22. "Seen but unnoticed," is from Garfinkel, *Studies in Ethnomethodology*, 36.

23. Smith, *The Everyday World as Problematic*, 2.

24. Ted R. Vaughan, "Crisis in Contemporary American Sociology: A Critique of the Discipline's Dominant Paradigm," in *A Critique of Contemporary American Sociology,* eds. Ted R. Vaughan, Gideon Sjoberg, and Larry T. Reynolds (Dix Hills, NY: General Hall, Inc., 1993), 10–53, on 37.

25. Gouldner, *Sociology and the Everyday Life*," 432.

26. Cf. Ulrich Beck, "The Cosmopolitan Condition: Why Methodological Nationalism Fails," *Theory, Culture & Society* 24, no. 7–8 (2007): 286–290. *Pace* Daniel Chernilo, "The Critique of Methodological Nationalism: Theory and History," *Thesis Eleven* 106, no. 1 (2011): 98–111; Daniel Chernilo, "Classical Sociology and the Nation-State: A Reinterpretation," *Journal of Classical Sociology* 8, no. 1 (2008): 27–43.

27. Gouldner, Sociology and the Everyday Life Life," 432.

28. Gouldner, "Sociology and the Everyday Life," 432.

29. D. H. Wrong, "The Oversocialized Conception of Man in Modern Sociology," *American Sociological Review* 26 (1961): 183–193; John Bellamy Foster, "Marx's Theory of Metabolic Rift: Classical Foundations for Environmental Sociology," *American Journal of Sociology* 105, no. 2 (September 1999): 366–405.

30. Alfred Sohn-Rethel, *Intellectual and Manual Labour: A Critique of Epistemology* (London: Macmillan, 1978); Thorpe and Jacobson, "Abstract Life, Abstract Labor, Abstract Mind," 59–62.

31. Karl Marx, *Capital: A Critique of Political Economy, Volume 1*, trans. Ben Fowkes (New York: Vintage, 1977), 125.

32. Klaus Ronneberger, "Contours and Convolutions of Everydayness: On the Reception of Henri Lefebvre in the Federal Republic of Germany," *Capitalism Nature Socialism* 13, no. 2 (2002): 42–57, on 48. See also Lizbeth Cohen, *A Consumers' Republic: The Politics of Mass Consumption in Postwar America* (New York: Vintage, 2008).

33. George Steinmetz, "Scientific Authority and the Transition to Post-Fordism: The Plausibility of Positivism in U.S. Sociology since 1945," In *The Politics of Method in the Human Sciences: Positivism and its Epistemological Others,* ed. George Steinmetz (Durham, NC: Duke University Press, 2005), 275–323, on 298–299. See also George Steinmetz and Ou-Byung Chae, "Sociology in an Era of Fragmentation: From the Sociology of Knowledge to the Philosophy of Science, and Back Again," *The Sociological Quarterly* 43, no. 1 (2002): 113–137.

34. Fredy Perlman, *The Reproduction of Daily Life* (London: Dark Star/Phoenix Press [orig. published 1969, date of reprint unknown]); Stefan Kipfer, "Urbanization, Everyday Life and the Survival of Capitalism: Lefebvre, Gramsci and the Problematic of Hegemony," *Capitalism Nature Socialism* 13, no. 2 (2002): 117–149. See also. E. Wayne Ross and Kevin D. Vinson, "Social Justice Requires a Revolution of Everyday Life," in César Augusto Rossatto, Ricky Lee Allen, Marc Pruyn eds, *Reinventing Critical Pedagogy* (Rowman and Littlefield, 2006), 143–156, on 147–150; Michael E. Gardiner, *Critiques of Everyday Life* (London: Routledge, 2000).

35. Wolfe, "New Directions," 156–157. See also E. Wayne Ross and Kevin D. Vinson, "Social Justice Requires a Revolution of Everyday Life," in César Augusto Rossatto, Ricky Lee Allen, Marc Pruyn eds, *Reinventing Critical Pedagogy* (Lanham, MD: Rowman and Littlefield, 2006), 143–156, on 147–150.

36. Cf. Peter Bratsis, *Everyday Life and the State* (Abingdon, Oxon, UK: Routledge, 2016), 44–48.

37. Sohn-Rethel, *Intellectual and Manual Labour.*

38. Howard Brick, *Transcending Capitalism: Visions of a New Society in American Thought* (Ithaca, NY: Cornell University Press, 2006), 13.

39. On the relationship between ideology and sociology as being "among the new terms with which the modern consciousness begins to think," see Alvin W. Gouldner, *The Dialectic of Ideology and Technology: The Origins, Grammar, and Future of Ideology* (New York: The Seabury Press, 1976), 196.

40. Leon Bramson, *The Political Context of Sociology* (Princeton: Princeton University Press, 1961), 12. See also Robert A. Nisbet, *The Sociological Tradition* (New York: Basic Book, 1966).

41. Cf. Steven Seidman, *Liberalism and the Origins of European Social Theory* (Berkeley: University of California Press, 1983), 10.

42. Quoted in Krishan Kumar, *Prophecy and Progress: The Sociology of Industrial and Post-Industrial Society* (London: Allen Lane, 1978), 29.

43. Gertrud Lenzer, "Postscript: Mind-Forged Manacles: August Comte and the Future," in Gertrud Lenzer ed., *Auguste Comte and Positivism: The Essential Writings* (New Brunswick, NJ: Transaction Publishers, 1998), 493–519, on 513.

44. Lenzer, "Introduction: August Comte and Modern Positivism," in Gertrud Lenzer ed., *Auguste Comte and Positivism*, xxxi–lxxxii, on xlvii.

45. Herbert Spencer, "Reasons for Dissenting from the Philosophy of M. Comte," (1864), https://www.marxists.org/reference/subject/philosophy/works/en/ spencer.htm; See also Sydney Eisen, "Herbert Spencer and the Spectre of Comte," *Journal of British Studies* 7, no. 1 (1967): 48–67.

46. Cf. Göran Therborn, *Science, Class and Society: On the Formation of Sociology and Historical Materialism* (London: NLB, 1976), 143.

47. Tipple, *The Capitalist Revolution*, 338.

48. Wolfe, "New Directions in Marxist Theory," 154.

49. Wolfe, "New Directions in Marxist Theory," 154.

50. Eric J. Hobsbawm, *The Invention of Tradition* (Cambridge: Cambridge University Press, 1983). See also George L. Mosse, *The Nationalization of the Masses: Political Symbolism and Mass Movements in Germany from the Napoleonic Wars through the Third Reich* (New York: H. Fertig, 1975).

51. Zimmerman, "German Sociology and Empire," 169.

52. Zimmerman, "German Sociology and Empire," 169.

53. Goldman, *Max Weber and Thomas Mann*; Goldman, *Politics, Death, and the Devil: Self and Power in Max Weber and Thomas Mann*.

54. Eric Hobsbawm, "From Social History to the History of Society," *Daedalus* 100, no. 1 (Winter, 1971): 20–45, esp. 40–41; Cf. Eugen Weber, *Peasants into Frenchmen: The Modernization of Rural France, 1870-1914* (Stanford, CA: Stanford University Press, 1976), 113.

55. Karl Marx, *Capital, Volume One* (New York: Vintage Books, 1977), 477. See also Torkil Lauesen, *The Principal Contradiction* (Montreal, Canada: Kersplebedeb, 2020), 13–18.

56. Karl Marx and Frederick Engels, *Manifesto of the Communist Party* (Moscow: Progress Publishers, 1986), 36.

57. Cf. Jacques Bidet, *Foucault with Marx*, trans. Steven Corcoran (London: Zed Books, 2016); Bob Fine, "Struggles Against Discipline: The Theory and Politics of Michel Foucault," *Capital & Class* 9 (1979): 75–96; Dario Melossi, "Between Struggles and Discipline: Marx and Foucault on Penality and the Critique of Political Economy," in *The Political Economy of Punishment Today* (London: Routledge, 2017), 23–46; Michael Hardt, "The Global Society of Control," *Discourse* 20, no. 3 (Fall 1998): 139–152.

58. Karl Marx, *The Poverty of Philosophy* (New York: International Publishers), 1963), 54; E. P. Thompson, "Time, Work Discipline, and Industrial Capitalism," *Past & Present* 38 (December 1967): 56–97. Cf. Barbara Adam, "Modern Times: The Technology Connection and its Implications for Social Theory," *Time & Society* 1, no. 2 (1992): 175–191.

59. Cf. Stanley Cohen and Andrew Scull eds, *Social Control and the State* (New York: St. Martin's Press, 1983).

60. Karl Polanyi, *The Great Transformation* (Boston, MA: Beacon Press, 2001).

61. Pierre Bourdieu, *Acts of Resistance: Against the New Myths of Our Time* (Cambridge: Polity Press, 1998).

62. Karl Marx, *Capital, Volume 1: A Critique of Political Economy*, trans. Ben Fowkes (New York: Vintage Books, 1977), 381.

63. Hannah Holleman, Robert W. McChesney, John Bellamy Foster and R. Jamil Jonna, "The Penal State in an Age of Crisis," *Monthly Review* 61, no. 2 (June 1, 2009), https://monthlyreview.org/2009/06/01/the-penal-state-in-an-age-of-crisis/.

64. Fred Block, "The Ruling Class Does Not Rule," *Socialist Revolution* 33 (May-June) (1977): 6–28.

65. Block, "The Ruling Class Does Not Rule," 22–23.

66. Michael Billig, *Banal Nationalism* (London: Sage, 1995).

67. Henri Lefebvre, *Everyday Life in the Modern World*, trans. Sacha Rabinovitch (London: Allen Lane The Penguin Press, 1971). See also Charles Thorpe, "Alienation as Death: Technology, Capital, and the Degradation of Everyday Life in Elmer Rice's *The Adding Machine*," *Science as Culture* 18, no. 3 (2009): 261–279.

68. Lefebvre, *Everyday Life in the Modern World*, 24. Gouldner compares Lefebvre's notion of everyday life with that of ethnomethodology: Gouldner, "Sociology and the Everyday Life," 417–418.

69. Christopher Caudwell, *The Concept of Freedom* (London: Lawrence and Wishart, 1965), 210.

70. Anthony Giddens, "Erving Goffman as a Systematic Social Theorist," in P. Drew and A. Wooton eds, *Erving Goffman: Exploring the Interaction Order* (Oxford: Polity Press/Basil Blackwell, 1985), 250–279; Eviatar Zerubavel, *Hidden Rhythms: Schedules and Calendars in Social Life* (Chicago: University of Chicago Press, 1981).

71. Lefebvre, *Everyday Life in the Modern World*, 68–109.

72. J. K. Galbraith, *The New Industrial State* (Boston: Houghton Mifflin, 1971). See also Raniero Panzieri, "Surplus Value and Planning: Notes on the Reading of Capital," in Conference of Socialist Economics ed, *The Labour Process and Class Strategies* (London: Conference of Socialist Economics, 1976), 4–25.

73. Howard Brick, *Transcending Capitalism: Visions of a New Society in Modern American Thought* (Ithaca, NY: Cornell University Press, 2006). For a recent iteration of this kind of technocratic reformism, see Lane Kenworthy, *Social Democratic Capitalism* (Oxford: Oxford University Press, 2020), which makes a strong empirical case for reforms that could equalize the economy, improve quality of life, and thereby make for a good society; if only, that is, there was a ruling class with any interest in such a thing.

74. Alvin W. Gouldner, *The Future of the Intellectuals and the Rise of the New Class* (New York: The Seabury Press, 1979).

75. Mats Alvesson, *Organization Theory and Technocratic Consciousness: Rationality, Ideology, and Quality of Work* (Berlin: Walter de Gruyter, 1987); D. Gvishiani, *Organization and Management: A Sociological Analysis of Western*

Theories (Moscow: Progress Publishers, 1972); Boris Kagarlitsky, *The Dialectic of Change*, trans. Rick Simon (London: Verso, 1990), 57–109.

76. The question of technocracy intersects with new class theory: Pat Walker ed., *Between Labor and Capital* (Montreal: Black Rose Books, 1978); Hansfried Kellner and Frank W. Heuberger ed., *Hidden Technocrats: The New Class and New Capitalism* (New Brunswick: Transaction Publishers, 1992); Michael Lind, *The New Class War: Saving Democracy from the Managerial Elite* (New York: Portfolio/Penguin, 2020); Beverly H. Burris, *Technocracy at Work* (Albany, NY: State University of New York Press, 1993); Donald Clark Hodges, *Class Politics in the Information Age* Urbana: University of Illinois Press, 2000); Frank Fischer, *Technocracy and the Politics of Expertise* (London: Sage, 1990); Jeffrey Friedman, *Power Without Knowledge: A Critique of Technocracy* (Oxford: Oxford University Press, 2019); King and Szelenyi, *Theories of the New Class*.

77. Alvin W. Gouldner, *The Coming Crisis of Western Sociology* (New York: Equinox, 1971), 92 (emphasis in original).

78. Fred Block, "The Ruling Class Does Not Rule."

79. See the concept of the "Keynesian-Westphalian frame" in Nancy Fraser ed, *Fortunes of Feminism: From State-Managed Capitalism to Neoliberal Crisis* (London: Verso, 2013), 189.

80. Cf. Christopher Newfield, *Unmaking the Public University: the Forty-Year Assault on the Middle Class* (Cambridge, MA: Harvard University Press, 2008).

81. Gouldner, *Coming Crisis*, 92–93.

82. Gouldner, *Coming Crisis*, 155.

83. Auguste Comte, "The First System: Cours de Philosophie Positive (1930-1842)," in Gertrud Lenzer ed, *Auguste Comte and Positivism: The Essential Writings* (New Brunswick, NJ: Transaction Publishers, 1998), 71–306, on 83.

84. On the demise of social planning and the militarization of planning during and after World War II, see Andrew Abbott and James T. Sparrow, "Hot War, Cold War: The Structures of Sociological Action, 1940-1955," in Craig Calhoun ed, *Sociology in America: A History* (Chicago: University of Chicago Press, 2007), 281–313, on 298–300.

85. Herman Schwendinger and Julia R. Schwendinger, *The Sociologists of the Chair: A Radical Analysis of the Formative Years of North American Sociology, 1883-1992* (New York: Basic Books, 1974).

86. Herbert Marcuse, *Reason and Revolution: Hegel and the Rise of Social Theory* (Boston: Beacon Press, 1960).

87. Liu, *Virtue Hoarders*.

88. Finn Bowring, "From Mass Worker to Multitude: A Theoretical Contextualization of Hardt and Negri's Empire," *Capital & Class* 28, no. 2 (July 2004): 101–132.

89. Doug McAdam, "From Relevance to Irrelevance: The Curious Impact of the Sixties on Public Sociology," in Calhoun ed, *Sociology in America*, 411–426, on 411.

90. Stephen Turner, *American Sociology: From Pre-Disciplinary to Post-Normal* (New York: Palgrave Macmillan, 2014), 47–48. See also Stephen P. Turner and

Jonathan H. Turner, *The Impossible Science: An Institutional Analysis of American Sociology* (London: Sage, 1990), 137–138.

91. Simon Clarke, "New Utopias for Old: Fordist Dreams and Post-Fordist Fantasies," *Capital & Class* 42 (1990): 131–155. Cf. Greg Grandin, *Fordlandia: The Rise and Fall of Henry Ford's Forgotten Jungle City* (New York: Metropolitan Books, 2009); Matt Vidal, "Postfordism as a dysfunctional accumulation regime: a comparative analysis of the USA, the UK and Germany," *Work, Employment & Society* 27, no. 3 (2013): 451–471.

92. Steinmetz, "Scientific Authority and the Transition to Post-Fordism," 296.

93. Steinmetz, "Scientific Authority and the Transition to Post-Fordism," 296.

94. Ian Welsh, *Mobilising Modernity: The Nuclear Moment* (London: Routledge, 2000).

95. Bob Johnson, *Carbon Nation: Fossil Fuels in the Making of American Culture* (Lawrence, KS: University Press of Kansas, 2014), xv–xxix.

96. Elizabeth Shove, *Comfort, Cleanliness, and Convenience: The Social Organization of Normality* (Berg, 2003).

97. Jacques Ellul, *The Technological Society* (New York: Vintage Books, 1967).

98. Giddens, *Contemporary Critique*, 173. See also Thorpe and Jacobson, "Life Politics, Nature, and the State," 102.

99. Barbara Adam, *Timescapes of Modernity: The Environment and Invisible Hazards* (London: Routledge, 1998).

100. Harry F. Dahms, "The Matrix Trilogy as Critical Theory of Alienation: Communicating a Message of Radical Transformation," *Transdisciplinary Journal of Emergence* 3, no. 1 (2005): 108–124.

101. Lefebvre, *Everyday Life in the Modern World*, 24.

102. Godfrey Reggio, *Koyaanisqatsi* (film) (Santa Fe, NM: Institute for Regional Education, 1982).

103. Roger Keil, "'Commonsense Neoliberalism': Progressive Conservative Urbanism in Toronto, Canada," *Antipode* 34, no. 3 (2002): 578–601, on 583.

104. Richard Hoggart, *The Uses of Literacy: Changing Patterns in English Mass Culture* (Fair Lawn, NJ: Essential Books, 1957).

105. Marx, *Capital, Volume One*, 381, 477.

106. Harry Braverman, *Labor and Monopoly Capital: The Degradation of Work in the Twentieth Century* (New York: Monthly Review Press, 1974), quoting 344.

107. Stephen Meyer, "Adapting the Immigrant to the Line: Americanization in the Ford Factory, 1914-1921," *Journal of Social History* 14, no. 1 (Autumn, 1980): 67–82; Clarence Hooker, "Ford's Sociology Department and the Americanization Campaign and the Manufacture of Popular Culture among Assembly Line Workers c.1910-1917," *Journal of American Culture* 20, 1 (Spring 1997): 47–53; Georgios Paris Loizides, " 'Making Men' at Ford: Ethnicity, Race, and Americanization during the Progressive Era," *Michigan Sociological Review* 21 (Fall 2007): 109–148; F. J. Weed, "The Sociological Department at the Colorado Fuel and Iron Company, 1901 to 1907: Scientific Paternalism and Industrial Control," *Journal of the History of the Behavioral Sciences* 41, no. 3 (2005): 269–284. Thanks to Dorothy Howard for bringing the latter article to my attention.

108. Julian B. Carter, *The Heart of Whiteness: Normal Sexuality and Race in America, 1880-1940* (Durham, NC: Duke University Press, 2007). See also Lennard Davis, *Enforcing Normalcy: Disability, Deafness, and the Body* (London: Verso, 1995); Amy L. Brandzel, *Against Citizenship: The Violence of the Normative* (Urbana: University of Illinois Press, 2016).

109. Anastacia Marx de Salcedo, *Combat-Ready Kitchen: How the U.S. Military Shapes the Way You Eat* (New York: Current, 2015).

110. John Kenneth Galbraith, *The Affluent Society* (London: Hamish Hamilton, 1958).

111. Kevin Boyle writes, "The New Deal wasn't a failed or fumbled attempt to create a collective form of economic citizenship. It was a largely successful attempt to give the federal government the power it needed to restore economic stability and promote growth through mass purchasing power": Boyle, "Why Is There No Social Democracy in America?" *International Labor and Working-Class History* 74 (Fall, 2008): 33–37, quoting 35.

112. Habermas, "Technology and Science as 'Ideology'," 113.

113. Hillel Ticktin, "The Decline of Capitalism," *Critique: A Journal of Socialist Theory* 23, no. 1 (1995): 153–158.

114. Massimo De Angelis, *Keynesianism, Social Conflict and Political Economy* (Houndmills, Basingstoke, UK: Macmillan Press, 2000), 50–60, 75–96, 148–149, 172; Michael Kalecki, "Political Aspects of Full Employment," *Political Quarterly* 14, no. 4 (1943): 322–331. See also Antonio Negri, "Keynes and the Capitalist Theory of the State Post-1929," in Antonio Negri ed., *Revolution Retrieved: Writings on Marx, Keynes, Capitalist Crisis and New Social Subjects* (London: Red Notes, 1988), 5–42.

115. Bowring, "From the Mass Worker to the Multitude."

116. Charles Thorpe, "Political Economy of the Manhattan Project," in David Tyfield, Rebecca Lave, Samuel Randalls, and Charles Thorpe eds, *The Routledge Handbook of the Political Economy of Science* (London: Routledge, 2017), 43–56.

117. Audra J. Wolfe, *Freedom's Laboratory: The Cold War Struggle for the Soul of Science* (Baltimore, MD: Johns Hopkins University Press, 2018).

118. Michael K. Honey, *To the Promised Land: Martin Luther King and the Fight for Economic Justice* (New York: W. W. Norton and Co., 2018).

119. Lauren Rebecca Sklaroff, *Black Culture and the New Deal: The Quest for Civil Rights in the Roosevelt Era* (Durham: University of North Carolina Press, 2009), 2, 28, 241; Dona Cooper Hamilton and Charles V. Hamilton, "The Dual Agenda of African American Organizations Since the New Deal: Social Welfare Policies and Civil Rights," *Political Science Quarterly* 107, no. 3 (Autumn 1992): 435–452.

120. Mary L. Dudziak, *Cold War Civil Rights: Race and the Image of American Democracy* (Princeton: Princeton University Press, 2011).

121. Brenda Gayle Plummer, *In Search of Power: African Americans in the Era of Decolonization, 1956-1974* (Cambridge: Cambridge University Press, 2013).

122. McCoy, *Shadows of the American Century*. Saccarelli and Varadarajan. *Imperialism.*

123. David North, "The Trump Coup and the Rise of Fascism: Where is America Going?" *World Socialist Web Site*, January 19, 2021, https://www.wsws.org/en/articles/2021/01/19/dnor-j19.html.

124. North, "The Trump Coup."

125. Nick Beams, "The Rise of Financial Parasitism and the Emergence of Fascism," *World Socialist Web Site*, January 26, 2021, https://www.wsws.org/en/articles/2021/01/26/para-j26.html.

126. Beams, "The Rise of Financial Parasitism"; Barry Grey, "Bailout of US Corporations Continues While Workers See Little Relief," *World Socialist Web Site*, April 9, 2020, https://www.wsws.org/en/articles/2020/04/09/bail-a09.html. Cf. John Bellamy Foster and Fred Magdoff, *The Great Financial Crisis: Causes and Consequences* (New York: Monthly Review Press, 2009).

127. Gouldner, *Coming Crisis*.

128. Anthony Giddens, *Profiles and Critiques in Social Theory* (Berkeley: University of California Press, 1982), 3.

129. Richard Lee Deaton, "The Two Masks of Alvin Ward Gouldner: Angry Outsider and Intellectual Street Fighter—Reflections of an Undutiful Son," in James J. Chriss ed, *Confronting Gouldner: Sociology and Political Activism* (Chicago: Haymarket Books, 2015), vii–xxxiii, on xxviii. See also William Buxton, *Talcott Parsons and the Capitalist Nation-State: Political Sociology as a Strategic Vocation* (Toronto: University of Toronto Press, 1985).

130. Irving Louis Horowitz, *The Decomposition of Sociology* (New York: Oxford University Press, 1994).

131. Daniel T. Rodgers, *Age of Fracture* (Cambridge, MA: The Belknap Press of Harvard University Press), 89; David J. Hess, "Neoliberalism and the History of STS Theory: Toward a Reflexive Sociology." *Social Epistemology* 27, no. 2 (2013): 177–193; Josh Whitford, "Pragmatism and the Untenable Dualism of Means and Ends: Why Rational Choice Theory Does Not Deserve Paradigmatic Privilege," *Theory and Society* 31, no. 3 (June 2002): 325–363; Scott Lash and John Urry. "The Dissolution of the Social?" In Mark Wardell and Stephen P. Turner *Sociological Theory in Transition* (London: Routledge, 1986), 95–110.

132. H. M. Collins and Graham Cox, "Recovering Relativity: Did Prophecy Fail?" *Social Studies of Science* 6 (1976): 423–444, on 437.

133. Sumner, *Sociology of Deviance*, 266–267.

134. Zygmunt Bauman, *Modernity and Ambivalence* (Cambridge: Polity Press, 1991).

135. Gouldner, *Coming Crisis*, 160.

136. Gouldner, *Coming Crisis*, 284–285.

137. Daniel Bell, *The Cultural Contradictions of Capitalism* (New York: Basic Books, 1976); Scott Lash and John Urry, *The End of Organized Capitalism* (Cambridge: Polity Press, 1987); Lauren Langman, "From Subject to Citizen to Consumer: Embodiment and the Mediation of Hegemony," in Richard Harvey Brown ed, *The Politics of Selfhood; Bodies and Identities in Global Capitalism* (University of Minnesota Press, 2003), 167–188; Robert Lifton, *The Protean Self: Human Resilience in an Age of Fragmentation* (New York: Basic Books, 1993); Richard Sennett, *The*

Corrosion of Character: the Personal Consequences of Work in the New Capitalism
(New York: W. W. Norton and Co., 1998); Fred Turner: *From Counterculture to
Cyberculture: Stewart Brand, The Whole Earth Network, and the Rise of Digital
Utopianism* (Chicago: University of Chicago Press, 2006); Luc Boltanski and Eve
Chiapello, *The New Spirit of Capitalism* (London: Verso, 2005); Grace Elizabeth
Hale, *A Nation of Outsiders: How the White Middle Class Fell in Love with Rebellion
in Postwar America* (Oxford: Oxford University Press, 2011), 6. Cf. Christopher
Newfield, "'Innovation' Discourse and the Neoliberal University: Top Ten Reasons
to Abolish Disruptive Innovation," in William Callison and Zachary Manfredi eds,
Mutant Neoliberalism: Market Rule and Political Rupture (New York: Fordham
University Press, 2020), 244–268.

138. Rodgers, *Age of Fracture*, 8, 39, 220.

139. Clara Elisabetta Mattei, "Keynesianism, Technocracy and Class Struggle,"
Journal of Cultural Economy 11, no. 5 (2018): 476–479, on 476.

140. Geoff Mann, *In the Long Run We are All Dead: Keynesianism, Political
Economy, and Revolution* (New York: Verso, 2017), 23; quoted in Mattei,
"Keynesianism," 476.

141. Negri, "Keynes and the Capitalist Theory of the State post-1929," 14.

142. On Weber's conceptions of will and subjectivity and their relation to his
political project, see Harvey Goldman, *Calling and the Shaping of Self* and *Politics,
Death and the Devil*.

143. Keynes, quoted in Negri, "Keynes and the Capitalist Theory of the State," 16.

144. Cf. David Blackbourn and Geoff Eley, *The Peculiarities of German History:
Bourgeois Society and Politics in Nineteenth-Century Germany* (Oxford: Oxford
University Press, 1984).

145. Zygmunt Bauman, *Modernity and the Holocaust* (Ithaca, NY: Cornell
University Press, 2000).

146. Dragstedt and Slaughter, *State, Power and Bureaucracy*, 35.

147. Thorpe, "Violence and the Scientific Vocation"; R. B. J. Walker, "Violence,
Modernity, Silence: From Max Weber to International Relations," in David Campbell
and Michael Dillon eds, *The Political Subject of Violence* (Manchester: Manchester
University Press, 1993), 137–160.

148. Mosse, *German Jews*.

149. Wolfe, *Limits of Legitimacy*, 314.

150. Goldman, *Politics, Death, and the Devil*.

151. Negri, "Keynes and the Capitalist Theory of the State," 9–10.

152. Wolfe, *Limits of Legitimacy*, 103.

153. Brick, *Transcending Capitalism*, 122.

154. Weber, *Protestant Ethic*, 214–215, note 145; Robert K. Merton, *Science,
Technology and Society in Seventeenth-Century England* (New York: Howard Fertig/
Harper Torchbooks, 1970); Steven Shapin, "Understanding the Merton Thesis," *Isis*
79, no. 4 (December 1988): 594–605.

155. Shapin, *Scientific Life*, 47–92.

156. David Riesman, *The Lonely Crowd: A Study of the Changing American
Character* (New Haven, CT: Yale University Press, 1965).

157. Ezrahi, *Descent of Icarus.*

158. David Paul Haney, *The Americanization of Social Science* (Philadelphia, PA: Temple University Press, 2008), 3. Samuel Z. Klausner and Victor M. Lidz eds, *The Nationalization of the Social Sciences* (Philadelphia: University of Pennsylvania Press, 1986).

159. Stephen P. Turner and Jonathan H. Turner, *The Impossible Science: An Institutional Analysis of American Sociology* (Newbury Park, CA: Sage Publications, 1990), 134. Cf. Mark Solovey. *Shaky Foundations: The Politics-Patronage-Social Science Nexus in Cold War America* (Piscataway: Rutgers University Press, 2013); Mark Solovey and Hamilton Cravens, *Cold War Social Science: Knowledge Production, Liberal Democracy, and Human Nature* (New York: Palgrave Macmillan, 2012); Mark Solovey, *Social Science for What?: Battles over Public Funding for the "Other Sciences" at the National Science Foundation* (Cambridge: The MIT Press, 2020).

160. Cf. Samuel Z. Klausner, "The Bid to Nationalize American Social Science," in Klausner and Lidz, *Nationalization of the Social Sciences*, 3–39, esp. 21, 31–32; Henry W. Riecken, "Underdogging: The Early Career of the Social Sciences in the NSF," in Klausner and Lidz, *Nationalization of the Social Sciences*, 209–225, esp. 213. See also Abbott and Sparrow, "Hot War, Cold War," 309–310; Mike Forrest Keen, *Stalking Sociologists: J. Edgar Hoover's FBI Surveillance of American Sociology* (New Brunswick, NJ: Transaction Publishers, 2004); John McCumber, *The Philosophy Scare: The Politics of Reason in the Early Cold War* (Chicago: University of Chicago Press, 2016); George A. Reisch, *How the Cold War Transformed Philosophy of Science: To the Icy Slopes of Logic* (Cambridge: Cambridge University Press, 2005).

161. Andrew Abbott rightly denies that Chicago was atheoretical. But he says that it avoided conceptual abstractions, which is precisely what distinguishes Parsons, as Gouldner emphasizes. See Andrew Abbott, *Department & Discipline: Chicago Sociology at One Hundred* (Chicago: University of Chicago Press, 1999), 196–197.

162. Brick, *Transcending Capitalism*, 14.

163. Brick, *Transcending Capitalism*, 14.

164. David J. Hess "Neoliberalism and the History of STS Theory: Toward a Reflexive Sociology," *Social Epistemology* 27, no. 2 (2013): 177–193.

165. Lauren Langman, "Dionysus—Child of Tomorrow," *Youth & Society* 3, 1 (1971): 80–99; Lauren Langman, "After Marcuse: Subjectivity—From Repression to Consumption and Beyond," *Radical Philosophy Review* 20, no. 1 (2017): 75–105.

166. On Martin Luther King Jr. and social liberalism, see Brick, *Transcending Capitalism*, 12.

167. Irving Louis Horowitz, *The Decomposition of Sociology* (New York: Oxford University Press, 1993), 6, 15, 19, 180.

168. Horowitz, *Decomposition*, 17, 21.

169. Horowitz, *Decomposition*, 176, 204.

170. Vaughan, "Crisis in Contemporary American Sociology," 21–23. George Steinmetz, "The Cultural Contradictions of Irving Louis Horowitz," *Michigan Quarterly Review* 44 no. 3 (2005): 496–505.

171. Alvin W. Gouldner, "The Sociologist as Partisan: Sociology and the Welfare State," in Alvin W. Gouldner, *For Sociology: Renewal and Critique in Sociology Today* (New York: Basic Books, 1973), 27–68, quoting 49.

172. Gouldner, "The Sociologist as Partisan," 48.

173. Chriss, *Alvin W. Gouldner*, 79.

174. Arlene Stein, "Discipline and Publish: Public Sociology in an Age of Professionalization," in J. David Knottnerus and Bernard Phillips eds, *Bureaucratic Culture and Escalating World Problems: Advancing the Sociological Imagination* (Boulder, CO: Paradigm Publishers, 2009), 156–171, on 160.

175. Thomas Frank, *Listen Liberal: Or, Whatever Happened to the Party of the People?* (New York: Picador, 2017).

176. Gouldner, "The Sociologist as Partisan," 55.

177. Kenan Malik, *Multiculturalism and its Discontents: Rethinking Diversity After 9/11* (London: Seagull Books, 2013), 61 (emphasis in original).

178. Janet Afary and Kevin B Anderson, *Foucault and the Iranian Revolution: Gender and the Seductions of Islamism* (Chicago: University of Chicago Press, 2005).

179. Gouldner, "Sociologist as Partisan," 37.

180. Cf. Langman, "Dionysus: Child of Tomorrow"; Alvin Gouldner and Richard Peterson, *Notes on Technology and the Moral Order* (Indianapolis, IN: Bobbs-Merrill, 1962).

181. Liu, *Virtue Hoarders*, 12. See also Rebecca Fisher ed., *Managing Democracy, Managing Dissent: Capitalism, Democracy and the Organisation of Consent* (London: Corporate Watch, 2013). Cf. Caroline W. Lee, *Do-It-Yourself Democracy: The Rise of the Public Engagement Industry* (Oxford: Oxford University Press, 2015); Charles Thorpe and Jane Gregory. "Producing the Post-Fordist Public: The Political Economy of Public Engagement with Science." *Science as Culture* 19, no. 3 (2010): 273–301.

182. Kagarlitsky, *Between Class and Discourse*, 17–18.

183. Jo Littler, *Against Meritocracy: Culture, Power, and the Myths of Mobility* (London: Routledge, 2017); Liu, *Virtue Hoarders*; Matt Huber, "March 2020 and the Professional Managerial Class," *Medium* (blog), March 31, 2020, https://medium.com/@Matthuber78/march-2020-and-the-professional-managerial-class-f874334ab99a; Scipio Sattler, "How Warren, and the Professional Class Left Undermined Sanders 2020," *Collide*, July 23, 2020, https://www.collidemag.com/post/how-warren-and-professional-class-left-undermined-sanders-2020; Anderson-Connolly, *A Leftist Critique of the Principles of Identity*; Domhoff, *Diversity in the Power Elite*; David Livermore, "What Diversity Matters Most," *Management Issues*, September 23, 2015, https://www.management-issues.com/opinion/7099/what-diversity-matters-most; Eric London, "Identity Politics and the Growth of Inequality within Racial Minorities," *World Socialist Web Site*, October 7, 2017, https://www.wsws.org/en/articles/2017/10/07/pers-o07.html; Eric London, "The New York Times on Race and Class: What

Determines Social Mobility in America?" *World Socialist Web Site*, April 5, 2018, https://www.wsws.org/en/articles/2018/04/05/ineq-a05.html.

Niles Niemuth, "Race, Class and Social Conflict in the United States," *World Socialist Web Site*, September 5, 2021, https://www.wsws.org/en/articles/2021/09/06/race-s06.html; Andrea Peters, "The 'Racial Wealth Gap' Narrative Obscures Reality of Class Divide in the US," *World Socialist Web Site*, June 28, 2021, https://www.wsws.org/en/articles/2021/06/29/gapr-j29.html; David Walsh, "The Socioeconomic Basis of Identity Politics: Inequality and the Rise of an African American Elite," *World Socialist Web Site*, August 30, 2016, https://www.wsws.org/en/articles/2016/08/30/pers-a30.html.

184. Hiawatha Bray, "MIT Cancels Speech by University of Chicago Professor Following Backlash," *Boston Globe*, October 13, 2021, https://www.bostonglobe.com/2021/10/13/business/mit-cancels-speech-by-university-chicago-professor-following-backlash/.

185. Nancy Fraser, *Fortunes of Feminism: From State-Managed Capitalism to Neoliberal Crisis* (London: Verso, 2013); Liu, *Virtue Hoarders*, 12.

186. Arlie Russell Hochschild, *The Managed Heart: Commercialization of Human Feeling* (Berkeley: University of California Press, 1983); Frank Furedi, *What's Happened to the University? A Sociological Exploration of its Infantilisation* (London: Routledge, 2017).

187. Alan Wolfe, "The New Class Comes Home," in Edith Kurzweil and William Phillips eds, *Our Country, Our Culture: The Politics of Political Correctness* (New York: Partisan Review Press, 1994), 283–291, on 285.

188. UCSD chancellor Pradeep Khosla (co-signed by senior administrators) to All Academics, Students, and Staff at UC San Diego, "A Message to Black Faculty, Staff and Students," June 5, 2020; Toby Reese, "Drone Valley: The University of California and the Business of High-Tech Slaughter," *World Socialist Web Site*, September 12, 2016, https://www.wsws.org/en/articles/2016/09/12/ucsd-s12.html; Pradeep K. Khosla, Biography, Office of the Chancellor, https://chancellor.ucsd.edu/chancellor-khosla/khosla-biography (accessed October 12, 2021); Neda Atanasoski, *Humanitarian Violence: The U.S. Deployment of Diversity* (Minneapolis: University of Minnesota Press, 2013); Alex Rubinstein, "Intersectional Imperialism: A Wholesome Menace," *RT*, March 21, 2021, https://www.rt.com/op-ed/518645-intersectional-imperialism-wholesome-menace/.

189. Cf. Brook Kelly-Green, "Why Black Lives Matter to Philanthropy," Ford Foundation (July 19, 2016), https://www.fordfoundation.org/just-matters/just-matters/posts/why-black-lives-matter-to-philanthropy/; Gabriel Black, "Billionaires Back Black Lives Matter," *World Socialist Web Site*, October 11, 2016, https://www.wsws.org/en/articles/2016/10/11/pers-o11.html; Trévon Austin, "Cashing in on Racialist Politics: Black Lives Matter Foundation Raised $90 Million in 2020," *World Socialist Web Site*, February 26, 2021, https://www.wsws.org/en/articles/2021/02/27/blmm-f27.html; J. C. Pan, "Will Big Philanthropy Defang Our Radical Moment," *The New Republic*, July 17, 2020, https://newrepublic.com/article/158545/will-big-philanthropy-defang-radical-moment; Touré Reed, "Why Liberals Separate Race from

Class," *Jacobin*, August 22, 2015, https://www.jacobinmag.com/2015/08/bernie
-sanders-black-lives-matter-civil-rights-movement/.

190. Liu, *Virtue Hoarders*, 74.

191. Thornton McEnery, "Jamie Dimon Drops into Mt. Kisco Chase Branch,
Takes a Knee with Staff," *New York Post*, June 5, 2020, https://nypost.com/2020/06
/05/mending-jpm-chief-drops-into-mt-kisco-chase-branch/; Cf. Roger Lowenstein,
"Jamie Dimon: America's Least-Hated Banker," *The New York Times Magazine*,
December 1, 2010, https://www.nytimes.com/2010/12/05/magazine/05Dimon-t.html;
Amy Goodman, "The Policing of Occupy Wall Street: We are Watching," *The
Guardian*, October 5, 2011, https://www.theguardian.com/commentisfree/cifamerica
/2011/oct/05/policing-occupy-wall-street-amy-goodman.

192. Stanley Aronowitz, "Against the Liberal State: ACT-UP and the Emergence
of Postmodern Politics," in Linda Nicholson and Steven Seidman eds, *Social
Postmodernism: Beyond Identity Politics* (Cambridge: Cambridge University Press,
1995), 357–383, quoting 374.

193. Furedi, *What's Happened to the University?*, quoting 28, see also 42. See also
Kristiina Brunila & Leena-Maija Rossi "Identity Politics, the Ethos of Vulnerability,
and Education," *Educational Philosophy and Theory* 50, no. 3 (2018): 287–298; Frank
Furedi, *Therapy Culture: Cultivating Vulnerability in an Uncertain Age* (London:
Routledge, 2004), 90. See also Roger Foster, "Therapeutic Culture, Authenticity
and Neo-liberalism," *History of the Human Sciences* 29, no. 1 (2016): 99–116; Bill
Durodié, "Fear and Terror in a Post-Political Age," *Government and Opposition*
42, no. 3 (2007): 427–450; Frank Furedi, "Is it Justice? Therapeutic History and
the Politics of Recognition," in Ewen Speed, Joanna Moncrieff, Mark Rapley eds,
De-Medicalizing Misery II: Society, Politics and the Mental Health Industry (London:
Palgrave Macmillan, 2014), 1–18. See also J. E. Elliott, "Insourcing Dissent: Brand
English in the Entrepreneurial University," *Telos* 187 (2019): 129–155. On paternal-
ism and clientelism supported by identity politics arguments for targeted benefits
rather than modern universal welfare provision, see Kagarlitsky, *Between Class and
Discourse*, 17–18.

194. Erving Goffman, "On Cooling the Mark Out: Some Aspects of Adaptation to
Failure," *Psychiatry* 15, no. 4 (1952): 451–463. See also Schmidt, *Disciplined Minds*,
193–202.

195. Nicos Poulantzas, quoted in Clyde W. Barrow, *Toward a Critical Theory
of States: The Poulantzas-Miliband Debate After Globalization* (Albany: State
University of New York Press, 2016), 164–165.

196. Cf. Gouldner, "Romanticism and Classicism: Deep Structures in Social
Science," in Alvin W. Gouldner ed., *For Sociology*, 323–366.

197. Ivan T. Berend, "Foucault and the Welfare State," *European Review* 13, no.
4 (October 2005): 551–556; Daniel Zamora, "Foucault's Responsibility," *Jacobin*,
December 15, 2014, https://jacobinmag.com/2014/12/michel-foucault-responsibility
-socialist; Magnus Paulsen Hansen, "Foucault's Flirt? Neoliberalism, the Left and the
Welfare State: a Commentary on La dernière leçon de Michel Foucault and Critiquer
Foucault," *Foucault Studies* 20 (December 2015): 291–306; Gabriel Rockhill, "Foucault:

The Faux Radical," *The Philosophical Salon, Los Angeles Review of Books*, October 12, 2020, http://thephilosophicalsalon.com/foucault-the-faux-radical/.

198. Mike Savage and Roger Burrows, "The Coming Crisis of Empirical Sociology," *Sociology* 41, no. 5 (2007): 885–899. Roger Burrows and Mike Savage, "After the Crisis? Big Data and the Methodological Challenges of Empirical Sociology," *Big Data & Society* 1, no. 1 (April-June 2014): 1–6; William Housley, Rob Procter, Adam Edwards , Peter Burnap , Matthew Williams, Luke Sloan, Omer Rana, Jeffrey Morgan, Alex Voss, and Anita Greenhill, "Big and Broad Data and Sociological Imagination: A Collaborative Response," *Big Data & Society* 1, no. 2 (July–September 2014): 1–15.

199. Zuboff, *Surveillance Capitalism*, 499.

200. Reese, "Drone Valley"; Eli Berman, Joseph H. Felter, Jacob N. Shapiro, and Vestal McIntyre, *Small Wars, Big Data: the Information Revolution in Modern Conflict* (Princeton: Princeton University Press, 2018); Callinicos, *New Mandarins*. Cf. Henry T. Nash, "The Bureaucratization of Homicide," *Bulletin of the Atomic Scientists* 36, no. 4 (1980): 22–27.

201. Bauman, *Intimations of Postmodernity*, 106.

202. Bauman, *Intimations of Postmodernity*, 106.

203. Gouldner, *Coming Crisis*, 390–395.

204. Michael Rectenwald, *Springtime for Snowflakes: Social Justice and Its Postmodern Parentage, An Academic's Memoir* (London: New English Review Press, 2018); Helen Pluckrose and James Lindsay, *Cynical Theories; How Activist Scholarship Made Everything about Race, Gender, and Identity* (Durham, NC: Pitchstone Publishing, 2020); Liu, *Virtue Hoarders*, 73.

205. Gouldner, *Future of the Intellectuals*, 37.

206. Vivek Ramaswamy, *Woke, Inc.: Inside Corporate America's Social Justice Scam* (New York: Center Street, 2021); Thomas Frank, *One Market Under God: Extreme Capitalism, Market Populism, and the End of Economic Democracy* (New York: Doubleday, 2000). See also David Walsh, "The Socioeconomic Basis of Identity Politics," *World Socialist Web Site*, August 30, 2016, https://www.wsws .org/en/articles/2016/08/30/pers-a30.html; Eric London, "Wealth Distribution in the United States and the Politics of the Pseudo-Left," *World Socialist Web Site*, January 18, 2017, https://www.wsws.org/en/articles/2017/01/18/pers-j18.html; Eric London and David North, "Further Observations on Social Inequality and the Politics of the Pseudo-Left," *World Socialist Web Site*, January 26, 2017, https://www.wsws.org/ en/articles/2017/01/26/comm-j26.html; Matthew Stewart, *The 9.9 Percent: The New Aristocracy that is Entrenching Inequality and Warping our Culture* (New York: Simon and Schuster, 2021), 207–236. See also Richard Anderson-Connolly, *A Leftist Critique of the Principles of Identity, Diversity, and Multiculturalism* (Lanham, MD: Lexington Books, 2019).

207. Wolfe, *Limits of Legitimacy*, 331.

208. John David Skretny, *The Ironies of Affirmative Action: Politics, Culture, and Justice in America* (Chicago: University of Chicago Press, 1996), 89. See also Richard L. Zweigenhaft and G. William Domhoff, *Diversity in the Power*

Elite: Ironies and Unfulfilled Promises (Lanham, MD: Rowman and Littlefield, 2018), 191.

209. Noliwe M. Roosk, *White Money, Black Power: The Surprising History of African American Studies and the Crisis of Race in Higher Education* (Boston, MA: Beacon Press, 2006); Fabio Rojas, *From Black Power to Black Studies: How a Radical Social Movement became an Academic Discipline* (Baltimore, MD: Johns Hopkins University Press, 2007), 164. See also Cedric Johnson, *Revolutionaries to Race Leaders: Black Power and the Making of African American Politics* (Minneapolis: University of Minnesota Press, 2007).

210. Liu, *Virtue Hoarders*, 2–3.

211. Readings, *The University in Ruins*, 44–88.

212. Robert S. Westman, "The 'Two Cultures' Question and the Historiography of Science in the Early Decades of the Salk Institute for Biological Studies," *Sartoniana* 32 (2019): 43–86.

213. Gouldner, *Dialectic of Ideology and Technology*, 188.

214. Jean-Francois Lyotard, *The Postmodern Condition: A Report on Knowledge*, trans. Geoff Bennington and Brian Massumi (Minneapolis: University of Minnesota Press, 1993); Charles Thorpe, "Postmodern Neo-Romanticism and The End of History in Margaret Atwood's MaddAddam Trilogy," *Soundings* 103, no. 2 (2020): 216–242.

215. Charles Thorpe, "Capitalism, Audit, and the Demise of the Humanistic Academy," *Workplace: A Journal for Academic Labor* 15 (September 2008): 103–125; Connor, *Tragedy of American Science*; Ralph Fevre, *The Demoralization of Western Culture: Social Theory and the Dilemmas of Modern Living* (London: Bloomsbury Publishing, 2000). Cf. Shapin, *The Scientific Life*.

216. Ziman, *Real Science*; David John Frank and John W. Meyer. *The University and the Global Knowledge Society* (Princeton: Princeton University Press, 2021). See also Elliott, "Insourcing Dissent"; Masao Miyoshi, "Sites of Resistance in the Global Economy," *Boundary* 2, no. 1 (Spring, 1995): 61–84.

217. Boris Kagarlitsky, *Between Class and Discourse*, 35, 37.

218. Kagarlitsky, *Between Class and Discourse*, 51. Cf. Alvin W. Gouldner, *Against Fragmentation: The Origins of Marxism and the Sociology of Intellectuals* (Oxford: Oxford University Press, 1985), 297.

219. David L. Eng, Judith Halberstam, and José Esteban Muñoz, "What's Queer about Queer Studies," *Social Text* 23, no. 3–4 (Fall-Winter 2005): 1–17, on 1 (emphasis in original). See also Amy L. Brandzel, *Against Citizenship: The Violence of the Normative* (Urbana: University of Illinois Press, 2016); Pluckrose and Lindsay, *Cynical Theories*, 89.

220. Jack Halberstam, "Strategy of Wildness," *Critique & Praxis* 13, no. 13 (February 25, 2019), http://blogs.law.columbia.edu/praxis1313/jack-halberstam-strategy-of-wildness/. Damon R. Young, "Public Thinker: Jack Halberstam on Wildness, Anarchy, and Growing up Punk," *Public Books* (March 26, 2019), https://www.publicbooks.org/public-thinker-jack-halberstam-on-wildness-anarchy-and-growing-up-punk/. See also Jack Halberstam, *Gaga Feminism: Sex, Gender, and the End of Normal* (Boston: Beacon Press, 2013).

221. Liu, *Virtue Hoarders*, 26.

222. Cf. Gane, *Max Weber and Postmodern Theory*.

223. Frances Stonor Saunders, *Who Paid the Piper? The CIA and the Cultural Cold War* (London: Granta Books, 1999); Michael Barker, "Why the CIA Cares about Marxism," *Counterpunch*, June 15, 2017, https://www.counterpunch.org /2017/06/15/why-the-cia-cares-about-marxism/; Gabriel Rockhill, "The CIA Reads French Theory: On the Intellectual Labor of Dismantling the Cultural Left," *The Philosophical Salon, Los Angeles Review of Books*, February 28, 2017, http:// thephilosophicalsalon.com/the-cia-reads-french-theory-on-the-intellectual-labor-of -dismantling-the-cultural-left/; Domhoff, *Diversity in the Power Elite*; Anderson-Connolly, *Leftist Critique of the Principles of Identity*.

Bibliography

Abbott, Andrew. *Department & Discipline: Chicago Sociology at One Hundred.* Chicago: University of Chicago Press, 1999.

Abbott, Andrew, and James T. Sparrow. "Hot War, Cold War: The Structures of Sociological Action, 1940–1955." In *Sociology in America: A History*, edited by Craig Calhoun, 281–313. Chicago: University of Chicago Press, 2007.

Ackerman, Spencer. *Reign of Terror: How the 9/11 Era Destabilized America and Produced Trump.* New York: Viking, 2021.

Adam, Barbara. *Timescapes of Modernity: The Environment and Invisible Hazards.* London: Routledge, 1998.

Adams, Matthew. "Hypernormalised? Heathrow Plan is Proof that We Live in a Catastrophic Fantasyland." *The Ecologist,* October 26, 2016. https://theecologist.org/2016/oct/26/hypernormalised-heathrow-plan-proof-we-exist-catastrophic-fantasyland.

Afary, Janet, and Kevin B. Anderson. *Foucault and the Iranian Revolution: Gender and the Seductions of Islamism.* Chicago: University of Chicago Press, 2005.

Agamben, Giorgio. *State of Exception.* Translated by Kevin Attell. Chicago: University of Chicago Press, 2005.

Ahmad, Sultan, and Abdul Qadir Sediqi. "U.S. Drone Strike Kills 30 Pine Nut Farm Workers in Afghanistan." *Reuters*, September 19, 2019. https://www.reuters.com/article/us-afghanistan-attack-drones/u-s-drone-strike-kills-30-pine-nut-farm-workers-in-afghanistan-idUSKBN1W40NW.

Akbar, Jay. "Cannibal 'Moderate' Syrian Rebel Who Cut Out and Ate an Assad Soldier's Heart and Liver is Killed 'After his Convoy was Ambushed'." *The Daily Mail*, April 5, 2016. https://www.dailymail.co.uk/news/article-3524976/CANNIBAL-moderate-Syrian-rebel-cut-ate-Assad-soldier-s-heart-liver-killed.html.

Althusser, Louis. "Ideology and Ideological State Apparatuses." In *Lenin and Philosophy and Other Essays*, 127–186. New York: Monthly Review Press, 1971.

Alvesson, Mats. *Organization Theory and Technocratic Consciousness: Rationality, Ideology, and Quality of Work.* Berlin: Walter de Gruyter, 1987.

Ames, Mark. *Going Postal: Rage, Murder and Rebellion.* New York: Soft Skull, 2005.

Amnesty International. "With Whom are Many U.S. Police Departments Training? With a Chronic Human Rights Violator – Israel." *Amnesty International*, August 25, 2016. https://www.amnestyusa.org/with-whom-are-many-u-s-police-departments-training-with-a-chronic-human-rights-violator-israel/.

Amos, Howard. "Hermitage Re-Starts Clocks Stopped at the Moment Bolsheviks Seized Power." *The Calvert Journal*, October 26, 2017. https://www.calvertjournal.com/articles/show/9170/hermitage-re-starts-clocks-stopped-russian-revolution.

Ansari, Alya, and Mitch Hernandez. "Business Always as Usual: Hypernormalization and Pandemic Labor." *Society for the Anthropology of Work*, June 3, 2020. https://doi.org/10.21428/1d6be30e.cc25e869.

Apeldoorn, Bastiaan van, Naná de Graaff, and Henk Overbeek. "The Rebound of the Capitalist State: The Rearticulation of the State-Capital Nexus in the Global Crisis." In *The State-Capital Nexus in the Global Crisis: Rebound of the Capitalist State*, edited by Bastiaan van Apeldoorn, Naná de Graaff and Henk Overbeek, 5–35. London: Routledge, 2014.

Aravindan, Aradhana, and James Mackenzie. "From China to Germany, Floods Expose Climate Vulnerability." *Reuters*, July 22, 2021. https://www.reuters.com/business/environment/china-germany-floods-expose-climate-vulnerability-2021-07-22/.

Aronowitz, Stanley. *Science as Power: Discourse and Ideology in Modern Society.* Minneapolis: University of Minnesota Press, 1988.

Aronowitz, Stanley. "Against the Liberal State: ACT-UP and the Emergence of Postmodern Politics." In *Social Postmodernism: Beyond Identity Politics*, edited by Linda Nicholson and Steven Seidman, 357–383. Cambridge: Cambridge University Press, 1995.

Atanasoski, Neda. *Humanitarian Violence: The U.S. Deployment of Diversity.* Minneapolis: University of Minnesota Press, 2013.

Auken, Bill Van. "The US War and Occupation of Iraq—the Murder of a Society." *World Socialist Web Site*, May 19, 2007. https://www.wsws.org/en/articles/2007/05/iraq-m19.html.

Auken, Bill Van. "The Atrocities of ISIS and the US Wars of Sociocide." *World Socialist Web Site*, August 26, 2015. https://www.wsws.org/en/articles/2015/08/26/pers-a26.html.

Auken, Bill Van. "Trump's War Crime Pardons: Cultivating a Fascistic Base in the Military." *World Socialist Web Site*, November 27, 2019. https://www.wsws.org/en/articles/2019/11/27/pers-n27.html.

Austin, Trévon. "The US Mortality Crisis: CDC Reports Extraordinary Drop in Life Expectancy." *World Socialist Web Site*, November 30, 2018. https://www.wsws.org/en/articles/2018/11/30/cdcr-n30.html.

Austin, Trévon. "Cashing in on Racialist Politics: Black Lives Matter Foundation Raised $90 Million in 2020." *World Socialist Web Site*, February 26, 2021. https://www.wsws.org/en/articles/2021/02/27/blmm-f27.html.

Austin, Trévon. "Democrats Let US Eviction Moratorium Expire, Pushing Millions of Families to the Brink." *World Socialist Web Site*, July 30, 2021. https://www.wsws.org/en/articles/2021/07/31/pers-j31.html.

Ay, Karl-Ludwig. "Max Weber: A German Intellectual and the Question of War Guilt After the Great War." In *Max Weber and the Culture of Anarchy*, edited by Sam Whimster, 110–128. Houndmills, Basingstoke, UK: Mamillan, 1999.

Bacevich, Andrew J. *The New American Militarism: How Americans are Seduced by War*. Oxford: Oxford University Press, 2005.

Bailey, Beth. "The Army in the Marketplace: Recruiting and All-Volunteer Force." *The Journal of American History* 94, no. 1 (June 2007): 47–74.

Balibar, Étienne. *Violence and Civility: On the Limits of Political Philosophy*. Translated by G. M. Goshgarian. New York: Columbia University Press, 2016.

Balogh, Brian. *Chain Reaction: Expert Debate and Public Participation in American Commercial Nuclear Power 1945–1975*. Cambridge: Cambridge University Press, 1991.

Barker, Michael. "Why the CIA Cares About Marxism." *Counterpunch*, June 15, 2017. https://www.counterpunch.org/2017/06/15/why-the-cia-cares-about-marxism/.

Barrett, Michelle, and Mary McIntosh. *The Anti-Social Family*. London: Verso, 2015.

Barrow, Clyde W. *Universities and the Capitalist State: Corporate Liberalism and the Reconstruction of American Higher Education, 1894–1928*. Madison: The University of Wisconsin Press, 1990.

Barrow Clyde W. *Toward a Critical Theory of States: The Poulantzas-Miliband Debate After Globalization*. Albany: State University of New York Press, 2016.

Bates, Thomas R. "Gramsci and the Theory of Hegemony." *Journal of the History of Ideas* 36, no. 2 (1975): 351–366.

Baudrillard, Jean. *America*. London: Verso, 1988.

Baudrillard, Jean. *Simulacra and Simulation*. Ann Arbor: University of Michigan Press, 1994.

Bauman, Zygmunt. "The Phenomenon of Norbert Elias." *Sociology* 13 (1977): 117–135.

Bauman, Zygmunt. *Legislators and Interpreters: On Modernity, Post-Modernity and Intellectuals*. Cambridge: Polity Press, 1987.

Bauman, Zygmunt. *Freedom*. Milton Keynes, UK: Open University Press, 1988.

Bauman, Zygmunt. *Modernity and Ambivalence*. Cambridge: Polity Press, 1991.

Bauman, Zygmunt. *Intimations of Post-Modernity: Culture as the Ideology of Intellectuals*. London: Routledge, 1992.

Bauman, Zygmunt. *Globalization: The Human Consequences*. New York: Columbia University Press, 1998.

Bauman, Zygmunt. *Liquid Modernity*. Cambridge: Polity Press, 2000.

Bauman, Zygmunt. *Modernity and the Holocaust*. Ithaca, NY: Cornell University Press, 2000.

Bauman, Zygmunt. *Wasted Lives: Modernity and its Outcasts*. Cambridge: Polity Press, 2004.

Bauman, Zygmunt. *Liquid Life*. Cambridge: Polity Press, 2005.

Bauman, Zygmunt. *Liquid Times: Living in an Age of Uncertainty*. Cambridge: Polity Press, 2006.

BBC News. "9/11 Attacks: US to Reveal Key Name in Saudi Lawsuit." *BBC News*, September 13, 2019. https://www.bbc.com/news/world-us-canada-49686128.

BBC News. "Texas Snow: Mayor Quits After 'Only Strong Will Survive' Post." *BBC News*, February 17, 2021. https://www.bbc.com/news/world-us-canada-56100743.

Beams, Nick. "The Significance and Implications of Globalisation: A Marxist Assessment." *World Socialist Web Site*, January 4, 1998. https://www.wsws.org/en/articles/1998/01/glob-j04.html.

Beams, Nick. "The Rise of Financial Parasitism and the Emergence of Fascism." *World Socialist Web Site*, January 26, 2021. https://www.wsws.org/en/articles/2021/01/26/para-j26.html.

Beams, Nick. "50 Years Since the End of the Bretton Woods Monetary System." *World Socialist Web Site*, August 13, 2021. https://www.wsws.org/en/articles/2021/08/14/wood-a14.html.

Beck, Jared H. *What Happened to Bernie Sanders?* New York: Hot Books, 2018.

Beck, Ulrich. "The Cosmopolitan Condition: Why Methodological Nationalism Fails." *Theory, Culture & Society* 24, no. 7–8 (2007): 286–290.

Beck, Ulrich. *World at Risk*, trans. Ciaran Cronin. Cambridge: Polity Press, 2009.

Becker, Ernest. *The Denial of Death*. New York: The Free Press, 1997.

Beckett, Katherine, and Steve Herbert. *Banished: The New Social Control in Urban America*. Oxford: Oxford University Press, 2011.

Beckett, Lois. "What the Arrests of Beverly Hills Residents Say About the US Capitol Attack." *The Guardian*, February 25, 2021. https://www.theguardian.com/us-news/2021/feb/25/beverly-hills-arrests-us-capitol-attack#:~:text=From%20lockdown%20protests%20to%20the,conduct%20in%20a%20capitol%20building.

Bell, Daniel. *The End of Ideology: The Exhaustion of Political Ideas in the Fifties*. Glencoe, IL: The Free Press, 1960.

Ben-David, Joseph. "Review of Edward Shils ed., *Max Weber on Universities: The Power of the State and the Dignity of the Academic Calling in Imperial Germany*." *American Journal of Sociology* 80, no. 6 (May 1975): 1463–1468.

Berend, Ivan T. "Foucault and the Welfare State." *European Review* 13, no. 4 (October 2005): 551–556.

Berger, Peter. *The Sacred Canopy: Elements of a Sociological Theory of Religion*. New York: Anchor, 1990.

Berman, Elizabeth Pop. *Creating the Market University: How Academic Science Became an Economic Engine*. Princeton, NJ: Princeton University Press, 2012.

Berman, Marshall. *All that is Solid Melts into Air: The Experience of Modernity*. New York: Simon and Schuster, 1982.

Berman, Sheri. "Populism Is a Problem. Elitist Technocrats Aren't the Solution." *Foreign Policy*, December 20, 2017. https://foreignpolicy.com/2017/12/20/populism-is-a-problem-elitist-technocrats-arent-the-solution/.

Betz, Hans-Georg. "Postmodernism and the New Middle Class." *Theory, Culture & Society* 9, no. 2 (1992): 93–114.

Bevins, Vincent. *The Jakarta Method: Washington's Anticommunist Crusade and the Mass Murder Program that Shaped Our World*. PublicAffairs, 2020.

Bidet, Jacques. *Foucault with Marx*. Translated by Steven Corcoran. London: Zed Books, 2016.

Biernacki, Richard. *Reinventing Evidence in Social Inquiry: Decoding Facts and Variables*. New York: Palgrave Macmillan, 2012.

Billig, Michael. *Banal Nationalism*. London: Sage, 1995.

Bittman, Michael. "A Bourgeois Marx? Max Weber's Theory of Capitalist Society." *Thesis Eleven* 15, no. 1 (1986): 81–91.

Black, Gabriel. "Billionaires Back Black Lives Matter." *World Socialist Web Site*, October 11, 2016. https://www.wsws.org/en/articles/2016/10/11/pers-o11.html.

Blackbourn, David, and Geoff Eley. *The Peculiarities of German History: Bourgeois Society and Politics in Nineteenth-Century Germany*. Oxford: Oxford University Press, 1984.

Blackburn, Robin, ed. *Ideology in Social Science: Readings in Critical Social Theory*. New York: Vintage Books, 1973.

Blanchflower, David G. *Not Working: Where Have All the Good Jobs Gone*. Princeton, NJ: Princeton University Press, 2019.

Block, Fred. "The Ruling Class Does Not Rule." *Socialist Revolution* 33 (May–June) (1977): 6–28.

Bluhdorn, Ingolfür, and Ian Welsh. "Eco-Politics Beyond the Paradigm of Sustainability: A Conceptual Framework and Research Agenda." *Environmental Politics* 16, no. 2 (2007): 185–205.

Bluhdorn, Ingolfür, and Ian Welsh, eds. *The Politics of Unsustainability: Eco-Politics in the Post-Ecologist Era*. London: Routledge, 2013.

Blumenthal, Max. *The Management of Savagery: How America's National Security State Fueled the Rise of Al Qaeda, ISIS, and Donald Trump*. London: Verso, 2019.

BMJ, Editorial. "Covid-19: Social Murder, They Wrote –Elected, Unaccountable, and Unrepentant." *BMJ* 372, no. 314 (February 4, 2021): 372.

Boggs, Carl. *Intellectuals and the Crisis of Modernity*. Albany: State University of New York Press, 1993.

Boggs, Carl. *Fascism Old and New: American Politics at the Crossroads*. New York: Routledge, 2018.

Böller, Florian, and Welf Werner, eds. *Hegemonic Transition: Global Economic and Security Orders in the Age of Trump*. Cham, Switzerland: Palgrave Macmillan, 2021.

Boltanski, Luc, and Eve Chiapello. *The New Spirit of Capitalism*. London: Verso, 2005.

Borger, Julian. "CIA Forges Unity in Diversity: Everybody Hates Their 'Woke' Recruitment Ad." *The Guardian*, May 4, 2021. https://www.theguardian.com/us-news/2021/may/04/cia-woke-recruitment-ad.

Bosman, Julie, Sophie Kasakove, and Daniel Victor. "U.S. Life Expectancy Plunged in 2020, Especially for Black and Hispanic Americans." *The New York Times,* July 21, 2021. https://www.nytimes.com/2021/07/21/us/american-life-expectancy-report.html.

Bound, Kirsten, Tom Saunders, James Wilsdon, and Jonathan Adams. *China's Absorptive State: Research, Innovation and the Prospects for China-UK Collaboration.* London: NESTA, 2013.

Bourdieu, Pierre. *Outline of a Theory of Practice.* Cambridge: Cambridge University Press, 1977.

Bourdieu, Pierre. *Acts of Resistance: Against the New Myths of Our Time.* Cambridge: Polity Press, 1998.

Bourdieu, Pierre. "The Invisible Hand of the Powerful." In *Firing Back: Against the Tyranny of the Market 2*, translated by Loic Wacquant, 26–37. London: Verso, 2003.

Bowring, Finn. "From Mass Worker to Multitude: A Theoretical Contextualization of Hardt and Negri's *Empire.*" *Capital & Class* 28, no. 2 (July 2004): 101–132.

Bowring, Finn. "Negative and Positive Freedom: Lessons from, and to, Sociology." *Sociology* 49, no. 1 (2015): 156–171.

Boyer, Dominic, and Alexei Yurchak. "American Stiob: Or, What Late-Socialist Aesthetics of Parody Reveal About Contemporary Political Culture in the West." *Cultural Anthropology* 25, no. 2 (2010): 179–221.

Boyle, Kevin. "Why Is There No Social Democracy in America?" *International Labor and Working-Class History* 74 (Fall, 2008): 33–37.

Bramson, Leon. *The Political Context of Sociology.* Princeton, NJ: Princeton University Press, 1961.

Brandzel, Amy L. *Against Citizenship: The Violence of the Normative.* Urbana: University of Illinois Press, 2016.

Bratich, Jack. *Conspiracy Panics: Political Rationality and Popular Culture.* Albany: State University of New York Press, 2008.

Bratich, Jack. "'Give Me Liberty or Give Me Covid!' Anti-Lockdown Protests as Necropopulist Downsurgency." *Cultural Studies* 35, no. 2–3 (2021): 257–265.

Bratsis, Peter. *Everyday Life and the State.* Abingdon, Oxon, UK: Routledge, 2016.

Braverman, Harry. *Labor and Monopoly Capital: The Degradation of Work in the Twentieth Century.* New York: Monthly Review Press, 1974.

Brenner, Robert. *The Economics of Global Turbulence: The Advanced Capitalist Economies from Long Boom to Long Downturn, 1945–2005.* London: Verso, 2006.

Brick, Howard. *Transcending Capitalism: Visions of a New Society in American Thought.* Ithaca, NY: Cornell University Press, 2006.

Briggs, Raymond. *When the Wind Blows.* London: S. French, 1983.

Brown, Wendy. *Undoing the Demos: Neoliberalism's Stealth Revolution.* New York: Zone Books, 2015.

Brown, Wendy. *In the Ruins of Neoliberalism: The Rise of Antidemocratic Politics in the West.* New York: Columbia University Press, 2019.

Brunila, Kristiina, and Leena-Maija Rossi. "Identity Politics, the Ethos of Vulnerability, and Education." *Educational Philosophy and Theory* 50, no. 3 (2018): 287–298.

Bunyard, Tom. *Debord, Time and Spectacle: Hegelian Marxism and Situationist Theory.* Chicago, IL: Haymarket Books, 2018.

Burawoy, Michael. *Manufacturing Consent: Changes in the Labor Process Under Monopoly Capitalism.* Chicago: University of Chicago Press, 1979.

Burris, Beverly H. *Technocracy at Work*. Albany: State University of New York Press, 1993.

Burrows, Roger, and Mike Savage. "After the Crisis? Big Data and the Methodological Challenges of Empirical Sociology." *Big Data & Society* 1, no. 1 (April–June 2014): 1–6.

Buschendorf, Christa, Astrid Franke, and Johannes Voels. *Civilizing and Decivilizing Processes: Figurational Approaches to American Culture*. Newcastle, UK: Cambridge Scholars Publishing, 2001.

Bush, George H. W. "State of the Union Address." January 29, 1991, Public Papers of the Presidents of the United States. https://www.presidency.ucsb.edu/documents /address-before-joint-session-the-congress-the-state-the-union-1.

Buxton, William. *Talcott Parsons and the Capitalist Nation-State: Political Sociology as a Strategic Vocation*. Toronto, ON: University of Toronto Press, 1985.

Caffentzis, George. "Throwing Away the Ladder: The Universities in the Crisis." *Zerowork* 1 (1975): 128–142.

Calhoun, Craig, ed. *Sociology in America: A History*. Chicago: University of Chicago Press, 2007.

Callinicos, Alex. *The New Mandarins of American Power*. Cambridge: Polity Press, 2003.

Callinicos, Alex. *Universities in a Neoliberal World*. London: Bookmarks, 2006.

Campbell, John L. *American Discontent: The Rise of Donald Trump and the Decline of the Golden Age*. Oxford. Oxford University Press, 2018

Campbell, Stephen. "Anthropology and the Social Factory." *Dialectical Anthropology* 42 (2018): 227–239.

Cantwell, Brendan, and Ilkka Kauppinen. *Academic Capitalism in the Age of Globalization*. Baltimore, MD: Johns Hopkins University Press, 2014.

Carley, Robert F. *Culture & Tactics: Gramsci, Race, and the Politics of Practice*. Albany: State University of New York Press, 2019.

Carlson, Jennifer. *Citizen Protectors: The Everyday Politics of Guns in an Age of Decline*. New York: Oxford University Press, 2015.

Carroll, Patrick. *Science, Culture, and Modern State-Formation*. Berkeley: University of California Press, 2006.

Carson, Rachel. *Silent Spring*. Boston, MA: Houghton Mifflin, 1962.

Carter, Julian B. *The Heart of Whiteness: Normal Sexuality and Race in America, 1880–1940*. Durham, NC: Duke University Press, 2007.

Cassano, Graham, and Richard A. Dello Buono, eds. *Crisis, Politics, and Critical Sociology*. Chicago, IL: Haymarket, 2012.

Caudwell, Christopher. *The Crisis in Physics*. London: John Lane The Bodley Head, 1939.

Caudwell, Christopher. *The Concept of Freedom*. London: Lawrence and Wishart, 1965.

Caudwell, Christopher. *Romance and Realism: A Study in English Bourgeois Literature*. Edited by Samuel Hynes. Princeton, NJ: Princeton University Press, 1970.

Cavalletto, George, and Catherine Silver. "Opening/Closing the Sociological Mind to Psychoanalysis." In *The Unhappy Divorce of Sociology and Psychoanalysis:*

Diverse Perspectives on the Psychosocial, edited by Lynn Chancer and John Andrews, 17–53. New York: Palgrave Macmillan, 2014.

Chamayou, Gregoire. *A Theory of the Drone.* New York: The New Press, 2015.

Chang, Gordon C., and Hugh Mehan. "Why We Must Attack Iraq: Bush's Reasoning Practices and Argumentation System." *Discourse & Society* 19, no. 4 (2008): 453–482.

Chariton, Jordan, and Jenn Dize. "How a Flurry of Suspicious Phone Calls Sent Investigators on Rick Snyder's Trail." *The Intercept,* January 13, 2021. https://theintercept.com/2021/01/13/flint-michigan-rick-snyder-legionnaires/.

Charles, Daniel. *Master Mind: The Rise and Fall of Fritz Haber, the Nobel Laureate Who Launched the Age of Chemical Warfare.* New York: HarperCollins, 2005.

Chenoweth, Erica, and Jeremy Pressman. "Black Lives Matter Protests Were Overwhelmingly Peaceful, Our Research Finds." Harvard Radcliffe Institute, October 20, 2020. https://www.radcliffe.harvard.edu/news-and-ideas/black-lives-matter-protesters-were-overwhelmingly-peaceful-our-research-finds.

Chernilo, Daniel. "Classical Sociology and the Nation-State: A Reinterpretation." *Journal of Classical Sociology* 8, no. 1 (2008): 27–43.

Chernilo, Daniel. "The Critique of Methodological Nationalism: Theory and History." *Thesis Eleven* 106, no. 1 (2011): 98–111.

Chernilo, Daniel. "Beyond the Nation? Or Back to It? Current Trends in the Sociology of Nations and Nationalism." *Sociology* 54, no. 6 (2020): 1072–1087.

Chriss, James J. *Alvin W. Gouldner: Sociologist and Outlaw Marxist.* Aldershot: Ashgate, 1999.

Chriss, James J. *Confronting Gouldner: Sociology and Political Activism.* Leiden: Brill, 2015.

Cicourel, Aaron. *Method and Measurement in Sociology.* New York: Free Press of Glencoe, 1967.

Clarke, Simon, and Paul Hoggett. "The Empire of Fear: The American Political Psyche and the Culture of Paranoia." *Psychodynamic Practice* 10, no. 1, 89–106.

Clegg, John, and Adaner Usmani. "The Economic Origins of Mass Incarceration." *Catalyst* 3, no. 3 (Fall 2019). https://catalyst-journal.com/2019/12/the-economic-origins-of-mass-incarceration.

Cliff, Tony. "Perspectives of the Permanent War Economy." *Socialist Review* 6, no. 8 (May 1957). https://www.marxists.org/archive/cliff/works/1957/05/perm-war.htm.

Cohen, Lizbeth. *A Consumers' Republic: The Politics of Mass Consumption in Postwar America.* New York: Vintage, 2008.

Cohen, Philip N. "The American Sociological Association is Collapsing and its Organization is a Perpetual Stagnation Machine." *Family Inequality* (blog), March 21, 2021. https://familyinequality.wordpress.com/2021/03/28/the-american-sociological-association-is-collapsing-and-its-organization-is-a-perpetual-stagnation-machine/.

Collins, Chuck. *The Wealth Hoarders: How Billionaires Pay Millions to Hide Trillions.* Cambridge: Polity Press, 2021.

Collins, Harry M. "Socialness and the Undersocialized Conception of Society." *Science, Technology and Human Values* 23, no. 4 (Autumn 1998): 494–516.

Collins, Harry M. *Artifictional Intelligence: Against Humanity's Surrender to Computers.* Cambridge: Polity Press, 2018.

Collins, Harry M. *Forms of Life: The Method and Meaning of Sociology.* Cambridge, MA: The MIT Press, 2019.

Collins, Harry M., and Graham Cox. "Recovering Relativity: Did Prophecy Fail?" *Social Studies of Science* 6 (1976): 423–444.

Collins, Harry M., and Martin Kusch, *The Shape of Actions: What Humans and Machines Can Do.* Cambridge, MA: MIT Press, 1998.

Connor, Clifford D. *A People's History of Science: Miners, Midwives, and "Low Mechanicks."* New York: Nation Books, 2005.

Connor, Clifford D. *The Tragedy of American Science: From Truman to Trump.* Chicago, IL: Haymarket, 2020.

Cooley, Alexander, and Daniel Nixon. *Exit from Hegemony: The Unraveling of American Global Order.* Oxford: Oxford University Press, 2020.

Cooper, Ryan. "Trump's False Lafayette Square Exoneration." *The Week,* June 11, 2021. https://theweek.com/donald-trump/1001404/lafayette-square-clearing -inspector-general-report.

Cordle, Daniel. *States of Suspense: The Nuclear Age, Postmodernism and United States Fiction and Prose.* Manchester: Manchester University Press, 2008.

Cryle, Peter, and Elizabeth Stephens. *Normality: A Critical Genealogy.* Chicago: University of Chicago Press, 2017.

Curtis, Adam, *HyperNormalisation* (film). BBC, 2016.

Cypher, James M. "From Military Keynesianism to Global Neoliberal Militarism." *Monthly Review,* June 1, 2007. https://monthlyreview.org/2007/06/01/from-mili-tary-keynesianism-to-global-neoliberal-militarism/.

Dahms, Harry F. "The Matrix Trilogy as Critical Theory of Alienation: Communicating a Message of Radical Transformation." *Transdisciplinary Journal of Emergence* 3, no. 1 (2005): 108–124.

Damon, Andre. "Trump vs. the Democrats: Two Reactionary Factions Fight over Foreign Policy." *World Socialist Web Site*, July 16, 2018. https://www.wsws.org/ en/articles/2018/07/16/pers-j16.html.

Davidson, Helen. "Mallacoota Fire: Images of 'Mayhem' and 'Armageddon' as Bushfires Rage." *The Guardian*, December 30, 2019. https://www.theguardian .com/australia-news/2019/dec/31/mallacoota-fire-mayhem-armageddon-bushfires -rage-victoria-east-gippsland.

Davis, Mike. *City of Quartz: Excavating the Future in Los Angeles.* New York: Vintage Books, 1992.

Davis, Mike. *The Monster Enters: COVID-19, Avian Flu and the Plagues of Capitalism.* New York: OR Books, 2020.

Davis, Mike, and Daniel Bertram Monk, eds. *Evil Paradises: Dreamworlds of Neoliberalism.* New York: New Press, 2007.

Davis, Lennard J. *Enforcing Normalcy: Disability, Deafness, and the Body.* London: Verso, 1995.

De Angelis, Massimo. *Keynesianism, Social Conflict and Political Economy.* Houndmills, Basingstoke, UK: Macmillan Press, 2000.

Deaton, Richard Lee. "The Two Masks of Alvin Ward Gouldner: Angry Outsider and Intellectual Street Fighter – Reflections of an Undutiful Son." In *Confronting Gouldner*, edited by James J. Chriss, vii–xxxiii. Leiden; Brill, 2015.

Debord, Guy. *Society of the Spectacle*. London: Black and Red, 2002.

Debord, Guy. *Comments on the Society of the Spectacle*. London: Verso, 2011.

Deneen, Patrick J. *Why Liberalism Failed*. New Haven, CT: Yale University Press, 2018.

Derber, Charles. *The Wilding of America: Money, Mayhem, and the New American Dream*. New York: Worth Publishers, 2004.

Derber, Charles. *The Sociopathic Society*. New York: Routledge, 2015.

Derber, Charles, William A. Schwartz, and Yale Magrass. *Power in the Highest Degree: Professionals and the Rise of a New Mandarin Order*. Oxford: Oxford University Press, 1990.

Derber, Charles, and Yale R. Magrass. *Bully Nation: How the American Establishment Creates a Bullying Society*. Lawerence: University of Kansas Press, 2017.

Derysh, Igor. "Joe Biden to Rich Donors: 'Nothing Would Fundamentally Change' if He's Elected." *Salon,* June 19, 2019. https://www.salon.com/2019/06/19/joe-biden-to-rich-donors-nothing-would-fundamentally-change-if-hes-elected/.

De Swaan, Abram. *The Management of Normality: Critical Essays in Health and Welfare*. London: Routledge, 1990.

Democracy Now! "Vaccine Apartheid: Marc Lamont Hill, Mitchell Plitnick on Israel's 'Indifference to Palestinian Health'." *Democracy Now!*, March 4, 2021. https://www.democracynow.org/2021/3/4/vaccine_rollout_palestinian_territories_israel.

Diggins, John Patrick. *The Lost Soul of American Politics: Virtue, Self-Interest and the Foundations of Liberalism*. New York: Basic Books, 1984.

Diggins, John Patrick. *Max Weber: Politics and the Spirit of Tragedy*. New York: Basic Books, 1996.

Domhoff, G. William. *The Corporate Rich and the Power Elite in the Twentieth Century: How They Won, Why Liberals and Labor Lost*. New York: Routledge, 2020.

Doubt, Keith. *Sociocide: Reflections on Today's Wars*. Lanham, MD: Rowman and Littlefield, 2021.

Douglas, Jack. *The Social Meanings of Suicide*. Princeton, NJ: Princeton University Press, 1967.

Douglas, Jack, ed. *Understanding Everyday Life: Toward the Reconstruction of Sociological Knowledge*. Chicago, IL: Aldine, 1970.

Dragstedt, Albert, and Cliff Slaughter. *State, Power and Bureaucracy: A Marxist Critique of Sociological Theories*. London: New Park Publications, 1981.

Drury, Shadia. "The Postmodern Face of American Exceptionalism." In *Radical Intellectuals and the Subversion of Progressive Politics: The Betrayal of Politics*, edited by Gregory Smulewicz-Zucker and Michael J. Thompson, 16–32. New York: Palgrave Macmillan, 2015.

Dudziak, Mary L. *Cold War Civil Rights: Race and the Image of American Democracy*. Princeton, NJ: Princeton University Press, 2011.

Durkheim, Emile. "The Dualism of Human Nature and its Social Conditions." (Reprinted in) *Durkheimian Studies* 11 (2005): 35–45.

Durodié, Bill. "Fear and Terror in a Post-Political Age." *Government and Opposition* 42, no. 3 (2007): 427–450.

Dyer-Witheford, Nick. *Cyber-Marx: Cycles and Circuits of Struggle in High-Technology Capitalism*. Urbana: University of Illinois Press, 1999.

Dyer-Witheford, Nick. "Digital Labour, Species-Becoming, and the Global Worker." *Ephemera: Theory & Politics in Organization* 10, no. 3/4 (2010): 484–503.

The Economist. "The Antidote to Civilisational Collapse: An Interview with the Documentary Filmmaker Adam Curtis." *The Economist*, December 6, 2018. https://www.economist.com/open-future/2018/12/06/the-antidote-to-civilisational -collapse.

Ehrenreich, Barbara. *Fear of Falling: The Inner Life of the Middle Class*. New York: HarperPerennial, 1990.

Ehrenreich, Barbara, and John Ehrenreich. "The Professional-Managerial Class." In *Beyond Labor and Capital*, edited by Pat Walker, 5–45. Montréal, QC: Black Rose Books, 1978.

Eisen, Sydney. "Herbert Spencer and the Spectre of Comte." *Journal of British Studies* 7, no. 1 (1967): 48–67.

Elias, Norbert. *What is Sociology?* Translated by Stephen Mennell. New York: Columbia University Press, 1978.

Elias, Norbert. *The Civilizing Process*. Oxford: Wiley-Blackwell, 1994.

Elias, Norbert. *The Germans: Power Struggles and the Development of Habitus in the Nineteenth and Twentieth Centuries*. Cambridge: Cambridge University Press, 1996.

Elliott, J. E. "Insourcing Dissent: Brand English in the Entrepreneurial University." *Telos* 187 (Summer 2019): 129–155.

Ellis, Anthony. "A De-civilizing Reversal or System Normal? Rising Lethal Violence in Post-Recession Austerity United Kingdom." *British Journal of Criminology* 59 (2019): 862–878.

Ellul, Jacques. *The Technological Society*. New York: Vintage Books, 1967.

Emery, Theo. *Hellfire Boys: The Birth of the U.S. Chemical Warfare Service and the Race for the World's Deadliest Weapons*. New York: Little, Brown and Co., 2017.

Engelhardt, Tom. *The End of Victory Culture: Cold War America and the Disillusioning of a Generation*. Amherst: University Massachusetts Press, 2007.

Engels, Frederick. "Speech at the Grave of Karl Marx." March 17, 1883. https://www .marxists.org/archive/marx/works/1883/death/burial.htm.

Engels, Frederick. *Dialectics of Nature*. Translated by Clemens Dutt. New York: International Publishers, 1940.

Engels, Friedrich. *The Condition of the Working Class in England*. Edited by David McLellan. Oxford: Oxford University Press, 1993.

Erdely, Sabrina Rubin. "The Rape of Petty Officer Blumer: Inside the Military's Culture of Sex Abuse, Denial and Cover Up." *Rolling Stone*, February 14, 2013. https://www.rollingstone.com/politics/politics-news/the-rape-of-petty-offi-cer-blumer-99154/.

Esposito, Luigi, and Laura L. Finley. "Beyond Gun Control: Examining Neoliberalism, Pro-gun Politics and Gun Violence in the United States." *Theory in Action* 7, no. 2 (April 2014): 74–103.

Evans, Brad, and Henry A. Giroux. *Disposable Futures: The Seduction of Violence in the Age of Spectacle*. San Francisco, CA: City Lights Books, 2015.

Ezrahi, Yaron. *The Descent of Icarus: Science and the Transformation of Contemporary Democracy*. Cambridge, MA: Harvard University Press, 1990.

Fairclough, Norman. *New Labour, New Language?* London: Routledge, 2000.

Federici, Silvia. *Beyond the Periphery of the Skin: Rethinking, Remaking, and Reclaiming the Body in Contemporary Capitalism*. Oakland, CA: PM Press, 2020.

Federspiel, Frederik, and Mohammad Ali. "The Cholera Outbreak in Yemen: Lessons Learned and Way Forward." *BMC Public Health* 18 (2018): 1138–1146. https://www.ncbi.nlm.nih.gov/pmc/articles/PMC6278080/.

Feenberg, Andrew. *Critical Theory of Technology*. Oxford: Oxford University Press, 1991.

Fevre, Ralph. *The Demoralization of Western Culture: Social Theory and the Dilemmas of Modern Living*. London: Bloomsbury Publishing, 2000.

Findell, Elizabeth. "Full Death Toll from Texas Storm Could Take Months to Determine." *Wall Street Journal*, February 23, 2021. https://www.wsj.com/articles/full-death-toll-from-texas-storm-could-take-months-to-determine-11614107708#:~:text=Power%20had%20been%20restored%20in,according%20to%20the%20Associated%20Press.

Fine, Bob. "Struggles Against Discipline: The Theory and Politics of Michel Foucault." *Capital & Class* 9 (1979): 75–96.

Fischer, Frank. *Citizens, Experts, and the Environment: The Politics of Local Knowledge*. Durham, NC: Duke University Press, 2000.

Fisher, Mark. *Capitalist Realism: Is There No Alternative?* London: Zero Books, 2009.

Fisher, Rebecca, ed. *Managing Democracy, Managing Dissent: Capitalism, Democracy and the Organisation of Consent*. London: Corporate Watch, 2013.

Fisher, Rebecca. "The Paradox of Democratic Capitalism: An Historical View." In *Managing Democracy, Managing Dissent: Capitalism, Democracy and the Organisation of Consent*, edited by Fisher, Rebecca, 15–45. London: Corporate Watch, 2013.

Fleming, Peter, and Andre Spicer. "Working at a Cynical Distance: Implications for Power, Subjectivity and Resistance." *Organization* 18, no. 1 (2003): 157–179.

Fletcher, Jonathan, *Violence and Civilization: An Introduction to the Work of Norbert Elias*. Cambridge: Polity Press, 1997.

Foster, John Bellamy. "Marx's Theory of Metabolic Rift: Classical Foundations for Environmental Sociology." *American Journal of Sociology* 105, no. 2 (September 1999): 366–405.

Forman, Paul. "The Primacy of Science in Modernity, of Technology in Postmodernity, and of Ideology in the History of Technology." *History and Technology* 23, no. 1–2 (2007): 1–152.

Forman, Paul. "On the Historical Forms of Knowledge Production and Curation: Modernity Entailed Disciplinarity, Postmodernity Entails Antidisciplinarity." *Osiris* 27, no. 1 (2012): 56–97.

Foster, John Bellamy. "Marx's Theory of Metabolic Rift: Classical Foundations for Environmental Sociology." *American Journal of Sociology* 105, no. 2 (September 1999): 366–405.

Foster, John Bellamy. *Naked Imperialism: The US Pursuit of Global Dominance.* New York: Monthly Review Press, 2006.

Foster, John Bellamy, and Fred Magdoff. *The Great Financial Crisis: Causes and Consequences* New York: Monthly Review Press, 2009.

Foster, Roger. "Therapeutic Culture, Authenticity and Neo-Liberalism." *History of the Human Sciences* 29, no. 1 (2016): 99–116.

Frank, David John, and John W. Meyer. *The University and the Global Knowledge Society.* Princeton, NJ: Princeton University Press, 2021.

Frank, Thomas. *One Market Under God: Extreme Capitalism, Market Populism, and the End of Economic Democracy.* New York: Doubleday, 2000.

Frank, Thomas. *Listen Liberal: Or, Whatever Happened to the Party of the People?* New York: Picador, 2017.

Frankel, Todd C. "A Majority of the People Arrested for Capitol Riot had a History of Financial Trouble." *The Washington Post*, February 10, 2021. https://www.washingtonpost.com/business/2021/02/10/capitol-insurrectionists-jenna-ryan-financial-problems/.

Fraser, Nancy. *Fortunes of Feminism: From State-Managed Capitalism to Neoliberal Crisis.* London: Verso, 2013.

Fraser, Nancy, interviewed by Martin Mosquera. "Nancy Fraser: Cannibal Capitalism is On Our Horizon." *Jacobin*, September 10, 2021. https://jacobinmag.com/2021/09/nancy-fraser-cannibal-capitalism-interview.

Freedman, Robert, ed. *Marx on Economics.* Harmondsworth: Penguin, 1961.

Friedman, Jeffrey. *Power without Knowledge: A Critique of Technocracy.* Oxford: Oxford University Press, 2019.

Fromm, Erich. *The Sane Society.* New York: Holt, Rinehart and Winston, 1955.

Fromm, Erich. *The Heart of Man: Its Genius for Good and Evil.* New York: Harper and Row, 1964.

Fromm, Erich. *Escape from Freedom.* New York: Henry Holt and Co., 1969.

Fromm, Erich. *The Anatomy of Human Destructiveness.* New York: Holt, Rinehart and Winston, 1973.

Fuller, Steve. *Thomas Kuhn: A Philosophical History for Our Times.* Chicago: University of Chicago Press, 2000.

Fukuyama, Francis. "The End of History?" *The National Interest* 16 (Summer 1989): 3–18.

Funtowicz, S. O., and J. Ravetz. "The Good, the True and the Post-Modern." *Futures* 24, no. 10 (December 1992): 963–976.

Furedi, Frank. "So Much for the 'Peace Dividend'." *Living Marxism* (October 1990): 14–19.

Furedi, Frank. *Therapy Culture: Cultivating Vulnerability in an Uncertain Age.* London: Routledge, 2004.

Furedi, Frank. *Where Have All the Intellectuals Gone?* London: Continuum. 2005.

Furedi, Frank. "Is it Justice? Therapeutic History and the Politics of Recognition." In *De-Medicalizing Misery II: Society, Politics and the Mental Health Industry,* edited by Ewen Speed, Joanna Moncrieff, and Mark Rapley, 1–18. London: Palgrave Macmillan, 2014.

Furedi, Frank. *What's Happened to the University? A Sociological Exploration of its Infantilisation.* London: Routledge, 2017.

Furedi, Frank. *Why Borders Matter: Why Humanity Must Relearn the Art of Drawing Boundaries.* London: Routledge, 2020.

Furedi, Frank, Roger Kimball, Raymond Tallis, and Robert Whelan. *From Two Cultures to No Culture: C. P. Snow's 'Two Cultures' Fifty Years On.* London: Civitas, 2009.

Galbraith, James K. *The Predator State: How Conservatives Abandoned the Free Market and Why Liberals Should Too.* New York: The Free Press, 2008.

Galbraith, James K. *The End of Normal: The Great Crisis and the Future of Growth.* New York: Simon and Schuster, 2014.

Galbraith, John Kenneth. *The Affluent Society.* London: Hamish Hamilton, 1958.

Galbraith, John Kenneth. *The New Industrial State.* Boston: Houghton Mifflin, 1971.

Galtung, Johan. "Violence, Peace, and Peace Research." *Journal of Peace Research* 6, no. 3 (1969): 167–191.

Gamble, Andrew. *The Free Economy and the Strong State: The Politics of Thatcherism.* Basingstoke, UK: Macmillan Education, 1988.

Gane, Nicholas. *Max Weber and Postmodern Theory: Rationalization versus Re-enchantment.* Houndmills, Basingstoke, UK: Palgrave Macmillan, 2004.

Gardiner, Michael E. *Critiques of Everyday Life.* London: Routledge, 2000.

Garfinkel, Harold. *Studies in Ethnomethodology.* Cambridge: Polity Press, 1984.

Garland, David. *The Culture of Control: Crime and Social Order in Contemporary Society.* Oxford: Oxford University Press, 2001.

Gee, Alistair, and Dani Anguiano. "Last Day in Paradise: The Untold Story of How a Fire Swallowed a Town." *The Guardian*, December 20, 2018. https://www.the-guardian.com/environment/2018/dec/20/last-day-in-paradise-california-deadliest-fire-untold-story-survivors.

Gellner, Ernest. *Nations and Nationalism.* Ithaca, NY: Cornell University Press, 1983.

Gerth, Hans, and C. Wright Mills. "Introduction: The Man and His Work." In *From Max Weber: Essays in Sociology*, edited by H. H. Gerth and C. Wright Mills, 1–74. New York: Oxford University Press, 1958.

Ghamari-Tabrizi, Sharon. *The Worlds of Herman Kahn: The Intuitive Science of Thermonuclear War.* Cambridge, MA: Harvard University Press, 2005.

Giddens, Anthony. *A Contemporary Critique of Historical Materialism, Volume 1: Power, Property and the State.* London: Macmillan, 1981.

Giddens, Anthony. *Profiles and Critiques in Social Theory.* Berkeley: University of California Press, 1982.

Giddens, Anthony. *The Constitution of Society: Outline of a Theory of Structuration.* Berkeley: University of California Press, 1984.

Giddens, Anthony. "Erving Goffman as a Systematic Social Theorist." In *Erving Goffman: Exploring the Interaction Order,* edited by. P. Drew and A. Wooton, 250–279. Oxford: Polity Press/Basil Blackwell, 1985.

Giddens, Anthony. *The Nation-State and Violence: Volume II of a Contemporary Critique of Historical Materialism.* Berkeley: University of California Press, 1987.

Giddens, Anthony. *The Consequences of Modernity.* Stanford: Stanford University Press, 1990.

Giddens, Anthony. *Modernity and Self-Identity: Self and Society in the Late Modern Age.* Stanford, CA: Stanford University Press, 1991.

Giddens, Anthony. "Living in a Post-Traditional Society." In *Reflexive Modernization: Politics, Tradition and Aesthetics in the Modern Social Order,* edited by Ulrich Beck, Anthony Giddens, and Scott Lash, 56–109. Stanford: Stanford University Press, 1994.

Giddens, Anthony. *In Defence of Sociology: Essays, Interpretations and Rejoinders.* Cambridge: Polity Press, 1996.

Gill, Rosalind, and Andy Pratt. "In the Social Factory? Immaterial Labour, Precariousness and Cultural Work." *Theory, Culture & Society* 25, no. 7–8 (December 2008): 1–30.

Gillespie, Tarleton. *Custodians of the Internet: Platforms, Content Moderation, and the Hidden Decisions that Shape Social Media.* New Haven, CT: Yale University Press, 2021.

Gilman-Opalsky, Richard. "Why New Socialist Theory Needs Guy Debord: On the Practice of Radical Philosophy." In *Crisis, Politics, and Critical Sociology,* edited by Graham Cassano and Richard A. Bello Buono Cassano, 109–134. Chicago: Haymarket, 2012,

Gilmore, Ruth Wilson. *Golden Gulag: Prisons, Surplus, Crisis, and Opposition in Globalizing California.* University of California Press, 2007.

Ginsberg, Benjamin. *The Fall of the Faculty: The Rise of the All-Administrative University and Why it Matters.* Oxford: Oxford University Press, 2011.

Giroux, Henry A. *Theory and Resistance in Education: Pedagogy for the Opposition.* Praeger, 1983.

Giroux, Henry A. *Teachers as Intellectuals: Toward a Critical Pedagogy of Learning.* Praeger, 1988.

Giroux, Henry A. "Racial Injustice and Disposable Youth in the Age of Zero Tolerance." *Qualitative Studies in Education* 16, no. 4 (July–August 2003): 553–565.

Giroux, Henry A. "Zero Tolerance, Domestic Militarization, and the War Against Youth." *Social Justice* 30, no. 2 (2003): 59–65.

Giroux, Henry A. *Beyond the Spectacle of Terrorism: Global Uncertainty and the Challenge of the New Media.* New York: Routledge, 2006.

Giroux, Henry A. *Stormy Weather: Katrina and the Politics of Disposability.* Boulder, CO: Paradigm Publishers, 2006.

Giroux, Henry A. "Bare Pedagogy and the Scourge of Neoliberalism: Rethinking Higher Education as a Democratic Public Sphere." *The Education Forum* 74, no. 3 (2010): 184–196.

Giroux, Henry A. *The Mouse that Roared: Disney and the End of Innocence.* Lanham, MD: Rowman and Littlefield, 2010.

Giroux, Henry A. "Neoliberal's War Against Teachers in Dark Times." *Cultural Studies ←→ Critical Methodologies* 13, no. 6 (2013): 458–468.

Giroux, Henry A. *The University in Chains: Confronting the Military-Industrial-Academic Complex.* New York: Routledge, 2015.

Giroux, Henry A. *Twilight of the Social: Resurgent Politics in an Age of Disposability.* New York: Routledge, 2015.

Giroux, Henry A. "When Schools Become Dead Zones of the Imagination: A Critical Pedagogy Manifesto." *The High School Journal* 99, no. 4 (Summer 2016): 351–359.

Giroux, Henry A. *Terror of Neoliberalism: Authoritarianism and the Eclipse of Democracy.* New York: Routledge, 2018.

Glazebrook, Dan. *Divide and Ruin: The West's Imperial Strategy in an Age of Crisis.* San Francisco, CA: Liberation Media, 2013.

Goffman, Erving. "On Cooling the Mark Out: Some Aspects of Adaptation to Failure." *Psychiatry* 15, no. 4 (1952): 451–463.

Golden, Daniel. *Spy Schools: How the CIA, FBI, and Foreign Intelligence Secretly Exploit America's Universities.* New York: Henry Holt and Co., 2017.

Goldman, Harvey. *Max Weber and Thomas Mann: Calling and the Shaping of Self.* Berkeley: University of California Press, 1988.

Goldman, Harvey. *Politics, Death, and the Devil: Self and Power in Max Weber and Thomas Mann.* Berkeley: University of California Press, 1992.

Glynos, Jason, Robin Klimecki, and Hugh Willmott. "Cooling Out the Marks: The Ideology and Politics of the Financial Crisis." *Journal of Cultural Economy* 5, no. 3 (2012): 297–320.

Goffman, Erving. "On Cooling the Mark Out: Some Aspects of Adaptation to Failure." *Psychiatry* 15, no. 4 (1952): 451–463.

Goffman, Erving. *Encounters: Two Studies in the Sociology of Interaction.* Indianapolis, IN: Bobbs Merrill, 1961.

Goffman, Erving. *Relations in Public: Microstudies of the Public Order.* New York: Basic Books, 1971.

Goodman, Amy. "The Policing of Occupy Wall Street: We Are Watching." *The Guardian.* October 5, 2011. https://www.theguardian.com/commentisfree/cifamerica/2011/oct/05/policing-occupy-wall-street-amy-goodman.

Gouldner, Alvin W. "Cosmopolitans and Locals: Toward an Analysis of Latent Social Roles-I." *Administrative Science Quarterly* 2, no. 3 (1957): 281–306.

Gouldner, Alvin W. "Cosmopolitans and Locals: Toward an Analysis of Latent Social Roles. II." *Administrative Science Quarterly* 2, no. 4 (1958): 444–480.

Gouldner, Alvin W., and R. Peterson. *Notes on Technology and the Moral Order.* Indianapolis, IN: Bobbs-Merrill, 1962.

Gouldner, Alvin W. *The Coming Crisis of Western Sociology.* New York: Equinox, 1971.

Gouldner, Alvin W. *For Sociology: Renewal and Critique in Sociology Today.* New York: Basic Book, Inc., 1973.

Gouldner, Alvin W. "Anti-Minotaur: The Myth of a Value-Free Sociology." In *For Sociology: Renewal and Critique in Sociology Today,* edited by Alvin W. Gouldner, 3–26. New York: Basic Book, Inc., 1973.

Gouldner, Alvin W. "The Sociologist as Partisan: Sociology and the Welfare State." In *For Sociology: Renewal and Critique in Sociology Today,* edited by Alvin W. Gouldner, 27–68. New York: Basic Book, Inc., 1973.

Gouldner, Alvin W. "Romanticism and Classicism: Deep Structures in Social Science." In *For Sociology: Renewal and Critique in Sociology Today,* edited by Alvin W. Gouldner, 323–366. New York: Basic Book, Inc.

Gouldner, Alvin W. "Sociology and the Everyday Life." In *The Idea of Social Structure: Papers in Honor of Robert K. Merton,* edited by Lewis A. Coser, 417–432. New York: Harcourt Brace Jovanovich, 1975.

Gouldner, Alvin W. *The Dialectic of Ideology and Technology: The Origins, Grammar, and Future of Ideology.* New York: The Seabury Press, 1976.

Gouldner, Alvin W. *The Future of Intellectuals and the Rise of the New Class.* New York: Continuum, 1979.

Gouldner, Alvin W. *Against Fragmentation: The Origins of Marxism and the Sociology of Intellectuals.* Oxford: Oxford University Press, 1985.

Gramlich, John. "What the Data Says (and Doesn't Say) About Crime in the United States." Pew Research Center, December 20, 2020. https://www.pewresearch.org/fact-tank/2020/11/20/facts-about-crime-in-the-u-s/.

Gramsci, Antonio. *Selections from the Prison Notebooks of Antonio Gramsci.* Edited and translated by Quintin Hoare and Geoffrey Nowell-Smith. London: Lawrence & Wishart, 1971.

Grandin, Greg. *Fordlandia: The Rise and Fall of Henry Ford's Forgotten Jungle City.* New York: Metropolitan Books, 2009.

Gregory, Jane, and Simon Lock. "The Evolution of 'Public Understanding of Science: Public Engagement as a Tool of Science Policy in the UK." *Sociology Compass* 2, no. 4 (July 2008): 1252–1265.

Grey, Barry. "Senate Report on Wall Street Crash: The Criminalization of the American Ruling Class." *World Socialist Web Site.* April 18, 2011. https://www.wsws.org/en/articles/2011/04/pers-a18.html.

Guardian Staff and Agencies. "Clinton Lawyer Charged with Lying to FBI During Trump-Russia Inquiry." *The Guardian,* September 16, 2021. https://www.theguardian.com/us-news/2021/sep/16/michael-sussmann-clinton-lawyer-charged-lying-fbi-trump-russia.

Gvishiani, D. *Organization and Management: A Sociological Analysis of Western Theories.* Moscow: Progress Publishers, 1972.

Habermas, Jürgen. "Technology and Science as 'Ideology'." In *Toward a Rational Society: Student Protest, Science, and Politics,* 81–122. Boston: Beacon Press, 1971.

Habermas, Jürgen. *Legitimation Crisis.* Translated by Thomas McCarthy. Boston: Beacon Press, 1975.

Hale, Grace Elizabeth. *A Nation of Outsiders: How the White Middle Class Fell in Love with Rebellion in Postwar America.* Oxford: Oxford University Press, 2011.

Hall, Steve, Simon Winlow, and Craig Ancrum, *Criminal Identities and Consumer Culture: Crime, Exclusion and the New Culture of Narcissism.* Devon, UK: Willan, 2013.

Hall, Stuart, Chas Critcher, Tony Jefferson, John Clarke, and Brian Roberts. *Policing the Crisis: Mugging, the State, and Law and Order.* New York: Holmes and Meier Publishers, 1978.

Halliday, Terence C., and Morris Janowitz. *Sociology and its Publics: The Forms and Fates of Disciplinary Organization.* Chicago: University of Chicago Press, 1992.

Halliwell, Martin. *Therapeutic Revolutions: Medicine, Psychiatry, and American Culture, 1945–1970.* Rutgers University Press, 2013.

Halsey, A. H. *Decline of Donnish Dominion: The British Academic Professions in the Twentieth Century.* Oxford: Clarendon Press, 1995.

Hamann, Julian. "Boundary Work Between Two Cultures: Demarcating the Modern *Geisteswissenschaften.*" *History of the Humanities* 3, no. 1 (Spring 2018): 27–38.

Hamilton, Dona Cooper, and Charles V. Hamilton. "The Dual Agenda of African American Organizations Since the New Deal: Social Welfare Policies and Civil Rights." *Political Science Quarterly* 107, no. 3 (Autumn 1992): 435–452.

Hamnett, Chris. "A World Turned Upside Down: The Rise of China and the Relative Economic Decline of the West." *Area Development & Policy* 3, no. 2 (2018): 223–240.

Haney, David Paul. *The Americanization of Social Science: Intellectuals and Public Responsibility in the Postwar United States.* Philadelphia, PA: Temple University Press, 2008.

Hansen, Magnus Paulsen. "Foucault's Flirt? Neoliberalism, the Left and the Welfare State: A Commentary on *La dernière leçon de Michel Foucault* and *Critiquer Foucault.*" *Foucault Studies* 20 (December 2015): 291–306.

Harcourt, Bernard E. *The Counterrevolution: How Our Government Went to War Against its Own Citizens.* New York: Basic Books, 2018.

Hardt, Michael. "The Global Society of Control." *Discourse* 20, no. 3 (Fall 1998): 139–152.

Harvie, David. "Alienation, Class, and Enclosure in UK Universities." *Capital and Class* 24, no. 2 (2000): 103–132.

Harvie, David, and Massimo de Angelis. "Cognitive Capitalism and the Rat Race: How Capital Measures Immaterial Labour in British Universities." *Historical Materialism* 17, no. 3 (2009): 3–30.

Haskell, Thomas L. "Professionalism *versus* Capitalism: R. H. Tawney, Emile Durkheim, and C. S. Peirce on the Disinterestedness of Professional Communities." In *The Authority of Experts: Studies in History and Theory,* edited by Thomas L. Haskell, 180–225. Bloomington: Indiana University Press, 1984.

Haynes, Jeffrey. *From Huntington to Trump: Thirty Years of the Clash of Civilizations.* Lanham, MD: Lexington Books, 2019.

Head, Mike. "Corporate Blueprint Predicts 'Death' of Higher Education in Australia." *World Socialist Web Site*, August 19, 2021. https://www.wsws.org/en/articles/2021 /08/20/unis-a20.html.

Hedges, Chris. *Death of the Liberal Class*. New York: Nation Books, 2010.

Hedges, Chris. *War is a Force that Gives Us Meaning*. New York: Public Affairs, 2014.

Henwood, Doug. "Take Me to Your Leader: The Rot of the American Ruling Class." *Jacobin*, April 27, 2021. https://jacobinmag.com/2021/04/take-me-to-your-leader -the-rot-of-the-american-ruling-class.

Herman, Edward S., and Noam Chomsky. *Manufacturing Consent: The Political Economy of the Mass Media*. New York: Pantheon Books, 2002.

Hersch, Seymour. *The Killing of Osama bin Laden*. London: Verso, 2017.

Hess, David J. "Neoliberalism and the History of STS Theory: Toward a Reflexive Sociology." *Social Epistemology* 27, no. 2 (2013): 177–193.

Hilbert, Richard A. *The Classical Roots of Ethnomethodology: Durkheim, Weber, and Garfinkel*. Chapel Hill: University of North Carolina Press, 1992.

Hinton, Elizabeth. *From the War on Poverty to the War on Crime: The Making of Mass Incarceration in America*. Cambridge, MA: Harvard University Press, 2016.

Hobsbawm, Eric J. *The Invention of Tradition*. Cambridge: Cambridge University Press, 1983.

Hochschild, Arlie Russell. *The Managed Heart. Commercialization of Human Feeling*. Berkeley: University of California Press, 1983.

Hochull, Alex, George Hoare, and Philip Cunliffe. *The End of the End of History: Politics in the Twenty-First Century*. London: Zero Books, 2021.

Hodges, Donald Clark. *Class Politics in the Information Age*. Urbana: University of Illinois Press, 2000.

Hoggart, Richard. *The Uses of Literacy: Changing Patterns in English Mass Culture*. Fair Lawn, NJ: Essential Books, 1957.

Holleman, Hannah, Robert W. McChesney, John Bellamy Foster, and R. Jamil Jonna. "The Penal State in an Age of Crisis." *Monthly Review* 61, no. 2 (June 1, 2009). https://monthlyreview.org/2009/06/01/the-penal-state-in-an-age-of-crisis/.

Hollinger, David. "Money and Academic Freedom a Half Century After McCarthyism: Universities amid the Force Fields of Capital." In *Unfettered Expression,* edited by Peggie Hollingsworth, 161–184. Ann Arbor: University of Michigan Press, 2000.

Holmwood, John. "Sociology's Misfortune: Disciplines, Interdisciplinarity and the Impact of Audit Culture." *British Journal of Sociology* 61, no. 4 (December 2010): 639–658.

Holmwood, John. "The University, Democracy and the Public Sphere." *British Journal of Sociology of Education* 38, no. 7 (2017): 927–942.

Honey, Michael K. *To the Promised Land: Martin Luther King and the Fight for Economic Justice*. New York: W. W. Norton and Co., 2018.

Hooker, Clarence. "Ford's Sociology Department and the Americanization Campaign and the Manufacture of Popular Culture among Line Assembly Workers c.1910– 1917." *Journal of American Culture* 20, no. 1 (Spring 1997): 47–53.

Horkheimer, Max, and Theodor W. Adorno. *Dialectic of Enlightenment: Philosophical Fragments*. Stanford, CA: Stanford University Press, 2002.

Horowitz, Irving Louis. *The Decomposition of Sociology*. New York: Oxford University Press, 1994.

House, James S. "Culminating Crisis of American Sociology and its Role in Social Science and Public Policy: An Autobiographical, Multimethod, Reflexive Perspective." *Annual Review of Sociology* 45 (2019): 1–26.

Housley, William, Rob Procter, Adam Edwards, Peter Burnap, Matthew Williams, Luke Sloan, Omer Rana, Jeffrey Morgan, Alex Voss, and Anita Greenhill. "Big and Broad Data and Sociological Imagination: A Collaborative Response." *Big Data & Society* 1, no. 2 (July–September 2014): 1–15.

Huber, Matt. "March 2020 and the Professional Managerial Class." *Medium* (blog), March 31, 2020. https://medium.com/@Matthuber78/march-2020-and-the-professional-managerial-class-f874334ab99a.

Hudis, Peter. "The Attack on Voting Rights – A Test for Everyone on the Left." *International Marxist-Humanist*, June 28, 2021. https://imhojournal.org/articles/the-attack-on-voting-rights-a-test-for-everyone-on-the-left/.

Hume, Mike. "The New Age of Imperialism." *Living Marxism* 25 (November 1990): 4–7.

Huntington, Samuel P. *The Clash of Civilizations and the Remaking of World Order*. New York: Touchstone, 1996.

Hutchins, Edwin. *Cognition in the Wild*. Cambridge, MA: MIT Press, 1995.

Ipperciel, Donald. "The Paradox of Normalcy in the Frankfurt School." *Symposium: Canadian Journal of Continental Philosophy* II, no. 1 (1998): 37–59.

James, Malcolm, and Sivamohan Valluvan. "Coronavirus Conjuncture: Nationalism and Pandemic States." *Sociology* 54, no. 6 (2020): 1238–1250.

Jameson, Frederic. "Future City." *New Left Review* 21 (May–June 2003): 76–77.

Jeffreys, Sheila. *Gender Hurts: A Feminist Analysis of the Politics of Transgenderism*. London: Routledge, 2014.

Jencks, Christopher, and David Riesman. *The Academic Revolution*. Chicago: University of Chicago Press, 1977.

Johnson, Bob. *Carbon Nation: Fossil Fuels in the Making of American Culture*. University Press of Kansas, 2014.

Johnson, Chalmers. *The Sorrows of Empire: Militarism, Secrecy, and the End of the Republic*. New York: Owl Books, 2004.

Joyce, Helen. *Trans: When Ideology Meets Reality*. London: Oneworld, 2021.

Kagarlitsky, Boris. *The Dialectic of Change*. Translated by Rick Simon. London: Verso, 1990.

Kagarlitsky, Boris. *Between Class and Discourse: Left Intellectuals in Defence of Capitalism*. London: Routledge, 2020.

Kalecki, Michael. "Political Aspects of Full Employment." *Political Quarterly* 14, no. 4 (1943): 322–331.

Keen, Mike Forrest. *Stalking Sociologists: J. Edgar Hoover's FBI Surveillance of American Sociology*. New Brunswick, NJ: Transaction Publishers, 2004.

Keil, Roger. "'Commonsense Neoliberalism': Progressive Conservative Urbanism in Toronto, Canada." *Antipode* 34, no. 3 (2007): 578–601.

Kellner, Hansfried, and Frank W. Heuberger, eds. *Hidden Technocrats: The New Class and New Capitalism.* New Brunswick, NJ: Transaction Publishers, 1992.

Kelly-Green, Brook. "Why Black Lives Matter to Philanthropy." Ford Foundation. July 19, 2016. https://www.fordfoundation.org/just-matters/just-matters/posts/why -black-lives-matter-to-philanthropy/.

Kenworthy, Lane. *Social Democratic Capitalism.* Oxford: Oxford University Press, 2020.

King, Lawrence, and Iván Szelényi. *Theories of the New Class.* Minneapolis: University of Minnesota Press, 2004.

Kinnvall, Catarina. "Globalization and Religious Nationalism: Self, Identity, and the Search for Ontological Security." *Political Psychology* 25, no. 5 (2004): 741–767.

Kipfer, Stefan. "Urbanization, Everyday Life and the Survival of Capitalism: Lefebvre, Gramsci and the Problematic of Hegemony." *Capitalism Nature Socialism* 13, no. 2 (2002): 117–149.

Klausen, Jytte. *War and Welfare: Europe and the United States, 1945 to the Present.* New York: Palgrave Macmillan, 1998.

Klausner, Samuel Z. "The Bid to Nationalize American Social Science." In *Nationalization of the Social Sciences*, edited by Samuel Z. Klausner and Victor M. Lidz, 3–39. Philadelphia: University of Pennsylvania Press, 1986.

Klausner, Samuel Z., and Victor M. Lidz, eds. *The Nationalization of the Social Sciences.* Philadelphia: University of Pennsylvania Press, 1986.

Klein, Ezra. "Joe Biden's Promise: A Return to Normalcy." *Vox*, March 20, 2019. https://www.vox.com/policy-and-politics/2019/5/20/18631452/joe-biden-2020 -presidential-announcement-speech.

Klein, Naomi. *The Shock Doctrine: The Rise of Disaster Capitalism.* New York: Picador, 2008.

Kloos, Peter. "The Dialectics of Globalization and Localization." In *The Ends of Globalization: Bringing Society Back In,* edited by Don Kalb, Marco van der Land, Richard Staring, Bart van Steenbergen, and Nico Wilterdink, 281–297. Lanham, MD: Rowman and Littlefield, 2000.

Kocka, Jurgen. *Facing Total War: German Society 1914–1918.* Leamington Spa: Berg Publishers, 1984.

Kuhn, Thomas. *The Structure of Scientific Revolutions.* Chicago: University of Chicago Press, 1970.

Kumar, Deepa. *Islamophobia and the Politics of Empire: Twenty Years After 9/11.* Chicago, IL: Haymarket Books, 2012.

Kumar, Deepa. "After 9/11, the US Tried to Force its Will on the World. It Failed." *Jacobin,* September 12, 2021. https://www.jacobinmag.com/2021/09/9-11-us -imperialism-orientalism-neocon-middle-east-intervention-war-foreign-policy -security-islamic-terrorism.

Kupchik, Aaron, and Torin Monahan. "The New American School: Preparation for Post-Industrial Discipline." *British Journal of Sociology of Education* 27, no. 5 (2006): 617–631.

Kuttner, Rober. *Can Democracy Survive Global Capitalism?* New York: W. W. Norton and Co., 2018.

LaFree, Gary. *Losing Legitimacy: Street Crime and the Decline of Social Institutions in America.* Boulder, CO: Westview Press, 1998.

LaFree, Gary, Karise Curtis, and David McDowall. "How Effective are Our 'Better Angels'? Assessing Country-Level Declines in Homicide Since 1950." *European Journal of Criminology* 12, no. 4 (2015): 482–504.

Laing, R. D. *Knots.* London: Tavistock, 1970.

Langley, Chris. *Soldiers in the Laboratory: Military Involvement in Science & Technology, and Some Alternative.* Edited by Stuart Parkinson and Philip Webber. Lancaster, UK: Scientists for Global Responsibility, 2005.

Langman, Lauren. "From Subject to Citizen to Consumer: Embodiment and the Mediation of Hegemony." In *The Politics of Selfhood; Bodies and Identities in Global Capitalism,* edited by Richard Harvey Brown, 167–188. University of Minnesota Press, 2003.

Langman, Lauren. "After Marcuse: Subjectivity—From Repression to Consumption and Beyond." *Radical Philosophy Review* 20, no. 1 (2017): 75–105.

Langman, Lauren. "The Dialectic of Populism and Cosmopolitanism." In *Cosmopolitanism in Hard Times,* edited by Vincenzo Cicchelli and Syvlie Mesure, 339–354. Leiden: Brill, 2020.

Langman, Lauren, and George Lundskow. *God, Guns, Gold and Glory: American Character and its Discontents.* Leiden: Brill, 2016.

Langman, Lauren, and George Lundskow. "Social Character, Social Change, and the Social Future." In *Erich Fromm's Critical Theory: Hope, Humanism, and the Future,* edited by Kieran Durkin and Joan Braune, 194–215. London: Bloomsbury Academic, 2020.

Langman, Lauren, and Maureen Ryan. "Capitalism and the Carnival Character: The Escape from Reality." *Critical Sociology* 35, no. 4 (2009): 471–492.

Lantier, Alex and Andre Damon, "The Response of the Ruling Class to the Coronavirus Pandemic: Malign Neglect." *World Socialist Web Site* (March 14, 2020), https://www.wsws.org/en/articles/2020/03/14/pers-m14.html.

Lasch, Christopher. *The Culture of Narcissism: American Life in an Age of Diminishing Expectations.* New York: W. W. Norton and Co., 1978.

Lash, Scott, and John Urry. *The End of Organized Capitalism.* Cambridge: Polity Press, 1987.

Lash, Scott, and John Urry. "The Dissolution of the Social?" In *Sociological Theory in Transition,* edited by Mark Wardell and Stephen P. Turner, 95–110. London: Routledge, 2014.

Latham, Michael E. *Modernization as Ideology: American Social Science and "Nation-Building" in the Kennedy Era.* Chapel Hill: University of North Carolina Press, 2000.

Latzer, Barry. *The Rise and Fall of Violent Crime in America.* New York: Encounter, 2017.

Laub, Zachary. "Debating the Legality of the Post-9/11 'Forever War'." *Council on Foreign Relations,* January 12, 2017. https://www.cfr.org/expert-roundup/debating-legality-post-911-forever-war.

Lawrence, Chase. "Eleven Million US Families Face Eviction as CDC Moratorium Expires." *World Socialist Web Site,* July 27, 2021. https://www.wsws.org/en/articles/2021/07/28/evic-j28.html.

Le Billon, Philippe, ed. *The Geopolitics of Resource Wars: Resource Dependence, Governance and Violence.* Abingdon, Oxon: Routledge, 2015.

Lee, Caroline W. *Do-It-Yourself Democracy: The Rise of the Public Engagement Industry.* Oxford: Oxford University Press, 2015.

Lefebvre, Henri. *Everyday Life in the Modern World.* Translated by Sacha Rabinovitch. London: Allen Lane, The Penguin Press, 1971.

Lenin, V. I. *Imperialism: The Highest Stage of Capitalism, a Popular Outline.* New York: International Publishers, 1939.

Lenin, V. I. "The State and Revolution." In *The Lenin Anthology,* edited by Robert C. Tucker. New York: W. W. Norton and Co., 1975.

Lenzer, Gertrud, ed. *Auguste Comte and Positivism: The Essential Writings.* New Brunswick, NJ: Transaction Publishers, 1998.

Leonard, Eileen. *Crime, Inequality, and Power.* New York: Routledge, 2015.

Levy, Carl. "Max Weber, Anarchism and Libertarian Culture: Personality and Power Politics." In *Max Weber and the Culture of Anarchy,* edited by Sam Whimster, 83–109. Houndmills, Basingstoke, UK: Mamillan, 1999.

Lifton, Robert. *The Protean Self: Human Resilience in an Age of Fragmentation.* New York: Basic Books, 1993.

Lind, Michael. *The New Class War: Saving Democracy from the Managerial Elite.* New York: Portfolio/Penguin, 2020.

Lind, Michael. "The New National American Elite." *Tablet,* January 19, 2021. https://www.tabletmag.com/sections/news/articles/new-national-american-elite.

Lindseth, Brian. *From Radioactive Fallout to Environmental Critique: Ecology and the Politics of Cold War Science.* PhD Dissertation, University of California, San Diego, 2013.

Lindseth, Brian. "Nuclear War, Radioactive Rats, and the Ecology of Exterminism." In *Animals and War,* edited by Ryan Hediger, 151–174. Leiden: Brill, 2013.

Liptak, Kevin. "Biden Defends Pulling US Out of Afghanistan as Taliban Advances: 'We Did Not Go to Afghanistan to Nation-Build'." *CNN,* July 8, 2021. https://www.cnn.com/2021/07/08/politics/biden-afghanistan-speech/index.html.

Littler, Jo. *Against Meritocracy: Culture, Power and the Myths of Mobility.* London: Routledge, 2017.

Liu, Catherine. *Virtue Hoarders: The Case Against the Professional Managerial Class.* Minneapolis: University of Minnesota Press, 2021.

Livermore, David. "What Diversity Matters Most." *Management Issues,* September 23, 2015. https://www.management-issues.com/opinion/7099/what-diversity-matters-most.

Loizides, Georgios Paris. "'Making Men' at Ford: Ethnicity, Race, and Americanization During the Progressive Era." *Michigan Sociological Review* 21 (Fall 2007): 109–148.

London, Eric. "Wealth Distribution in the United States and the Politics of the Pseudo-Left." *World Socialist Web Site,* January 18, 2017. https://www.wsws.org/en/articles/2017/01/18/pers-j18.html.

London, Eric, and David North. "Further Observations on Social Inequality and the Politics of the Pseudo-Left." *World Socialist Web Site*, January 26, 2017. https://www.wsws.org/en/articles/2017/01/26/comm-j26.html.

London, Eric. "Identity Politics and the Growth of Inequality within Racial Minorities." *World Socialist Web Site,* October 7, 2017. https://www.wsws.org/en/articles/2017/10/07/pers-o07.html.

London, Eric. "The New York Times on Race and Class: What Determines Social Mobility in America?" *World Socialist Web Site,* April 5, 2018. https://www.wsws.org/en/articles/2018/04/05/ineq-a05.html.

Lopez, German. "2020's Historic Surge in Murders, Explained." *Vox*, March 25, 2021. https://www.vox.com/22344713/murder-violent-crime-spike-surge-2020-covid-19-coronavirus.

Lowenstein, Roger. "Jamie Dimon: America's Least-Hated Banker." *The New York Times Magazine*, December 1, 2010. https://www.nytimes.com/2010/12/05/magazine/05Dimon-t.html.

Lukács, György. *The Destruction of Reason.* London: Merlin, 1980.

Lukes, Steven. *Power: A Radical View.* London: Macmillan, 1974.

Lyne, Charlie. "Hypernormalisation: Adam Curtis Plots a Path from Syria to Trump, via Jane Fonda." *The Guardian*, October 15, 2016. https://www.theguardian.com/tv-and-radio/2016/oct/15/hypernormalisation-adam-curtis-trump-putin-syria.

Lyotard, Jean-Francois. *The Postmodern Condition: A Report on Knowledge.* Translated by Geoff Bennington and Brian Massumi. Minneapolis University of Minnesota Press, 1993.

Mackenzie, G. Calvin, and Robert Weisbrot. *The Liberal Hour: Washington and the Politics of Change in the 1960s.* New York: Penguin, 2008.

MacLean, Nancy. *Democracy in Chains: The Deep History of the Radical Right's Stealth Plan for America.* New York: Viking, 2017.

Macpherson, C. B. *The Political Theory of Possessive Individualism.* Oxford: Clarendon Press, 1962.

MacQueen, Graeme. *The 2001 Anthrax Deception: The Case for a Domestic Conspiracy.* Atlanta, GA: Clarity Press, 2014.

Malik, Kenan. *Multiculturalism and its Discontents: Rethinking Diversity After 9/11.* London: Seagull Books, 2013.

Mandel, Ernest. "The Changing Role of the Bourgeois University." Speech delivered at Rijks Universiteit Leiden on the occasion of its 79th anniversary, June 1970. Published as a pamphlet by the Spartacus League, London 1971. https://www.marxists.org/archive/mandel/1970/06/university.htm.

Mandel, Ernest. *Power and Money: A Marxist Theory of Bureaucracy.* London: Verso, 1992.

Mann, Geoff. *In the Long Run We are All Dead: Keynesianism, Political Economy, and Revolution.* New York: Verso, 2017.

Marcuse, Herbert. *Reason and Revolution: Hegel and the Rise of Social Theory.* Boston: Beacon Press, 1960.

Marcuse, Herbert. *One-Dimensional Man: Studies in the Ideology of Advanced Industrial Society.* Boston: Beacon Press, 1964.

Marcuse, Herbert. "Industrialization and Capitalism." *New Left Review* 30 (March–April 1965): 3–17.

Martin, Jonathan. "Biden Always Had a Simple Message. He Rode It to the Nomination." *New York Times*, August 21, 2020. https://www.nytimes.com/2020/08/21/us/politics/Joe-Biden-Democratic-nominee.html.

Martin, Patrick. "Edward Gallagher, Donald Trump and America's Criminal Wars." *World Socialist Web Site*, December 30, 2019. https://www.wsws.org/en/articles/2019/12/30/pers-d30.html.

Marx, Karl. *The Economic and Philosophic Manuscripts of 1844.* Edited by Dirk Struik, translated by Martin Milligan. New York: International Publishers, 1964.

Marx, Karl. "On the Jewish Question." In *Writings of the Young Marx on Philosophy and Society*, edited and translated by Lloyd D. Easton and Kurt Guddat, 216–248. Garden City, NY: Anchor Books, 1967.

Marx, Karl. *Grundrisse: Foundations of the Critique of Political Economy.* Translated by Martin Nicolaus. New York: Penguin Books, 1973.

Marx, Karl. *Capital, Volume 1: A Critique of Political Economy.* Translated by Ben Fowkes. New York: Vintage Books, 1977.

Marx, Karl, and Frederick Engels. *Manifesto of the Communist Party.* Moscow: Progress Publishers, 1986.

Mateus, Benjamin. "Behind the Epidemic of Police Killings in America: Class, Poverty and Race." *World Socialist Web Site*, December 20, 2018. https://www.wsws.org/en/articles/2018/12/20/kill-d20.html.

Mattei, Clara Elisabetta. "Keynesianism, Technocracy and Class Struggle." *Journal of Cultural Economy* 11, no. 5 (2018): 476–479.

May, Elaine Tyler. *Homeward Bound: American Families in the Cold War Era.* New York: Basic Books, 1999.

Mayer, Jane. *Dark Money: The Hidden History of the Billionaires behind the Rise of the Radical Right.* New York: Anchor, 2016.

Mayer, Jane. "The Reclusive Hedge-Fund Tycoon behind the Trump Presidency." *The New Yorker,* March 17, 2017. https://www.newyorker.com/magazine/2017/03/27/the-reclusive-hedge-fund-tycoon-behind-the-trump-presidency.

McAdam, Doug. "From Relevance to Irrelevance: The Curious Impact of the Sixties on Public Sociology." In *Sociology in America: A History*, edited by Craig Calhoun, 411–426. Chicago: University of Chicago Press, 2007.

McCarthy, Rory. "Taliban Order Bin Laden to Leave." *The Guardian*, September 27, 2001. https://www.theguardian.com/world/2001/sep/28/afghanistan.terrorism1?INTCMP=ILCNETTXT3487.

McCarthy, Rory. "New Offer on Bin Laden." *The Guardian*, October 16, 2001. https://www.theguardian.com/world/2001/oct/17/afghanistan.terrorism11?fb=optOut.

McCoy, Alfred W. *In the Shadows of the American Century: The Rise and Decline of US Global Power.* Chicago, IL: Haymarket, 2017.

McCumber, John. *The Philosophy Scare: The Politics of Reason in the Early Cold War*. Chicago: University of Chicago Press, 2016.

McEnery, Thornton. "Jamie Dimon Drops into Mt. Kisco Chase Branch, Takes a Knee with Staff." *New York Post*, June 5, 2020. https://nypost.com/2020/06/05/mending-jpm-chief-drops-into-mt-kisco-chase-branch/.

McGirr, Lisa. *Suburban Warriors: The Origins of the New American Right*. Princeton, NJ: Princeton University Press, 2001.

McMurty, John. *Cancer Capitalism: From Crisis to Cure*. London: Verso, 2013.

Medecins Sans Frontieres. "On 3 October 2015, US Airstrikes Destroyed Our Trauma Hospital in Kunduz, Afghanistan, Killing 42 People." *Medecins San Frontieres*, n.d. https://www.msf.org/kunduz-hospital-attack-depth.

Mehan, Hugh, and Houston Wood. *The Reality of Ethnomethodology*. New York: John Wiley and Sons, 1975.

Melman, Seymour. *Pentagon Capitalism: The Political Economy of War*. New York: McGraw-Hill, 1970.

Melossi, Dario. "Between Struggles and Discipline: Marx and Foucault on Penality and the Critique of Political Economy." In *The Political Economy of Punishment Today*, edited by Dario Melossi et al., 23–46. London: Routledge, 2017.

Merton, Robert K. "The Role-Set: Problems in Sociological Theory." *The British Journal of Sociology* 8, no. 2 (1957): 106–120.

Merton, Robert K. *Science, Technology and Society in Seventeenth-Century England*. New York: Howard Fertig/Harper Torchbooks, 1970.

Merton, Robert K. "Insiders and Outsiders: A Chapter in the Sociology of Knowledge." *The American Journal of Sociology* 78, no. 1 (1972): 9–47.

Merton, Robert K. *The Sociology of Science: Theoretical and Empirical Investigations*. Chicago: University of Chicago Press, 1973.

Mészáros, István. *The Challenge and Burden of Historical Time: Socialism in the Twenty-First Century*. New York: Monthly Review Press, 2009.

Meyer, Stephen. "Adapting the Immigrant to the Line: Americanization in the Ford Factory, 1914–1921." *Journal of Social History* 14, no. 1 (Autumn 1980): 67–82.

Mills, C. Wright. *White Collar; the American Middle Classes*. New York: Oxford University Press, 1951.

Mills, C. Wright. *The Causes of World War Three*. New York: Simon and Schuster, 1958.

Mills, C. Wright. *The Sociological Imagination*. New York: Oxford University Press, 1959.

Mirowski, Phillip. *Science-Mart: Privatizing American Science*. Cambridge, MA: Harvard University Press, 2011.

Mirowski, Philip. *Never Let a Serious Crisis Go to Waste: How Neoliberalism Survived the Financial Crisis*. London: Verso, 2014.

Misztal, Barbara A. "Normality and Trust in Goffman's Theory of Interaction Order." *Sociological Theory* 19, no. 3 (November, 2001): 312–324.

Miyoshi, Masao. "Sites of Resistance in the Global Economy." *boundary 2* 22, no. 1 (Spring 1995): 61–84.

Mommsen, Wolfgang J. *Max Weber and German Politics, 1890–1920.* Chicago: University of Chicago Press, 1984.

Moore, Kelly. *Disrupting Science: Social Movements, American Science, and the Politics of the Military, 1945–1975.* Princeton, NJ: Princeton University Press, 2008.

Moore, Kelly, Daniel Lee Kleinman, David Hess, and Scott Frickel. "Science and Neoliberal Globalization: A Political Sociological Approach." *Theory & Society* 40, no. 5 (2011): 505–532.

Moore, Ryan. *Sells Like Teen Spirit: Music, Youth Culture, and Social Crisis.* New York: New York University Press, 2010.

Mosse, George L. *The Nationalization of the Masses: Political Symbolism and Mass Movements in Germany from the Napoleonic Wars through the Third Reich.* New York: H. Fertig, 1975.

Mosse, George L. *German Jews Beyond Judaism.* Bloomington, IN: Indiana University Press, 1985.

Mosse, George L. *Nationalism and Sexuality: Middle-Class Morality and Sexual Norms in Modern Europe.* Madison: University of Wisconsin Press, 2020.

Mounk, Yascha. "What an Audacious Hoax Reveals About Academia." *The Atlantic,* October 5, 2018. https://www.theatlantic.com/ideas/archive/2018/10/new-sokal -hoax/572212/.

Mouzelis, Nicos. *Sociological Theory: What Went Wrong? Diagnosis and Remedies.* London: Routledge, 1995.

Mukerji, Chandra. *A Fragile Power: Scientists and the State.* Princeton, NJ: Princeton University Press, 1989.

Mukerji, Chandra. *Territorial Ambitions and the Gardens of Versailles.* Cambridge: Cambridge University Press, 1997.

Mumford, Lewis. *The Pentagon of Power: The Myth of the Machine Volume II.* New York: Harcourt, Brace, Jovanovich, 1970.

Murray, Robert K. *The Politics of Normalcy: Governmental Theory and Practice in the Harding-Coolidge Era.* New York: Norton, 1973.

Nash, Henry T. "The Bureaucratization of Homicide." *Bulletin of the Atomic Scientists* 36, no. 4 (1980): 22–27.

National Commission on Terrorist Attacks upon the United States. *9/11 Commission Report.* New York: Barnes and Noble, 2006.

National Research Council. *Strategic Engagement in Global S&T: Opportunities for Defense Research.* Washington, DC: The National Academies Press, 2014.

Negri, Antonio. *Revolution Retrieved: Writings on Marx, Keynes, Capitalist Crisis and New Social Subjects.* London: Red Notes, 1988.

Negri, Antonio. "Keynes and the Capitalist Theory of the State Post-1929." In *Revolution Retrieved: Writings on Marx, Keynes, Capitalist Crisis and New Social Subjects,* edited by Antonio Negri, 5–42. London: Red Notes, 1988.

Negri, Antonio. "Crisis of the Planner-State: Communism and Revolutionary Organisation." In *Revolution Retrieved: Writings on Marx, Keynes, Capitalist Crisis and New Social Subjects,* edited by Antonio Negri, 97–148. London: Red Notes, 1988.

Newfield, Christopher. *Unmaking the Public University: The Forty-Year Assault on the Middle Class*. Cambridge, MA: Harvard University Press, 2008.

Newfield, Christopher. "'Innovation' Discourse and the Neoliberal University: Top Ten Reasons to Abolish Disruptive Innovation." In *Mutant Neoliberalism: Market Rule and Political Rupture*, edited by William Callison and Zachary Manfredi, 244–268. New York: Fordham University Press, 2020.

New York Times. "Impeachment Trial Day 3 Highlights: Prosecutors Rest Their Case, Warning Trump 'Can Do this Again' if He Is Not Convicted." *New York Times*, February 22, 2021. https://www.nytimes.com/live/2021/02/11/us/impeachment-trial.

New York Times. "F.B.I. Finds Contact Between Proud Boys Member and Trump Associate Before Riot." *New York Times*, March 5, 2021. https://www.nytimes.com/2021/03/05/us/politics/trump-proud-boys-capitol-riot.html.

New York Times Editorial Board. "The C.I.A.'s Reckless Breach of Trust." *New York Times,* July 31, 2014. https://www.nytimes.com/2014/08/01/opinion/The-CIAs-Reckless-Breach-of-Trust.html.

Niemuth, Niles. "Race, Class and Social Conflict in the United States." *World Socialist Web Site*, September 5, 2021. https://www.wsws.org/en/articles/2021/09/06/race-s06.html.

Nisbet, Robert A. *The Sociological Tradition*. New York: Basic Book, 1966.

Noble, David. "Command Performance: A Perspective on the Social and Economic Consequences of Military Enterprise." In *Military Enterprise and Technological Change*, edited by Merritt Roe Smith, 329–346. Cambridge, MA: MIT Press, 1985.

Noggle, Burl. *Into the Twenties: The United States from Armistice to Normalcy*. Urbana: University of Illinois Press, 1974.

North, David. *The Crisis of American Democracy: The Presidential Elections of 2000 and 2004*. Oak Park, MI: Mehring Press, 2004.

North, David. "The Capitalist Crisis and the Return of History." *World Socialist Web Site,* March 26, 2009. https://www.wsws.org/en/articles/2009/03/dnor-m26.html.

North, David. *The Russian Revolution and the Unfinished Twentieth Century*. New York: Mehring Books, 2014.

North, David. *The Frankfurt School, Postmodernism and the Politics of the Pseudo-Left: A Marxist Critique*. Oak Park, MI: Mehring Books, 2015.

North, David. *A Quarter Century of War: The U.S. Drive for Global Hegemony 1990–2016*. Oak Park, MI: Mehring Press, 2016.

North, David. "The Trump Coup and the Rise of Fascism: Where is America Going?" *World Socialist Web Site,* January 19, 2021. https://www.wsws.org/en/articles/2021/01/19/dnor-j19.html.

Oakes, Walter J. "Toward a Permanent War Economy?" *Politics* (February, 1944): 11–17.

O'Connor, Alice. *Poverty Knowledge: Social Science, Social Policy, and the Poor in Twentieth-Century U.S. History*. Princeton, NJ: Princeton University Press, 2001.

Oreskes, Naomi. "How Earth Science has Become a Social Science." *Historical Social Research/Historische Sozialforschung* 40, no. 2 (152) (2015): 246–270.

Orwell, George. "Review of *The Road to Serfdom* by F. A. Hayek, *The Mirror of the Past* by K. Zilliacus." In *As I Please, 1943–1946*, 117–119. Jaffrey, NH: David R. Godine, 2000.

Osterweil, Willie. "The Drone of Permanent War." *Dissent*, March 21, 2012. https://www.dissentmagazine.org/blog/the-drone-of-permanent-war.

Pan, J. C. "Will Big Philanthropy Defang Our Radical Moment." *The New Republic*, July 17, 2020. https://newrepublic.com/article/158545/will-big-philanthropy-defang-radical-moment.

Panitch, Leo, and Colin Leys. *Morbid Symptoms: Health Under Capitalism*. New York: Monthly Review Press, 2010.

Panzieri, Raniero. "Surplus Value and Planning: Notes on the Reading of Capital." In *The Labour Process and Class Strategies*, edited by Conference of Socialist Economics, 4–25. London: Conference of Socialist Economics, 1976.

Parenti, Michael. *Lockdown America: Police and Prisons in the Age of Crisis*. London: Verso, 2008.

Passas, Nikos. "Global Anomie, Dysnomie, and Economic Crime: Hidden Consequences of Neoliberalism in Russia and Around the World." *Social Justice* 27, no. 2 (Summer 2000): 16–44.

Pateman, Carole. *The Problem of Political Obligation: A Critique of Liberal Theory*. Cambridge: Polity Press, 1985.

Perelman, Michael. *Manufacturing Discontent: The Trap of Individualism in Corporate Society*. London: Pluto Press, 2005.

Perlman, Fredy. *The Reproduction of Daily Life*. London: Dark Star/Phoenix Press. Orig. published 1969, date of reprint unknown.

Peters, Andrea. "The 'Racial Wealth Gap' Narrative Obscures Reality of Class Divide in the US." *World Socialist Web Site,* June 28, 2021. https://www.wsws.org/en/articles/2021/06/29/gapr-j29.html.

Petras, James. *The End of the Republic and the Delusion of Empire*. Atlanta, GA: Clarity Press, 2016.

Phillips, Bernard, and Louis C. Johnston. *The Invisible Crisis of Contemporary Society: Reconstructing Sociology's Fundamental Assumptions*. Boulder, CO: Paradigm Publishers, 2007.

Phillips, Peter. *Giants: The Global Power Elite*. New York: Seven Stories Press, 2018.

Pilger, John, and Alan Lowery. *The War You Don't See*. UK: Dartmouth Films, 2010.

Plummer, Brenda Gayle. *In Search of Power: African Americans in the Era of Decolonization, 1956–1974*. Cambridge: Cambridge University Press, 2013.

Plumpe, Werner. "Carl Duisberg, the End of World War I, and the Birth of Social Partnership from the Spirit of Defeat." In *German Economic and Business History in the Nineteenth and Twentieth Centuries*, 305–332. Palgrave Macmillan, 2016.

Polanyi, Karl. *The Great Transformation: The Political and Economic Origins of Our Time*. Boston, MA: Beacon Press, 1957.

Popalzai, Ehsan, Nilly Kohzad, and Ivana Kottasová. "A Strike Targeting Taliban Kills 40 Civilians at a Wedding Next Door." *CNN*, September 25, 2019. https://www.cnn.com/2019/09/23/asia/afghanistan-wedding-attack-intl/index.html.

Prashad, Vijay. "We Suffer from an Incurable Disease Called Hope." *TriContinental Newsletter* 48 (November 6, 2020). https://www.thetricontinental.org/newsletterissue/48-covid-vaccines/.

Pratt, John. "Towards the Decivilizing of Punishment?" *Social and Legal Studies* 7, no. 4 (December 1998): 487–515.

Pressman, Jack D. "Human Salvage: Why Psychosurgery Worked in 1949 (and Not Now)." In *Last Resort: Psychosurgery and the Limits of Medicine*. Cambridge: Cambridge University Press, 1998.

Proctor, Robert. *Value-Free Science? Purity and Power in Modern Knowledge*. Cambridge, MA: Harvard University Press, 1991.

Putney, Snell, and Gail J. Putney. *The Adjusted American: Normal Neuroses in Individual and Society*. New York: Harper Colophon Books, 1964.

Rahn, Wendy M., and John E. Transue. "Social Trust and Value Change: The Decline of Social Capital in American Youth, 1976–1995." *Political Psychology* 19, no. 3 (September 1998): 545–565.

Ramaswamy, Vivek. *Woke, Inc.: Inside Corporate America's Social Justice Scam*. New York: Center Street, 2021.

Randall, Kate. "CDC Report: Biggest Drop in US Life Expectancy Since World War II." *World Socialist Web Site*, February 19, 2021. https://www.wsws.org/en/articles/2021/02/19/pers-f19.html.

Ranulf, Svend. *Moral Indignation and Middle Class Psychology: A Sociological Study*. New York: Schocken Books, 1964.

Ratner, Carl. "Pathological Normalcy: A Construct for Comprehending and Overcoming Psychological Aspects of Alienation." *The Humanistic Psychologist* 42, no. 3 (2014): 298–303.

Ravetz, Jerome R., and S. O. Funtowicz. "Science for the Post-Normal Age." *Futures* 25, no. 7 (September 1993): 735–755.

Readings, Bill. *The University in Ruins*. Cambridge: Harvard University Press, 1996.

Rectenwald, Michael. *Springtime for Snowflakes: Social Justice and its Postmodern Parentage. An Academic's Memoir*. Nashville, TN: New English Review Press, 2018.

Rectenwald, Michael. *Google Archipelago: The Digital Gulag and the Simulation of Freedom* Nashville, TN: New English Review Press, 2019.

Reed, Touré. "Why Liberals Separate Race from Class." *Jacobin*, August 22, 2015. https://www.jacobinmag.com/2015/08/bernie-sanders-black-lives-matter-civil-rights-movement/.

Reese, Toby. "Drone Valley: The University of California and the Business of High-Tech Slaughter." *World Socialist Web Site*, September 12, 2016. https://www.wsws.org/en/articles/2016/09/12/ucsd-s12.html.

Reggio, Godfrey. *Koyaanisqatsi* (film). Santa Fe, NM: Institute for Regional Education, 1982.

Reid, Roddey. "Bullying in US Public Culture, Or, Gothic Terror in the Full Light of Day." *TOPIA: Canadian Journal of Cultural Studies* 20 (Fall 2008): 129–150.

Reid, Roddey. *Confronting Political Intimidation and Public Bullying: A Citizen's Handbook for the Trump Era and Beyond*. Santa Barbara, CA: Amazon Self-Publishing, 2017.

Reiner, Robert. "What's Left? The Prospects for Social Democratic Criminology." *Crime, Media, Culture* 8, no. 2(2012): 135–150.

Reisch, George A. *How the Cold War Transformed Philosophy of Science: To the Icy Slopes of Logic*. Cambridge: Cambridge University Press, 2005.

Reisch, George A. *The Politics of Paradigms: Thomas S. Kuhn, James B. Conant, and the Cold War "Struggle for Men's Minds."* Albany: State University of New York Press, 2019.

Richardson, Theresa R. *The Century of the Child: The Mental Hygiene Movement & Social Policy in the United States & Canada*. Albany: State University of New York Press, 1989.

Riecken, Henry W. "Underdogging: The Early Career of the Social Sciences in the NSF." In *Nationalization of the Social Sciences*, edited by Samuel Z. Klausner and Victor M. Lidz, 209–225. Philadelphia: University of Pennsylvania Press, 1986.

Riesman, David. *The Lonely Crowd: A Study of the Changing American Character.* New Haven, CT: Yale University Press, 1965.

Ringer, Fritz. *The Decline of the German Mandarins: The German Academic Community, 1890–1933*. Cambridge, MA: Harvard University Press, 1969.

Ritschel, Chelsea. "Ruth Bader Ginsburg Said People Will See this Period in American History as 'An Aberration'." *The Independent*, September 19, 2020. https://www.independent.co.uk/news/world/americas/ruth-bader-ginsburg-rbg -trump-aberration-supreme-court-a9143781.html.

Robinson, Susan L., and Matias Nestore. "Education Cleavages, or Market Society and the Rise of Authoritarian Populism?" *Globalisation, Societies, and Education*, published online, July 19, 2021. https://doi.org/10.1080/14767724 .2021.1955662.

Robinson, William I. "Global Capitalist Crisis and Twenty-First Century Fascism: Beyond the Trump Hype." *Science & Society* 83, no. 2 (April 2019): 155–183.

Robinson, William I. *Into the Tempest: Essays on the New Global Capitalism*. Chicago, IL: Haymarket, 2019.

Robinson, William I., and Mario Barrera. "Global Capitalism and Twenty-First Century Fascism: A US Case Study." *Race & Class* 53, no. 3 (2012): 4–29.

Rockhill, Gabriel. "The CIA Reads French Theory: On the Intellectual Labor of Dismantling the Cultural Left." *The Philosophical Salon, Los Angeles Review of Books*, February 28, 2017. http://thephilosophicalsalon.com/the-cia-reads-french -theory-on-the-intellectual-labor-of-dismantling-the-cultural-left/.

Rockhill, Gabriel. "Foucault: The Faux Radical." *The Philosophical Salon, Los Angeles Review of Books.* October 12, 2020. http://thephilosophicalsalon.com/foucault-the-faux-radical/.

Rodgers, Daniel T. *Age of Fracture.* Cambridge, MA: The Belknap Press of Harvard University Press, 2011.

Rogovin, V. Z. *Stalin's Terror of 1937–1938: Political Genocide in the USSR.* Oak Park, MI: Mehring Books, 2009.

Ronneberger, Klaus. "Contours and Convolutions of Everydayness: On the Reception of Henri Lefebvre in the Federal Republic of Germany." *Capitalism Nature Socialism* 13, no. 2 (2002): 42–57.

Rose, Lisle A. *Farewell to Prosperity: Wealth, Identity, and Conflict in Postwar America.* Columbia: University of Missouri Press, 2014.

Rosenblatt, Daniel. "Stuff the Professional Managerial Class Likes: 'Distinction' for an Egalitarian Elite." *Anthropological Quarterly* 86, no. 2 (2013): 589–623.

Ross, E. Wayne, and Kevin D. Vinson. "Social Justice Requires a Revolution of Everyday Life." In *Reinventing Critical Pedagogy*, edited by César Augusto Rossatto, Ricky Lee Allen, and Marc Pruyn, 143–156. Lanham, MD: Rowman and Littlefield, 2006.

Rostker, Bernard. "The Evolution of the All-Volunteer Force." RAND Research Brief, n.d. https://www.rand.org/pubs/research_briefs/RB9195.html.

Rubinstein, Alex. "Intersectional Imperialism: A Wholesome Menace." *RT,* March 21, 2021. https://www.rt.com/op-ed/518645-intersectional-imperialism-wholesome-menace/.

Russell, James W. "A Left Weberian Road to Identity Politics." In *Crisis, Politics, and Critical Sociology*, edited by Graham Cassano and Richard A. Dello Buono Cassano, 37–44. Chicago: Haymarket, 2012

Saccarelli, Emanuele, and Latha Varadarajan. *Imperialism: Past and Present.* New York: Oxford University Press, 2015.

Salcedo, Anastacia Marx de. *Combat-Ready Kitchen: How the U.S. Military Shapes the Way You Eat.* New York: Current, 2015.

Sanbonmatsu, John. "Postmodernism and the Corruption of the Critical Intelligentsia." In *Radical Intellectuals and the Subversion of Progressive Politics: The Betrayal of Politics*, edited by Gregory Smulewicz-Zucker and Michael J. Thompson, 33–68. New York: Palgrave Macmillan, 2015.

Sardar, Ziauddin. *The Postnormal Times Reader.* Herndon, VA: International Institute for Islamic Thought and the Centre for Postnormal Policy & Futures Studies, 2017.

Sardar, Ziauddin. "Welcome to Postnormal Times." In *The Postnormal Times Reader*, edited by Ziauddin Sardar, 47–70. Herndon, VA: International Institute for Islamic Thought and the Centre for Postnormal Policy & Futures Studies, 2017.

Sassen, Saskia. *Expulsions: Brutality and Complexity in the Global Economy.* Cambridge, MA: The Belknap Press of Harvard University Press, 2014.

Sassen, Saskia. "Predatory Logics: Going Well Beyond Inequality." In *Twenty-First Century Inequality and Capitalism: Piketty, Marx and Beyond*, edited by Lauren Langman and David A. Smith, 64–85. Chicago, IL: Haymarket Books, 2017.

Sattler, Scipio. "How Warren, and the Professional Class Left Undermined Sanders 2020." *Collide,* July 23, 2020. https://www.collidemag.com/post/how-warren-and -professional-class-left-undermined-sanders-2020.

Saunders, Frances Stonor. *Who Paid the Piper? The CIA and the Cultural Cold War.* London: Granta Books, 1999.

Savage, Charlie. *Power Wars: Inside Obama's Post-9/11 Presidency.* New York: Little, Brown and Co., 2015.

Savage, Mike, and Roger Burrows. "The Coming Crisis of Empirical Sociology." *Sociology* 41, no. 5 (2007): 885–899.

Scahill, Jeremy. *Dirty Wars: The World is a Battlefield.* New York: Nation Books, 2013.

Schaffer, Simon. "Babbage's Intelligence: Calculating Engines and the Factory System." *Critical Inquiry* 21, no. 1 (1994): 203–227.

Schmidt, Jeff. *Disciplined Minds: A Critical Look at Salaried Professionals and the Soul-Battering System that Shapes their Lives.* Lanham, MD: Rowman and Littlefield, 2000.

Schmitt, Eric. "Lloyd Austin Ramps up the Fight Against Right-Wing Extremism within the Military." *New York Times,* February 3, 2021. https://www.nytimes.com /2021/02/03/us/lloyd-austin-extremism-military.html.

Schriftgiesser, Karl. *This was Normalcy: An Account of Party Politics During Twelve Republican Years: 1920–1932.* New York: Little Brown, 1948.

Schwendinger, Herman, and Julia Schwendinger. *The Sociologists of the Chair: A Radical Analysis of the Formative Years of North American Sociology (1883–1992).* New York: Basic Books, 1974.

Schwendinger, Herman, and Julia Schwendinger. *Homeland Fascism: Corporatist Government in the New American Century.* Surrey, BC: Thought Crimes, 2016.

Scott, James C. *Seeing Like a State : How Certain Schemes to Improve the Human Condition Have Failed.* New Haven, CT: Yale University Press, 1998.

Scott, Peter Dale. *The American Deep State: Wall Street, Big Oil, and the Attack on U.S. Democracy.* Lanham, MD: Rowman and Littlefield, 2015.

Scott, Susie, and Charles Thorpe. "The Sociological Imagination of R. D. Laing." *Sociological Theory* 24, no. 4 (2006): 331–352.

Scranton, Roy. "I've Said Goodbye to 'Normal.' You Should Too." *The New York Times,* January 25, 2001. https://www.nytimes.com/2021/01/25/opinion/new-nor-mal-climate-catastrophes.html?searchResultPosition=1.

Scranton, Roy. *Learning to Die in the Anthropocene: Reflections on the End of a Civilization.* San Francisco, CA: City Lights Books, 2015.

Scranton, Roy. *War Porn.* New York: Soho Press, 2016.

Scull, Andrew. "The Mental Health Sector and the Social Sciences in Post-World War II USA, Part 2: The Impact of Federal Research Funding and the Drugs Revolution." *History of Psychiatry* 22, no. 3 (2011): 268–284.

Seidman, Steven. *Liberalism and the Origins of European Social Theory.* Berkeley: University of California Press, 1983.

Selfa, Lawrence. *The Democrats: A Critical History.* Chicago, IL: Haymarket, 2012.

Sengupta, Kim. "Syrian Civil War: The Day I Met the Organ Eating Cannibal Rebel Abu Sakkar's Fearsome Followers." *The Independent*, May 10, 2013. https://www.independent.co.uk/news/world/middle-east/syrian-civil-war-day-i-met-organ-eating-cannibal-rebel-abu-sakkar-s-fearsome-followers-8617828.html.

Sennett, Richard. *The Corrosion of Character : The Personal Consequences of Work in the New Capitalism*. New York: W. W. Norton and Co., 1998.

Shafir, Gershon. "The Incongruity Between Destiny and Merit: Max Weber on Meaningful Existence and Modernity." *The British Journal of Sociology* 36, no. 4 (1985): 516–530.

Shafir, Gershon. "Opinion: Two Decades After 9/11, Many Questions are Left Unanswered: Moral Panics Leave a Trail of Catastrophic Results." *The San Diego Union-Tribune,* September 9, 2021. https://www.sandiegouniontribune.com/opinion/commentary/story/2021-09-09/911-questions-afghanistan-taliban.

Shafir, Gershon, and Alison Brysk. "The Globalization of Rights: From Citizenship to Human Rights." *Citizenship Studies* 10, no. 3 (2006): 275–287.

Shafir, Gershon, Everard Meade, and William J Aceves. *Lessons and Legacies of the War on Terror: From Moral Panic to Permanent War*. Abingdon, Oxon: Routledge, 2013.

Shapin, Steven. "Understanding the Merton Thesis." *Isis* 79, no. 4 (December 1988): 594–605.

Shapin, Steven. "Hyper-Professionalism and the Crisis of Readership in the History of Science." *Isis* 96, no. 2 (2005): 238–243.

Shapin, Steven. *The Scientific Life: A Moral History of a Late Modern Vocation*. Chicago: University of Chicago Press, 2010.

Shapin, Steven. "Weber's *Science as a Vocation*: A Moment in the History of 'Is' and 'Ought'." *Journal of Classical Sociology* 19, no. 3 (August 2019): 290–307.

Shapin, Steven, and Barry Barnes. "Head and Hand: Rhetorical Resources in British Pedagogical Writing, 1770–1850." *Oxford Review of Education* 2, no. 3 (1976): 231–254.

Shi, David Emory, and George Brown Tindall. *America: A Narrative History*. New York: W. W. Norton and Co., 2016.

Shlaes, Amity. *Great Society: A New History*. New York: Harper, 2019.

Shove, Elizabeth. *Comfort, Cleanliness, and Convenience: The Social Organization of Normality*. Oxford: Berg, 2003.

Shupak, Greg. "Afghanistan was Never a Good War." *Jacobin*, September 11, 2021. https://www.jacobinmag.com/2021/09/afghanistan-war-united-states-taliban-civilian-deaths.

Siang Low, Remy Yi. "Education As/Against Cruelty: On Etienne Balibar's Violence and Civility." *Educational Philosophy and Theory* 51, no. 6 (2019): 640–649.

Simmel, Georg. *Conflict: The Web of Group-Affiliations*. New York: Free Press, 1964.

Simon, Jonathan. *Governing through Crime: How the War on Crime Transformed American Democracy and Created a Culture of Fear*. Oxford: Oxford University Press, 2007.

Singer, Thomas. "Extinction Anxiety and Collective Madness: Marjorie Taylor Greene, Facemasks, Extreme Sports and Reddit/Gamestock." *Moyers on Democracy*, February 3, 2021. https://billmoyers.com/story/extinction-anxiety-and -collective-madness/.

Sjoberg, Gideon, and Ted R. Vaughan. "The Bureaucratization of Sociology: Its Impact on Theory and Research." In *A Critique of Contemporary of American Sociology*, edited by Ted R. Vaughan, Gideon Sjoberg, and Larry T. Reynolds, 54–113. Dix Hills, NY: General Hall, Inc., 1993.

Sklaroff, Lauren Rebecca. *Black Culture and the New Deal: The Quest for Civil Rights in the Roosevelt Era*. University of North Carolina Press, 2009.

Slaughter, Sheila, and Larry Leslie. *Academic Capitalism: Politics, Policies, and the Entrepreneurial University*. Baltimore, MD: Johns Hopkins University Press, 1997.

Smith, David Geoffrey. *Trying to Teach in a Season of Great Untruth: Globalization, Empire and the Crises of Pedagogy*. Rotterdam, The Netherlands: Sense Publishers, 2006.

Smith, Dennis. *The Chicago School: A Liberal Critique of Capitalism*. New York: St. Martin's Press, 1988.

Smith, Dorothy E. *The Everyday World as Problematic: A Feminist Sociology*. Milton Keynes: The Open University Press, 1987.

Smith, Laurence D. *Behaviorism and Logical Positivism: A Reassessment of the Alliance*. Stanford, CA: Stanford University Press, 1986.

Smith, Merritt Roe, and Leo Marx, eds. *Does Technology Drive History?: The Dilemma of Technological Determinism*. Cambridge, MA: MIT Press, 1994.

Smulewicz-Zucker, Gregory, and Michael J. Thompson, *Radical Intellectuals and the Subversion of Progressive Politics: The Betrayal of Politics*. New York: Palgrave Macmillan, 2015.

Snow, C. P. *The Two Cultures*. Cambridge: Cambridge University Press, 1993.

Sohn-Rethel, Alfred. *Intellectual and Manual Labour: A Critique of Epistemology*. London: Macmillan, 1978.

Soling, Cevin D. *The War on Kids*. Documentary Film, 2009.

Solon, Olivia. "Amazon Patents Wristband that Tracks Warehouse Workers' Movements." *The Guardian*, January 31 2018. https://www.theguardian.com/tech-nology/2018/jan/31/amazon-warehouse-wristband-tracking.

Solovey, Mark, and Hamilton Cravens, *Cold War Social Science: Knowledge Production, Liberal Democracy, and Human Nature*. New York: Palgrave Macmillan, 2012.

Solovey, Mark. *Shaky Foundations: The Politics-Patronage-Social Science Nexus in Cold War America*. Piscataway, NJ: Rutgers University Press, 2013.

Solovey, Mark. *Social Science for What?: Battles over Public Funding for the "Other Sciences" at the National Science Foundation*. Cambridge, MA: MIT Press, 2020.

Sontag, Deborah. "Video Is a Window into a Terror Suspect's Isolation." *New York Times*, December 4, 2006. https://www.nytimes.com/2006/12/04/us/04detain .html.

Sorkin, Michael. *Variations on a Theme Park: The New American City and the End of Public Space.* New York: Hill and Wang, 1992.

Spencer, Herbert. "Reasons for Dissenting from the Philosophy of M. Comte." 1864. https://www.marxists.org/reference/subject/philosophy/works/en/spencer.htm.

Steger, Manfred B., and Ravi K. Roy. *Neoliberalism: A Very Short Introduction.* Oxford: Oxford University Press, 2010.

Stein, Arlene. "Discipline and Publish: Public Sociology in an Age of Professionalization." In *Bureaucratic Culture and Escalating World Problems: Advancing the Sociological Imagination,* edited by J. David Knottnerus and Bernard Phillips, 156–171. Boulder, CO: Paradigm Publishers, 2009.

Stein, Howard F. *Beneath the Crust of Culture: Psychoanalytic Anthropology and the Cultural Unconscious in American Life.* Amsterdam: Rodopi, 2004.

Steinmetz, George. "Scientific Authority and the Transition to Post-Fordism: The Plausibility of Positivism in U.S. Sociology Since 1945." In *The Politics of Method in the Human Sciences: Positivism and its Epistemological Others,* edited by George Steinmetz, 275–323. Durham, NC: Duke University Press, 2005.

Steinmetz, George. "The Cultural Contradictions of Irving Louis Horowitz," *Michigan Quarterly Review* 44 no. 3 (2005): 496–505.

Steinmetz, George, and Ou-Byung Chae. "Sociology in an Era of Fragmentation: From the Sociology of Knowledge to the Philosophy of Science, and Back Again." *The Sociological Quarterly* 43, no. 1 (2002): 113–137.

Stephens, Elizabeth. "Post-Normal: Crisis and the End of the Ordinary." *Media International Australia* 177, no. 1 (2020): 92–102.

Stewart, Matthew. *The 9.9 Percent: The New Aristocracy that is Entrenching Inequality and Warping Our Culture.* New York: Simon and Schuster, 2021.

Stock, Kathleen. *Material Girls: Why Reality Matters for Feminism.* London: Fleet, 2021.

Storm, Jason Ãnanda Josephson. "A Note on the Dating of Max Weber's 'Science as a Vocation'." *Absolute Disruption: Theory After Postmodernism* (blog), October 24, 2017. https://absolute-disruption.com/2017/10/24/a-note-on-the-dating-of-max-webers-science-as-a-vocation/#_ednref3.

Sullivan, Eileen, Dave Montgomery, and Brian Pietsch. "Texas is Ending its Mask Mandate and Will Allow All Businesses to Fully Re-Open." *New York Times,* March 2, 2021. https://www.nytimes.com/2021/03/02/world/greg-abbott-texas-masks-reopening.html.

Sünker, Heinz. "Childhood Between Individualization and Institutionalization." In *Individualization in Childhood and Adolescence,* edited by Georg Neubauer and Klaus Hurrelmann, 37–52. Berlin: Walter de Gruyter, 2012.

Symonds, Michael, and Jason Pudsey. "The Concept of 'Paradox' in the Work of Max Weber." *Theory, Culture, and Society* 42, no. 2 (2008): 223–241.

Tavernise, Sabrina, and Abby Goodnough. "American Life Expectancy Rises for First Time in Four Years." *New York Times,* January 30, 2020. https://www.nytimes.com/2020/01/30/us/us-life-expectancy.html.

Teeple, Gary. *Globalization and the Decline of Social Reform: Into the Twenty-First Century.* Amherst, NY: Humanity Books, 2000.

Therborn, Göran. *Science, Class and Society: On the Formation of Sociology and Historical Materialism.* London: NLB, 1976.

Theweleit, Klaus. *Male Fantasies.* Cambridge: Polity Press, 1987.

Thompson. Michael J. *The Domestication of Critical Theory.* London: Rowman and Littlefield, 2016.

Thorpe, Charles. "Science Against Modernism: The Relevance of the Social Theory of Michael Polanyi." *British Journal of Sociology* 52, no. 1 (March 2001): 19–35.

Thorpe, Charles. "Violence and the Scientific Vocation." *Theory, Culture and Society* 21, no. 3 (2004): 59–84.

Thorpe, Charles. *Oppenheimer: The Tragic Intellect.* Chicago: University of Chicago Press, 2006.

Thorpe, Charles. "Review of *The Worlds of Herman Kahn: The Intuitive Science of Thermonuclear War*, by Sharon Ghamari-Tabrizi." *Journal of Historical Biography* 3 (Spring 2008): 134–140.

Thorpe, Charles. "Capitalism, Audit and the Demise of the Humanistic Academy." *Workplace: A Journal for Academic Labor* 15 (September 2008): 103–125.

Thorpe, Charles. "Alienation as Death: Technology, Capital, and the Degradation of Everyday Life in Elmer Rice's *The Adding Machine*." *Science as Culture* 18, no. 3 (2009): 261–279.

Thorpe, Charles. "Review of Daniel Cordle, *States of Suspense: The Nuclear Age, Postmodernism and United States Fiction and Prose*." British Society for Literature and Science, published online 2009. https://www.bsls.ac.uk/reviews/modern-and-contemporary/daniel-cordle-states-of-suspense/.

Thorpe, Charles. "Science and Political Power." *Metascience* 19, no. 3 (2010): 433–439.

Thorpe, Charles. "Death of a Salesman: Petit-Bourgeois Dread in Philip K. Dick's Mainstream Fiction." *Science-Fiction Studies* 38, no. 3 (2011): 412–434.

Thorpe, Charles. *Necroculture.* New York: Palgrave Macmillan, 2016.

Thorpe, Charles. "Political Economy of the Manhattan Project." In *The Routledge Handbook of the Political Economy of Science*, edited by David Tyfield et al., 43–56. London: Routledge, 2017.

Thorpe, Charles. "The Carnival King of Capital." *Fast Capitalism* 17, no. 1 (2020): 87–108.

Thorpe, Charles. "Escape from Reflexivity: Fromm and Giddens on Individualism, Anxiety, and Authoritarianism." In *Erich Fromm's Critical Theory*, edited by Joane Braune and Kieran Durkin, 166–193. Bloomsbury Publishing, 2020.

Thorpe, Charles. "Postmodern Neo-Romanticism and the End of History in Margaret Atwood's MaddAddam Trilogy." *Soundings* 103, no. 2 (2020): 216–242.

Thorpe, Charles. "Science, Technology, and Life Politics Beyond the Market." *Journal of Responsible Innovation* 7, no. S1 (2020): 553–573.

Thorpe, Charles. "Toward Species Being." *Logos: A Journal of Modern Society & Culture* (Summer 2021). http://logosjournal.com/2021/toward-species-being/.

Thorpe, Charles, and Brynna Jacobson. "Life Politics, Nature and the State: Giddens' Sociological Theory and the Politics of Climate Change." *The British Journal of Sociology* 64, no. 1 (2013): 99–122.

Thorpe, Charles, and Brynna Jacobson. "Abstract Life, Abstract Labor, Abstract Mind." In *The Capitalist Commodification of Animals*, edited by Brett Clark and Tamar Diana Wilson, 59–105. UK: Emerald Publishing Limited, 2020.

Thorpe, Charles, and Jane Gregory. "Producing the Post-Fordist Public: The Political Economy of Public Engagement with Science." *Science as Culture* 19, no. 3 (2010): 273–301.

Thorpe, Rebecca U. *The American Warfare State: The Domestic Politics of Military Spending*. Chicago: University of Chicago Press, 2014.

Thrush, Glenn. "Pelosi Playing Defense on Torture." *Politico,* April 27, 2009. https://www.politico.com/story/2009/04/pelosi-playing-defense-on-torture -021724.

Thrush, Glenn, Mathew Goldstein, and Connor Dogherty. "Eviction Freeze Set to Lapse as Biden Housing Aid Effort Lags." *New York Times,* August 1, 2021. https://www.nytimes.com/2021/07/31/us/politics/eviction-moratorium-biden -housing-aid.html.

Ticktin, Hillel. "The Decline of Capitalism." *Critique: A Journal of Socialist Theory* 23, no. 1 (1995): 153–158.

Tipple, John. *The Capitalist Revolution: A History of American Social Thought, 1890–1919*. New York: Pegasus, 1970.

Toddonio, Patrice. "CIA Director Nominee Supported Destruction of Torture Tapes." *PBS,* May 9, 2018. https://www.pbs.org/wgbh/frontline/article/cia-director-nomi- nee-supported-destruction-of-torture-tapes/.

Tönnies, Ferdinand. *Community and Society (Gemeinschaft und Gesellschaft)*. New Brunswick, NJ: Transaction Publishers, 1993.

Tribe, Keith. "Commerce, Science and the Modern University." In *Organizing Modernity: New Weberian Perspectives on Work, Organization and Society*, edited by Larry J. Ray and Michael Reed, 141–157. London: Routledge, 1994.

Tribe, Keith. "Max Weber's 'Science as a Vocation': Context, Genesis, Structure." *Sociologica* 12, no. 1 (2018): 125–136.

Triebert, Christian, Ben Decker, Derek Watkins, Arielle Ray, and Stella Cooper. "First They Guarded Roger Stone. Then They Joined the Capitol Attack." *New York Times*, February 14, 2021. https://www.nytimes.com/interactive/2021/02/14 /us/roger-stone-capitol-riot.html.

Tronti, Mario. *Workers and Capital*. Translated by David Broder. London: Verso, 2019.

Trotsky, Leon. *War and the Fourth International*. Translated by Sara Webe. Originally published as a pamphlet by Pioneer Publishers, July 10, 1934. https:// www.marxists.org/archive/trotsky/1934/06/warfi.htm.

Trotsky, Leon. "Once Again on the 'Crisis of Marxism." In *Writings of Leon Trotsky 1938–39,* edited by George Breitman, 204–206. New York: Pathfinder Press, 1974.

Trotsky, Leon. *The Death Agony of Capitalism and the Tasks of the Fourth International: The Transitional Program*. New York: Labor Publications, 1981.

Turner, Fred. *From Counterculture to Cyberculture: Stewart Brand, the Whole Earth Network, and the Rise of Digital Utopianism*. Chicago: University of Chicago Press, 2006.

Turner, Stephen P. "The Strange Life and Hard Times of the Concept of General Theory in Sociology: A Short History of Hope." In *Postmodernism and Social Theory: The Debate Over General Theory,* edited by Steven Seidman and David G. Wagner, 101–133. Cambridge, MA: Blackwell, 1992.

Turner, Stephen P. *American Sociology: From Pre-Disciplinary to Post-Normal.* London: Palgrave Macmillan, 2014.

Turner, Stephen P. "The Road from 'Vocation': Weber and Weblen on the Purposelessness of Scholarship." *Journal of Classical Sociology* 19, no. 3 (2019): 229–253, esp. 238–242.

Turner, Stephen P., and Jonathan H. Turner. *The Impossible Science: An Institutional Analysis of American Sociology.* Newbury Park, CA: Sage Publications, 1990.

Tyfield, David, Rebecca Lave, Samuel Randalls, and Charles Thorpe, eds. *The Routledge Handbook of the Political Economy of Science.* London: Routledge, 2017.

Varki, Ajit, and Danny Brower. *Denial: Self-Deception, False Belief and the Origins of the Human Mind.* New York: Twelve, 2013.

Vaughan, Ted R., and Gideon Sjoberg. "Human Rights Theory and the Classical Sociological Tradition." In *Sociological Theory in Transition,* edited by Mark Wardell and Stephen P. Turner, 127–141. London: Routledge, 1986.

Vaughan, Ted R. "Crisis in Contemporary American Sociology: A Critique of the Discipline's Dominant Paradigm." In *A Critique of Contemporary American Sociology,* edited by Ted R Vaughan et al., 10 53. Dix Hills, NY: General Hall, Inc., 1993.

Vaughan, Ted R., Gideon Sjoberg, and Larry T. Reynolds. *A Critique of Contemporary American Sociology.* Dix Hills, NY: General Hall, Inc., 1993.

Veblen, Thorstein. *The Engineers and the Price System.* New York: B. W. Huebsch, 1921.

Veblen, Thorstein. *The Higher Learning in America: A Memorandum on the Conduct of Universities by Business Men.* New York: A. M. Kelley, 1965.

Vidal, Matt. "Postfordism as a Dysfunctional Accumulation Regime: A Comparative Analysis of the USA, the UK and Germany." *Work, Employment & Society* 27, no. 3 (2013): 451–471.

Virilio, Paul. *Popular Defense & Ecological Struggles.* New York: Semiotexte, 1990.

Virilio, Paul. *The Information Bomb.* Translated by Chris Turner. London: Verso, 2006.

Wallin, J. E. Wallace. *Personality Maladjustments and Mental Hygiene: A Textbook for Students of Mental Hygiene, Psychology, Education, Sociology, and Counseling.* 2nd ed. New York: McGraw-Hill, 1949.

Walker, Pat, ed. *Between Labor and Capital.* Montreal, QC: Black Rose Books, 1978.

Walker, R. B. J. "Violence, Modernity, Silence: From Max Weber to International Relations." In *The Political Subject of Violence,* edited by David Campbell and Michael Dillon, 137–160. Manchester: Manchester University Press, 1993.

Walkowitz, Daniel J. "The Conundrum of the Middle-Class Worker in the Twentieth-Century United States: Professional-Managerial Workers' (Folk) Dance Around Class." In *The Making of the Middle-Class: Toward a Transnational History,* edited by A. Ricardo López and Barbara Weinstein, 121–140. New York: Duke University Press, 2012.

Walsh, David. "The Socioeconomic Basis of Identity Politics: Inequality and the Rise of an African American Elite." *World Socialist Web Site*, August 30, 2016. https://www.wsws.org/en/articles/2016/08/30/pers-a30.html.

Ward, Alexander. "Welcome to Joe Biden's Somalia War." *Politico*, July 21, 2021. https://www.politico.com/newsletters/national-security-daily/2021/07/21/welcome-to-joe-bidens-somalia-war-493679.

Watson, Ben, and Bradley Peniston. "US at War in 7 Countries — Including Niger; US Army Rebuilds Afghan Firebases; F-35s to India?; and Just a Bit More..." *Defense One*, March 15, 2018. https://www.defenseone.com/news/2018/03/the-d-brief-march-15-2018/146688/.

Weber, Max. *From Max Weber: Essays in Sociology*. Edited by Hans H. Gerth and C. Wright Mills. New York: Oxford University Press, 1958.

Weber, Max. "Science as a Vocation." In *From Max Weber: Essays in Sociology*, edited by H. H. Gerth and C. Wright Mills, 129–156. New York: Oxford University Press.

Weber, Max. "Politics as a Vocation." In *From Max Weber: Essays in Sociology*, edited by H. H. Gerth and C. Wright Mills, 77–128. New York: Oxford University Press.

Weber, Max. "Bureaucracy." In *From Max Weber: Essays in Sociology*, edited by H. H. Gerth and C. Wright Mills, 196–244. New York: Oxford University Press.

Weber, Max. *The Protestant Ethic and the Spirit of Capitalism*. London: Routledge, 1992.

Weber, Max. *The Vocation Lectures*. Edited by David Owen and Tracy Strong. New York: Hackett, 2004.

Weed, F. J. "The Sociological Department at the Colorado Fuel and Iron Company, 1901 to 1907: Scientific Paternalism and Industrial Control." *Journal of the History of the Behavioral Sciences* 41, no. 3 (2005): 269–284.

Weinberg, Julius. *Edward Alsworth Ross and the Sociology of Progressivism*. Madison: The State Historical Society of Wisconsin, 1972.

Wellerstein, Alex. "The Hawaii Alert was an Accident. The Dread it Inspired wasn't." *Washington Post*, January 16, 2018. https://www.washingtonpost.com/news/posteverything/wp/2018/01/16/the-hawaii-alert-was-an-accident-the-dread-it-inspired-wasnt/.

Welsh, Ian. *Mobilising Modernity: The Nuclear Moment*. London: Routledge, 2000.

Westbrook, Robert B. *John Dewey and American Democracy*. Ithaca, NY: Cornell University Press, 1993.

Westman, Robert S. "The 'Two Cultures' Question and the Historiography of Science in the Early Decades of the Salk Institute for Biological Studies." *Sartoniana* 32 (2019): 43–86.

Whimster, Sam. "Introduction to Weber, Asconsa and Anarchism." In *Max Weber and the Culture of Anarchy*, edited by Sam Whimster, 1–40. Houndmills, Basingstoke, UK: Macmillan, 1999.

Whimster, Sam, ed. *Max Weber and the Culture of Anarchy*. Houndmills, Basingstoke, UK: Macmillan, 1999.

Whitford, Josh. "Pragmatism and the Untenable Dualism of Means and Ends: Why Rational Choice Theory Does Not Deserve Paradigmatic Privilege." *Theory and Society* 31, no. 3 (June 2002): 325–363.

Wiebe, Robert H. *Who We Are: A History of Popular Nationalism*. Princeton, NJ: Princeton University Press, 2002.

Wieder, D. Lawrence. "Ethnomethodology and Ethnosociology." *Mid-American Review of Sociology* 2, no. 1 (1977): 1–18.

Wills, Gary. *Bomb Power: The Modern Presidency and the National Security State*. New York: Penguin, 2010.

Wilsdon, James, and James Keeley. *China: The Next Science Superpower?* London: Demos, 2007.

Wilson, William Julius. *When Work Disappears: The World of the New Urban Poor*. New York: Vintage, 1997.

Winch, Peter. *The Idea of a Social Science and its Relation to Philosophy*. London: Routledge & Kegan Paul, 1958.

Winner, Langdon. *Autonomous Technology: Technics-Out-of-Control as a Theme in Political Thought*. Cambridge, MA: MIT Press, 1977.

Wolfe, Alan. "New Directions in the Marxist Theory of Politics." *Politics & Society* 4 no. 2 (Winter 1974): 131–159.

Wolfe, Alan. *The Limits of Legitimacy: Political Contradictions of Contemporary Capitalism*. New York: The Free Press, 1977.

Wolfe, Alan. "Weak Sociology/Strong Sociologists: Consequences and Contradictions of a Field in Turmoil." *Social Research* 59, no. 4 (1992): 759–779.

Wolfe, Alan. "The New Class Comes Home." In *Our Country, Our Culture: The Politics of Political Correctness*, edited by Edith Kurzweil and William Phillips, 283–291. New York: Partisan Review Press, 1994.

Wolfe, Alan. *One Nation, After All: What Middle-Class Americans Really Think About, God, Country, Family, Racism, Welfare, Immigration, Homosexuality, Work, the Right, the Left, and Each Other*. New York: Viking, 1998.

Wolfe, Alan. *Return to Greatness: How America Lost its Sense of Purpose and What It Needs to Do to Recover It*. Princeton, NJ: Princeton University Press, 2005.

Wolfe, Alan. "So Right Together." *The New Republic*, February 11, 2016. https://newrepublic.com/article/129013/right-together-exit-right-oppenheimer.

Wolfe, Alan. *The Politics of Petulance: America in an Age of Immaturity*. Chicago: The University of Chicago Press, 2018.

Wolfe, Audra J. *Freedom's Laboratory: The Cold War Struggle for the Soul of Science*. Baltimore, MD: Johns Hopkins University Press, 2018.

Women's Liberation Front. "CA Women's Prisons Anticipate Pregnancy After Forcing Women to be Housed with Men." *Women's Liberation Front*, July 15, 2021. https://www.womensliberationfront.org/news/ca-womens-prisons-anticipate-pregnancy-sb123.

Woodward, Bob, and Robert Costa. *Peril*. New York: Simon and Schuster, 2021.

Worth, Owen. *Morbid Symptoms: The Global Rise of the Far-Right*. London: Zed Books, 2019.

Wright, Susan, and Cris Shore, *Death of the Public University?: Uncertain Futures for Higher Education in the Knowledge Economy*. New York: Berghahn Books, 2017.

Wrong, D. H. "The Oversocialized Conception of Man in Modern Sociology." *American Sociological Review* 26 (1961): 183–193.

Yurchak, Alexei. *Everything was Forever, Until it was No More: The Last Soviet Generation*. Princeton, NJ: Princeton University Press, 2013.

Zammito, John H. *A Nice Derangement of Epistemes: Post-Positivism in the Study of Science from Quine to Latour*. Chicago: University of Chicago Press, 2004.

Zamora, Daniel. "Foucault's Responsibility." *Jacobin*, December 15, 2014. https://jacobinmag.com/2014/12/michel-foucault-responsibility-socialist.

Zenko, Micah. "Obama Discusses Targeted Killing of U.S. Citizens During Google+ Hangout." *Council on Foreign Relations* (blog), February 15, 2013. https://www.cfr.org/blog/obama-discusses-targeted-killing-us-citizens-during-google-hangout.

Zerubavel, Eviatar. *Hidden Rhythms: Schedules and Calendars in Social Life*. Chicago: University of Chicago Press, 1981.

Ziman, John. *Real Science: What it Is and What it Means*. Cambridge: Cambridge University, 2000.

Zimmerman, Andrew. "German Sociology and Empire: From Internal Colonization to Overseas Colonization and Back Again." In *Sociology & Empire: The Imperial Entanglements of a Discipline*, edited by George Steinmetz, 166–187. Durham, NC: Duke University Press, 2013.

Žižek, Slavoj. *Living in the End Times*. London: Verso, 2011.

Zuboff, Shoshana. *The Age of Surveillance Capitalism*. London: Profile, 2019.

Zunz, Olivier. *Why the American Century?* Chicago: University of Chicago Press, 1998.

Index

About the Author

Charles Thorpe is professor of sociology at the University of California, San Diego. He has taught at Cardiff University and University College London. He is the author of *Oppenheimer: The Tragic Intellect* (University of Chicago Press, 2006) and *Necroculture* (Palgrave Macmillan, 2006) and coeditor of *The Routledge Handbook of the Political Economy of Science* (Routledge, 2017).

www.ingramcontent.com/pod-product-compliance
Lightning Source LLC
Chambersburg PA
CBHW022302280326
41932CB00010B/949